A MIDSUMMER NIGHT'S DREAM IN CONTEXT

Anthem Perspectives in Literature

Titles in the **Anthem Perspectives in Literature** series are designed to contextualize classic works of literature for readers today within their original social and cultural environments. The books present historical, biographical, political, artistic, moral, religious and philosophical material from the period that enable readers to understand a text's meaning as it would have struck the original audience. These approachable but informative books aim to uncover the period and the people for whom the texts were written, their values and views, their anxieties and demons, what made them laugh and cry, their loves and hates. The series is targeted at high-achieving A Level, International Baccalaureate and Advanced Placement pupils, undergraduates following Shakespeare and Renaissance drama modules and an intellectually curious audience.

A MIDSUMMER NIGHT'S DREAM IN CONTEXT

MAGIC, MADNESS AND MAYHEM

Keith Linley

ANTHEM PRESS

Anthem Press
An imprint of Wimbledon Publishing Company
www.anthempress.com

This edition first published in UK and USA 2016
by ANTHEM PRESS
75–76 Blackfriars Road, London SE1 8HA, UK
or PO Box 9779, London SW19 7ZG, UK
and
244 Madison Ave #116, New York, NY 10016, USA

British Library Cataloguing-in-Publication Data
A catalogue record for this book is available from the British Library.

Library of Congress Cataloging-in-Publication Data
A catalog record for this book has been requested.

ISBN-13: 978-1-78308-555-2 (Pbk)
ISBN-10: 1-78308-555-X (Pbk)

This title is also available as an e-book.

CONTENTS

INTRODUCTION

About This Book

This book concentrates on the contexts from which the play emerges, those characteristics of life in Elizabethan England which are reflected in the values and views William Shakespeare brings to the text and which affect how a contemporary might have responded to it. The central context comprises the writer, the text, the audience and all the views, values and beliefs held by the writer and audience and encapsulated in the text. These values are the prime concern of this book. There is a secondary context that is also a focus. A play does not suddenly come into being without having a background. It does not exist in vacuo. It will have its own unique features, but has characteristics inherited from its author and generic traits derived from the writing of its time, particularly from the drama.

Other secondary contexts – the actors, the acting space, the social mix of any one audience – do not figure in this study except as occasional incidentals. There are tertiary contexts, such as the afterlife of the text (its printed form, how subsequent ages interpreted it, performed it, changed it – its performance history). There is also the critical backstory (the profile showing how critics of subsequent times bring their agendas and the values and prejudices of their period to analysis of the text). These are referenced incidentally where they seem useful and relevant, but are not a major concern. Any scholarly edition of *A Midsummer Night's Dream* will cover these areas in greater detail.

The book is for students preparing assignments and examinations for Shakespeare modules. The marking criteria at any level explicitly or implicitly require that students show a consistently well-developed and consistently detailed understanding of the significance and influence of contexts in which literary texts are written and understood. This means responding to the play in the ways Shakespeare's audience would have done. The following material will enable you to acquire a surer grasp of this cultural context – the social-political conditions from which the play emerged, the literary profile prevailing when it was written and its religious-moral dimension. The setting is ostensibly pagan, with ancient Greek names for the courtly characters and references to the gods and goddesses of the classical world, but this is merely a literary fashion of Shakespeare's time and is not meant to be taken seriously or literally. Furthermore, since the play was written in an age of faith, when the Bible's teachings and sermons heard in church formed part of every man and woman's mindset, it is vital to recreate those factors, for the actions of the characters will be assessed by Christian criteria. You may not agree with the values of the time or the views propounded in the play, but you do need to understand how belief mediated the possible responses of the audience that watched the play in 1595–6. A key concept in this book's approach is that *Dream* is full of sins, transgressions, boundary crossing and rule breaking in the personal world and, in less dominant ways, in the public and political arena as well. Alerted to the transgressive behaviour of Egeus, Hermia and Lysander in the opening scene, an audience member, who would not know the story (as it is largely the author's fabrication), would expect they be punished. Though biblical values would be applied to the action, there is much more going on scene by scene than a series of echoes of or allusions to what the Bible says about virtue and vice. Interwoven are concerns about rule of self (a recurrent theme in all the comedies), patriarchy and paternal rule, the dangers of appetite unrestrained and the inconsistency, unpredictability and sheer oddness of love.

What Is a Context?

Any document – literary or non-literary – comes from an environment and has that environment embedded in it, overtly and covertly. Its context is its DNA, the conditions which produced it; the biographical, social, political, historical, cultural circumstances which form it; and the values operating within it and affecting the experience of it. A text in isolation is simply an accumulation of words carrying growing, developing meanings as the writing/ performance progresses. It is two dimensional, a lexical, grammatical construct and the sum of its literal contents. It has meaning. We can understand what it is about, how its characters interact and how their conflicts lead to crises which may or may not be resolved, but context provides a third dimension, making meaning comprehensible within the cultural values of the time. Context is the sum of all the influences the writer brings to the text and all the influences the viewer/reader deploys in experiencing it. This book concentrates on the archaeology of the play, recovering how it would have been understood in 1596, recovering the special flavour and prevailing attitudes of the time and displaying the factors that shaped its meaning for that time and that audience. A *Midsummer Night's Dream in Context* offers the views, prejudices, controversies and basic beliefs buried in the play – all the significations of society embedded in the text that added together make it what Shakespeare intended it to be or as closely as we can be reasonably sure. Recovering the mindset, nuances and values Shakespeare intentionally or unconsciously works into *Dream*, and how his audience would have interpreted them, means unearthing and recreating the Elizabethan period. To achieve that a range of aspects is considered, but two key contextual areas dominate the approach of this book: the religious and the sociopolitical. The multiple transgressions represented in the play would have been interpreted by the audience in terms of the scriptural upbringing most of them would have had and in the light of their ideas on how the gentry should behave. The social range of the cast spreads from a duke who rules the state, through the younger generation of the gentry, to the ordinary artisans of Athens. It excludes the rising bourgeoisie, but includes a whole parallel range of supernatural figures spreading from the king and queen of the fairies down to the queen's attendant servants Mustardseed and Moth. The play automatically activates some political considerations related to kingship and rule. We are invited to judge Theseus as a leader, a man manager and as an arbitrator of a personal problem that crops up in his court. We also have to consider the behaviour of those other rulers of the fairy world. The nature of rule and rulers were subjects which were constantly debated in pre-Civil War England. Here Shakespeare presents rule through a series of fictional states (Athens, Fairyland and gentry conduct) and, though they are of limited scope in this piece as compared with the history plays, they have some small specific relevance to the hothouse court of Elizabeth I because they relate to conduct, the conduct of supposedly better educated, better brought-up people from the rank that called itself 'the better sort'.

Cultural historians aim to recover 'the commonplaces, the unargued presuppositions' and 'the imperative need, in any comparative discussions of epochs, [is] first to decide what the norm of the epoch is'.[1] Once the typical and orthodox values are established, it is then essential to register significant divergences from them. Sin, subversion, transgression and reversals abound in the play and part 1 looks broadly at the contemporary 'world view', the inherited past, the normative value system, which shaped how Elizabethans thought about God, the world, sin, virtue, death, the Devil, the social structure, family, gender relationships, social change and political matters.

---

1 Tillyard, *The English Renaissance: Fact or Fiction?*, 27, 28.

This establishes the orthodox understandings and expectations of the time so that the subversions of natural order and hierarchy displayed onstage can be seen in their ethical framework. Part 2 discusses contemporary contexts – politics, literature, authority and morality – that enhance and clarify some issues the play addresses. It does this by looking, in separate chapters, at comedy as a genre, at aspects of the central characters, at perception and deception and at views on love. Connections are also made between the play and the wider literary world. Most importantly, the book considers the religious beliefs informing the likely judgements made of the actions viewed and suggests a number of sociopolitical allusions giving the drama a topical dimension. It is not known where the play was first performed – at The Globe public arena, the Blackfriars indoor theatre, at court or at a private house in celebration of an aristocratic marriage. The latter is the critics' favourite, but none can agree to which high-end couple's union it was meant as a compliment.

Crucial to the religious context are moral frameworks against which conduct in the play would have been measured – the Ten Commandments, the Seven Deadly Sins, the Seven Cardinal Virtues, the Corporal and Spiritual Works of Mercy – the ethical framework in which the action is set and by which it is to be judged. (These are discussed in chapters 3 and 4.) These ethical contexts decode the hidden nuances and inflexions of meaning by which a contemporary audience would have mediated their responses to the madcap story of lovers eloping and getting lost in the woods. There would have been many different responses to the attitude of Egeus, the actions of the lovers and the interventions of Puck and Oberon, but in the area of the religious and moral values there would have been many shared reactions.

A gulf always exists between what people are supposed to do or believe and what they actually do or believe. Machiavelli's version of the traditional 'mirror for princes' claimed,

> I have thought it proper to represent things as they are in real truth, rather than as they are imagined. [...] the gulf between how one should live and how one does live is so wide that a man who neglects what is actually done for what should be done learns the way to self-destruction rather than self-preservation.[2]

Ignorance, indifference, rebelliousness, purposeful wickedness, laziness and weakness account for these discrepancies. No one in the audience would have missed the fact that Hermia breaks the commandment to honour her

---

2 Niccolo Machiavelli, *The Prince*, 15, 90-1.

father and breaks the law in running off to get married illegally. Neither would they have missed the excessively punitive threats of Egeus. Those sorts of actions were expected in a comedy. Comedy thrives on normality pushed to an extreme. Though the actions portrayed were not morally acceptable they reflect what happened in real life: the putting of personal obsession and private will before paternal, filial and marital responsibilities. The tension between what people should do and what they actually do creates dramatic conflicts not just for the characters but also for the audience, who may be torn between endorsing the lovers yet feeling they ought to be condemned. And the questions remain: should they be laughing at any of it and how can they not laugh at such a mad mixture of mistakes?

Further Reading

Useful Editions

A Midsummer Night's Dream (ed. R. A. Foakes, New Cambridge Shakespeare, 1994).
A Midsummer Night's Dream (ed. Harold Brooks, Arden Shakespeare, 1979).
A Midsummer Night's Dream (ed. Stanley Wells, Penguin Shakespeare, 2005).

Critical Works

Regina Buccola, ed., A Midsummer Night's Dream: A Critical Guide (2010).
Jan Kott, Shakespeare Our Contemporary, 1965.
Alexander Leggatt, Shakespeare's Comedy of Love, 1974.
A Midsummer Night's Dream: New Casebook (ed. Richard Dutton, 1995).
Shakespeare: A Midsummer Night's Dream (Casebook Series, ed. Anthony Price, 1983)
Emma Smith, ed., Shakespeare's Comedies: A Guide to Criticism, 2008.
John Palmer, Comic Characters of Shakespeare, 1946.
John Dover Wilson, Shakespeare's Happy Comedies, 1962.

Articles

Kenneth Burke, 'Why A Midsummer Night's Dream?', Shakespeare Quarterly 57, no. 3 (2006).
Alan Lewis, 'Reading Shakespeare's Cupid', Criticism 47, no. 2 (2005).
Ania Loomba, 'The Great Indian Vanishing Trick – Colonialism, Property and the Family in A Midsummer Night's Dream'. In A Feminist Companion to Shakespeare, 2000.
Deborah Baker Wyrick, 'The Ass Motif in The Comedy of Errors and A Midsummer Night's Dream', Shakespeare Quarterly 33 (1982).

Note: All quotes are from the Arden edition.

PART I

THE INHERITED PAST

PROLOGUE

The Setting

The audience would be restless with excitement. If the first performance was for a wedding party they would be well fed, well wined, in a merry mood after the music and singing during the marriage banquet and looking forward to dancing after the play. There would be an expectation of amusement to finish the evening before the ritual of attending the bride and groom to their bedchamber. If the play was part of nuptial festivities then the audience would be in an excitable state anyway, ready to laugh at anything and susceptible to accepting fantastical happenings. And how appropriate the piece to be performed would be – the madcap mistakes of a night focused on love and marriage. There would be similar expectations for a public staging, only the social range would be wider. The Elizabethan popular audience had a natural love of clowning, slapstick and the mayhem that was released when the rules of society were relaxed, broken or subverted. A play set on Midsummer Night and structured as a dream would be fun and full of the resonances associated with a festal day that had age-old overtones of love, marriage, misrule and jollity. Midsummer was traditionally celebrated with dancing and feasting and always involved secret assignations in the woods later when it was dark. Indeed, *A Midsummer Night's Dream* is a play with a bit of everything – magic, moonlight, mayhem, love's mad entanglements, fairies, mistakes, mechanicals as mummers – all set in the spookiness of the woods at midnight and all of it provoking laughter. Wherever it was first played and for whom, it was a fun-filled festivity, a celebration of the follies of man and the incorrigible persistence of the impulse of men and women to pair up, wrangle, break up, wrangle more and reunite. There is a wise duke, a stern father, four soppy sloppy lovers, a mischievous sprite, a magic flower, a vengeful king of the fairies, his beautiful queen and a gobby weaver who has his head changed into an ass's head. 'Cupid is a knavish lad' (3.2.40) indeed, for the partner changes of the lovers become hilarious. The play starts with a sentimental romantic pair declaring their passion and lamenting the obstacles to their being happy. The backstory narrative (*protasis*) is given in part by Egeus and further by Hermia and Lysander as they relate the progress of their love.[1] It also informs us that before the play began a second couple were also in love, but they are not so happily paired, for though they once loved each other, the man has switched his attraction to the young woman in the first pairing, so the happy duo has become an awkward trio with one sad solo character. Numerous tensions are generated by the man of the second couple transferring his affections to his previous love's friend, while the woman continues to love him. These tensions are comic for the audience but upsetting for the characters involved. Lost already?

The confusions are part of the comedy. Let's put the love situation more simply: Lysander loves Hermia and she loves him, and Demetrius loved Helena and she still loves him. 'Loves' is rather understating it. She dotes on Demetrius, 'Dotes in idolatry' (1.1.109). Demetrius now claims he loves Hermia. This leaves Helena alone. And this is before they even get to the woods where matters get even more complicated. By the mistaken action of Puck with the magic flower and its juice we see a situation where Lysander transfers his 'love' to Helena, while Demetrius returns to his love of Helena, and Hermia is left alone, still loving Lysander. This reversal of the opening position with a change in the young woman left isolated, forces Hermia to experience how her friend had felt. That should be salutary, feeling what it is like to be jilted, learning to feel what another has experienced. It should extend her understanding and sympathy and make her appreciate the good luck she had had. A loves B and B loves A is not dramatic – unless there is an obstacle. A loves B loves A, and C loves D loves C is equally dull. But if A loves B loves A, and C loves D but D loves A, that has distinct theatrical possibilities – either for tragedy or comedy. If A loves B but B loves C, and C loves D and D loves C, that too has dramatic potential. This succession of love situations is what the play's narrative follows, where A = Hermia, B = Lysander, C = Helena and D = Demetrius.

The whole process is like the movements of a dance. Indeed it is the oldest dance in the world – Cupid's quadrille. Take your partners. The married couple for whom perhaps the play is being performed, have taken their partner. There may well have been others among the audience who are still

---

1 *Protasis* is a device for filling in information about events that happened outside the time frame of a text. Most commonly it is relayed by a character reporting from memory what has previously taken place.

in the throes of the certainty of Love's uncertainties. There were others, older viewers, to whom the mistakes of the night were a distant but still amusing memory of their own part in Love's comedy. By the end of act 4 Lysander's love is returned to Hermia by an antidote to the love juice, and Demetrius's magically induced return of love to Helena is left in place. Thus all partners are now in their original pairing and the courtship dance is over. Bow and curtsy. With their marriages in act 5 a new dance begins, but that is the afterlife of the story. 'Lord, what fools these mortals be' (3.2.115). What the audience was about to watch was a mad carnival of a play, but with some dark threats looming at its shadowy edges.

The play becomes part of the official public record on 8 October 1600 when Thomas Fisher entered it in the Stationers' Register. Before the end of the year he published the text (First Quarto, Q1). The title page claims the play had been 'sundry times publicly acted'. This suggests that after a possible private first performance as part of high-society wedding celebrations, the play entered the repertoire of the Chamberlain's Men and was possibly played at The Theatre or The Curtain. It may have been staged at the newly opened Globe, depending on just when the play was written and when it assumed public status. The phrase 'sundry times acted' was a formula often used, and not necessarily strictly accurate. Claiming 'sundry' performances might well be intended to encourage book sales. Critical consensus speculatively puts composition between 1594 and 1596. Until 1596 William Shakespeare was based at Burbage's The Theatre.[2] From 1596–8 the troupe performed at the nearby Curtain, moving in 1599 to the newly constructed Globe, south of the river. Thus 'sundry times' could mean performance at any or all three venues. It was not usual in those times for any piece to be acted in a run. After one performance the play would be put aside to be recalled at a later date if it was popular.

The first recorded showing was during the Christmas/New Year festivities at the court of the new king, James I, on 1 January 1604. The courtier Dudley Carlton writes in a letter to John Chamberlain about the acting of 'a play of Robin goode-fellow'.[3] If this is Shakespeare's piece, already Puck's magic had seemingly translated the play into his own. Several internal topical references suggest composition between 1594 and 1596, and there is an allusion to Edmund Spenser's *Epithalamion*, which was published 1595.[4] Since the play is focused on the misadventures of love's voyage and a final arrival safely in the haven of marriage, it has become axiomatic that the piece was written to be

2 Built in 1576 in Shoreditch just outside the city wall, north of Bishopsgate.
3 Chambers, *William Shakespeare: A Study of Facts and Problems*, II. 329.
4 An *epithalamion* was a poem celebrating a marriage.

performed as part of the entertainment at an aristocratic marriage. That has triggered the idea that Elizabeth I might have been present, a notion further encouraged by the reference to 'the imperial votaress' (2.1.163) as alluding to the Virgin Queen. Neither the monarch's presence nor a specific wedding can be verified, but Elizabeth Vere's union with the Earl of Derby (26 January 1595) and that of 18-year-old Elizabeth Carey's with Lord Thomas Berkeley (19 February 1596) have been argued for.[5] The latter involved the granddaughter of the Lord Chamberlain, Henry Carey, first Baron Hunsdon, cousin to the queen and patron of the players to whom Shakespeare was attached. The Lord Chamberlain's Men, formed in 1594, was the company in which Shakespeare acted, for which he wrote and in which he bought a share. The bride's father, George Carey, succeeded to the title in 1596 and as Chamberlain took on the patronage of the acting company. The wedding ceremony took place in Blackfriars, which had a private theatre constructed within the building. It would have been an appropriate offering to the couple, commissioned by either the bride's grandfather or father or both, and a suitable compliment from writer to patron. It has also been suggested the play was specially commissioned by the queen to celebrate the Feast of St John (24 June), which coincides with the summer solstice and midsummer. No definitive evidence exists to prove when, where or for whom (if anyone) the piece was written and performed.

It is not essential that the piece was performed first on Midsummer Night, though if it was, that would have added a further frisson to the expectations of the audience given the mass of traditional community ceremonies, superstitions and folklore attached to that night. What is beyond doubt is that the piece is festive and ends, after tribulation, mistakes and much misrule, as a celebration of marriage. It is a wedding blessing, a hymeneal good luck charm and probably did grace a specific occasion.[6]

Whether the play was performed on the evening before Midsummer Day, on the day itself (24 June) or at another time, the title alone would have aroused excitement. Since pagan times the middle of summer was the occasion for a range of unusual and sometimes spectacular activities. From long ages past bonfires were lit on Midsummer Eve, or cartwheels stuffed with straw, ignited and rolled downhill. Young people leapt over the embers of the

---

5 A. L. Rowse (*William Shakespeare: A Biography*) sees 'no reason to doubt that *A Midsummer Night's Dream* was produced to grace the occasion' of the Countess of Southampton's wedding to Sir Thomas Heneage on 2 May 1594 (205). There is no documentation to prove that this or any other wedding was the occasion that called forth the piece, but it seems a strong possibility.

6 Hymen was the ancient Greek god of marriage.

fires, and there was singing, dancing and feasting and certainly illicit kissing, cuddling and coupling.

The fires were believed to frighten away evil spirits and to cleanse the poisonous air, thus protecting the all-important crops. Houses were decked with greenery, and the richer folk offered food to their neighbours.[7] Herbs picked on Midsummer Day were thought to have specially increased medicinal potency, and various other rituals were carried out by young women to ascertain who their husband would be. Though the early Reformation had officially banished many of the rites associated with the summer solstice as being pagan, superstitious and too closely connected with witchcraft, country folk persisted in celebrating them.[8] It was another of those periods when misrule was liberated, allowing the people to indulge themselves in wilder activities than the usually prescriptive customs of daily life, drudging work and the expected sober conduct of good Christians. The period had powerful practical and spiritual dimensions. It was the peak of sunshine hours before the slow diminishing of daylight into autumn and winter. The sun was at its high point of strength, and the corn and fruit crops were reaching their fullness before the process of ripening led to autumn harvest. Since 85 per cent of the population lived in the country and were in one way or another dependent on agriculture, such good luck rituals were of great importance. In an age when science hardly existed, superstition was all people had to fall back on. Bad harvests meant famine, hardship, unemployment and death. Anything that might bring good luck was worth trying, however pagan its origins. This led inevitably to confrontations with the zealous new Protestant clergy, who regarded the bonfires particularly as being counter to religion and a remnant of papistry. The fire festivals largely disappeared from East Anglia, the south-east and a swathe of lands from the Thames Valley westwards to Gloucestershire. Outside this heartland of the new faith the old customs lived on, though they were slowly receding. It was still a contentious matter in 1591 when a vicar in Shrewsbury finally got the town bailiffs to ban the bonfires and the maypoles.[9] That the cleansing, luck-bringing, protective beliefs clustered round Midsummer fires continued to have power through to the nineteenth century is a sign of the continuing importance of agriculture in preindustrial Britain and the stubborn resilience of vestigial superstitions. The belief in the insecticide value of the heat generated by the fires bears witness to the

---

7 See Stow, *The Survey of London*, 90–1.
8 Some of the nobility also kept alive the old festivities. Bess of Hardwick for example celebrated with May dances, morris dancing, the Fool and the Hobby Horse on her Derbyshire estates (Lovell, *Bess of Hardwick*, 394).
9 Cited in Hutton, *The Stations of the Sun*, 316.

very slow improvement in people's understanding of the biological threats to farming. Titania's speech about the adverse effects of her quarrel with Oberon (2.1.81–116) indicates how vulnerable to bad weather country life and food production were. The fires that would bring the hope-for good luck were timed to precede the July–August tendency for destructive rain, storms, crop blights and animal diseases. They were also believed to ward off the huge increase in insects that could devastate crops. The fairy element in *Dream* marks the ambiguous, but persisting, status of magic throughout the whole period. The regular failure of harvests in the 1590s, due to bad summer weather, is reflected in Titania's speech and is also a reminder of how in desperate times people resort to superstition in the hope of better fortune. Poor harvests meant a shortage of corn, meant a shortage of bread, meant high bread prices, meant hunger and starvation for the poorest. Hoarding grain and other foodstuffs was an indictable offence.[10]

The play may not even have been intended for Midsummer performance at all. Theseus tries to fob off Egeus's complaints about his daughter being in the woods with Lysander and the others by saying,

> No doubt they rose up early, to observe
> The rite of May. (4.1.131–2)

This is either a mistake by Shakespeare or a joke by Theseus intended to say to Egeus, 'I know it's not the first of May, but you must accept whatever I say it is and whatever my ruling on your daughter. I am Duke and my power is absolute'.

The respectable Philostrate, the 'usual manager of mirth', organizes the wedding entertainments. He is a Master of the Revels, much like Sir Edmund Tilney, who was overseer of court festivities from 1581 to 1610. But in the dominant central portion of the play Puck presides as a Lord of Misrule, loosing mischief and mayhem for the audience's pleasure. Anarchy and carnival are the characteristics of his reign, while balance and order epitomize Theseus's rule.[11] But it has to be said that Puck is an undemonized sprite, full of mischief

---

10 Recent research has discovered legal documents pertaining to Shakespeare being fined for hoarding food, presumably to sell at inflated prices (*Sunday Times*, 31 March 2013). His role as a moneylender puts a hypocritical slant on his comments about usurers and tarnishes his stance as someone concerned for the poor.

11 Russian linguist Mikhail Bakhtin identified *carnivalization*, turning order and hierarchy upside down, mocking established views and institutions, as a liberating strand in literature. It preexisted his theory by centuries and remained in the Elizabethan period in Boy Bishops and Lords of Misrule set up in university colleges and Inns of Court. It persists in the Venice Carnival. The church disapproved strongly. See Stow, 86.

and pranks but not the malicious devil of Reginald Scot's description.[12] The fairies too are benign. Oberon's vindictiveness is targeted only against the wife he wishes to punish for opposing his patriarchal dominance. The resolution of that gender clash heralds and precedes the human unions. Nothing must, in the end, distract from the celebration of the positive.

---

12 In *Discovery of Witchcraft* (1584). See chap. 12.

Chapter 1

THE HISTORICAL CONTEXT

1.1 The Elizabethan Context: An Overview

In 1558 Elizabeth I assumed the crown of England. This inaugurated a period of relative peace, commercial and imperial expansion and growing national confidence, lasting until her death in 1603. It was also a period overshadowed by continuing religious frictions that were often extreme, sometimes violent. *A Midsummer Night's Dream* (hereafter called *Dream*), written in the mid-to-late 1590s, is therefore Elizabethan though its values reflect those of the late Middle Ages intermixed with those of the Renaissance.

In the wider European literary and political contexts, the period is the High Renaissance. Historians today call it Early Modern because many features of it are recognizably modern while being early in the evolution that shaped our world, but medieval views (particularly as regard conduct, the pervasiveness of religion and attitudes to sin and virtue) endured and coexisted with the Humanism of influential writers like Baldassare Castiglione and Erasmus that had originated on the continent.

Elizabeth, of the Tudor family, much loved, respected and feared, was a strong ruler, indeed strong enough to suppress the addressing of many problems which by her successor's time had become irresolvable. At times a sharply incisive intellect drove her political decisions. At others, caprice and temper made her a dangerous and unreliable force, all the more feared because of her cruelty and absolutism. She could be irritatingly resistant to making important decisions, but always knew where her best interests lay. The peace of her reign was constantly overshadowed by fears of Catholic outrage – against the queen herself or against society in general – or foreign invasion. Externally, the Spanish posed a considerable but diminishing threat to her tenure of the crown. Internally, Catholic opposition had been increased after the Pope declared Elizabeth a bastard and heretic and tacitly encouraged individual assassination attempts against her or state military action. This opposition had outwardly been blunted by the defeat of the Armada (1588), but the great bane of her reign was the claim of Mary Queen of Scots to have a stronger right to the throne of England than her cousin.

Associated with Mary's claim was the constant, very real fear of assassination plots for she provided a focus for discontented Catholics and a ready replacement on the throne.[1] Perhaps with reluctance on Elizabeth's part, but certainly with relief, Mary was eventually executed in 1587 after implication in the Babington plot.

The Tudors (Henry VII, Henry VIII, Edward VI, Mary I, Elizabeth I) ruled from 1485 to 1603. Though dysfunctional and brutally absolutist, they successfully brought stability after the turmoil of the Wars of the Roses (though there were various short-lived rebellions against them). Questions of succession, the nature of rulers, the use and limits of monarchical power, the precariousness of power, the influence of court and the qualities of courtiers were matters that concerned people throughout the period. These matters hardly affect the mood of *Dream*, which is a largely festive mix of many sorts of comedy, but there are some issues around leadership and maintaining order. These emerge through the conduct of Oberon, through Theseus and his handling of Egeus's harsh patriarchy, and through Egeus's attitude to disposing of his daughter in marriage or to death. They are parodied in the problems Peter Quince has curbing Bottom's anarchic enthusiasms and Oberon's inept control of Puck's irrepressible mischievousness. The limited effects reason and balanced judgement can have on unrestrainable passions and the extent to which paternal rule may be allowed before it becomes unreasonable and cruel, were ongoing, much-debated problems of the time and would continue to be so into the next century. They are pushed to the margins of the play as the madcap happenings in the woods take over and the happy ending banishes all qualms.

Religion was a major conflict area, with Dissenters fighting for freedom from tight central control by the newly established English Church and Catholics trying to avoid the threats to their worship and, in some cases, actively seeking to topple the Protestant monarch. The religious fractures of the age have no place in the crazy jollity of this piece, but biblically originated religious-moral values do. Carnival, misrule, mistakes and entanglements drive the play, but the use of magic does raise the problem of the Anglican Church's view of superstition and its opposition to entrenched beliefs in a

---

1 There was an attempt to shoot the queen on her barge on the Thames. The Ridolfi plot (1570) planned to replace her with Mary Queen of Scots, as did the Throgmorton (1583) and Babington (1586) plots. There were also the Don John Plot (1577) and the Somerville (1583), Parry (1584) and Lopez plots (1594).

world of spirits, goblins and witches. The effects on society and individual morality of the wealth that the new capitalism and the expansion of trade were creating, were also beginning to worry Elizabethan writers. This new individualism and the accompanying greed it promoted have no place either in *Dream*, but in the clash between the wilful self-regard both of romance and paternal authoritarianism (evident in the clash between Hermia and her father) we can see the beginnings of the crumbling of old ways and the embryonic emergence of new individualism. But in its overall effect *Dream* is a holiday from all the pressing anxieties of the day. Almost – for there are some shadows.

Henry VIII's great achievement (and cause of trouble) was breaking with the Catholic Church of Rome and setting up the Church of England. This inaugurated a period of seismic change called the English Reformation. There was some limited alliance with the continental Protestant Reformation led by Martin Luther, but in many ways the English went their own way. Monasteries and convents were dissolved and the infrastructure of Catholicism banished. Altars were stripped of ornaments (leaving only the cross and flanking candles and sometimes not even these), churches emptied of statues and relics, and many murals whitewashed over, scratched out or defaced. New church services and prayers were conducted in English rather than Latin. New English translations of the Bible began to appear and there was a Book of Common Prayer to be used in all parish churches. Holy shrines and saints' days were done away with as idols and superstitions. The vicar was to be the only intermediary between a person and God. After the nine-day reign of Lady Jane Grey and a brief fiery and bloody return to Catholicism under Mary I (1553–8), Elizabeth succeeded and bedding in the new church continued. But the reforms provoked opposition which fuelled ongoing tensions. The freedom of an English church, supposedly stripped back to its simple original faith, encouraged the rise of more extreme reforming Protestant sects (not always to the liking of the infant established church). These groups were called Non-Conformists, Independents or Dissenters. They included Puritans, Calvinists and Presbyterians – all Protestant, but with doctrinal differences. Some eccentric and freaky sects grew up too – like the Anabaptists, the Brownists and the Family of Love.[2] Religion and the tensions between different sects was a persistently present consideration at this time, but despite all the official changes, the essential beliefs in sin, virtue, salvation, the centrality of Christ and the ubiquity of the Devil (the idea that he was everywhere, looking to tempt man) were the same as they always had been, as were the

2 After Jean Calvin the radical French Protestant reformer.

beliefs that entry into Heaven was the reward of virtue, that punishment and possible perdition followed sin, and that the world was in decline and would shortly come to an end. In *Dream* Shakespeare hovers on the edge of a magic that sometimes has the frightening appearance of diabolic possession. The most extreme example is the transformation of Bottom's head. The funniest physical humour in the play is at the same time the most visually disturbing. Laughter saves the situation. The monstrous apparition that Bottom presents with his ass's head is diverted from diabolism by the down-to-earth, silly things he says and by the knowledge it will be reversed by Oberon when he is ready. But that understanding is suspended and delayed long enough to hint at the cruel potential that lurks underneath love and magic. We see a number of occasions where supposed love turns very hateful and shows its dark side.

The political discourse concerned with kingship is another persistent feature of the time. Elizabeth (adoringly nicknamed 'Gloriana') ruled from 1558, a time long enough to establish her as an icon, particularly as she headed up strong opposition (and victory) against the Spanish.[3] But while external threats were repulsed, the period was one of unstoppable internal changes. Often feared by her ministers and courtiers, Elizabeth was much loved by the mass of her people. But her fearsome conduct repressed or slowed the discussion of many sociopolitical issues that needed addressing. In the economic-commercial world too inexorable changes were slowly emerging. These gradually altered the profile and mood of society. Religion, commerce, growing industrialization, an increase of manufacture, social relationships, kingship and rule were all changing.[4] One unchanging feature of the period was the unceasing rise in prices, particularly of food. This brought an unceasing decline in the living standards of the poor, for wages did not rise. The rich and the rising middle class could cope with inflation, but the state of the poor deteriorated. Enclosure of arable land (very labour intensive) and its conversion to sheep farming (requiring less labour), raised unemployment among the 'lower orders' or 'baser sort' who constituted the largest proportion (between 80 and 85 per cent) of the 4–5 million population. Rising numbers of poor put greater burdens on poor relief in small, struggling rural communities, adding to the elite's fear of some monumental uprising of the disenchanted. Most of the population worked on the land, though increasing numbers were

---

3 After a character in Spenser's *The Faerie Queen*.

4 Niccolò Machiavelli had referred to 'the great changes and variations, beyond human imagining, which we have experienced and experience every day' (*The Prince*, 130; written 1513, published 1532). He was referring to Italy, but circumstances were similar in England. In 1596 the European world had not completely morphed from its medieval past.

moving to the few existing cities. Later ages looked back on the Elizabethan era as a 'Golden Age' and talked of 'Merry England'. It was not, except for a small elite of rich, privileged aristocrats – the very group which forms the court characters in the play, and the same social group which probably watched the first performance. Also beginning to enjoy greater luxury and comfort were canny merchants (making fortunes from trading in exotic goods from the 'New Worlds' of Asia and the Americas) and those manufacturers making luxury goods for the aristocracy and the increasingly wealthy, acquisitive 'middling sort'. The emotional detachment of the governing classes from awareness of the state of the poor was a resonant feature of contemporary England. On Sunday 13 March 1603, 11 days before Elizabeth died, the Puritan divine Richard Stock delivered a Lent sermon at the Pulpit Cross in St Paul's churchyard, commenting,

> I have lived here some few years, and every year I have heard an exceed-
> ing outcry of the poor that they are much oppressed of the rich of this
> city [...] All or most charges are raised [...] wherein the burden is more
> heavy upon a mechanical or handicraft poor man than upon an alder-
> man.[5]

Economic difficulties, poverty, social conflict, religious dissent and politi-cal tensions relating to the role and nature of monarchy and the role and authority of Parliament all remained unresolved. Charismatic, strong rul-ers like Elizabeth carry their followers with them, generating loyalty though often through an element of fear. Emerging problems are ignored or masked, because the ruler prevents them being discussed and councillors are afraid to raise them. Elizabeth, for example, passed several laws that made it treason to even discuss who might succeed her. This persistent refusal to face the succes-sion problem, strengthened by legislation making discussion of the succession treasonable (the 1571 Treason Act and in 1581 another reinforcing it), began to look like a very human failure to acknowledge, address and resolve a serious matter for fear of contemplating her own mortality. A polity needs an active ruler, engaged with the key problems (the 'larger picture') but also with day-to-day petty matters and responding according to careful reason, not knee-jerk stop-gap reactions. States need rulers engaged physically and sympathetically with the people, not reclusive scholars shut in their libraries improving their mind (like Prospero in *The Tempest*), or reluctant to exercise laws that are punitive for fear of losing the people's love (like Duke Vincentio in *Measure*

5 Quoted in De Lisle, *After Elizabeth*, 111.

for Measure) or reacting with cruel autocratic anger when thwarted (King Lear and James I). Theseus does react immediately to try and arbitrate the problem between Egeus and his rebellious daughter, though he should have taken more time to consider how to defuse the situation. His failure to resolve the problem forces Lysander to set up the elopement plan. Had matters been smoothed over, however, there would be no play.

Monarchical commitment and a readiness to seek advice was part of the circumspection expected of a ruler. Elizabeth was notoriously difficult to advise. Favourites attempted it, but rarely got very far. William Cecil, Lord Burghley (the queen's secretary), was perhaps the only effective politician to approach the queen and influence her thinking.[6] Strong, purposeful, central rule – in other words, caprice and diktat – were how Elizabeth administered her realm. Yet she did make regular progresses through the country and did meet her people. Theseus has done this (see 5.1.93–105) and shows a readiness to indulge his people as witness his attitude to the appallingly bad performance of 'Pyramus and Thisbe'. Though he is privately, in conversation with the courtly snobs, patronizingly disparaging of the acting, he accepts the play as an offering of loyalty:

> For never anything can be amiss
> When simpleness and duty tender it. (5.1.82–3)

It is a form of hypocrisy, being smilingly pleasant to them but criticizing them behind their backs. It is courtesy to accept a gift with apparent gratitude. It is the thought of wanting to put on a play for their duke that counts, not the quality of the acting. Theseus's hypocrisy is part of the role of a public figure.

All the problems and developments of Elizabeth's reign would persist and worsen under her successor. Commerce and manufacture expanded rapidly (triggering a rise in the middle class that provided and serviced the new trades and crafts). Attitudes to religion, a desired freedom from church authority, began developing into resistance, and science began slowly to displace old superstitions and belief in magic. Like all times of transition, the Elizabethan period and the seventeenth century were exciting times for some but unsettling for most, profitable for a few but a struggle for the majority. As always, the rich found ways to get richer, and the poor got poorer. The courtly ranks and working men are evident in *Dream*, but with no sense of the tensions that were growing in the real Elizabethan polity. The lovers betray some upper-rank snobbery while the play-within-the-play is being performed, but the mechanicals express only love and loyalty to the Duke. Gradually

---

6 He served her for most of her reign, twice as Secretary, then as Lord High Treasurer.

the poor found men to speak up for them in the corridors of power, in the villages of England and the overcrowded streets of the cities, but it was a dangerous step to take to oppose, question or open debate with the queen. In 1559, very soon after her accession, Elizabeth had issued a proclamation forbidding plays to discuss 'matters of religion or of the governance of the estate of the Commonwealth'. Such concerns were the province of 'grave and discreet persons', 'men of authority, learning and wisdom', not to be aired before or by the general public.[7]

The public rituals of monarchy are of their nature theatrical and therefore artificial and false, but the day-to-day running of a state is founded in the dullness of bureaucratic minutiae. The trick is to know where the make-believe ends and reality begins. Elizabeth certainly had the reputation of being a good public relations person. She could be dogmatic, autocratic and occasionally physically violent at court, but was friendly and personable in meeting her people. More Egeus in her orthodox dictatorial manner she could nevertheless play the Duke's more easy-going sympathetic style.

Her reign was still much overshadowed by the past. The Virgin Queen, married to her state, supportive of Anglican religion, was assailed by political and religious problems. Numerous plots to assassinate her troubled her reign. Catholic opposition to her and to her church was a constant threat undercutting the growing confidence of a people beginning to define itself by its separateness from and differentness to the Catholic continent. Theseus has none of these difficulties. They are outside the scope of the play. It is holiday time in Athens, and a royal wedding is to be celebrated.

7 Wickham, Berry, Ingram (eds.), *English Professional Theatre, 1530–1660,* 51.

Chapter 2

THE ELIZABETHAN WORLD ORDER: FROM DIVINITY TO DUST

Strict hierarchy (everything having its place according to its importance in God's order) and organic harmony (everything being part of a whole and having a function to perform) were the overriding principles of the broad orthodox background to how the audience thought their universe was structured (cosmology), how they saw God and religion (theology) and how their place in the order of things was organized (sociology). The disorders and disharmonies upsetting roles and expectations in *Dream* stem from Hermia's initial transgression in opposing her father's choice of husband and in his dogmatic determination to enforce patriarchy and have his way. Indeed the disharmony starts further back with Hermia's involvement with Lysander. Young women in those days did not have as much freedom as they do today to independently initiate personal relationships. It is a deep father/daughter, male/female opposition. It also incorporates a deep conflict between nature and man's artificially imposed morality.

Egeus accuses Lysander not only of having stolen Hermia's heart but also of having 'turn'd her obedience (which is due to me)/To stubborn harshness (1.1.37–80). The hoped-for happy harmony Theseus envisages in marrying his erstwhile enemy and prisoner, Hippolyta, is impossible until several reversals of orthodox hierarchy are returned to natural order. Theseus is able to make his own choice in marriage, but the progression of his situation from enmity to love is a foreshadowing of the dissensions that will disturb the lovers and amuse the audience.

From inauspicious beginnings his journey has ended in lovers meeting.[1] The audience will probably have a sentimental interest in whether the four young people they see before them will end up in similar happiness. Though Egeus is,

1 'Journeys end in lovers meeting', *Twelfth Night*, 2.3.42.

by law and custom, entitled to arrange his daughter's marriage and enforce its solemnization, he contravenes humanist teaching in being very heavy-handed and transgressing expected parental affection. The potential death sentence is a piece of unrealistic theatrical nonsense and excess invented to bring tension and suspense into the situation. The orthodoxy of paternal power is displayed in a bad light and in an extreme form, but the conduct of the young couples is equally counter to courteous behaviour. Loss of order and its restoration, at the heart of the play, is an essential ingredient of comedy, though in real society such disorder is deeply unsettling and not a matter for laughter.

Hermia is a stock character from classical comedy – the wayward child determined to have their lover. Usually in Roman comedy this is a young man in love (*adulescens amator*) who infuriates his miserly father by his choice of partner. The angry old man (*senex iratus*) is there in Egeus, but Shakespeare innovates by making his wayward child a young woman.

Breaking the commandment requiring she honour her father, Hermia and Lysander subvert authority and obedience by falling in love without her father's agreement and then further transgress by eloping and planning to marry without parental consent. That was illegal in Shakespeare's time. In act 2 the audience learns that the source of the human dissension is the conflict in the spirit world between a husband and wife, Oberon and Titania. Their unresolved animosity (significantly focused on a child, a surrogate for the infant they do not themselves have) has turned the natural world upside down. The unseasonable weather is not simply a topical reference to the heavy rains of 1594. It shows that the macrocosmic disorder of the elements creates a reflective, complementary disorder in the human microcosm. This is evidenced in Egeus and Hermia's situation where love and deference are overturned and in the seasonal changes and the effects on the social and agricultural activities of the human world. Once the fairy world is normalized and there is peace between the king and queen, hierarchy in the mortal world will be restored to its orthodox order. The initiating trope of the dissension brought by Egeus and the disruption brought to and by the lovers is fully explained and described by the weather disruptions listed by Titania (2.1.81–117). The source of the transgressions and reversals is clearly stated:

> And this same progeny of evils comes
> From our debate, from our dissension;
> We are their parents and original. (2.1.115–17)

This linking of the macrocosm with the microcosm, the idea that the spiritual dimension is connected to, has correspondence with and has an influence over the fleshly world, is central to Renaissance thought about order, hierarchy, nature and God. The disruptions witnessed in the court in Athens act as enveloping emblematic metaphors of a world turned upside down. A series of other reversals are presented before the play reaches a degree of harmony. The most visually alarming reversal is Bottom's metamorphosis into an ass/man monster. Such reversals of normal order, such deformities of nature, were unsettling to an audience that followed a strict etiquette of precedence, where social power depended on a high-ranked person's lofty place in the hierarchy being seen (in clothing and other signs of wealth, title, rank and office, in the imposing appearance of their home, in the size of their estate) and accepted as superior by those below them in society. This was 'a society obsessed with hierarchy'.[2] It was neurotically attached to the idea that social order was imposed by God, was highly religious, but at the same time it was believed that magic really existed and that storms, tempests, famines, plagues and epidemics, riots and rebellions, and bodily deformities were sent by God to punish sins.

Everyone was fairly clear where they were in the universal order, the Great Chain of Being. God ruled all, was omnipotent (all powerful) and omniscient (all knowing). Man was inferior to God, Christ, the Holy Ghost, all the angels, apostles, saints, the Virgin Mary and all the blessed, but superior to all animals, birds, fish, plants and minerals. God ruled heaven, kings (princes, dukes, counts) ruled on earth and fathers ruled families like God at home. Theseus, hoping to divert Hermia's defiance into conformity, reminds her, 'Your father should be as a god' (1.1.47). The chain stretched from God through all the hierarchies of existence to the very bottom in descending order of importance – from divinity to dust – all interconnected as contributory parts of God's creation. The chain links were each a separate group of beings, creatures or objects, each connected to the one before and the one after, semi-separate, dependent but partly independent, both separate and part of something greater. Within each link there was a hierarchy. The human link contained three different ranks – 'the better sort' (kings, nobles, gentry), the 'middling sort' (merchants, shopkeepers, farmers) and the 'baser sort', or lower orders (artisans, peasants, beggars). The word 'class' was not used then, but these ranks, degrees or stations represent our upper, middle and lower classes as we know them today.

2.1 Cosmology

When thinking of creation, of the cosmos, in astronomical terms, medieval and Renaissance man saw the universe as an all-enveloping godliness that

2 Beier, *Masterless Men*, 125.

incorporated Heaven, the human world and Hell.[3] The universe was thought to be a set of revolving, concentric, transparent crystal spheres, one inside the other, and each containing a planet. It was a geocentric model, with the earth in the middle encased in its sphere, enveloped by the moon's sphere, and then by Mercury, Venus, the sun, Mars, Jupiter and Saturn, like the rings of an onion.[4] Each of these bodies in its sphere circled the earth at different orbital angles and different speeds. The fairy Puck meets at the beginning of act 2 describes wandering everywhere 'swifter than the moon's sphere' (2.1.7), and Puck himself refers to 'Venus in her glimmering sphere' (3.2.61). These are planets that could sometimes be seen with the naked eye orbiting in their crystal spheres and increasingly observed through the new device the telescope.

After Saturn came the firmament or fixed stars (divided into 12 seasonal zodiac sectors). Next were the 'waters [...] above the firmament' (Genesis 1:7), then the tenth sphere, the Primum Mobile (the first mover), driving the spheres. Finally, enveloping everything was the all-surrounding empyrean, the domain that was all God's and all God – heaven. Here the Deity was accompanied by the angels, saints and the blessed. The set of concentric crystal balls was imagined by some to hang from the lip of heaven by a gold chain. This cosmological organization, called the Ptolemaic system, was formulated by the second-century AD Egyptian astronomer/geographer Ptolemy. In Tudor times his *Cosmographia* (Geography of the universe) was still recommended by Sir Thomas Elyot for boys to learn about the spheres.[5]

A man could see the stars and sometimes some of the planets, but not beyond, his vision being blocked by the 'waters'. As the empyrean (Heaven), the destination for the virtuous saved, was thus made invisible, people needed a visualizable image. It was easier to imagine the blessed 'living' in a celestial city rather than existing vaguely and spiritually in the heavenly ether, so the idea grew of a fortified city with towers and 12 gates made of different substances. At the gate of pearl St Peter supposedly received each approaching soul and consulted his 'Book of Life', recording all the good and evil a person had done, to see if the soul was worthy of entry. Medieval paintings show the *civitatis Dei* (city of God) resembling the walled cities of Italy, France or Germany. Painters often simply depicted the city they knew.

---

3 The Catholic Church had imagined another level – Mount Purgatory – as a sort of halfway house between earth and Heaven. It was for venial sinners who, after death, could purge their souls of sin and make themselves suitable for Heaven. Masses, paid for by money left in wills, were believed to assist in cleansing the soul of the departed. Protestantism saw this as a corrupt money-making scheme and doctrinally suspect. It banished the idea from its own teachings.

4 Uranus was only discovered in 1781.

5 In *The Boke Named the Governour* (1531).

Figure 2.1 The Ptolemaic System
Source: Adapted from the engraving for Apian, *Cosmographicus liber* (*Book of the universe*, 1524). Enclosing the spheres is the '*Coelum Empireum Habitacium Dei et Omnium Electorum*' (Empyrean sky, home of God and all the elect, that is, those judged worthy of heaven).

This system was beginning to be undermined. The great Copernican revolution, supported by Galileo Galilei, Johannes Kepler and others, put the sun at the heart of the universe. Entering the public domain with Nicolaus Copernicus's study *De Revolutionibus Orbium Coelestium* (On the revolutions of the celestial spheres, 1542), the idea was only slowly accepted by scientists and took even longer to filter down to the mass of ordinary people. Dissemination was impeded by church authorities and the slow information spread of those times. In 1603 Sir Christopher Heydon, displaying his knowledge of the new advances, declared, 'Whether (as Copernicus saith) the sun be the centre of the world, the astrologer careth not'.[6] This statement references the triple belief system in which most people lived: (1) Christian doctrine existing uneasily alongside (2) the new astronomy and sciences and (3) old semi-magical beliefs in

6 Quoted in Keith Thomas, *Religion and the Decline of Magic*, 414.

the authenticity of astrology. Heliocentrism, opposed by the scepticism of some astronomers (like John Dee), was frighteningly repressed by very conservative, dogmatic churches. The Catholic Church's Inquisition enforced conformity persuasively with thumbscrews, the rack and many other grisly tortures. The English Church had its own courts to question and punish deviations from customary practice and belief. Visitations within their diocese enabled bishops to keep vicars and congregations in line. Serious infractions could be brought before the Star Chamber or investigated by the Church Commission.[7] Torture was endemic in Protestant Britain too.

Other beliefs concerning the structure of our world were being transformed. Ferdinand Magellan's circumnavigation of the world in 1522 without falling off the edge showed the flat earth theory was inaccurate. Sir Francis Drake's 1580 voyage brought this home more directly to British people when the queen permitted an exhibition to publicize his discoveries. A map displayed at Whitehall Palace made the spherical world graphically clear. But how many people saw it? Shakespeare knew of the new development in thinking about the world's shape as evidenced by Puck's referring to putting 'a girdle round about the earth' (2.1. 175) and Lear's demand the gods 'strike flat the thick rotundity of the earth' (*King Lear*, 3.2. 7). He clearly also knew much about the travel writing describing the discovery and conquest of the Americas. To most people, unenlightened by the new discoveries, the earth's roundness and the centrality of the sun were unimportant and perhaps still unknown. In an age when the nearest town was often as alien as the moon, the 'New Worlds' were places of fantasy and nightmare, inhabited by unnatural beings like the cannibal *anthropophagi* 'whose heads/Do grow beneath their shoulders' (*Othello*, 1.3. 144–5) and a whole bestiary of strange animals.[8] As long as the sun rose to grow corn, ripen fruit and assist in telling the time and the season, most people were indifferent to and largely ignorant of new discoveries. The centre of their universe was their village. The world of Puck and the fairies is the Old World of the ancient fields and the more ancient woods around them, a world of mystery and magic not quite banished by the new religion. The ordinary farmer or villager knew the stars and some of the planets but thought of them as belonging to the mystical world of superstition, astrology, weather lore and magic rather than to the measurable, explicable world of science and astronomy.

7 A court comprising privy councillors and judges, instituted to try cases of suspected treason by powerful lords whom the ordinary courts were unable to bring to book. Under the Stuarts it became a means of curbing the Crown's political opponents, most of whom belonged to the dissenting religions.

8 A tribe with eyes in their shoulders and a mouth in their chest was reported by Sir Walter Raleigh after his 1595 trip to Guiana and recorded in Richard Hakluyt's *Voyages*, viii.

It is that Old World of spirits that is conjured up by Shakespeare to make a fun spectacle. But it is a world of frightening shadows and unsettling possibilities – a world where demons lurked and fairies were not necessarily benign.

2.2 The Great Chain of Being

Earthly creation was thought to be arranged in a set of hierarchical links that made the world order. Man was at the top, followed by animals, birds, fish, plants and minerals. Each stratum of existence was internally organized in order of importance. Man was the pinnacle of God's animal creation, though not entirely perfect. Flawed by original sin, with animal weaknesses (appetites) and negative passions, he was nevertheless part angel, endowed with soul, reason, language, intelligence and sensitivity. A human being acting morally was an imitation of Christ. Choosing the left-hand way, the path of sin, he resembled the Devil. The conflict between these two aspects made man an angel with horns, but the tensions between virtue and passion, the perpetual *psychomachia* of life, sparked the interest of literature.[9]

The Great Chain of Being was a construct of human imagination helping people from the early medieval period to the Renaissance picture how the universe was put together socially and how it worked physically. It was a general view still held by the majority of people in Shakespeare's time, though its physical structure was increasingly challenged by new astronomical research and by socio-economic changes. Most people still thought the universe was geocentric. The Renaissance is regarded as a time of change, new learning and new knowledge. Men were discovering new lands and new ways of thinking about God and society, but this only slowly affected everyday life. The iconoclastic, rationalist, free-thinking Renaissance Man, daringly breaking through barriers, questioning old orthodoxies, was an oddity often in conflict with the authorities, especially the church. Such men were confined to small minority groups of progressive artists/scientists/intellectuals.[10] The sixteenth-century Everyman was conservative, backward

---

9 *Psychomachia* is the struggle between good and evil for the mind/soul of man. Often portrayed on stage as a good angel and a bad angel, advising or tempting the protagonist (as in *Dr. Faustus*), by the 1600s they lost their allegorical state and were integrated into secularized characters, like a good friend/false friend or wise, disinterested adviser and flattering self-seeker.

10 Such a network of astrologers, mathematicians, atheists and navigators is discussed in Christopher Hill, *Intellectual Origins of the English Revolution*, chap. 4. There was an uncertain mix of genuine scientific discovery and superstition and magic among these groups. The 'Wizard Earl' of Northumberland, one of the Raleigh group, experimented in alchemy.

looking in his beliefs and daily lifestyle. If literate, he would have few books apart from a Bible.[11] He still went to the wise woman for semi-magical medical help, believed in divination, went to an astrologer to predict a suitable day for travelling or a suitable mate, and still believed the Chain of Being was constructed by God.

Hierarchically arranged, reflecting descending importance, usefulness and perfection, the chain was sometimes imagined instead as a ladder, the *scala naturae* (ladder of nature). The ladder image was agreeable to Christian thinkers because it suggested rising toward the divine (or descending toward perdition), as each person was supposed to do by a life of virtue that would cleanse away their earthly faults, purifying them as they metaphorically climbed rung by rung to a holiness that prepared their soul for heaven. The title of Walter Hilton's book *The Ladder of Perfection* (written between 1386 and 1396) reflects the image of the step-by-step rise from sin to virtue, presented as a spiritual journey toward the peace given by Christ and the peace which is Christ. He is the perfection achieved by climbing the ladder, reached by denying the primacy of the 'anti-Trinity' of mind, reason and will, and trusting faith alone.[12] In the busy, corrupt world of the 1590s, the same belief persisted among the godly sort.[13] These were not just fervent Puritan zealots but rather those ordinary folk who believed their Christian duty was to live the good life. The good life meant not the carnal life of fleshly pleasures but instead the hard-working, devoted life of the family man or woman, who struggled through their days with the example of Christ as their perpetual model. It is important not to underplay the general piety of most people at this time. They listened frequently to preachers of different sorts and attended church regularly. The literate bought, borrowed, read or had read to them the religious pamphlets pouring off the presses. The production of printed pamphlets accelerated from a trickle to a flood by the Civil War.[14] Though people lived physically 'by the rule of the flesh', as St Augustine put it, they were dominated by 'the rule of the spirit'.[15] While many lived dedicated Christian lives, others lived at various intermediate stages ranging from occasionally lapsing piety to a more sinful existence,

---

11 Literacy was accelerating and cheap books and pamphlets, increasingly numerous, were sold at the door by itinerant, general goods dealers called chapmen.

12 Its reliance on mind, reason and will marks the Renaissance's divergence from medievalism.

13 The word 'godly' is used throughout to mean those with faith and not just Puritans.

14 The church tried to keep track of unlicensed presses producing heretical or treasonable matter, but smuggled imports from Holland and the mobility of printers made it very difficult to police thought.

15 *City of God*, 548.

less concerned with virtue, more interested in bodily pleasures and shading down toward outright irreligion, atheism and criminality. This vast spectrum was much represented in the city comedies of the 1600s and in the revenge tragedies (1580s–1630s). Shakespeare's problem plays (*Troilus and Cressida*, 1601–2; *All's Well That Ends Well*, 1602–4; *Measure for Measure*, 1604) and the late romances (*Pericles*, 1608–9; *Cymbeline*, 1609–10; *The Winter's Tale*, 1610–11; *The Tempest*, 1611) are all concerned with the ethical complexities and ambiguities focused in the tensions between flesh and spirit.[16] *Dream*, though it mocks some of the pretensions of the court, is a more light-hearted venture, lacking the cynicism and satire that would soon permeate Shakespeare's work. It does nevertheless address questions of conduct in areas that were of contemporary interest, and the audience's responses would have largely been made within a Christian, Bible-based context.

The chain image was equally apt in suggesting an unbroken interconnection. Between the Creator and dust are all the many phases of existence. Originating in the pre-Christian philosophy of Plato and Aristotle, this idea of hierarchies reflects a Western obsession with taxonomy (classification). In medieval times Christian theology assimilated the heavenly hierarchy to fit above the feudal system of human society and the descending levels of the rest of creation. Below earthly life (physically and morally) came the hierarchy of hell traditionally thought to be in the bowels of the earth. In his *Inferno* (1321) Dante placed it below Gehenna, the rubbish dump outside Jerusalem.[17] The orderliness of God's creation was so embedded in people's minds that any disassembling of it was like an attack on the foundations of life and faith. Order was part of everything and the maintenance of order was a form of worship, an acceptance of God as the author of that order. Within each dominion – Heaven, earth, Hell – there was a series of graduated structures. Even angels were ranked. In Christian thought the domains of heaven and hell, equivalents of the classical world's Olympus (home of the gods) and Hades (the underworld, the place of the dead), had their inhabitants ranked according to priority and power like the various types of earthly creation. All three realms had rulers, and below them were ranks of diminishing power and diminishing virtue.

Hierarchy of Heaven – God > Christ > the Holy Ghost > seraphim > cherubim > thrones > dominations > principalities > powers > virtues >

16 For a full discussion of romance as a literary subgenre, see chap. 13, sec. 4. Literature of the time.

17 In the Book of Revelation, Hell is underground. In John Milton's *Paradise Lost* (1667), Hell is specially created by God from the materials of chaos to receive the falling angels after their defeat and expulsion from Heaven.

archangels > angels > the Virgin Mary > the disciples > the saints > the blessed (saved, elect, good souls admitted to heaven after a virtuous life)[18]

Praying to saints as intercessors for some particular concern was intermittently still practised in Protestant England. Though the church disapproved, having banished such idolatry, it took generations to change a mindset integral to thought and belief for centuries.

Hierarchy of Earth – man > animals > birds > fish > plants > rocks/minerals

Hierarchy of Hell – Devil > First Hierarchy (nobility of hell): named devils like Beelzebub, Mephistopheles, Mammon, Belial and so forth > Second Hierarchy: demons > goblins > imps > incubi/succubi[19] > familiars

Familiars are spirits acting as assistants to witches/wizards. Often they were in animal form. A black cat is commonly thought to be the standard witch's demon familiar, but records include frogs, dogs and toads, and demonic forms.[20] They could take human shape too.

Seventeenth-century witch confessions regularly describe a good-looking blonde-haired young man, but with giveaway cloven hoofs. A familiar attached to a necromancer/witch was thought to be a malevolent servant/assistant imp/demon, a limb of Satan, sometimes even Satan himself. If it was benevolent and assisted a white wizard/cunning woman it was sometimes called a fairy. The latter could have mischievous tendencies like Puck. They were capable of appearing as three-dimensional forms or remaining invisible. Often they were thought to be of human size, but could be tiny too, as are the elves Titania mentions, wearing coats made of bats' wings (2.2.4–5). Ariel, in his song in *The Tempest* (5.1.), claims 'in a cowslip's bell I lie,/On a bat's back I do fly'. Just where to place the fairies in the hierarchy is difficult. Just as magic occupied an ambiguous role in the thinking of the time – opposed by church and law, but resorted to regularly by all sectors of society – so too did fairies. In *The Tempest*, Ariel, Prospero's spirit familiar, is essentially benevolent, imprisoned by the witch Sycorax for having a moral sense 'too delicate/To act her earthy and abhorr'd commands' (1.2.272–3). While the majority of the population saw black magic as malevolent and diabolic, they saw white magic as benign

---

18 The angelic host was formalized by St Thomas Aquinas, one of the seminal Christian thinkers of the medieval period. Hell's hierarchy is variously organized by different writers. Matthew (12:24) calls Beelzebub 'the prince of the devils'.

19 An incubus was a male demon believed to have sex with sleeping women. A succubus was a female demon having sex with sleeping men. This provided an explanation for people's sex dreams. It was the forces of evil tempting you.

20 James I, in *Demonologie* (1597), describes the Devil himself appearing 'either in likeness of a dog, a Catte, an Ape, or such-like other beast; or else to answere by a voice onlie', 19.

and helpful. The law and the church saw both forms as illicit, dangerous and punishable. Ariel is a spirit of air and fire (qualities associated with the divine) rather than of earth and water (heavy qualities suited to darker arts). The cast list describes him as an 'airy spirit'. He flies swiftly over distances (as far as the Bermudas), is able to flame amazement and 'burn in many places' and leave the ship 'all afire with me', but also acts as an all-purpose spirit/servant associated with water and earth too. Puck too flies swiftly and far ('I'll put a girdle round the earth/In forty minutes', 2.1.175–6), can make himself invisible, can imitate voices, and (the only piece of spectacular magic he achieves by himself) turn a man's head into that of an ass. None of the fairies does or threatens harm. The commonest questionable act they were traditionally thought to commit was abduction. There are many folk tales from around the country telling of humans who were taken by the fairies. Some disappeared for good, others came back telling of a visit to fairyland. Like gypsies, fairies were often blamed for the theft of children. Being a fairy child exchanged for a human infant was a frequently made excuse for a child's strange, wayward or inexplicable behaviour. Puck's confederates are benign spirits. They are all controlled/commanded by the king or queen, neither of whom makes malefic magic. They are at odds with each other, and Oberon's trick to make her fall in love with 'some vile thing' (2.2.33) is cruel, but it is only ever envisaged as a temporary state that he can use to gain the changeling boy and then reverse. Far from intending any harm to humans, he attempts to intervene for the good. It is Puck's mistake that leads to humour and further complications. Puck has mastery of the powers of nature, can change his shape, become invisible, bring down a fog, transform a human head, induce sleep, but is unable to discern the relationship between Hermia and Lysander. Even fairies are not omniscient. The magic involved in his accounts to the fairy (2.1.), for all its elements of petty mischief-making, is theurgical.[21] Was fairy magic good or evil? It depended on your religious viewpoint. Some would condemn Puck outright as a sprite, as a non-human and as a breaker of Nature's laws. Many others, among the ordinary country folk of the time, would see him as sometimes vengeful, sometimes playful, sometimes helpful; a vestige of pre-Christian beliefs that the natural world was inhabited by spirits.

2.3 Human Hierarchy

Society was arranged in three main ranks, degrees or orders – the 'better sort', the 'middling sort' and the 'baser sort' ('lower orders', 'commoners'). It was

---

21 Theurgy is magic designed to call up and use good spirits. It was used to discover the secrets of the universe and to approach closer to God.

thought those of the highest rank were there by the grace of God and were therefore automatically considered to be more virtuous and more intelligent. They certainly thought themselves superior. The lower orders were thought to be naturally sinful, the middle ranks dour money-grubbers. The three-tier medieval feudal system (those who fight, those who pray, those who work) was refined during the Renaissance. The remaining clergy personnel, diminished by the Dissolution of the Monasteries, were assimilated into the upper ranks. 'Those who work' split into two – 'the middling sort' and 'commoners'. Both had to work in order to live, as opposed to the idle rich living off inherited fortunes and the income from their landholdings. The middling sort included the important expanding new masses of bourgeois entrepreneurs (bankers, projectors (speculators), merchants, wealthy clothiers, industrial manufacturers) that hardly existed before, but which were driving the astonishing explosion of culture, commerce and capitalism that was the Renaissance. As money and investment spread through the arteries of European trading, so the bourgeoisie expanded. This rising class was to be a vital feature in Elizabethan-Jacobean social change, hugely increasing the numbers of the middling sort, creating confusion about whether money-powerful 'merchant princes' and 'captains of industry' belonged within the middling rank or among the better sort.[22] In *Dream* the top tier includes Theseus, Hippolyta, Egeus and the lovers. The middle rank is not represented at all, except perhaps in the person of Philostrate, the Master of the Revels. He is a higher species of servant in the palace, part of the administration, but may be a courtier and of the better sort.

The baser sort are present in the mechanicals who are artisans with special skills (weaver, joiner and so on) and referred to in the mixed group of country folk Puck has played tricks on. The fairies too have a hierarchy, though it is limited to just the royal couple and the rest as their attendants. They form a household though it is not currently a bonded and happy one. Puck is Oberon's specific servant, not quite a domestic steward and not quite a personal body servant. He is clearly something more than a general attendant like Mustardseed, Cobweb and Co., acting as a 'fixer' or personal assistant and having a close bond with his master.

In general terms, the old, simple world of the Middle Ages, unified in religion by Catholicism and unified socially by the simplicity of the feudal system, was morphing into dynamic new forms. Rising wealth created new social classifications. Developing industries created new roles and services. The broad social stratifications were still the same, but within them the three levels were diversifying into complex new divisions while social/political/

---

22 Jacobean comes from the Latin word for James (*Jacobus*) and refers to Elizabeth's successor, James I.

commercial interactions were changing in destabilizing, disturbing ways with which many could not easily cope. *Dream*, as a probable wedding celebration piece, does not address the current social tensions. It does reflect an earlier form of community bonding whereby local people, ordinary workmen, would visit the houses of loftier folk and perform simple plays (mummings or guisings). These were accompanied by music, songs, dances and were a gift of loyalty made at seasonal times like Christmas or New Year, or to celebrate the lord of the manor's birthday or a family wedding. From the beginning, when Quince suggests putting on the 'Pyramus' play, it is a spontaneous display of love for the Duke. What it also does, minimally, during the performance, is allow the courtly characters (Theseus and Hippolyta included) to make some snobbish, mocking remarks on the amateur nature of the acting and by implication the uncultured nature of the actors. The audience will remember the many shortcomings of the lovers and make due assessment of them in the light of their illegitimate superior attitude. It is fools mocking fools, but the courtly lovers betray base conduct in their snobbishness, while the baser mechanicals display uncommon and simple love. It is yet another reversal in a play full of unexpected upside-down happenings. The 'Pyramus' play focuses implicitly on the contrast between the workmen of Athens, their sincere loyalty and simple lives and the idle and artificial lives of the courtly characters – between the old values of virtue and loyalty in Quince and Bottom and the new, self-obsessed younger generation. Theseus's court is only represented by the lovers, Egeus and Philostrate.[23] The latter is a court servant responsible for arranging entertainment. Master of the Revels was a royal appointment and was therefore a post of some authority. Philostrate's short list of possible items for the wedding entertainment is an amusing mix of types inappropriate for a marriage and is perhaps Shakespeare poking fun at the censors as well as referencing the hierarchy that existed among types of literature. Hierarchy applied in everything. What is here only a hint of tensions between the ranks would become a major theme in the plays of the 1600s as the governing elite detached itself more and more from the rest of the population. This process was already advanced by the end of Elizabeth's reign.

The state of official corruption was highlighted in the oration delivered to James I on his arrival in the City. It demanded, 'No more shall bribes blind the eyes of the wise, nor gold be reputed the common measure of a man's worth'. The burden of monopolies, generating taxes that went into the pockets of the monopoly owner, was described as 'most odious and unjust' and sucking the marrow out of the life of the people. Elizabeth had promised to deal with

---

23 This is the name Arcite assumes in Chaucer's 'The Knight's Tale', when he returns in disguise to Athens to serve Theseus.

the corrupt and burdensome matter of monopolies, but the Commission set up to do so had made little progress by the time of her death. The legal profession too is indicted: 'Unconscionable lawyers and greedy officers shall no longer spin out the poor man's cause in length to his undoing and the delay of justice'. The speaker demanded benefices no longer be sold, the nobility be encouraged to shoulder their responsibilities to the poor, and placemen rebuked for their 'abuse [of] the authority of his Majesty to their private gain and greatness'.[24] Anti-court satire is minimal in *Dream*, but exists in the young lovers, spoiled by privilege and the comforts of wealth. Like so many of the courtiers surrounding Elizabeth they have nothing to do so get entangled in love affairs. It is nature too, the young inevitably attracted to each other – swapping partners, falling out, making friends again, falling out again. Cupid's quadrille. The queen was always losing her temper with her gentlewomen for their flirting (and worse), sometimes striking them, sometimes dismissing them out of hand. These spoiled darlings, the four lovers, are offensively snooty about the failings of the lower sort and their acting, but blind to their own failings. Theseus, at least has the grace and wise experience to put that in the perspective of the 'great clerks' (men of great learning) who stumbled and stuttered over welcome speeches they should have delivered with practiced ease (5.1.93–103). And he has some sense too that the thought, the gesture, behind the mechanicals' play is of more count than the quality of the performance.

2.4 The Social Pyramid of Power

Each man was placed within different hierarchies relating to (1) society in general, (2) work and (3) family. It is usual nowadays to see human hierarchies as layered pyramids. This simple sociological model classifies according to priority, power and function. First you had a place in the social pyramid (better, middling, lower sorts), and within every rank there was a hierarchy with its duties and each with its role to play. At work you were in another pyramid where position depended on age, experience, seniority, qualification and success. Within the family pyramid an unmarried man was subordinate to his father and other male elders. Once married, he was still subordinate within his extended patrilineal family but ruled his own nuclear family – wife, children, servants.

---

24 Nichols, *The Progresses, Processions, and Magnificent Festivities of James the First*, 128–32. 'Placemen' were those who held court or government posts, often through family influence, often through flattery. A benefice was a post in a parish, a vicar's living. Priests often accumulated more than one in order to increase their income.

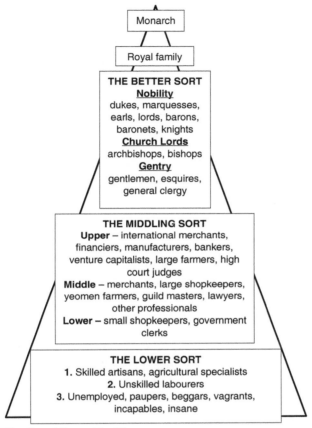

Figure 2.2 The Social Pyramid of Power

For each of these social structures obedience to those above was paramount, resistance to change was the default attitude and threats to order were seen as blasphemy defying God's arrangement. Those with the most to lose were the most in favour of things staying the same, and so in history and literature noblemen and kings promote order and hierarchy as God ordained and not to be overthrown; maintaining the status quo guaranteed the perpetuation of their power and privilege. The Bible, as so often, authorizes this view: 'Remember them that have the rule over you' (Hebrews 13:7) and the commandment 'Honour thy father and thy mother'. Hermia's usurpation of her father's right to choose her husband gives a blasphemous, order-threatening edge to the original driver of the plot. This is reinforced as she agrees to Lysander's plan to elope. She is both right and wrong. Right to pursue the growing humanist impulse to allow offspring a say in the choice of marriage partner, wrong to bullishly go ahead with opposing her father. This collision of different views must have been increasingly common, but the law is on Egeus's side. To marry without parental consent was illegal, but the urge to pair is a primal instinct, an example of a natural force that disregards morality. Hermia will be punished for this subversion by the temporary misery she experiences when she believes Lysander is dead and then learns that he has rejected her.

At the pyramid's pinnacle the ruler reflected God's dominance. The idea of Divine Right is founded on the belief that kings are chosen by God as his representatives on earth. This endows monarchs with immense psychological (or superstitious) influence and protection. As God's vice-regent a king could no more be questioned, tried, imprisoned or executed than you might think of questioning or dethroning God. In 1528 William Tyndale, a radical thorn in the church's side, affirmed in *Obedience of a Christian Man*:

> He that judgeth the King, judgeth God and damneth God's law and ordinance […] the King is, in this world, without law; and may at his lust [will] do right or wrong, and shall give accounts to God alone. (39)

A queen was regarded in a similar light. Though there was some resistance to Elizabeth initially (because of her religion and her gender), her stalwart behaviour gradually changed that. In some senses, as married to her state and refusing to marry, she had unsexed herself. She could become aggressively angry when opposed, but that was the way of monarchs, a reflection of the wrath of God. The queen's will was sufficient for anything to be done unquestioningly by willing courtiers. It was the magic password for absolute power.

Elizabeth's will could be implacable and she frequently acted outside the law. Here we encounter the uneasy tension between the divine aura attributed to kings and the daily experience of their human failings. Theseus could no doubt be autocratic. Some of the audience would know him from accounts (in Ovid and Plutarch) of his many exploits, military campaigns and amatory conquests.[25] He defeated the Amazons, captured Hippolyta and refers to returning victorious from Thebes (5.1.51). Oddly, his greatest exploit, the slaying of the Minotaur, is not mentioned. His legend also has various stories of his sexual encounters (2.1.78–80). The duke presented, however, is moderate, wise, circumspect, a mature figure about to settle into marriage. His patriarchalism is more benign, calm and flexible than Egeus's. Given the ritualistic, emotional reverence accorded to monarchs, customary obedience

---

25 He is most well known for killing the Minotaur. His amatory exploits involve numerous
    stories of his abandoning his women.

to hierarchical superiors and his apparent humanism, the audience would almost certainly endorse his conduct.

2.5 The Better Sort

Below the king come the royal family, the nobility and gentry. The descending ranks of the nobility – dukes, marquesses, earls, viscounts, barons, baronets, knights – were highly stratified, jealously preserving distinctions of precedence. This upper section included archbishops and bishops, men of immense power and wealth. Part of the upper sort, but untitled, was the gentry – men eligible to be called esquire and gentleman – ranked upper, middle and lower according to size of fortune, size of landholding, civic profile and ancientness of family title. They traditionally tended to live on their country estates, but were by the 1590s beginning to spend more of their time in London. This was a growing trend among the younger generation of gentry families whose sons were entered at one of the several Inns of Court (though not necessarily studying seriously). Many more hung about the court, hoping to get a government place or catch an heiress.

The better sort, the quality, was the governing elite. What did they actually do? Some of the titled nobility were ministers, privy councillors, government officers, Members of Parliament, army or navy officers (when there was a war) or local magistrates. Those with estates might manage them (though probably deputed a steward who did most of the actual administration). They were essentially idle, a leisured class pursuing their own pleasures (hunting, gambling, drinking, whoring, lounging about at court, visiting each other, being idle and bored), a do-nothing aristocracy doing nothing. The cowardly villain, Lord Segasto (in *Mucedorus*), in answer to the question 'What's your occupation?' replies, 'No occupation, I liue vpon my lands'.[26] Yet they had clear social duties as outlined in the Works of Corporal Mercy (chapter 4). Segasto may live (that is, gain income) from his estate, but in fact lives at the court and is affianced to Princess Amadine. He appears then to have trapped his heiress. Increasingly there were men who never had an estate (or had lost it through debt) but still called themselves gentlemen on the grounds of having (or having had) some sort of independent means, university education, officer rank, skill with weapons, no need (or intention) to work for a living, gentry parents and a coat of arms. The city comedies of Thomas Dekker, Thomas Middleton, Thomas Heywood and Ben Jonson are filled with impoverished gentlemen, living on the edge of high society, scrounging meals, hustling for an heiress or favour at court.

26 A romantic comedy (c. 1590).

The lovers appear to be at least of the gentry. Demetrius is called 'a worthy gentleman' (1.1.52) by Theseus and Hermia claims the same of Lysander. Speaking for himself Lysander enumerates some of the criteria required of gentry status; he is of good descent ('well deriv'd'), has property ('well posses'd') and claims his 'fortunes every way as fairly rank'd' as those of Demetrius. What the audience subsequently sees of both these gentlemen is not entirely positive. Both are prepared to do wrong in order to achieve their aims, and both are quarrelsome and petty. Demetrius is guilty of bad faith in declaring love for Helena, winning her devout love in return and then rejecting her as he switches his affections. Helena's idolatry of him is blasphemous and excessive, therefore sinful, but that does not excuse his inconstancy. What makes his situation worse is that there is no explanation for his change of heart. Is it simply that Hermia is more attractive? That would make him a shallow man influenced by looks. Some men are. Is he a rake, unwilling to commit himself and seeking the pleasure of a new conquest? Many young gentleman behaved thus. Are his feelings genuine affection? A possibility is that his change of focus is motivated by material considerations. Perhaps Egeus's estate and fortune are greater and the match therefore more advantageous. Young gentlemen of the time were guilty of all three motives. There is some suggestion that his change is simply due to the unpredictable, waywardness of sexual attraction. He once fancied Helena and then one day found he suddenly fancied Hermia instead.

This is a court drama centred on the privileged, with the mechanicals as a version of rustic clown humour to offset the supposed elegance and wit of the courtly characters. Bottom and his companions are of 'the baser sort', but, interestingly and significantly, their naivety (though laughed at by the lovers, by Puck, and by the audience) is outweighed by their goodness of heart. They make the courtly quartet look petty, narcissistic and spoiled. Their play-within-a-play parodies the immature and unreal fantasies of love displayed by the lovers. Though individual aristo-gentry characters in Shakespeare may have laudable qualities and conduct themselves suitably, many expose the increasing sense of the age that the governing elite was essentially no better morally than others of lesser rank and that in practical terms they often behaved badly and did not deserve the respect they demanded or the access to money and power they had traditionally monopolized.

The distinguishing material feature of the nobility and gentry was land ownership. Estates meant tenants (farmers and land workers) paying rents and farms generating edible or saleable produce. Rent rolls provided the basic unearned family income. Many titled men held sinecure government posts (requiring little actual work) enabling them to sell other places to family members, friends and political contacts who formed an obligated clientage. This nepotism (giving jobs to relatives), once a sin, now accepted, added to the growing grievances about court and government corruption. Wealth could be materially improved if the monarch gave or sold you a monopoly giving you control of the taxes and other charges on a commodity or service, like imports of wine, tobacco, sugar, spices, starch. This provided further opportunities for selling posts within the infrastructure.

The upper sort thought themselves superior in virtue, born with innate leadership abilities, with better moral qualities than other ranks. *Probitas* (physical and moral courage) was believed to pass through the male bloodline (a reason for ensuring the legitimacy of your heir), giving each generation the qualities of prowess, honour, magnanimity. Noble in rank, supposedly noble, courageous, generous in nature, they thought themselves deserving of respect from all below them. They were the contemporary evolution of the medieval warrior class, now demilitarized and without apparent function. Many were fine and decent people, living on their estate and doing their social-moral duties. Many others were simply weak personalities, extravagant, in debt, idle, sexually decadent, syphilitics, drunks, fools, inveterate gamblers, incompetent estate managers and indifferent to their role as social exemplars and leaders. The discrepancies between the expected conduct of the ranks and their actual behaviour were regular targets for satire. Knowing how to behave and actually conducting themselves decorously, respectfully, modestly, were two different matters. Running after the latest fashion or innovation was becoming a feature of court life, fed by leisure and the expanding availability of luxury goods as commerce and capitalism took hold in England. It was encouraged too by the increasingly closed nature of the court as a separate world in a protected bubble.

Contemporary plays are full of men claiming gentlemanly status, but behaving badly. Drunken, roistering, lecherous misconduct highlights serious discrepancies between the expected behaviour of aristo-gentry men and their actual comportment. Inconsistently, bad behaviour often coexisted with oversensitive alertness to offences to their honour. The phrase "'Pon my honour' is often used in plays of the time, but is often spoken by someone with no honour. Reacting to the slightest perceived insult to their conceived status and the respect they believed it deserved, that response was usually angry and violent. To assert their honour they often were drawn into dishonour by inflammable temper and a readiness to commit assault that often led to death. In an age when gentlemen habitually wore swords the ready resort to arms was all too easy, especially when alcohol played its part in the constant outbreaks of street and tavern brawls. This gives a very topical context to the swaggering braggadocio of the Montagu-Capulet bravo boys in *Romeo and Juliet*. In the mad atmosphere released in the woods, Lysander and Demetrius are ready to duel. This upper rank method of settling differences, often mocked in plays, might have a fatal outcome if it were not for Puck's comic interventions at the express command of Oberon. In Geoffrey Chaucer's 'The Knight's Tale', a minor source for the play, the rival lovers, Palamon and Arcite, are found fighting in the woods by Theseus. There the eventual outcome is tragic. Shakespeare is hinting at the silliness of thinking a love rivalry can be suitably settled by one side killing the other. It parallels the animal world where males fight to possess a female and suggests that in essence Lysander and Demetrius are not as noble as they like to think and humanity has not progressed far above the animal. Elizabethans were obsessed with genealogy and proving the ancientness of their noble or gentry origins. Many family trees, however, were fabricated, claiming spurious descent from Norman knights, Saxon thegns, the pre-Roman Trojan roots claimed for the British nobility by pseudohistorians like Geoffrey of Monmouth, even from Old Testament kings. Suitable payment to the College of Heralds bought you an 'authenticated' coat of arms and genealogy. A courtly audience knew full well that young men of titled or gentry background often behaved like rowdy boors and that some of them were currently watching the play – or probably ogling the female spectators.[27] In the 1600 city comedy *Eastward Ho!* Francis Quicksilver claims gentlemanly status because his mother was a gentlewoman and his father a senior Justice of the Peace. He feels it is beneath him being apprenticed to a goldsmith, and spends his time drinking, whoring and scamming money out of other gallants.[28] To him idleness, drunkenness, violence, sexual permissiveness and carelessness over money are gentlemanly markers:

> do nothing [...] be idle [...] Wipe thy bum with testons [sixpences; approximately 5p], and make ducks and drakes with shillings [10p]. [...] As I am a gentleman born, I'll be drunk, grow valiant, and beat thee.[29]

Golding, the industrious apprentice, scorns Quicksilver as 'a drunken whore-hunting rake-hell' (1.1.125). Sexual licence was common in the elite. A 'rake-hell' was a troublemaker and alludes to the gang mentality and hooliganism of the many unsupervised, upper-rank young men floating around London. Neither Demetrius nor Lysander is such a man. Or at least there is insufficient evidence to accuse them of rakish conduct. Such cynicism is out of place in

---

27 Public theatre audiences too knew how often flashy, attention-seeking gallants crowded the stage and interrupted performances.

28 Many aristo-gentry families put younger sons to professions and trades so they should have an income, since land and fortune were bequeathed to the eldest male.

29 1.1.114–16.

this play (though it was rightly displayed in other dramatic pieces). Their behaviour is more that of spoiled, badly behaved children than of Renaissance gentlemen.

Despite the intense stratification of society, dividing lines between social groups were becoming blurred by individual cases of social mobility, the proliferation of new knights (to accelerate under James I), growing bourgeois wealth and the increasing complexity of society. People became obsessively fussy about precedence, about being treated according to their rank and preserving (or creating) fine differences that made them feel superior.

Ambition is a subset of pride or vanity, so overambition is seen as pushy, selfish and sinful. Those born to great title and great place should still remain modestly humble. Similarly, those who rose to authority from humbler beginnings. A little ambition was proper use of your God-given talents. However, to avoid the hubris of becoming overproud of advancement, you should humbly thank God for the good fortune of your rise, downplaying the extent and effect of your own efforts. Some small degree of self-congratulatory hubris underlies Hermia's confidence in her relationship with Lysander and some slight tinge of pleasure may lurk behind her sense of how lucky she is compared to her unfortunate friend, Helena.

Political theorists and moral polemicists formulated programmes emphasizing the upper rank's duty to serve the state and the people. Elyot's *The Boke Named the Governour* (1531) proposed careful education combining a reverence for virtue and a readiness to assume social responsibilities. This meant residing on your estate, leading the community, helping the poor and establishing schools and almshouses, as enshrined in the Corporal and Spiritual Works of Mercy.[30] These justified living comfortably off income derived from the labours of tenant farmers and tenant labourers. Rank and privilege were counterbalanced by a requirement to put something back into the community, but one of the features of the growing new individualism was that civic spirit and charitable work were discarded by elite-group young men. This was assisted by the growing tendency of the governing class to gravitate to London and become detached from their locality. A responsible role for the ruling classes, built on a virtue-based humanist education, was promulgated by many writers throughout the decades leading to the Civil War, but the actual behaviour of many gentlemen conformed more to Viscount Conway's definition: 'We eat and drink and rise up to play and this is to live like a

---

30 'The great and their dependents seem to have fed on a gargantuan scale; and conspicuous waste was a feature here. (Though it is fair to say that the waste was supposed to go to the poor.)' (Davies, *Peace, Print and Protestantism*, 21). The key word here is 'supposed'.

gentleman; for what is a gentleman but his pleasure?"[31] Courtiers were docile yes-men and yes-women, obsequiously bowing and scraping at the monarch's whim. They were intent on pleasure and advancement. Advancement depended on others so they tended to be morally indifferent. To stand by principles could lose you favour and the pursuit of personal pleasures dulled the ability or willingness to make moral distinctions if acting on them threatened enjoyment.

2.6 The Middling Sort

The next layer down is the newly enlarged bourgeoisie or 'middling sort'. In the Middle Ages, the feudal system included them with 'those who work' (anyone earning a living – 90 per cent). This group had comprised everyone from day labourers to the wealthiest merchant. The country arrangement was village centred, with the lord of the manor (living in or near the village) governing and guarding his 'flock' of farmers and labourers like a shepherd guards and guides his sheep. The workers lived in or near the village, where the priest represented 'those who pray'. The professional 'middling sort' (lawyers, doctors, produce factors, clothiers) hardly existed in country areas, tending to cluster in market towns, and were numerically an insignificant demographic nationally. By the Renaissance the pattern had changed. With the growth of commerce and the growth of towns, the 'service' industries expanded and with them the numbers of the bourgeoisie. Eighty per cent of the population was still rural – farmers and labourers – but 15 per cent were now largely town-dwelling middle class. The growing bourgeoisie of Elizabeth's time was to expand much more in the trade boom of the seventeenth century. The remaining 5 per cent was the aristo-gentry. The upper ranks thought the middling sort were greedy, obsessed with making money and virtuous enough, but lacking taste, elegance, culture. They were mocked as 'cits' (citizens, city dwellers, that is, not landowners), derided as social climbers whose wives and daughters were snobbish, fashion mad, empty headed and easy prey for lascivious, gold-digging courtiers. Some were like that, but many were educated, cultivated people, looking after their families (especially their children) better than many of the nobility. Most were hard working, eager to put some comfort buffer between themselves and poverty, but showed civic spirit, were modest in lifestyle and personal behaviour, were pious and drove conservative church reform.

The rise of the middling sort was *the* big social change in Elizabethan-Jacobean England. Division into upper, middle and lower classifications distinguishes between, say, a very rich international merchant, the farmer

31 Cited in Stone, *The Crisis of the Aristocracy*, 27.

of a largish thriving farm and a small shopkeeper. The upper echelons were protocapitalists – merchant bankers, financiers, large-scale traders, major clothiers, wealthy manufacturers, leading lawyers and judges, and large-scale farmers; men of wealth and local (and increasingly national) power. The middle group would be comfortably wealthy merchants, middling size farmers, masters of guild trades, professionals like doctors and local attorneys, living in cathedral cities and market towns. The lower 'middling sort' were small shopkeepers, small farmers owning a little land and growing numbers of lowly paid metropolitan-based government clerks. What differentiated between the upper, middle and lower 'middling sort' was money. More money meant access to mayorships, masterships of guilds, alderman or councillor status. Money brought the capacity to invest in speculative enterprises and loan cash, thus becoming a sort of local banker or simply a moneylender. Usury (lending money at interest), a sin in medieval times, was acceptable by the seventeenth century, a natural development of the growing cash richness of the expanding commercial world. As the economy grew and fortunes were made and wasted, satire against moneylenders, money-amassing citizens, luxury, ostentation and the debt-fuelled lifestyles of parasite gentlemen, became regular features in contemporary plays.

The middle ranks looked up to the aristo-gentry and showed public respect. Privately they thought themselves morally better than the upper sort. Pious, hardworking, earning their living, living moderately, paying their debts, establishing schools and hospitals, doing civic duties and giving their children disciplined home lives, education and love, they saw the gentry and nobility as vain, idle, showy wastrels, parading in silks they did not always pay for, gambling, drinking, promiscuous and demanding deference not always deserved. Yet, many merchants longed to rise and put on the outer show of gentleman status – a fine country house, a coach and horses, fashionable clothes, social power. 'The old English gentry were powerfully reinforced [...] by an influx from the professional and mercantile classes. Lawyers, government officials, and successful merchants bought land not only to better their social standing but also to increase their incomes'.[32]

As England became a more active trading nation the middle ranks expanded, became wealthier and more upwardly mobile. Those at the very top could be awarded or buy titles. They tended also, with this status rise, to move into the country, selling their business, cutting themselves off from the taint of trade or distancing themselves from it by hiring a manager. Legislation restricting bourgeois land ownership was increasingly ignored,

---

32 Maurice Ashley, *England in the Seventeenth Century*, 18.

circumvented or simply not applied. The bourgeoisie was unstoppable, buying estates, thinking of themselves as equal to the nobility. Some became nobility. Money power enabled such men to push out the cash-strapped yeoman farmer. Agricultural depression led to many of these freemen, who owned their own farm, selling up to opportunist incoming merchants-turned landowners looking to add to their holdings. Small, independent farmers were also under pressure from some gentry buying them out to augment their estate.[33] Another expanding bourgeois group was top civil servants administering the proliferating departments of government. The three most prestigious power posts were those of Lord Treasurer, Lord Chancellor and the Queen's Secretary. These were political as well as royal household appointments. Below them was another internal pyramid of court power – the bureaucrats – reaching down to the lowliest 'base pen clerks'.[34] These serviced the royal palaces, but were also developing into the ever-growing numbers of Westminster-based government officers. The most junior bureaucrat dreamed of catching the eye of a superior or a titled courtier and being promoted. Once you were in a higher place your future was made. Place was gained by patrimony, patronage or purchase. A poor clerk without family connections or money to help him advance had to find a patron. It was difficult to penetrate 'the grand efflorescence of nepotism' if you could not buy promotion or inherit a post from your father.[35] The court was awash with idle young men seeking opportunities for advancement. In *Eastward Ho!* the idle apprentice, Quicksilver, cast off by his irate master, declares, 'I'll to the Court, another manner of place for maintenance [...] than the silly City!' (2.2.54–5).

If your courtier patron had some measure of power you were made. In the plots, counterplots and intrigues of the Elizabethan and Jacobean courts there are innumerable examples of servants ready to bear false witness, cheat, slander or kill to get on.

2.7 The Lower Orders

The mass of the population formed the broad base of the pyramid. Skilled artisans were at the top along with farm workers who had a specialism (shepherd, horse man, cattle man). The mechanicals are such men – weaver, joiner, carpenter, tinker, bellows-mender, tailor.

---

33 Maurice Ashley, *England in the Seventeenth Century*, 18.
34 Wilson, *State of England* (quoted in *Camden Miscellany*, vol. 16, 43).
35 Kishlansky, *A Monarchy Transformed: Britain 1603–1714*, 44, describing the huge network of family members given posts under the influence of the Duke of Buckingham, James I's favourite.

Apprentices, learning a trade or craft, would count themselves as being in the middle of the lower orders, but with diligence and industry aspired to become skilled in their craft, then masters of it, and move into guild membership and shop ownership, thus becoming bourgeois. Below was the mass of unskilled day labourers, with the unemployed, paupers, beggars, vagrants and the insane and incapable at the very bottom. Farm labourers were severely squeezed at this time. Their continuity of work was unreliable as they were for the most part day labourers hired according to a farmer's needs at any particular time. The family economy was thus irregular. Being taken on at one of the annual hiring airs could secure a year's work, but many unskilled labourers could only depend on short-term employment when a farmer needed hedges laid or cut, ditches dug or dredged, a batch of bricks made or some other rural activity that required muscle power. Being fit, with a good reputation for being a hard worker (and a good Christian) would be in your favour. To be known as a drunk, lazy and unreliable would make it hard to find regular employment.

Prices rose steeply throughout Elizabeth's reign. The purchase of basic foodstuffs, coal, wood, clothing, furniture became a challenge for the poor. Common land, where game could be caught, firewood gathered, vegetables cultivated and animals grazed, was being enclosed by greedy landowners. Thus the opportunity to augment comfort and the cooking pot was diminishing. The pauperized sector of society was growing alarmingly, not because of a high birth rate but because the changing economy caused 'casualties' falling out of working society into unemployment. The growing unemployed poor put pressure on local poor relief resources and represented a dangerous underclass with the potential for social unrest and riot. A 1597 law aimed at reducing poverty by banishing vagabonds to Newfoundland and the East and West Indies, but remiss or reluctant justices of the peace meant the law failed to reduce or repress the problem.

The lower orders were thought by those above them to be lazy, delinquent, ignorant, feckless and vicious (in the physically brutal and morally unsound senses). There was much truth in that, particularly among the growing numbers of urban poor. But commoners thought much the same of their so-called betters. And there was truth in that too. But there were hard-working men and women living godly lives and bringing up families despite hardships. Those living in the countryside were particularly susceptible to rent rises, fluctuations in labour needs, prices of produce and winter feed for livestock and changes in land usage brought about by local enclosure. A series of disastrous harvests in the 1590s exacerbated matters, bringing famine to many doors. Piety, thrift and frugality could not feed hungry children, nor could hard work and decent living protect you from market shifts caused by the greed of others in higher ranks. The queen and her self-satisfied courtly audience knew well that outside the comfort of Whitehall and Westminster beggars thronged the streets. There were about 12,000 in London in 1600. Some were indolent fraudsters preferring begging or thieving to work, but many were genuine victims of hard times. They were all the responsibility of those with wealth and rank and privilege. They were all morally and metaphorically (some literally) sons and daughters of the nobility. It was the job of the monarch and court to look after them. Most did not. Shakespeare was to roundly criticize the detachment of the rich from the poor in *King Lear* (1605–6) and *Measure for Measure* (1603). In the opening to *Coriolanus* (1607–9), the privileged senator Menenius and the arrogant Martius clash with the starving citizens of Rome:

> 1 *Citizen*: We are accounted poor citizens, the patricians good. What authority surfeits on would relieve us. If they would yield us but the superfluity while it were wholesome, we might guess they relieved us humanely. But they think we are too dear. The leanness that afflicts us, the object of our misery, is as an inventory to particularize their abundance. (1.1.13–19)

If the governing orders have responsibility to aid the poor, the poor have a duty of grateful, controlled conduct and respect for those above them. Bottom and crew clearly have a simple love for their duke. Their language register too is a social marker. As usual in Shakespeare, commoners speak in prose, while the courtly group speak in finely wrought verse, elegant and elevated with imagery and allusions that indicate their educated state. The mechanicals are presented as comic and clownish, though there is an element of instinctive human care and supportive comradeship in their treatment of each other. Social difference and tensions between the ranks are not major themes in *Dream*, but difference of degree is loosely present and relates to the duty of governorship, the Christian duty of charity, the concept that brothers (in Christ) and neighbours should take care of one another. Theseus shows something of this, but the young lovers seem unaware of any duty of respect for the actors of 'Pyramus and Thisbe'. While cringingly sycophantic to the duke they are mockingly dismissive of the working men trying so hard to show their loyalty. To Demetrius they are 'asses'. He is particularly vocal and negative in his comments, though Lysander too joins in making what they both think are clever, witty asides. Even Hippolyta is less than sympathetic to the amateurs' attempts and Theseus, though aware of the difference between intention and performance, is occasionally superior in his remarks. There is throughout a disturbing sense of lofty disdain from the courtly characters at odds with how they were expected to behave.

Their wit adds to the bluff humour of the poor acting and is perhaps suited to the play being written for a specific audience comprising people just like those witnessing the play-within-a-play. Thus we have the theatrical, emotionally heightened atmosphere of high-status people at a wedding feast watching high-status people at a wedding feast watching low characters performing a play. And the mechanical actors are watching and interacting with their fictional audience as well as watching the real audience watching them. A private performance in an aristocratic household would have an audience of the governing elite who might well echo the sniggering mockery made of Quince's prologue and the rest of the text and how it is realized. Would they also see how they were being exposed? Another level of irony, a further reflection of a reflection, is that the real audience would regard the actors as low. They were employees of the Lord Chamberlain, servants working for their living and their general reputation was not much higher than that of rogues and vagabonds. Yet, at the same time, the actors would also be observing and judging their audience and, in general, plays, as 'the abstract and brief chronicles of the time' (Hamlet, 2.2.520), presented, exposed and ridiculed the ruling elite.

2.8 The Theory of the Humours

There was a hierarchy of the inner man too. The head, like a monarch, ruled (theoretically) as a symbol of the primacy of reason. The major organs, like the nobility and gentry, came next as key to the functioning of the body. The limbs, like the commoners, were the mere labourers. This loose, imprecise image was less important than the connection of the body to the outer world; microcosm linked to the macrocosm. The alignment of stars, planets and the ascendant zodiac sign at the precise hour of your birth fixed your fate and personality, enabling predictions to be made concerning your future fortune. Different planets had influence over individual body organs, and whichever planet had dominance in the sky at the time of your birth was believed to influence your psychological profile. Some personalities were thought to reflect the influence of their birth planets and these were thought to be linked to gods or goddesses – jovial (Jove), martial (Mars), saturnine (Saturn), venerean (Venus), mercurial (Mercury).

From classical times until the end of the eighteenth century people believed that the body contained four fluids (humours) influencing personality, attitude and behaviour. This had been particularly developed by the Roman physician Galen and persisted into Renaissance times, though it was beginning to be modified by new scientific discoveries. While your astrological sign provided your broad personality characteristic, the proportions of the four humours determined more precisely your temperament. Whatever these proportions were at birth defined your healthy, normal state and your psychological type. The humours were phlegm, yellow bile (choler), blood and black bile. Four temperaments were associated with the humours. The phlegmatic person was normally easy going and stoical, remaining calm in crises and seeking rational solutions. Theseus as presented has some of these qualities. The choleric man was inclined to temper, was bossy, aggressive, ambitious and liked to take charge. Bottom shows this 'complexion' though his aggression is sublimated into enthusiasm. Egeus too has negative choleric aspects. The sanguine man (in whom blood predominated) tended to be positive, active, impulsive, pleasure seeking, self-confident, sociable, open, friendly and warm hearted. Bottom seems to have these qualities too. Those in whom black bile was dominant tended to be melancholic, negative, overly introverted and considerate of others but inclined toward pessimism about the imperfections of the world. Between these four cardinal types there were many permutations, explaining the huge variety of human character types and the range of emotional phases to which an individual might be subject.[36] Illness was thought due to increase or decrease in one fluid and led to (and explained) mood changes. The medical practices of bloodletting and purging were thought to rebalance the body, getting rid of an excess of one humour, while certain foods or drinks redressed deficiencies. Some natural philosophers (scientists and rationalists) were beginning to question this theory, believing parental attitudes, early life experiences and education formed personality. Some physicians were beginning to ascribe other causes to illnesses, though today's knowledge of chemical imbalances causing maladies and mental aberrations shows the humours theory was not entirely wrong. Belief in these characteristics led to 'humour' stereotypes in literature that were sources of comedy (grumpy fathers, shrewish wives, romantic lovers, bloodthirsty soldiers, gold-mad misers, sex-mad widows, scheming villains). The character flaws of tragic heroes and villains fall easily into these broad categories as well.[37] There were those who rejected astrological origins of personality and claimed they created their own destiny. In *King Lear* the Machiavellian individualist Edmund rejects the idea of the stars forming personality. Conceived 'under the dragon's tail' and born 'under Ursa Major' he would be expected to be 'rough and lecherous' (1.2), but he believes in himself as maker of his own destiny ('I should have been that I am had the maidenliest star in the firmament twinkled at my bastardizing'). It was a minority view.

36 Burton's *The Anatomy of Melancholy* (1621) explores this multiplicity of psychoemotional types.
37 Lily B. Campbell's *Shakespeare's Tragic Heroes* interprets heroic flaws from physiological diagnoses.

Because *Dream* is meant to be farcical fun, the humour characteristics are simple and superficial. The characterization too is simple and shallow. Exploration of deep psychological patterns is not part of this play. It is what people do that signifies and the consequences of their actions drive the plot and create comedy. There are some deeper issues related to patriarchy, arranged marriage and the oddities of love, but entertainment and laughter dominate.

Renaissance people believed in a network of complex correspondences flowing through the outer world and the inner world. All things were linked. The planets affected and reflected moods (the moon was particularly influential). Herbs and weather affected health (fogs were thought to carry poisons and disease) and certain organs were affected by particular types of food or drink and were also linked to moods and psychological states.

2.9 The Rest of Creation

Below humankind come the other animals – mammals, birds, fishes, insects – able to move, reproduce, experience appetites (hunger, thirst, heat, cold, sexual urges), with limited sensory responses, limited problem-solving intelligence, lacking capacity for a spiritual life, without ability to reason or make moral decisions. Animals were thought not to have souls, logic or language.

Animals were also ranged hierarchically though less precisely than humankind and often according to conflicting ideas about their nature. The lion topped the mammal world because of imagined links to courage, nobility and kingship (reflected in the use of lions as royal heraldic emblems). Machiavelli, who stared unblinkingly into the corrupt hearts of men, has a different take on lions. He asserts,

> As a prince is forced to know how to act like a beast, he should learn from the fox and the lion; because the lion is defenceless against traps and a fox is defenceless against wolves. Therefore one must be a fox in order to recognize traps, and a lion to frighten off wolves. Those who simply act like lions are stupid. So it follows that a prudent ruler cannot, and should not, honour his word when it places him at a disadvantage [...] If all men were good, this precept would not be good; but because men are wretched creatures who would not keep their word to you, you need not keep your word to them. [...] those who have known best how to imitate the fox have come off best. But one must know how to colour one's actions and to be a great liar and deceiver. Men are so simple, and

so much creatures of circumstance, that the deceiver will always find someone ready to be deceived.[38]

Wolves, jackals, hyenas and foxes were bottom of the rankings for their scavenging, savage, predatory, untrustworthy and devious nature.[39] Rats too were lowly rated. Tigers were noted for ferocity. A mother tiger's protectiveness of her young is admired but tigers could also display an unreliable, savage aspect – a quality ascribed to ruthless humans. Apes and goats were thought particularly lustful. Goats were also associated with the Devil for their horns and cloven feet. They were often pictured as part of black magic rituals. Reptiles were low in the hierarchy, snakes particularly being associated with evil, linked to temptation and original sin in the Bible. Frogs, toads and bats had witchcraft associations. Lowest of all were rats, mice and other vermin. Domesticated animals were ranked by usefulness. Dogs (guards and hunters), listed with the working creatures, could be highly prized. Elizabethan-Jacobean gentlemen discussed endlessly the qualities of their hunting dogs. Canine loyalty was highly regarded, but there were negatives – a fawning, flattering nature, greediness, readiness to follow anyone who fed them.[40] 'Whoreson dog' and 'cur' are common abusive epithets in plays. Hermia, angered by Demetrius saying he would give Lysander's carcase to his hounds rather than reunite him with her, loses her maidenly modesty and patience and abuses him: 'Out, dog! Out, cur!' (2.2.59). The insult is the worse for being made to someone who regards himself as a gentleman. The effects of the night, being lost, frightened and confused, leads all the lovers to betray less than courteous manners as they too are transformed by the less civilized atmosphere of nature into snapping, snarling animals. This fits with the wide-ranging animal references that abound in the woodland scenes. The range is drawn from all areas of living creatures, but there is a preponderance of negative images (frightening, savage, or evil) over positive or neutral images.

Birds were highly thought of because of flight's association with air, thought to be a divine element along with fire. Hierarchy applied again with the eagle as *the* hunting bird for an emperor, the gerfalcon for kings and other birds of prey, used for the chase, ranked according to their suitable social level; peregrine (nobility), goshawks (yeomen – landowning small-scale farmers),

38 *The Prince*, chap. 18, 99–100. Jonson had some knowledge of Machiavelli as evidenced in *Sejanus*. See Daniel C. Bourghner, '*Sejanus and Machiavelli*'. *Studies in English Literature, 1500–1900* 1, no. 2 (1961).
39 Plato commented, 'those who have deliberately preferred a life of irresponsible lawlessness and violence become wolves and hawks and kites' (*Phaedo*, 134).
40 'No animal fawns so much as a dog, and none is so faithful' (Erasmus, *Praise of Folly*, 134).

sparrow-hawks (priests) and the smallest hawk, the kestrel, for servants or knaves. Lower than birds of prey (including the owl, synonymous with wisdom) come the carrion eaters (vultures, crows, kites). They were thought of as lowly because they were scavengers, like hyenas in the mammal hierarchy.[41] Kites (combing rubbish tips in London) are always represented negatively, linked with the parasitical behaviour of those feeders and sycophants hanging around the households of men of power. The parasite (the yes-man toady, like Mosca in Jonson's *Volpone* and Oswald in *Lear*) was a familiar figure of scornful fun on stage, originating in Roman comedy and satirical poetry. A parasite was anyone attaching himself to a rich, powerful man in order to curry favour, be rewarded for running errands (including pimping) and flatter his master's self-esteem. At the very least he hoped to be invited to dinner, at most retained as a household member and personal assistant and fixer. Mosca, the paragon of parasites, is so called after the Latin for fly since flies are the lowest carrion-eaters. Volpone is named after the Latin for fox, since he is both devious and cunning. Jonson names his fortune hunters after allegorical animal figures in line with the medieval-Renaissance iconography of didactic beast fables – Voltore (a vulture-like advocate), Corbaccio (a raven miser) and Corvino (a crow merchant). Below the scavengers came the worm- and insect-eating birds and then the seed eaters. The peacock, in a class of its own, became the symbol of ostentatious vanity, pride in appearance and showiness. Abusive name-calling occurs plentifully in Jacobean drama, often involving animal/avian epithets that use negative characteristics associated with these creatures. A few animal epithets are positive, but linking human behaviour with animals is mostly negative, a reminder that the animal side of man was sinful – lustful, brutal, devious, greedy, slothful. The worst type of connection involves monsters – unnatural, mythical, animal hybrids. Puck describes Bottom translated as a monster ('My mistress with a monster is in love'. 3.2.6). The grotesque sight of an ass's head on a man's body, a reverse of the centaurs with their horse body and legs with human head and torso, is suitably unnatural enough to be called monstrous. It is the stuff of myth and nightmare, such as the dark Anglo-Saxon dreamings of beasts found in illuminated gospels, the multiplicity of strange hybrid creatures painted in the margins of medieval manuscripts and the ugly monster mutants in paintings of hell. These are the imaginings of mankind's worst fears. Though in one respect Bottom's appearance is pantomime comedy, in another respect it also suggests of course the forms the Devil takes and the darker side of life, the

---

41 Leviticus 11:14, cites kites among those fowls regarded as 'an abomination'.

fears that emerge in dreams, the monsters men can be made into by love or hate.

The word 'monster', applied to humans, connotes anyone behaving outside the acceptable parameters of civilized conduct and signifies an extreme shift from what is regarded as decent, normal human form and behaviour to brutal and uncivilized in manners and deformed in appearance. An ass-headed man is a travesty of nature. Medieval and Renaissance people believed outward ugliness expressed inner deformity and sinfulness. Beauty was thought a guarantee of inner grace and purity. In *The Tempest* Shakespeare has a savage, Caliban, described as being as deformed in mind as he is body. He is regularly called 'monster'. He represents the primitive savagery in man and the ungovernable sex drive of the brute, man reduced to his lowest, what King Lear calls 'unaccommodated man'. Another sort of monstrousness is released when the lovers quarrel in the woods. It is as if the restraints of normal consciousness are relaxed and the inner thoughts of Lysander's private criticisms of Hermia are cruelly voiced. They represent either how he might feel if he hated her or the negative aspects of her that he has already thought, but has repressed as being outweighed by the positives. It is what we all do when in love with someone. We become aware of those features of their behaviour that we do not like, but we put them to one side because our love is stronger than our criticisms. But in arguments such thoughts become weapons. Even more vicious are the poisonous recriminations spilled out by Hermia and Helena, long-repressed niggles and grievances from girlhood. Their nastiness is worse, however, for it is not caused by the magic juice. It is disturbingly natural and results from the situation triggered, ironically, by the misapplied love juice on the men's eyes. The release of these monsters shows how thin is the veneer of courtly, civilized behaviour, how thin the veil of some friendships. The smile of courtesy masks sharp teeth and these are often bared in Shakespeare at times of stress. The appearance of gentle, genteel conduct is often drawn aside to reveal the reality of the savage hidden underneath. This is a comedy and the lurch into seriousness is soon reversed, but the threat of death that looms with the two men marching off to duel with each other is a sharp little reminder that love and so-called love can provoke violent and hateful outcomes. There is Hermia's dream of a serpent eating her heart. The serpent has multiple meanings; it represents evil, sin and death as well as the lure of the phallus, the subliminal sexual longings of a young woman.[42] There is also the overhanging threat of Egeus's demand for her death if she refuses to marry the husband he has chosen. This shadow may recede from an audience's consciousness as the woodland wildness escalates,

42 See Norman N. Holland, 'Hermia's Dream', *Representing Shakespeare*.

but it comes back with a jolt in the light of dawn when the duke and his court discover the sleeping lovers. But then we remember Demetrius is left with the effects of the juice and loves Helena once again, so Egeus's argument is hobbled.

As explorers and exploiters opened up the world and contact was made with other cultures, questions began to be asked about just how truly civilized European society was with its institutionalized torture, witch burnings, the persistent wars, rampant urban sex trade and epidemic sexually transmitted diseases, assassinations, politically motivated executions and religion-based massacres. Its selfish, ruthlessly individualistic conduct, its predatory profit-driven capitalism, disregarding the ancient traditions of respect for the vulnerable, is another collision of old and new philosophies that casts doubts on European cultures and how much progress had been made in the achievement of virtue. Courtiers wore silks, adorned themselves in jewels, acted out elaborate rituals of etiquette, listened to intricate and beautiful music, read philosophy and poetry and watched charming and elegantly written plays. Manners had improved greatly. The surface gloss was supershiny, but people starved, thousands were homeless, syphilis raged, the plague still killed thousands, torture and brutal punishments were institutional and courts were hotbeds of promiscuity, intrigue, power struggles and murders. And over and above all this was the arrogant, bullying high-handedness of the better sort toward those 'beneath' them.

Transferring the action of the hub of the play to the woods at night banishes all possibility of pastoral nostalgia. The sudden entry of the fairy and Puck jolts the possibilities of the play into a whole new dimension and the increased use of animal imagery only adds to the edginess. The woodland scenes are hilarious but disturbing too. These are the woods of nightmare. Puck's account of his traditional mischief-making gives the promise of fun, but the very presence of these supernatural figures and the wrangle between the fairy rulers evokes the fear of trouble and evil. For all the playfulness of Puck some in the audience might feel uneasy watching representations of these creatures of nightmare. The church condemned all magic, black or white, and the uncertainty and unpredictability they represent was eerie and unsettling. The woods at night are a fearsome place and we need to remember that darkness then was truly dark; no street lighting, no reflected urban glow, would mitigate the depth of the blackness. Only the moon and stars would provide their spooky light in clearings. The rest of the wood, beneath the tree canopy, would be densely dark and thought to be full of goblins and sprites and the possibility of the Devil.

The final groupings of animals were the fish, reptiles, amphibians, insects, sessiles (unmoving shellfish). Fish were ranked low as water was thought to be a dull heavy element like earth. Reptiles, amphibians and insects were thought of as even lower, fleas and lice being seen as verminous like rats. Bees and ants were positively regarded for their industry and apparent social organization, which suggested something approaching intelligence. This period valued any form of corporate, civic or community cooperation as a mark of moral engagement with civilized behaviour.[43]

Lower still the plant world had only the ability to grow and reproduce. But it too had its hierarchy. Trees were at the top with the oak as the prime form – useful, because of its hardness, for building ships and houses – associated with stability, rootedness, imperturbable fortitude, Englishness. A king was seen as a great oak, sheltering his people as the tree did birds and insects. Shrubs and bushes came next, along with flowers. The rose was thought to be the most beautiful, associated with love and with the Virgin Mary (the rose without a thorn). The lily signified purity, chastity and death. There was a wide range of floral/herbal significations and symbolisms – pansies for thought, rosemary for remembrance, rue for repentance, violets for faithfulness, daisies for unhappy love and so on. Next came the useful plants – corn crops and herbs with their medicinal and edible uses. Ferns, weeds, moss and fungus were such basic forms they often furnish pejorative metaphors for useless, troublesome, threatening humans. The rising middle class were sometimes described as 'so many early mushrooms, whose best growth sprang from a dunghill'.[44]

At the bottom of creation were rocks and minerals. Even they were ranked by their values as gemstones, precious metals or their usefulness for building or yielding minerals. Pearls were much prized in the Renaissance – by Queen Elizabeth particularly – and long associated with purity. Among the metals gold was king, succeeded by silver, iron (and steel), bronze, copper and lead. Gold had particular power over the Renaissance imagination. It was the regal metal, used for crowns and sceptres, superior to silver and lowly lead. A high point in a nation's power was called a 'Golden Age'. Gold also had its negative side as a symbol of man's greed. It is the means to suborn, seduce and corrupt. Its corrupting power is most forcibly, comically and sadly expressed in Jonson's classic play *Volpone* (1606) where, blasphemously, gold has become Volpone's god. In *The White Devil* this idolatrous blasphemy is sharply described by Flamineo:

> O gold, what a god art thou! And O man, what a devil art thou to be tempted by that cursed mineral [...] there's nothing so holy but money will corrupt and putrify it. (3.3.21–8)

---

43 Plato regarded bees, wasps and ants as 'social and disciplined creatures' (*Phaedo*, 134).
44 Flamineo in Webster's *The White Devil* (1612), 3.3.49–50.

For Romeo gold is 'saint-seducing' (1.1.), and King Lear's reference to its power to corrupt justice is particularly pointed considering the persistent contemporary pleas for reforming and purifying public life and James I's ignoring of complaints about venial judges.

> Plate sin with gold,
> And the strong lance of justice hurtless breaks;
> Arm it in rags, a pigmy's straw does pierce it. (4.6)

Gold became a Renaissance obsession. People longed to own it, got it, wanted more, undertook dangerous voyages to find it and attacked Spanish galleons to steal it. Foolish speculators gave huge amounts of money and metal objects to alchemists experimenting to turn base metals into gold. Some seriously believed this possible. Others saw its potential for lucrative scams. This avaricious dream became the subject of Jonson's powerful satire on human greed, *The Alchemist* (1610). The exploration of America was triggered by the belief that limitless amounts of gold could be found there. Raleigh built a fantasized kingdom – El Dorado – where gold could be collected lying on the ground. There was gold to be found in South America, but not to be as easily acquired as Raleigh fooled himself and others into believing. Gold thread woven into cloth, gold jewellery and gold plates and drinking goblets all showed off your pride in your wealth. Pride was a deadly sin and display a vanity associated with pride. A base desire for gold may be behind Demetrius's switch of affection, if, as is probable, Hermia is an heiress.

Among rocks marble was most prized as a princely adornment for palaces, followed by granite, sandstone and limestone. Even lowly chalk and clay had their uses, though clay was connected metaphorically with man's mortality. Last of all are the particle forms – sand, gravel, soil, dust. Sand and gravel represented the precariousness of man's attempts to build a solid life. This is reflected in the biblical parable of the man who foolishly built his house on sand. Earth was thought a dull, heavy element, appropriately typifying man's last state: 'earth to earth, ashes to ashes, dust to dust'.[45]

2.10 Order

Not only were humans ranked in an order reflecting how they were valued but also the preservation of that order was seen as a guarantee of social harmony. Orderliness reflected, therefore affirmed, God's ordering of the universe. Disorder in the spirit world affects the human world in *Dream*,

---

45 'The Ordre For the Buriall of the Dead' (*Book of Common Prayer*), 82.

and when Oberon and Titania are ritually reharmonized then a restoration of order becomes possible among the humans. Order and hierarchy are present in the opening scene as Theseus, surrounded by silent courtiers, discusses his forthcoming marriage and then gives Philostrate his order for entertainment to be arranged. This calm orderliness is broken by Egeus, unsuitably noisy, angry and demanding in his complaint against his child. This is extended when Hermia argues her case – doubly transgressive in opposing her father and speaking up so aggressively. That would not be regarded as suitable for a woman and certainly not for a young woman and daughter.

Theseus remains calm in the face of Egeus and Hermia's provocative and disruptive demands. Dignity in a ruler was to be applauded, especially under provocation. Both Elizabeth and James I sometimes subverted hierarchy and decorum in public humiliation of great men. That could be a process of just punishment, part of the role of a ruler, but it was often rather the reaction and retaliation of personal anger and therefore unacceptable behaviour. Additionally, the increasingly elaborate ritualization of all aspects of the monarch's life meant nobles and titled men doing menial tasks. Some enjoyed the honour, some found it degrading but necessary to maintain their influence. This could also be seen as pride being suitably humble, learning to serve. Christ washing the feet of the disciples would be the biblical analogy. Sir Philip Gawdy describes the king's dinner served not by ordinary household servants but by titled courtiers:

> [The king] was serued wth great State. My Lo: of Southa [Southampton]: was caruer [carving the meat], my L. of Effingham Sewer, and my Lo: of Shrewsberry cup bearer, my poore selfe carried vp ij [2] dishes to his Maties [Majesty's] table.[46]

Courtiers struggled indecorously for these places, flattering, bribing and defaming rivals. Loss of favour unsettled the order of things by rearranging the tenancy of these posts. The tense uneasiness and jealous ever watchfulness of the court was something the audience well understood. Elizabeth's gentlewomen were a constantly simmering pot of jealousies and rivalries.[47] The normative subservience of Philostrate contrasts with the dissentient mood brought in by Egeus, but Theseus keeps the situation relatively calm and looks to deal with the *senex iratus* privately.

---

46 Sir Philip Gawdy, *The Letters of Sir Philip Gawdy*, 132. A sewer seated you at table and
   might also serve you.
47 See Tracy Borman, *Elizabeth's Women*.

THE ELIZABETHAN WORLD ORDER ·

The court was a precarious world; power and place struggles were everyday happenings. Loss of post meant shame, dishonour, loss of influence with the monarch and loss of valuable patronage saleable to those wanting your help accessing the queen or king. The court of Theseus seems decorous and orderly enough. The duke seems to have self-control, but Egeus's demand of the law threatens to destabilize an otherwise balanced, harmonious princely household. In the latter part of her life Elizabeth was increasingly volatile and unreliable. Fears about the end of her long reign, uncertainty about who would succeed, created a general mood of uneasiness in a society that believed the world in inevitable decline. Disharmony in the court would trigger anxiety in the outer world. This would worsen as hysterical anxieties clustered round the coming of the end of the century. The precariousness of the balances of power at the top, evident enough in the rise and fall of favourites, would soon be displayed more prominently when James I came to the throne. New monarchs usually brought in favourites, but James I gave unprecedented power to men regarded as foreigners. These anxieties were already felt in England before the queen even died. The Scottish usurpation would generate grievances to add to others accumulating around the wholesale Scots incursion into London and Whitehall. The Venetian ambassador, Giovanni Scaramelli, recounted how English courtiers complained,

> no Englishman, whatever his rank, can enter the Presence Chamber without being summoned, whereas the Scottish Lords have free entrée of the Privy Chamber, and more especially at the toilette; at which time they discuss proposals which, after dinner are submitted to the Council, in so high and mighty a fashion that no one has the courage to oppose them.[48]

James I's blatant favouritism had the effect of uniting rival English courtiers and politicians. Scaramelli observed, 'The English, who were at first divided amongst themselves, begin now to make common cause against the Scots'.[49] This weakness of the king worsened when favourites began to emerge, the Villiers faction gaining huge influence and huge amounts of money. The same had been experienced during the 'reigns' of Elizabeth's many favourites – Leicester, Essex, Raleigh and others. She regularly dismissed councillors who gave advice she disliked. The muddles and uncertainties of the lovers in

---

48 Quoted in De Lisle, 205. Scaramelli revealed to the Signory (the governing body of Venice) that English politicians, aristocrats and courtiers blamed the government for 'having sold England to the Scots'.
49 Quoted in De Lisle, 210.

the woods are amusing, but the unpredictability of anarchy and change is an unfunny echo of the instability of life at the real court and it is there in the opening scene in the fictional court before the woodland mayhem is even let loose.

This unstable atmosphere develops out of the chain of events set in motion by Egeus's anger and followed by that of Hermia, Demetrius, Lysander and Helena. It is then endorsed by the fury of Titania and Oberon, and the audience realizes that the domestic quarrel of the fairy king and queen is the cause of the dissension in Egeus's household. Michel de Montaigne's comment 'No passion disturbs the soundness of our judgement as anger does' echoes a theme schoolboys knew from studying Seneca's essay *De Ira* ('On Anger').[50] Elizabeth was well established as an intemperate, irascible monarch liable to burst into incandescent anger if opposed.[51] Hasty actions, un-thought-through, rash judgements are unwise. When the actor is a queen the consequences are national. In his essay 'On Anger', Bacon quotes Seneca: 'Anger is like ruin, which breaks itself upon that it falls'.[52] Egeus's anger is self-defeating and provokes reactions he did not want and appears not to have foreseen. Wrath is one of the Seven Deadly Sins. Ephesians 4:26 warns, 'Be angry, but sin not'. Luke 21:19 exhorts, 'In your patience possess ye your souls'. There are angry outbursts among the lovers, and some situations develop in the play that might threaten life and order and certainly disturb the happy humour of the comic mistakes made, but this is not a tragedy and the threats dissipate with the laughter. Keeping order, preserving the distinctions of rank, was essential and they are eventually restored.

Orderliness is given its most famous and detailed definition in *Troilus and Cressida* (1602). Ulysses upbraids the bickering Greek leaders for neglecting 'The specialty of rule'. If the clarity of 'degree' is blurred the unworthy will appear no different from the meritorious. 'The specialty of rule' is founded on the traditional belief that some were born to rule, the rest to obey. Ulysses points out that the whole universe follows ordained rules:

> The heavens themselves, the planets, and this centre,
> Observe degree, priority, and place,
> Insisture, course, proportion, season, form,
> Office, and custom, in all line of order. (1.3.85–8)

---

50 Montaigne, 'On Anger', 810.
51 A characteristic learned perhaps from her father and mother. See Borman, *Elizabeth's Women*, 39.
52 'Of Anger', 226. The translation is Bacon's.

If orderliness is disturbed,

> what plagues and what portents, what mutiny,
> What raging of the sea, shaking of the earth,
> Commotion in the winds. (1.3.96–8)

Disorder affects human society when rank is disrespected:

> O, when degree is shaked,
> Which is the ladder of all high designs,
> The enterprise is sick! How could communities,
> Degrees in schools, and brotherhoods in cities,
> Peaceful commerce from dividable shores,
> The primogenitive and due of birth,
> Prerogative of age, crowns, sceptres, laurels,
> But by degree, stand in authentic place? (1.3.101–8)

Order is the cement that bonds human society and Ulysses warns of the consequences of disassembling order:

> Take but degree away, untune that string,
> And hark what discord follows! each thing meets
> In mere oppugnancy: the bounded waters
> Should lift their bosoms higher than the shores,
> And make a sop of all this solid globe;
> Strength should be lord of imbecility,
> And the rude son should strike the father dead. (1.3.109–15)

Shakespeare was always concerned with order – nationally, socially, personally and spiritually. Rebellion, usurpation and collapse are political themes found in all his history plays (including the Roman ones). Disorder, excess, misrule figure too in his tragedies and comedies. Like many writers in the period, he was much preoccupied by questions relating to how society should be run. Loss of 'degree' means force would dominate society, justice would be lost and illegitimate power, will, appetite ('an universal wolf') would rule. In 1598, James I warned his son, 'beware yee wrest not the World to your owne appetite, as over many doe, making it like A Bell to sound as yee please to interpret'.[53] Oberon does not comply with this and is ready to wrest the world upside down in order to get what he wants. Ulysses uses images of natural order reversed, unnatural human behaviour and the dominance of sin. The

---

53 *Basilikon Doron*, 4. All quotes from EEBO Editions' reprint of the 1682 edition.

irony is that while theoretically God's Nature should be our model, history shows repeatedly that what is natural for man is that the strongest oppress the weak, the brutal take control, the ruthless rule and that mankind in general is unable to control his passions, appetites and the tendency to sin. The need and desire to cooperate creates society and unites community, but such bonding is often weak when faced by strong men ready to shed blood to gain power and backed by pitiless, armed henchmen. Shakespeare's history plays and tragedies show time after time how devious men gain power and how decency and virtue are slow to react. In the comedies, virtue, right thinking and right action win through and tragedy is averted, but there are always latent dangers in the plot situations that develop, dangers that could lead to misery if not death. These threats develop out of man's inability to control passion. In a Christian context, evil was thought ever present, the Devil constantly trying to tempt people into sin. Constant vigilance was crucial. Egeus and the lovers are not circumspect enough to be aware of the dangers inherent in what they bring about. And then the working of magic takes the matter entirely out of their hands. They become the playthings of unpredictability and the unintended consequences of mistakes.

The sixteenth century was much concerned with political theory. Playwrights, especially Shakespeare, picked up on the interest in how society was best to be administered. Sir Thomas More's *Utopia* (1516) fantasized an imaginary perfect state, Elyot's *The Boke Named the Governour* (1531) proposed a curriculum for educating leaders, and the various editions of *A Mirrour for Magistrates* (between 1559 and 1603) retold the exemplary stories of the failings of great men. Before becoming king of England, James I contributed two theoretical conduct books on kingship – *The True Law of Free Monarchies* (1598) and *Basilikon Doron* (1598). Sadly, though typically, there was a discrepancy between his ideas and his actions and both works exposed the shortcomings of Elizabeth too. The theory of order, the desire for peace and harmony were belied by the actualities of life. Order seemed continually under attack and the fear of disorder added to the growing angst the Elizabethans had about the approaching end of an era. The queen was close to death and the century too was dying. The end of a century always raised fears of disasters to come, especially in an age that believed the world was in decline and the end of the world imminent. Rising crime figures contributed to the general gloomy sense of decline and decay. These factors feed into those dramas which reflected the feeling of increased dishonesty, licentiousness, greed and brutality. The city comedies are peopled by petty criminals, shysters, cozeners, cony-catchers, usurers, legacy chasers, greedy merchants and braggart penniless heiress-hunting gentlemen. London itself emerges as the subject and often the setting of critical dramas in the 1590s.

Though foreign cities (especially Italian) also figure, the virulent satire, the abuses and 'ragged follies' are transparently English and associated with London. The astronomical increase in the crowded metropolitan population (200,000 in 1600; 575,000 in 1700) provided a huge variety of human types.[54] Writers revelled in portraying the seedier characters, enjoying their vitality while deprecating their immorality and trickiness. *Dream* is far less topically specific or cynical than *Hamlet*, *Measure for Measure* or *King Lear* and much less so than Jonson's comedies, but its overall mood still reflects those neurotic fears of collapse. *Dream* precedes these cynical-satirical outpourings, but the black mood was already building. It has no significant or lasting place in *Dream* though there are dark elements even in such a happy play.[55] Is it in fact a 'happy play'? It is a feature of this comedy that the sins and transgressions that destroy peace, harmony and lives in other dramas are successfully neutralized. But before they are, the mayhem has a destructive dimension and dissent and confusion dominate much of the action. To a cynical, mocking outsider, the mistakes, the anger released are comic, but the laughter has fear under it and disturbing reminders that our happiness is easily swept away by mischance, malign Fortune and human errors. It has to be said, however, that the Elizabethan period, though stable in so far as the queen reigned for 45 years, was constantly in fear of destabilization by Spanish invasion, wholesale Catholic insurrection or individual Catholic assassination of the queen. It was a very edgy time and such neurotic paranoia seeps into the atmosphere of many plays and is reflected in the frenetic action of even comedies. In 1572, after the Massacre of St Bartholomew in Paris, when possibly up to some 6,000 Protestants were slaughtered, the queen's printer published a book of penitential prayers in which something of the persistent anxiety of the Elizabethans is expressed:

> Oh Lord, the counsel of the wicked conspireth against us: and our ene-
> mies are daily in hand to swallow us up. They gape upon us with their
> mouths as it were ramping and roaring lions.[56]

Much of the fear was well founded and never quite went away, though the Tudor polity became more settled and secure as the reign went on. The Church of England became more solidly entrenched and recruited increasing numbers of the population, though it too faced constant attack from Catholics without and reformers within. The times were both settled and unsettled. Constant

---

54 Daunton, 137.
55 See Bevington, *'But we are spirits of another sort'*.
56 The prayer combines elements of Psalm 22.

vigilance was needed. There was the constant fight with the Devil and the constant fear of Spain and the Catholics. The young Francis Walsingham, even before he became Elizabeth's spymaster with a network of agents all over Europe and England, summed up the situation: 'there is less danger in fearing too much than too little'.[57] The feeling of being at siege, of being destabilized by the Antichrist in Rome, was there all the time. Any form of threat to hierarchy was very unsettling. This is the subliminal mood of *Dream*. For all the hilarity and comic mishap onstage, the action bespeaks nervousness and nightmare.

The geographical arrangements of the nation reflected the authoritarian orderly social structure. Divided into a network of counties, each with a sheriff or lord lieutenant, hierarchy imposed order on what might otherwise be, and sometimes was, a restless population. Below the sheriff, a patchwork of estates owned by rich, titled and powerful men, imposed local authority. The 'big house', often as large and impressive as a palace, carried powerful influence within the locality. Even if the noble owner was rarely there, his family and deputies had a proxy psychoemotional hold on the vicinage. Estates varied in size, but within reach (sometimes within the actual perimeter) of even the smallest would be villages, parishes and individual dwellings rented by families dependent on the landowner's good will.

Grandees often owned huge estates in different parts of the country, each providing income from rents and farm produce, but also extending the reach and control of the governing elite. Increasingly, though land gave status its value was diminishing. Landowners were becoming entrepreneur-employers exploiting mineral deposits on their domains and other natural advantages like water, timber, rush for thatching and clay for bricks. Men of lesser title and less money, with smaller estates, would still have dependent tenants and a home farm to provision the family. The gentry might only own one house, maybe a fortified manor, and their land might be no more than a small acreage surrounding the house, but as part of the ruling class – magistrates and justices of the peace – they further imposed the values of their privileged elite. The whole country was held down under this network of control. As Raleigh put it, 'The gentry are the garrisons of good order throughout the realm'.[58] Hierarchy penetrated parish churches where the better sort had boxed-in family pews near the pulpit, the middling sort sat on benches and the poor stood at the back. The gentry monopolized parish councils through the so-called 'select vestry' system that barred lower ranks from attending. Local politics was controlled by landed families and Parliament was 88 per cent upper orders

---

57 Quoted in Alford, *The Watchers. A Secret History of the Reign of Elizabeth I.* 54.
58 Quoted in Mortimer, *The Time Traveller's Guide to Elizabethan England*, 49.

and 12 per cent merchants and civic authorities. The top 5 per cent had the whole country under their nominal control. The few large cities – London, Bristol, Norwich, York – also had their networks of power, with aldermen, beadles, mayors and the wealthy liveried companies. Richard Stock's 1603 Lent sermon in St Paul's churchyard, directly addressed the Mayor of London, the aldermen, nobility and privy councillors:

> You are magistrates for the good of them that are under you, not to oppress them for your own ease. I would speak to him who is chief of the city for this year. What is past cannot be remedied, but for the future, as far as lies in your power, prevent these things.[59]

'The wealthier sort feared sudden uproars and tumults, and the needy and loose persons desired them'.[60] The gentry largely resided in the country while titled men spent much of their time at court and Parliament. In a period of high produce prices and little profit to be made from agriculture by any except the great farmers, landowners raised rents, reducing the profit margins of husbandmen holding leases from them and forcing many labourers into homeless unemployment. Increasingly gentry heirs and younger sons drifted to the capital, forming a large, shifting population of troublesome young men, some hanging about the court seeking posts or heiresses. They saw London as a pleasure ground, removed from immediate parental disapproval. Drinking, whoring, gambling, fighting, theatre-going and chasing rich merchants' daughters, they were generally a nuisance.

Many titled families were founded by men who, coming to power under Henry VIII, bought, or were given by the king, church lands that came onto the market at the Reformation. These once new families were now the old upper-rank families. A few titled dynasties could trace their ancestry to the Conquest. Most were of relatively recent authority, some paying the College of Heralds to manufacture fake genealogies that gave them more respectable and ancient descent. This network of power and privilege was intended to keep the queen's peace. It largely did so, despite outbursts of local unrest, but at the expense of the physical and political repression of the 'baser sort'. Generations of psychological pressure established a fear of the upper ranks, a belief that, like the king, they were part of God's order and that opposing them was a grave blasphemy, pitting your puny, sinful self against the divinely ordained state of creation. Associated with this fear was the belief that the

---

59 Historical Manuscripts Commission, *Calendar of the Manuscripts of … the Marquess of Salisbury*, vols. 12, 14, 15.
60 John Clapham, *Elizabeth of England* (eds. E. Plummer Read and C. Read), 98.

better sort were somehow endowed with special qualities, that they were a sort of magically superior species. *Dream* displays (as do many of Shakespeare's plays) the human frailties of the upper order.

The civil power was not the only repressive network controlling England. Hand in hand with government, often synonymous with it, the church attempted to guide conformity and forcibly dissuade dissent. In 1549 Thomas Cranmer, Archbishop of Canterbury, had reinforced this in upbraiding rebels: 'Though the magistrates be evil and very tyrants against the commonwealth and enemies to Christ's religion, yet the subjects must obey in all worldly things'.[61] This encouragement to submit even to injustice was repeated in the 1571 *Book of Homilies* in the sermon 'Against Disobedience and Wylful Rebellion'. The tyranny of a monarch was a divine punishment against a sinful people who should not 'shake off that curse at their owne hand'.[62] The attempt to identify hierarchical deference with submission to God is part of seeing the social order as God ordained. By making it an aspect of church doctrine the Anglican hierarchy aimed to curb rebellion, maintain power and enforce doctrinal uniformity. Social and religious submission to the established power structure, however unjust its actions, would work for the mass of fearful superstitious people. But opposition was slowly rising.

The state of Athens, as represented, is a simple polity. Theseus has complete control. He acts as the judiciary evidently since Egeus comes to him for judgement. There is some sort of gentry rank for Demetrius and Lysander are described as gentlemen. Egeus's rank is not revealed. He evidently has money, assumes the paternal role in arranging Hermia's marriage to a gentleman, has access to the ruler, accompanies Theseus on his hunting trip and therefore seems to be part of the court entourage. We may assume he is of the better sort. The middling sort seems entirely absent with only the artisan class present. It is altogether a simple fiction. The actual Athenian state was considerably more complex. This court comprises only unnamed, unspeaking 'Attendants', with Philostrate the only one to speak (24 lines) and be named.[63] His lines are all to do with the options for the wedding entertainment and an attempt to divert Theseus from choosing the 'Pyramus' play. This is then largely a courtly, upper rank entertainment, with clownish humour provided by Puck and the mechanicals. With typical Shakespearean nuanced ambiguity, the

61 Strype, rec. 114.

62 From 'An Homily Against Disobedience and Wylful Rebellion'. See Wootten, *Divine Right and Democracy: An Anthology of Political Writings in Stuart England*, 94–8.

63 The cast list and the characters entering at the start of scenes were organized by Rowe in his 1709 edition of Shakespeare's works. He calls the lovers 'young courtiers' and Egeus simply as 'Hermia's father'.

mechanicals, for all their stupidity and obvious mental shortcomings, are nicer people.

Each English diocese had a bishop responsible for ensuring priests and congregations followed the Anglican form of worship. These dioceses comprised some nine and a half to ten thousand parishes each (theoretically) with a priest. The average number of souls in country parishes was three hundred. In the less controllable, expanding cities it was 450. Pluralism (holding more than one living) was a growing practice whereby a poorly paid vicar could augment his stipend and an already rich one could add to his fortune.[64] Nonresident priests employed curate substitutes so there was religious presence to oversee the social and spiritual state of the congregants. The priest, representing the church's might, was a figure to be respected, part of the ruling Establishment, part of the control troika of magistrate, lord of the manor, priest. Often the lord of the manor was also a magistrate, thus narrowing the power base, and the vicar too might be of gentry origin, narrowing the power source even more. Part of the priestly power aura was education. The ability to read and write (though not all priests were highly literate) gave special, magical status. As mediator between this world and the next, he had immense psychological influence. Education made him able to advise about moral and practical matters, and his spiritual role made him a privileged mentor in areas related to living the virtuous life. In practice, many regarded the priest as representing an alien, elite culture and another form of repressive authority. Not everyone in a village would necessarily defer to the priest. Some vicars were ineffective – drunks, ignorant, more interested in hunting. Closet Catholics and Dissenters would only pay lip service. Puritan dissidents were slowly increasing in number and were increasingly vocally critical of the church. More worrying for the episcopal elite was the spread of vicars of Puritan sympathy. In the 1590s large numbers of progressive, radical-thinking young ordinands graduated from Cambridge University, adding yet another destabilizing factor to an age already undergoing disturbing changes. Principles absorbed from the lectures and writings of Cambridge don William Perkins inclined them to be less obsequious to their gentry parishioners and more mindful of the hardships of the poor, though some gentry families, sympathetic to reform, protected Puritan-minded vicars from church persecution.

Another source of anti-Establishment attacks was playwrights coming from the universities where they had contact with radical views. Vitriolic

---

64 Entering the priesthood was a common career path for younger sons of gentry families. Faith and devotion were not always their chief motives. Barred from inheriting by the custom of primogeniture, such men could access wealth and power by carefully targeted promotions within the ecclesiastical hierarchy.

in criticizing purse-proud citizens, their ostentatious wives, the explosion of greed, the obsession with luxury, vanity, lust, the idle and incompetent aristocracy and particularly those many ungentlemanly gentlemen buzzing like flies round the court, they also deplored the state of the lower orders. Though set firmly in the contemporary world their city comedies were essentially morality based, harking back to medieval values. Shakespeare tended to appear to avoid overt attacks on his own times by setting his plays in other countries or in other periods, but the Greek setting of *Dream* should not fool us into thinking the play is not about current issues or situated within contemporary values. The original audience would not be gulled either. The characters would probably not wear Athenian costume, but would look just like contemporary Elizabethans. Their conduct would certainly be judged by the religious and humanist ethics of the time.

James I expressed the principle that concern for 'the well-fare and peace of his people' identifies a king 'as their naturall father and kindly maister'. In 'subjecting his owne private affections and appetites to the weale and standing of his subjects', he shows himself better than the tyrannical king who 'thinketh his people ordained for him, a pray to his passions and inordinate appetites'.[65] Theseus shows a paternalistic concern for the plight of Hermia, attempts to gently persuade her to conform to the patriarchal view of a father's power, but is not stern when he finds her adamant. He has a fatherly, didactic tone in inviting the couples to join him in his wedding day and in guiding their thoughts during the play and extending his blessing on their futures.

Detachment from people encourages desensitization which leads to brutal attitudes to them. Rank divisions were becoming a growing tension in English society. They would worsen under James I and his son Charles I. Theseus shows a laudable benevolence both to the young courtiers and to the 'hard-handed men that work in Athens' (5.1.72). The lovers, however, appear not to be at all chastened by their experiences, are still full of themselves and mocking of the efforts of men who, if less elegant, less wealthy, less educated than themselves, are at least better hearted. Experiencing setbacks usually teaches characters a lesson. That appears not to have taken place here. Any courtly audience members should feel awkward watching the immune, self-confident brattishness of the lovers. They represent the idle and privileged who neglect their duty to help the poor and neglect showing God gratitude for being wealthy by not wasting their excess fortune on pointless extravagances but putting it to the good of the whole polity. The Bible authorized this: 'For unto whomsoever much is given, of him shall be much required' (Luke 12:48). The lovers play

---

at drama critics during the 'Pyramus' play, pointedly identifying a number of amusing conundrums related to reality and fiction and how to represent reality in fiction. Though their comments draw attention to the degree to which audiences suspend expectations of reality and how overblown the rhetoric of romances can be, the cruelty of their comments has social implications too. The lovers are too arrogantly egotistic to see that the language of Pyramus and Thisbe parodies their own highfalutin, sub-Petrarchan declarations of love. The middling and lower orders had obvious work to do to live, while those with wealth and rank did not need to work. However, the standard view was that 'none are less exempted from a calling than great men'.[66] The bible story of Dives and Lazarus (Luke 16:19), a popular text for sermons, told how the rich Dives refused to pass the crumbs off his table to the poor Lazarus. Dives dies, goes to Hell and in his sufferings sees Lazarus among the elect. The rich and powerful had a duty to be fathers to their neighbours, shepherds to the flock around them. Brathwait put it starkly: 'The higher place the heavier the charge'.[67] Many privileged lords and ladies sent unwanted food to the poor, endowed almshouses and schools and did other acts of charity. Many did not. Each new generation inheriting wealth needed reminding that

> charity [...] should flow
> From every generous and noble spirit,
> To orphans and to widows.[68]

The concept of *caritas* (love expressed through charitable acts), integral to medieval church teaching, derived from canon law's delineation of the basic duty of the rich to assist the needy. It was taken up in Protestant thinking too. Compassion was a necessary virtue in a Christian and essential for those who had never experienced adversity or affliction. The lovers show little compassion, but then the mechanicals may be seen as being in the play to act as mere butts of humour based on the snobberies and prejudices of the ranks toward each other and to amuse the privileged audience watching them while that audience reflects the shortcomings of the onstage courtiers. The governing ranks had detached themselves from the rest of society, living their own self-interested, selfish and narcissistic lives at court or isolated in their mansions on their estates. What a prick to the consciences of the pampered, self-obsessed courtiers in the audience the behaviour of the lovers would be throughout the play. Probably though, the audience would endorse

---

66 Brathwait, *The English Gentleman*, 115.
67 Brathwait, 115.
68 Webster, *The White Devil*, 3.2.64–6.

their behaviour. Mankind is never too ready to see its failings when displayed. Corrupt, ineffective and arrogant monarchy was another feature of the time and the period is full of admonitions to prince figures and nobility.[69] In 1609 the Earl of Northumberland wrote,

> There are certain works fit for every vocation; some for kings; some for noblemen; some for gentlemen; some for artificers; some for clowns [country people]; and some for beggars; [...] If everyone play his part well, that is allotted him, the commonwealth will be happy; if not then it will be deformed.[70]

God's judgement against Adam and Eve at the Fall condemned men to live by the sweat of their brow. Adam had a second chance. Saved from destruction by the mercy of God, he left Eden and sought salvation elsewhere. The lovers are given a second chance, saved by Oberon's essential benevolence toward them. The Bible is full of figures given a second chance and Ezekiel, Proverbs, Ecclesiastes, the Epistles to the Thessalonians and Timothy all strongly criticize idleness and recommend employment. That included kings and courtiers.

---

69 In the language of the time the word 'prince' was generically applied to anyone who had a role as ruler of a state, be that person count, duke, governor, prince, king or queen.
70 Percy, *Advice to His Son*, 119.

Chapter 3

SIN, DEATH AND THE PRINCE OF DARKNESS

Stand thou in rightwiseness and in dread, and make ready thy soul to temptation, for temptation is a man's life on the earth.[1]

An inescapable factor in every aspect of Elizabethan life was the ever-present sense of the ever-present possibility of sin. People's sinfulness was the greatest threat to order. The Elizabethans were neurotically alert to the temptations surrounding life. The conflicting Christian sects may have differed violently about matters of doctrine – ritual, liturgy, ornament, transubstantiation, confession and so on – but they shared basic beliefs when it came to right and wrong. Man was perpetually open to sin and temptation was all around him. The Devil was to be defied, and Christ was man's redeemer and the way to salvation. The moral bases of life were agreed.

The Ten Commandments (abridged from Exodus 20:19)

1. Thou shalt have no other gods before me.
2. Thou shalt not make unto thee any graven image.
3. Thou shalt not take the name of the Lord thy God in vain.
4. Remember the Sabbath day, to keep it holy.
5. Honour thy father and thy mother.
6. Thou shalt not kill.
7. Thou shalt not commit adultery.
8. Thou shalt not steal.
9. Thou shalt not bear false witness.
10. Thou shalt not covet […] any thing that is thy neighbour's.

1 Wycliffe, Prologue to the Apocalypse, 493.

The Seven Deadly Sins

1. **Pride** (arrogance, vanity, vainglory, hubris)
2. **Wrath** (anger, violence)
3. **Lust** (lechery, wantonness, lasciviousness)
4. **Envy** (covetousness)
5. **Greed** (avarice)
6. **Gluttony** (including drunkenness)
7. **Sloth** (laziness, despair)

Sin and Satan were as much a part of religious consciousness as the desire to emulate Jesus and live virtuously. The church's cultural monopoly meant even those indifferent to religion would acknowledge that faith was the common, underlying feature of life at all levels. The passing year was marked by religious festivals, each day was punctuated by aspects of faith, the parish church bell indicated the times of services, pious families gathered for morning and evening prayers and individuals might visit the church during the day. Schoolboys had communal classroom prayers with their teacher. A master craftsman, his journeymen and apprentices might start the working day with prayers. The formal ceremonies of their guild involved prayers, readings and sermon-like addresses. Children were taught the Bible, learned texts, creeds, catechisms and prayers and would kneel by their bedside to ask for protection during the dangerous hours of darkness. Those of weak faith attended Sunday service rather than be fined in a church court. Those not particularly pious in their everyday life had scriptural grounding as children and like everyone else would know how they were expected to behave as Christians and would be aware of biblical allusions, echoes and ethics in what their neighbours said and did. They would observe too how plays displayed, reinforced and debated the basic Christian values of society. The church was omnipresent. When you were born, married, committed adultery, defamed a neighbour, were rowdy, sharp-tongued and shrewish, or opened your shop on Sunday, the church was there approving or wagging its finger. You lived in public, your discovered sins were made public and your punishment would be public. Your misdemeanours would be spied out by constables, beadles, the watch, servants and neighbours and dealt with in the local church court. These wrongdoings dealt not just with religious matters like blasphemy, heresy, contempt for the vicar's authority or absence from service. Secular misdemeanours too came within the jurisdiction of the church and its officials: perjury, slander, incontinence (excessive sexuality, excessive gluttony, excessive anything), sorcery, adultery, domestic disputes, marital quarrels, probate of wills. Anglicans were rarely left to solve a problem alone. Individual conscience was too weak to deal with matters of sin and morality without help. In times of national or personal stress many people turned to the consolations offered by being part of communally held belief. When you were afraid of imminent disaster, the support of others was a coping mechanism; the church was a mental, spiritual and physical refuge.

All Shakespeare plays either verbally echo or allude to well-known biblical texts and are situated explicitly or implicitly within a value matrix of sins and virtues. Unspoken, indirect, implicit biblical contexts evoking Christian values, reactions and assessments are inescapable in the literature of the time. Christian values shadow the actions of *Dream*. The second agent in the mediation of a text – the responder (reader or viewer) – provided a religious assessment. The text may lack a direct allusion to or verbatim quotation from Christian dogma, but Shakespeare knew his audience would make the connections. The play is nominally set in legendary Athens, but this is a shallow fiction that provides the opportunity to give his characters classical-sounding names. This would appeal to a cultivated audience and lend an air of authority and courtliness. It was an established feature of comedies that the upper-rank characters bore Italianate or classical names. *Dream* is full too of references to classical deities. The setting and the names are merely a blind. The classical world – its literature, philosophy, history and mythology – was the lingua franca of learned discussion. It was the common depository for allusion as a result of the education of most of the male and some of the female audience. But it did not preclude that other parallel moral system – the Bible. In discussing the early humanist reformers of the 1520s, A. G. Dickens put it thus,

> It became a natural tendency in a classically-educated age to co-ordinate the teaching of the great pagan moralists with that of the New Testament, to see in Christianity a mode of this life rather than a way of salvation for the next, even to envisage a cool, reasonable religion, a Christianity without tears.[2]

Indeed the two systems overlapped considerably, but the value system by which the audience would be expected to judge actions, attitudes and outcomes was entirely Christian – and probably Protestant. Every scene provokes a Christianity-focused judgement of what is said and done. Whatever the level of engagement with faith, Christian upbringing triggered a vigorous conscious or subconscious religious reaction to everything seen. Debauched libertines

2 Dickens, *The English Reformation*, 101.

or audience members who had lost their religion still had vestigial memories of the values they had learned as children. The Bible was the standard of all conduct. To Protestants canon law and episcopal rules and regulations meant nothing: 'Christian doctrine and conduct have only one sure basis – the New Testament'.[3] Responses might vary according to education, upbringing, class, political and/or religious allegiance and experience of and attitude toward the world, but there would be broad agreement, since all the viewers – from the pit to the top gallery – shared this common Bible-based background. The ways in which time after time the characters offend the commandments or commit sins would be glaringly obvious to the audience. It is an absolutely fundamental aspect of the play, informing every other motif in it.

Life was a journey, a pilgrim's progress toward holiness and union with God or into sin and damnation in Hell. The journey from the court to the woods and back again was a testing time, a several hours in the wilderness (as opposed to 40 days), but also a confrontation with self, loss of self, with temptation, a coming face-to-face with fear, frenzy and disorientation, to destabilize complacent views and force a reassessment of society's established values. It is a reminder to the lovers that their cosy little privileged aristocratic world of Athens is not the only sphere of existence and that chaos is outside in the dark (and also lurking inside in the heart). Coming through the night of ordeal should lead to a new vision of the world, a new understanding of self and others. It should be a healing process that would regenerate the individuals morally, re-establish more firmly the bases of their relationships and reassert the orderly harmony of society in Athens.

From birth people were to pursue virtue, shun sin, imitate Christ, keep the soul pure and progress toward death, ready to pass through to the life everlasting. Earthly life was a transient state preparatory to the afterlife. In John Ford's late revenge tragedy *'Tis Pity She's a Whore* (c. 1629–31; hereafter called 'Tis Pity), when sexual sins and violent plots begin to gather and drive the drama, the character Richardetto states the basic situation of Christian existence: 'No life is blessèd but the way to heaven' (4.2.21) and encourages his niece to flee a vile world by entering a convent: 'Who dies a virgin lives a saint on earth' (4.2.28). The virtuous life gained Christ's favour and a state of grace. No advantage in the fleshly, physical world, neither crown nor coin, was of any value if you lacked grace. Ford presents even the standard view of good looks in a religious context:

Beauty that clothes the outside of the face
Is cursèd if it be not clothed with grace. (5.1.12–13)

3 Dickens, 124.

It is unclear whether the lovers have found or earned grace by their ordeal, but there is something of a new awareness in Demetrius as he implicitly renounces Hermia (and thereby destroys Egeus's case):

> My good lord, I wot not by what power –
> But by some power it is – my love to Hermia,
> Melted as the snow, seems to me now
> As the remembrance of an idle gaud
> Which in my childhood I did dote upon;
> And all the faith, all the virtue of my heart,
> The object and the pleasure of my eye,
> Is only Helena. To her my lord,
> Was I betroth'd ere I saw Hermia;
> But like a sickness did I loathe this food:
> But as in health, come to my natural taste,
> Now do I wish it, love it, long for it,
> And will evermore be true to it. (4.2.163–75)

This is a confession of aberrance and broken troth. Demetrius, we now learn, was betrothed to Helena. Their relationship was more than boy likes girl and girl likes boy. Betrothal was a formal and binding promise of intention to marry. It was usually made before relatives and friends, but was valid even if only made between the couple. Demetrius has committed a serious transgression in breaching his promise of marriage. He admits his judgement and feelings were wrong. He uses the image of illness and a return to health as if the perception of love for Hermia were an imbalance of spirit or humours that has now been physicked. The confession is a cleansing and a reassumption of grace. Uncontrolled appetite (a spiritual or physical imbalance) was something the church feared and punished. Lust was the most common everyday sin, but any of the Seven Deadly (or Mortal) Sins could damn you eternally if unrepented. Sexual liaison between either of the pairs of lovers is not at any point suggested, though premarital sex was common between formally and informally betrothed couples. Not endorsed by the church but grudgingly tolerated, premarital sex was beginning to be prosecuted more actively.[4] Shakespeare relied on his audience seeing the danger of youthful sexuality and the guiding restraint Christian morality offered. He relied too on their seeing how the court did not fit the moral framework of the time. A courtly audience, possibly more attentive than the social mix at the public theatres, had enough

---

4 For the growing prosecution of prenuptial sex, adultery and bastard birth, see Dabhoiwala, *The Origins of Sex: A History of the First Sexual Revolution*, 41.

biblical knowledge (even if their faith was weak) to put the actions and words before them into a moral context that reflected poorly on their own attitudes to love and fidelity, especially pertinent if the occasion of the performance was a wedding. The antics of the lovers reflect the intricate and entangled love games played out in Elizabeth's court, where, even when the queen was old, there were many young men and young women.

The permeating religious atmosphere of society made identifying sin instinctive. Sin was the Devil's portal, giving access to your soul to damn you. The Devil was a very real entity to people, not a metaphor of evil, but a very real horned, hoofed, forked tail and sulphurous presence. Progressive thinkers tried to internalize Satan as the evil in man, but most people believed he was a real creature with a physical body. His earthly work, assisted by legions of demons, imps, goblins, incubi and succubi, was devoted to corrupting man and thwarting God's will. The Book of Revelation describes 'the great dragon' who 'was cast out, that old serpent, called the Devil and Satan, which deceiveth the whole world' (22:9). In John's Gospel he is called 'the prince of this world' (22:31) and in II Corinthians 'god of this world (4:4), suggesting that the fleshly world of greed, brutality, cheating and lust (ever present in the plays of the 1590s and1600s) is the Devil's domain. Paul's Epistle to the Ephesians (2:2–3) goes further, placing the Devil firmly in this world, embodied in the waywardness and violence of men. Given the celebratory atmosphere of the play it is not surprising that the Devil has no place in *Dream*, though the introduction of magic and the fairies does flirt with the dangers of the supernatural. By transgressing decorous conduct and fleeing to the woods, the young courtiers commit sins – immodesty, disobedience, recklessness. The devils are loosed when Christian values and cultivated, civilized, sensitive and sympathetic behaviours are ignored. The lovers court danger by their venture. Real danger is unlikely to develop since, for all their immaturity, none of the characters is evil. Demetrius threatens to do harm to Helena, but runs away from her to avoid being tempted. His innate decency triumphs over anger and what it might lead to. Helena's immodesty too is saved by his gentlemanly behaviour. Dante defined nobility in terms of virtuous conduct not rank or title.[5] Baldassare Castiglione highlights this too when, during a discussion on what makes the best sort of courtier, he has Pallavicino remark that while some 'of the most noble blood, have been wicked in the extreme' there were 'many of humble birth, who, through their virtues, have won glory for their descendants'.[6] Conduct is the determinant of true nobility. Nobility of spirit, expressed in courteous, gentlemanly, noble behaviour, counts for more than

5 See Chaucer, *The Wife of Bath's Tale*, 1109–30.
6 Castiglione, *The Book of the Courtier*, 55.

all the titles, estates and cultured accomplishments a lady or gentleman may have. Both Lysander and Demetrius have sufficient virtue not to do any real ill, but do not behave entirely with dignity and are bad mannered, tetchy and untrustworthy. Lysander proposes an elopement and Demetrius is guilty of bad faith, but neither is evil.

Viewers would see the piece not simply as a traditional Roman comedy tale of true love opposed by an overstrict father, facing a test and surviving the interference and help of magic but also as a display of sins punished and redeemed by an act of mercy by an understanding ruler. Egeus does wrong and Hermia and Lysander do wrong. Their elopement turns into a nightmare, but their love is restored and Theseus's courage in setting aside the demand for the extreme judgement of the law called for by Egeus enables a happy ending. Though not written in the style of the earlier morality plays, the subject and ethics have similarities.

Vicars loved loosing their imaginations in sermons describing the workings of the Evil One and the torments of Hell awaiting unrepentant sinners. Creative writers too enjoyed the opportunities for fantasy descriptions offered by ideas of Hell, sin, death and the Devil. The awareness that sin is ever-present, that life is a persistent battle between good and evil and that the lure of vice has to be constantly rejected, would resonate in the shock and horror revealed in witch trials. Witchcraft was another subject on which King James I delivered his opinions. His *Demonologie* (1597) captures the contemporary mood of fear and suspicion.

Many artists painted representations of demons and the Devil gave visual concreteness to the fears haunting people. Hell and the sufferings of the damned were popular subjects. Hieronymous Bosch (1450–1516) graphically depicts the horrors of perdition in *The Last Judgement*.

Many medieval churches had depictions of 'Christ in Majesty' but in the late medieval period (in response perhaps to the holocaust of the Black Death) artists took to painting scenes of 'The Last Judgement'. Many (but not all) were scratched out or whitewashed over during the Reformation, but there were other means by which the idea of suffering was established in the minds of people. It was an age when hanged bodies were routinely publicly displayed strung up in chains, 'heretics' were burnt at the stake and traitors had their entrails cut out and burned in front of them. The rack, thumbscrew and strappado were regularly used to extract information. Noses were slit and ears cropped for criticizing royalty or the church, thieves were branded and blasphemers had their tongue pulled out or a hole bored in it. Birching, blinding and being broken on the wheel were simply part of institutionalized cruelty. The gruesome acts portrayed in plays reflect a violent culture. Sin against the state or sin against God – the painful retribution was similar.

These brutal punishments reflect the age and how people imagined the damned tortured in Hell.

Sermons threatening damnation and eternal torture for extreme sinners were a useful moral control device to frighten naughty children and were a moral corrective for adults, but there were those who did not care about hellfire and damnation, and those who did not believe in Hell. Christopher Marlowe's Faustus declares 'hell's a fable' (scene 5, line 128). Despite Mephistopheles asserting, 'This is hell, nor am I out of it' and 'where we are is hell', Faustus arrogantly laughs off the possibility:

> *Faustus*: Think'st thou that Faustus is so fond to imagine
> That, after this life, there is any pain?
> Tush, these are trifles and mere old wives' tales.
> *Mephistopheles*: But, Faustus, I am an instance to prove the contrary,
> For I am damn'd, and am now in hell.
> [...]
> *Faustus*: How! now in hell!
> Nay, an this be hell, I'll willingly be damn'd here. (scene 5, lines 134–44)

People were beginning to question Hell's existence, claiming this life was our Hell. In *'Tis Pity*, the reckless Giovanni, a scholar like Faustus, thinks reasoned argument can demolish the idea of Hell, and confidently announces to his confessor,

> The hell you oft have prompted is nought else
> But slavish and fond superstitious fear,
> And I could prove it too. (5.3.19–21)

The friar replies, 'Thy blindness slays thee'. Giovanni's trust in rational arguments led him to believe sex with his sister was permissible – a moral blindness. His actions result in spiritual death and physical slaughter. Most of the audience, if they thought about it, probably believed in both Heaven and Hell as real places of reward and punishment in the afterlife. Most, except extreme libertines, believed sin was everywhere and virtue needed to be cultivated. This would not have prevented most people from committing sins or encouraged living a particularly good life. Like most people they would probably experience guilt and fear, resolve to improve, then lapse into the normal not-very-bad-but-not-very-good everyday life. An affecting play might well prick their consciences – temporarily at least.

In *Lear* the mad king makes a brief mention of Hell in a comment on female lust that shifts from describing how from the waist down 'is all the fiend's' domain to a recognizable description of the Christian idea of the Devil's kingdom:

> There's hell, there's darkness,
> There is the sulphurous pit – burning, scalding,
> Stench, consumption. (4.6.)

In 'Tis Pity the friar, trying to frighten Annabella into repentance for fornication and incest, describes Hell:

> There is a place [...] in a black and hollow vault,
> Where day is never seen. There shines no sun,
> But flaming horror of consuming fires,
> A lightless sulphur, choked with smoky fogs
> Of an infected darkness. In this place
> Dwell many thousand thousand sundry sorts
> Of never-dying deaths: there damned souls
> Roar without pity [...] (3.6.8–16)

He continues with specific punishments meted out for specific sins:

> There are gluttons fed
> With toads and adders; there is burning oil
> Poured down the drunkard's throat, the usurer
> Is forced to sup whole draughts of molten gold;
> There is the murderer forever stabbed,
> Yet can he never die; there lies the wanton
> On racks of burning steel, whiles in his soul
> He feels the torment of his raging lust. (3.6.16–23)

3.1 Sin and Death

The Prince of Darkness was inexorably linked with temptation, reminders of what awaited after death and the very fact of death itself. In medieval and Renaissance art reminders of mortality are ubiquitous.[7] Skulls, skeletons and the Grim Reaper, appear regularly in paintings in churches and in the funerary furniture surrounding the congregation. Sin and death are linked as a

---

7 Lucifer was a prince of light before he fell. The Testaments call the Devil a prince and as darkness denotes sin joining the two terms is natural. Edgar's phrase 'The Prince of Darkness is a gentleman; Modo he's called, and Mahu' (King Lear, 3.4.) links evil with the sham politeness of gentlemen that masks devious intent.

hellish duo in opposition to Christ and the Holy Spirit. The everyday world was a minefield for the morally unwary, full of devils waiting for any hint of ungodly, impure thought. Momentary lapses – a nasty comment, bitchy gossip, a bad-tempered snappish reply, blasphemous expletives, temptations to gluttony, theft, the prickings of lust – were opportunities for 'the Enemy of Mankind'. Wary Christians prayed regularly for protection. Prayers at bedtime were especially important, calling guardian angels as night security. A habit grew of eventide self-examination of your day, casting up your account of good and bad acts, making resolutions to improve, repenting and praying for salvation. It was end-of-the-day quiet time for assessing how well you had passed the day and resolving to be better if need be. James I recommended,

> Remember ever once in the foure and twentie houres, either in the night, or when yee are at greatest quiet, to call yourself to account of all your last dayes actions, either wherein yee have committed things ye should not, or omitted the things yee should doe, either in your Christian or Kingly duty.[8]

A marginal note references I Corinthians 11:31: 'For if ye judge your selfe, ye shall not be judged'. Temptation to sin was everywhere and everyone knew 'the wages of sin is death' (Romans 6:23). You had to fight constantly to win the gift of eternal life through Jesus Christ. What made it more difficult was that you were born a sinner with the susceptibility to sin already in you. This original sin was the curse Adam and Eve's fall brought to mankind. Their disobedience meant that all successive generations were weakened by being open to temptation – a weakness played on by omnipresent devils. The radical Puritan and Cambridge don William Perkins asserted, 'All men are wholly corrupted with sinne through Adams fal: & so are become slaves of Sathan'.[9] This idea provoked a rich language of condemnation among moralists – pamphleteers or preachers – and a delight in describing the pains of Hell.

In the turbulent times when *Dream* was written there was no shortage of targets named as the source of sin. Women figured persistently, from Eve onwards, as the provokers of sin. Sin bred like disease in the growing capital. Disease itself was God's punishment for sin, not just the usual bodily sins of lust, gluttony and sloth but also pride in rank, the vanity of fashion, the greed of moneymaking. Society seemed to be falling apart. Crime was rising and sexual debauchery and alcoholism too. Heresy and religious dissent were rife.

---

8 *Basilikon*, 12–13.
9 *The Foundation of Christian Religion* (1591), sig. A4.

Anglicans blamed Puritans, Puritans blamed Anglicans and everyone blamed the Catholics, the Pope (the Antichrist), the French, the Spanish, the court and occasionally the queen.

Life was a battle to preserve your virtue and live like Christ, cleansing sin by prayer. Prayer would involve repentance and begging forgiveness ('Forgive us this day our daily trespasses'.).[10] Accumulated, unrepented sins, particularly grave ones, could damn you when you died, though repentance (even at the last minute) could save you. The terrified Faustus, about to be dragged down to Hell as payment of his side of the bargain with Satan, cries out,

> See, see where Christ's blood streams in the firmament!
> One drop would save my soul, half a drop.
> Ah, my Christ! Ah, rend not my heart for naming of my Christ!
> Yet will I call on him. (scene 19, lines 146–9)

Death was never far away in those days of plague and illnesses easily brought on by poor diet, unhealthy living conditions and ignorance of basic hygiene.[11] Infections were a leveller making no distinction between rich or poor, though the better off might be better protected by better food. The world was an insecure place, made more uncertain by persistent Puritan claims that epidemic diseases were punishment for tolerating Catholicism or changes to church ritual, the performance of plays, not keeping the Sabbath holy, the sinfulness of the court and the sinfulness of everyone in general.[12] There was no escape. Poverty, illness and sudden disaster were constant anxieties people lived with. As Michel de Montaigne put it, 'We do not know where death awaits us: so let us wait for it everywhere'.[13] Starting and ending the day with family prayers was part of that protection/salvation process and behaving piously during the day was another. James I advised his son, 'Pray [...] God would give you grace so to live, as yee may everie houre of your life be readie for death'.[14] This life, though the gift of a bountiful God, was short and merely a preparation for the life eternal, spent in the torments of Hell or among the blessings of Heaven.

10 The Lord's Prayer (*Book of Common Prayer*, 'An Ordre for Mattins', 7).
11 Nearly half of all babies never reached their first birthday. High mortality among teenagers affected not just the poor but also ended many direct dynastic lines. James I's eldest son, the promising and popular Prince Henry, would die aged 18 (probably of typhus). Shakespeare lost his only son aged 11. Jonson lost his first son aged 7.
12 The anonymous *Memorial* (addressed to James I on his accession) demanded the reintroduction of the Edwardian reforms, more practising preaching ministers, strict observance of the Sabbath, the banishment of the ring exchange in marriage and other 'superstitious' remnants of popery.
13 'To philosophize is to learn how to die', 96.
14 *Basilikon*, 13.

Increasingly in the seventeenth century small coteries of scientists and intellectuals questioned the authority and authenticity of the concepts of sin, damnation and salvation. Part of a growing rationalist movement, they encouraged cynicism, secularism and individualism. The idea that the individual was responsible for his own soul and for his personal relationship with God was refreshing and liberating, facilitating independence from an Anglican Church already as mired in corruption and entangled in the Establishment power structure as the Church of Rome had been. But individualism, emerging simultaneously with the capitalist practices of a profit-driven, go-getting, selfish commercial world, threatened old ideas of humble self-effacement and dedication to the community's good. This individualism discounted others, prioritized your needs, disconnected you from moral restraints and promoted a world where personal will and private appetite were the measure of actions, where villainy and ambition thrived. Traditional morality demanded the bad be punished in fiction. In real life villains often got away with skulduggery and dishonesty. Niccolò Machiavelli was demonized because his works 'openly and unfeignedly [...] describe what men do, and not what they ought to do'.[15] Once more, discrepancy between moral expectation and actual behaviour shows that rule breakers succeed. Man's unique features – the virtues of charity, mercy, sympathy, intellectual ability, reason and the emotional faculties (imagination, love, sympathy) – raised him above animals and closer to godlike status. But the pinnacle of God's earthly creation, part-divine, part-animal hybrid, was too easily tempted by fleshly failings. Mankind was God's second attempt after some of his first angelic creations rebelled with Satan. Because humans had animal traits life was a constant battle between the animal promptings of appetites and passions and the angelic demands of reason and virtue. The exploration of that struggle between our baser and our better nature is the domain of literature. The Ten Commandments, the Seven Deadly Sins and the Seven Virtues specifically address this need to fight the impulses toward lust, bloody acts, all violence, theft, gluttony and sloth. The presence of some of these appetites, even in minor forms, gives *Dream* its religious-ethical context. These conduct guidelines are implicit in all Elizabethan-Jacobean drama. Characters can be measured against them.

15 Bacon, *The Advancement of Learning* (1605), 157. Machiavelli's own words were, 'I have thought it proper to represent things as they are in real truth, rather than as they are imagined. [...] The gulf between how one should live and how one does live is so wide that a man who neglects what is actually done for what should be done learns the way to self- destruction rather than self-preservation' (*The Prince*, chap. 15, lines 90–1).

The list of sins, revised by Pope Gregory I in 590 AD, was used by Dante in his influential poem *The Divine Comedy* (1321). Originating in Catholicism, these mortal, capital or cardinal sins, were still much referred to by the very sin-conscious Anglican Protestants of Shakespeare's time and obsessively so by dissenting sectarians. They are cardinal because they were thought grave enough to require God to renew his grace to the sinner and for the sinner to show repentance before forgiveness could be shown. They are mortal or capital because they were serious enough to warrant death ('For the wages of sin is death'.). God was thought able to strike down great sinners by sudden death or to use human agents. The Book of Proverbs lists looking proud of yourself, lying, shedding innocent blood, having a heart ready to devise wickedness, having a readiness to do mischief and stirring trouble. St Paul offers a longer list, any of which will lose you the kingdom of God: adultery, fornication, uncleanness, lasciviousness, idolatry, witchcraft, hatred, variance, emulations, wrath, strife, seditions, heresies, envyings, murders, drunkenness, revellings 'and such like' (Epistle to the Galatians 5:19–21). Fornication was sex between a couple not married to each other. The principle was that sex should not take place at all unless permitted by the sacrament of matrimony. Elizabeth's court, for all her surveillance of her gentlewomen, was a hotbed of promiscuity, ambition, petty rivalry, plotting for promotion and blatant vanity and display. These failings and more would increase during the reign of the Stuart kings in the next century. Ranked below the Deadly Sins are many other negative behaviours and vices regarded as sinful, though less serious. These are called venial sins. Committing them would not lead to you losing the grace of God, and thus you could still be cleansed and saved – with effort on your part.

The idea of Hell as below the earth, imagined as a fiery pit structured like a funnel, is formalized by Dante in *L'Inferno* [Hell], the first part of *The Divine Comedy*. Each sin was tabulated and allocated its sector. The lower Dante goes in his visit to the nine circles of Hell, the worse the sins committed by the damned he meets. In 'Upper Hell' are those who committed sins of incontinence, failings effected by those constant enemies of mankind, the appetites. These mainly personal failings are in descending order – the lustful, the gluttonous, hoarders and spendthrifts, the wrathful, suicides. In 'Nether Hell' – getting closer to Satan at the bottom of the pit – are sinners who committed planned transgressions – fraud or acts of malice. In descending order they are panders and seducers (pimps and fornicators), flatterers, simoniacs (those who sold church offices), sorcerers, barrators (who abused the legal system to profit by groundless cases or false claims), hypocrites, thieves, those encouraging fraud, sowers of discord, falsifiers and traitors (to kindred, country, guests, their lord).[16] These broad definitions comprise a number of sins against the community and against probity in public office. Some of them are present in the play and the audience would easily identify them.

Pride was the first sin, committed by the Devil in thinking so well of himself he rebelled against God to replace him. As Lucifer ('the bright one'), he was God's favourite angel, but becoming ambitious, thinking that though God favoured him above the other angels he deserved even better and higher status, he rebelled, was defeated and cast out of Heaven. He and his co-conspirators fell through chaos into Hell, a fiery pit full of sulphur and smoke, specially created by God. Vanity is a form of pride. At a venial level it is conceit about your physical looks, clothes or status. In Stephen Bateman's *The Christall Glasse of Christian Reformation* (1584) the engraving *Pride* shows a well-dressed woman looking in a mirror. Her foot rests on a skull. Behind her is a winged, horned Devil, with clawed feet like a bird of prey, a man's torso, a balding skull-shaped head and a long curved beak of a nose. The accompanying description reads, 'The woman signifieth pride: the glasse in her hand flattery or deceate – the deuil behind her temptation: the death head which she setteth her foote upon, signifieth forgetfulness of the life to come, wherby commeth destruction'. Egeus has pride in his patriarchal power as does Oberon. Hermia and Lysander are proudly convinced they are right to elope. Bottom has overly high self-esteem, an overblown perception of his own worth. It is a minor failing in him, but one that irritates Quince as he tries to cast the play and is interrupted by Bottom wanting to play every character and immediately projecting himself into the different parts. This is vanity presented humorously. It harms no one. Bottom is much loved by his associates, though his ebullience is annoying to them at times. He is, however, punished through Puck's trick, though he accepts the oddest of situations without turning a hair. The arrogance of thinking yourself better than others is a small vanity until it becomes active disregard and bad treatment of others, behaving as if you were above common courtesy and the law. Bottom is not at this level of sin. It is another aspect of the comedy of the ass-head transformation that Bottom is not fazed at all by suddenly, in the middle of a wood, in the depth of the night, becoming the object of the amorous attentions of a beautiful woman and her fairy train. He takes it all in his stride and, though feeling he has grown 'marvellous hairy about the face' (4.1.24), seems unaware that he has an ass's head. The fool is perhaps the last to become aware of his folly. Bateman's view of 'Pride' has a verse heading that reads, 'When daintie dames hath whole delight: with proude

---

16 Sorcerers used occult, diabolic powers, as opposed to conjurors or white magicians (not intending evil), using natural magic, harnessing Nature's forces.

attyre themselves to [ar]ray/Pirasmos shineth in the sight: of glittering glass such fooles to fray [frighten]'.[17] This simply means that when a woman delights solely in ostentatious appearance, the Devil will appear reflected in her mirror to frighten her into remembrance of what is truly important in life.

Vanity related to appearance and fashion, and any reference to clothing as a distraction, is relevant to a peacock courtly audience whose wasteful extravagance on clothes was infamous. Personal display was a common target in drama and moralistic pamphlets. The most extensive and hysterically extreme attack is to be found in the Puritan Philip Stubbes's *Anatomie of Abuses* (1583). Ostentation is not in Shakespeare's sights in *Dream*, though it would be in many plays to follow. Pride is the besetting sin of those with power, privilege, rank and wealth (like the audience). In defeating Titania Oberon reinforces patriarchy, but behaves inappropriately for a husband and a king, proudly defending his prerogatives but failing to see how arrogant and overbearing he has been. The Bible required such people to disregard their advantages and be humbly ready to serve those whom it was their duty to help. Theseus seems to fit this model. A king is most likely to be proud, but overweening self-regard was rife among courtiers too. Bateman's second example of 'Pride' shows a rich man, fashionably dressed, striding past a beggar and ignoring the supplication for alms.

Power pride may be discerned in Oberon's determination to have his way over the changeling boy. The conflict between him and Titania is a domestic, personal power struggle, but also an attempt by the king to exert his superiority of rank over his wife to reassert and display his position as a man, husband and ruler. It is a stalemate opposition of two obstinate figures. It is man versus woman, husband versus wife. The row they have in act 2, scene 1 outlines the causes of their dissension, but it ends unresolved:

> *Oberon.* Give me that boy, and I will go with thee.
> *Titania.* Not for thy fairy kingdom. Fairies away!
> We shall chide downright if I longer stay. [*Exeunt Titania and her train.*] (2.1.143–5)

By the end of the play, however, unjustly and through trickery, Oberon manipulates a result that seems to reinforce his domination. Shakespeare is perhaps emphasizing to the newly married couple in his audience that it is the husband who ultimately has the superior status.

Wrath ranged from any tiny moment of anger that flares and soon dies away, through escalating losses of temper to the irrational rage that becomes violent

---

17 *Peirasmos* is the Greek word used in the New Testament to mean temptation or testing.

against someone else. This is relevant to those men in the audience ready to fall out and fight. Men (not just gentlemen) wore swords, carried concealed daggers and were prepared to use them. Too much wine, and tempers frayed easily – over cards, dice, women, a word taken the wrong way. The Day of Judgement was known as the *Dies Irae* (Day of Wrath, the term used in the Anglican Communion). It was the day when God's ultimate wrath would be shown, but in Him it was thought of as divine judgement and justice. The wrath of humans was a different matter, sometimes just, often merely private anger and a desire to retaliate.

Irascibility (a tendency to hot temper) is a sin liable to occur in any rank of society, but particularly among hot-headed young men. Those of rank and wealth were most susceptible to it, believing themselves superior to others and ready to defend any perceived slur against their honour. Bateman's engraving *Wrath* shows a helmeted, armed man carrying a sword and a flag. He sits astride a boar. He represents a standard view of anger as the soldier's key quality, but his flag bears a figure in ecclesiastical dress. In front of the boar a man stabs himself with a dagger and a stream of blood cascades to the ground. Behind the boar a woman raises her arms to the sky. The explanation reads, 'The boar signifieth Wrath, and the man on his backe mischief: the Pope in the Flag destruction, & the Flag vncertain religion, turning and changing with euery blast of winde: the man killing him selfe desperation: the woman madness'. Ira (anger) is commonly depicted at this time as a sword-bearing man.

Anger is the inciting emotion of *Dream*, is a major feature and drives the plot. Egeus's anger with Hermia's disobedience and hers with his dogmatic attitude set up the conflict situation essential to drama. Then add Lysander's anger with Demetrius for trying to move in on Hermia and Demetrius's anger with Lysander for standing in his way and his 'fury' as he follows the escapees to the woods. These different incidents of wrath are then matched by the overarching anger of the fairy king and queen. The wrath of gods and goddesses crowds the great classical texts that so influenced Elizabethan education and thinking. The plots of *The Iliad*, *The Odyssey* and *The Aeneid* all pivot on anger. Many of the stories in Ovid's *Metamorphoses* have their origins too in personal conflict. The dramatic change of mood that Egeus brings in act 1, scene 1 persists until it is resolved and disappears in parallel with Oberon's return to amity with his wife.

Lust was a universal sin, felt by both sexes, all ranks and most ages. The 'disease of lust' was to St Augustine persistently intrusive and the most destructive of the appetites.[18] John Donne defined 'our carnal affections, our

18 *Confessions*, bk. 8, sect. 7, p. 169.

concupiscencies' as 'those beasts [...] those brutish affections, that are in us [...] in sinning we lose this dominion over our selves'.[19] Necessary for the continuation of the species, the human sex drive was difficult to control. It concerned all churches. The sin of fornication was defined as any prohibited sex. Prohibited meant outside marriage. Consensual sex between two unmarried adults was forbidden. Sex with someone other than your husband or wife was both fornication and adultery. The intention to conceive a child was the only justification for intercourse within marriage. Sex for pleasure alone was lust and fornication. Lust comprised all unclean thoughts and unclean acts, including unnatural ones like bestiality, incest and homosexuality (condemned in Romans 1:26).

Masturbation, rape and sexual thoughts were all lust. A perceived growing libidinousness in society, with an increase in unwanted pregnancies in all ranks, worried preachers and playwrights alike. 'In political libels, lampoons, satires, and other forms of writing and action, upper-class immorality is almost inevitably the object of sharp disapproval, reflecting the growing grip of Protestant attitudes to sin, social order, and divine vengeance'.[20] The church's attitudes to sexuality focus on two problem areas; the medieval church's view of women as the source of sin (particularly the belief that women were naturally more lascivious than men) and the church's central principle that appetites (passions) made men more like animals than angels and needed to be controlled or suppressed. The Christian ascetic tradition required avoiding all excess: simple food, simple clothes, a focus on the spiritual rather than the carnal. Every deadly sin is a form of appetite developed to excess and reflected in the beast in man. In *'Tis Pity* calm reason is recommended to a jealous, vengeful husband: 'Sir you must be ruled by your reason and not by your fury: that were unhuman and beastly' (4.3.83–5). Unruly appetites (of different sorts) were the subject of play after play. Through the long period of the Middle Ages marriage was slowly established as a means of controlling and channelling lust. While theoretically chastity was regarded as preferable in order for full spiritual perfection to be achieved, it was gradually conceded that marriage was the second-best course if you could not effectively control your sexual impulses.[21] Marrying was preferable to engaging in promiscuity, but even within wedlock lust had to be restrained. Lust was a major topic for admonition in sermons and religious writing. Men and women even sat separately in church. The Puritans, though in favour of marriage, had

---

19 *Sermons*, 10 and 2.
20 Dabhoiwala, 42.
21 'If they cannot contain, let them marry: for it is better to marry than to burn' (St Paul, I Corinthians 7:9).

considerable difficulty with the whole area of sexuality. Criticism of rampant lust is recurrent in plays of the 1600s. *Measure for Measure, Hamlet, Othello* and *Troilus and Cressida* all express concern about female sexuality.

Sexuality has a part to play in *Dream*. Other dramatists (John Marston, Thomas Middleton, Thomas Dekker) addressed the nature and effects of lust too. For all the intricate euphemistic euphuism of their speeches, lust obviously underlies the love of Hermia and Lysander. It is part of the attraction between Theseus and Hippolyta, Pyramus and Thisbe, and the thwarted passion of Helena. The separation and estrangement of Oberon and Titania indicates a lust/love gone wrong. That they are arguing over 'ownership' of a changeling boy is not only a reflection of a gender power struggle but also a masking excuse that expresses their lack of their own progeny. They are both blindly opposed to each other at the beginning, unable to arbitrate their differences. That the repentant Titania, ashamed of her temporary straying into a form of grotesque, bestial lust for Bottom, should hand over the child as atonement, is perhaps an inadequate resolution of their problem of childlessness. Both Oberon and Titania treat the boy as a commodity, as a piece of property, and display the lust of ownership. An agreement to share the boy, to adopt him, might be a more rational answer. Handing him to Oberon merely reasserts orthodox male dominance as part of the play's return to normality. It is not a humanist outcome.

Envy or **covetousness** is jealous desire for what others have, a form of mental theft and discontent with the lot God gave you. Demetrius envies Lysander's fortune in being loved by Hermia. If he also has half a mind to her inheritance then he sees Lysander too as obstructing his access to her money. His explanation of the 'sickness' that drew him from Helena to Hermia does not address what it was about Hermia that attracted him. Perhaps it was only the greediness of a child coveting one thing and then rejecting it quickly for something else, unable to make up their mind or stay constant. Such vacillation of emotion commonly features in youthful 'love', wanting to possess one person and then another and another and another. The play is not interested in exploring deep psychological states, so there is little to go on and it is inappropriate to expect to find consistent and detailed explanations. The child in a sweetshop unable to decide what item to choose and choosing first one and then the other, is a characteristic of lustful young men. So too was the unspoken avarice for an heiress's wealth masquerading as love. Both motives were aspects of contemporary life in Elizabethan England among the upper ranks. Oberon clearly envies Titania's love for the changeling, feeling it denies him the primacy he regards as his due, and this shifts perhaps into jealousy that her love for the child diminishes the love she feels for him. This hints at the sometimes fraught change in family dynamics when a child is added to the previous double bond of husband and wife.

Helena betrays some signs of envying her friend's happiness ('How happy some o'er other some can be!/Through Athens I am thought as fair as she', 1.1.226–7). There is something of sibling rivalry in this, for though they are not technically sisters they have been very close. Helena's speech (3.2.195–216), with its history of their inseparability ('Like to a double cherry'), confirms this. This image hints they were also a symmetrical double of each other, separate as entities but identical and joined. When the audience first sees them, they spot similarities of dress, appearance, class, education and language style, but also differences – of height and colouring, and personal standing (one paired in love, the other abandoned and isolated). When each suspects the other of having suborned the men to mock her, then the suppressed jealousies of the past, and a sense of reproach at betrayal, emerge strongly.

Sibling rivalry is a frequent motif and motive in Shakespeare. It is doubly present in As You Like It with Orlando and his brother, and the exiled Duke and his brother. In Hamlet it focuses on Hamlet Senior and Claudius. In Much Ado there are Don Pedro and his bastard brother Don John. These rivalries all involve deceit, cheating and attempts to oust the hated rival, an actual murder of one brother by another (Hamlet), and a war between siblings (Much Ado). In Richard III the Duke of Gloucester is deeply envious of his handsome, golden, successful brother, Edward IV. In The Taming of the Shrew an older sister is jealous of the younger because she is seen as their father's pet. In Lear the long-held grievances of childhood surface in the jealousies of the king's three daughters and the conflict between a legitimate and an illegitimate brother. It is deeply disturbing to see how little love can exist within the family, or how testing times can open cracks rather than strengthen bonds. Egeus's attitude displays a lack of affection, and the sisterly love of the two young women is strained even before they leave Athens for the woods. Helena, possibly orphaned and alone (her father is mentioned but never discussed), seems to feel that Fortune has unjustly given Hermia all the luck. Her seemingly solid relationship has come to an end on Demetrius's part, yet her friend's is thriving. In different ways, and to different degrees of seriousness, Shakespeare reworks envy as an unsettling, potentially destructive aspect of family relationships. Sibling rivalry and envy make rich drama-generating themes. The early morality/chronicle play Gorboduc (1571) goes back to a period of British prehistory focusing on the rivalry of two brothers who are given half the kingdom by their father, Gorboduc, who is resigning from power. The plot pivots on sibling rivalry and succession. It involves civil war and fratricide. Envy too is a frequent theme in revenge plays. The Mary Tudor/Elizabeth relationship had had its uneasy jealousies and the Mary Queen of Scots/Elizabeth I cousin rivalry bedevilled English politics until the former was executed for yet another plot against the queen.

Greed and **gluttony** are sins of physical excess. Avarice (greed), or excessive desire for material goods or wealth, is the miser's sin, hoarding for its own sake. It is the sin of the moneymaker – the financier, speculator, entrepreneur – accumulating more than he needs. It is the sin of conquistador explorers like Sir Walter Raleigh and the Virginia Company, like the founders of the East India Company, looking to loot luxury materials from the Americas and Asia and make huge profits. From the religious standpoint it is the sin of the man who does not 'shake the superflux' (his unwanted excess food or money) to the needy, a theme much discussed in the increasingly hard times of the 1590s and 1600s. Gluttony is a bodily excess, largely applied to overindulgence in food and drink. It reminds that 'enough is as good as a feast'. As long as you had eaten and drunk in moderation, sufficient for the body's needs, anything more was unnecessary indulgence. The leftovers could be given to the old and the poor. It is the Dives and Lazarus story again, a story reminding the rich and comfortably off to do their duty to the community. It was part of the harmony of society, payment for deference, putting back into the community.

Excess was a moral hot point. Any form of excess was disapproved. The early church was built on moderation, on asceticism, fast days, lack of material possessions and the simple life. It failed to live up to that ideal, becoming a monolithic edifice of accumulated wealth, land, power, corruption and self-indulgence. Its decadence and worldliness triggered various reforming heresies violently suppressed in the name of preserving the faith, but actually defending Catholicism's monopoly hold over the people of Europe. The theoretical basis was moderation and simplicity. The Apollonian religion of ancient Greece had a tradition of controlled moderation. 'Nothing in excess' was inscribed on Apollo's temple in Delphi. The concept persisted. A late-fourteenth-century proverb said, 'There is measure in all things'. St Augustine wisely remarked that 'to some, total abstinence is easier than perfect moderation'.[22] The Puritans revitalized the traditions of asceticism, leading to them being seen as killjoys, but excess was a moral danger marker. In tragedy (classical and Elizabethan-Jacobean), once a character behaves with excess in any aspect of their life, disaster becomes possible. Excess of anger, of jealousy, of grief, of ambition, all figure as destructive flaws in *Lear*, *Othello*, *Hamlet* and *Macbeth*. In comedy too we find excesses – overstrict fathers, overangry old men, boastful soldiers, effusive lovers, lust-driven characters, drunks. Any form of obsessive/excessive behaviour is open to mockery. Bottom, Hermia, Lysander and Helena all display a degree of excess that becomes amusing. Puck's irrepressible but excessive need to make mischief is comic too, but it knows no bounds of moderation

---

22 *On the Good of Marriage*, chap. 21.

and borders on being dangerously disruptive. Egeus's anger is over the top and is both humorous and dangerous. In the end it is thwarted, but objectively his role as the stock angry father is funny if played in a melodramatic way. Bottom's persistent need to take the lead and play the knowledgeable man of the world becomes comic for he has no understanding of when to hold back and be modestly silent. The lovers amuse in a different key. Their duets, full of allusive references to other classical lovers and their problems, though voiced in a poetic register become a list, as each character attempts to keep up and follow the other. Shakespeare is both using and mocking the overelaborate speeches of court masques and the unreal language of Lyly's court comedies, but then love's excessive exaggerations were always amusing to Shakespeare. There is excess too in Oberon's cruel revenge on Titania, though again it is comic bordering on cruel. Comedy is usually cruel for the victim of the joke. As spectators, outside the action, not involved too closely and knowing it is only a fiction, we can laugh, though occasionally the suffering that a mistake or trick can cause may be too much to be acceptable. Emotional identification probably does not take place in watching *Dream*, for the characters are not three-dimensional enough for us to feel empathy. The aim of the piece is to entertain, to amuse, to instruct.

Virtuous, rational living was thought to be its own reward. Moderation, abstinence, chastity and renouncing and avoiding temptation were all ways to concentrate your devotion to God and virtue. None was much practised at court. The principle of moderation was integral to Christian belief from its beginnings. The simple life of John the Baptist, Jesus, the hermits of the Thebaid Desert and many saints prioritized spiritual cleansing over the demands of the body. Regular fasting and leading a frugal life were practices that continued in Protestant England. Periods of contemplation and prayer were encouraged as was the rejection of luxury. Excessive, ostentatious displays of your spirituality were sinful too. The showy overpiety of the Puritans is a common target in drama. The aim was to put the corrupting influence of this world into perspective. Diminishing its power over you gave you time to focus on the next world. But balance had to be kept. It was acceptable to work hard, enjoy your family, be an active, useful member of your community *and* take pleasure moderately in the good things of this world. Shakespeare is always subtextually smuggling in warnings for the audience.

Courtiers were an ostentatious, drunken, promiscuous, gambling-obsessed, garrulous and debt-ridden lot, mostly living away from home and thus neglecting their families and their local social duty, and needing more instruction than most. Given the sometimes noisy, inattentive, food-munching, giggling, gossiping nature of audiences, we can only hope that the courtly spectators of this play were more receptive to the lessons taught.

Another sort of excess – an overdeveloped laziness – **Sloth** was not just a disinclination to work but also a psychological/spiritual state of not bothering. Your duty to God was to work hard at your trade and at being virtuous. Many didactic stories and plays illustrate the spiritual and material rewards of industry. A popular one compared two apprentices – one, hard-working, gets on well in his trade and gains his master's daughter, while the other, idle, falls into bad habits and ends up in prison for debt. This is demonstrated in *Eastward Ho!* (1605). Industry not only meant working at your livelihood but also being a committed, active Christian, helping the community and actively working at guarding and improving your own spiritual state. The Latin word for sloth, *acedia* (or *accidia*), also applies to spiritual slothfulness or despair, the state in which you lost the belief that God cared for and watched over you. It was a state akin to melancholy or depression. Excessive grief and despair were forms of spiritual sloth.

The sins displayed in this play are not explicitly telegraphed, but are implicitly embedded in words and actions. A contemporary audience would be of the mindset to interpret the drama before them in the light of these moral waymarkers. It would also take the points made by Puck ('Lord, what fools these mortals be!', 3.2.115) and by Bottom ('reason and love keep little company together nowadays', 3.1.138–9) that mankind is a foolish species and that folly is always an expression of one sin or another.

Man had two qualities that none of the rest of creation shared: sensibilities and reason. Altruistic feelings of kindness and caring led to charity and showed in family love and community care which rationally accepted that some loss of self-will was needed if the benefits of group cooperation were to be accrued. It encompassed empathy, the ability to understand what others are feeling. Despite the positive aspects of some feelings there were many others that lured men into folly. Folly was the first step toward sin. It was, however, his ability to reason that raised him far above the animal world and drew him closer to the angels. It was the capacity to postulate action, speculate on causes, effects and consequences and then decide what course to take. Hamlet sums this up most aptly:

> What a piece of work is a man! How noble in reason! how infinite in faculty! in form, in moving, how express and admirable! in action how like an angel! in apprehension how like a god! the beauty of the world! the paragon of animals! (2.2.303–7)

This ideal Renaissance man, rational and civilized, had cultured accomplishments, could play and write music, write poems, dance well, converse easily and fluently, had impeccable manners and was cultivated and learned. All of this was very possible if you had education, position and money.

The year *Hamlet* described man's perfectibility, another picture of what man could be (and generally was) is voiced by the jester Feste (*Twelfth Night*, 1601) telling Viola/Cesario (a boy actor pretending to be a girl pretending to be a boy), 'Foolery Sir, does walk about the Orb like the Sun, it shines everywhere' (3.1.39–40). In theory rational, in practice foolish is Shakespeare's presentation of mankind. Everyone acknowledged man at his best – planning ahead; being practical and reasonable; using common sense; adjusting to changed circumstances; doing what was just and kind; constructing social agencies to fit the needs of a community; sympathetically desiring to redress imbalances of food, wealth and power caused by individual greed, laziness and intemperance, and formulating this into a judicial system; and developing a power hierarchy that theoretically enabled society to work effectively. It was the other aspect, however, the failure to achieve perfect social harmony and perfect personal government, that most exercised the pens and tongues of satirists and moralists. Acts of folly, the first steps on the road to sin, provided an endless, rich ground for descriptions of failure and prescriptions for improvement. Man's infinite capacity for spoiling things was a much more exciting, titillating, sensational and fruitful subject for dramatists and religious polemicists, than theorizing about ideal sociopolitical-personal structures. Silly judgements, making a fool of oneself, deceiving others, self-deception, trickery for gain, greed, the minefields of sex and love, power, money and outright wrongdoing provided a complex network of failed right conduct and a wonderful parade of fools. In *Dream* the working of magic eliminates, for a large part of the play, any possibility of acting rationally. The magic and the mistakes and confusions it creates take rational, balanced judgements and views out of the hands of most of the characters. They become puppet playthings of chance with no control over their lives.

This releases chaos and with chaos come misunderstandings, follies, sins – and humour. It is worth noting, however, that the nastiness of Hermia and Helena is not magic induced. It shows the personal viciousness that may lurk under the elegant clothes and pretty looks of two young gentlewomen. It shows how, under pressure, the veneer of civilized manners cracks. As Bacon said, 'Prosperity doth best discover vice, but adversity doth best discover virtue'.[23] Put people under pressure and unsuspected aspects of their character will emerge – not always noble ones.

The madcap pantomime of what happens in the woods is like commedia dell'arte slapstick farce, but with serious underlying issues. The helplessness

---

23 'Of Adversity', 75.

of the lovers is deeply disturbing for it displays the effects of appetite freed from rational decisions and makes them prey to sight sensations. It displays will devoid of consideration for others. Because they rely on their eyes for understanding, for attraction, they make misperceptions, misunderstanding what they are seeing and having their sight manipulated without their knowing. It is love gone mad, prompted by attraction alone, without sensitivity, without careful character assessment, driven by what the self wishes. Its logical outcome, in its most extreme form, is Titania's 'love' (or deluded fixation) for a monster. Theseus's detached analysis is that lovers, lunatics and poets 'are of imagination all compact' (5.1.8). That means they all think, feel and perceive the same way and that much of what they imagine is not real. This suggests that what we think of as love is itself a delusion. As long as the person we 'love' agrees with us the delusion works. But if the delusion breaks down and becomes not a mutual thing but separate, then there will be conflict. Hermia believes Lysander loves her, but finds herself rejected because his delusion has switched to Helena. The reality is that this is artificially induced, but no one in the group of four knows this. Yet it completely de-stabilizes Hermia and turns upside down a world she thought she knew. The audience knows the truth of the situation, but they are not part of the action. Our superior knowledge of just what is going on enables us to be amused at their confusion, though it may generate a sense of helplessness. We watch but are not able to step into the scene and explain. This is part of the magic of theatre, but also part of its closed nature. It is its own world and we are only spectators. This situation is a metaphor for our own blindness, our own failure to always see clearly, our own sense of being at the mercy of Fortune, luck, chance.

Chapter 4

THE SEVEN CARDINAL VIRTUES

If the Seven Deadly Sins were the warning signs for avoiding damnation, the Virtues were waymarkers to salvation.

The Seven Cardinal Virtues

1. **Temperance** (abstinence, moderation)
2. **Prudence** (providence, foresight, circumspection, consideration, wise conduct)
3. **Justice** (justice, equity, fair judgement)
4. **Fortitude** (strength under pressure)
5. **Faith** (piety, duty to and belief in God)
6. **Hope** (hope of salvation)
7. **Charity** (love of, benevolence to, others)

A godly life won a heavenly crown. If life was a journey and each person a pilgrim on the highway, conduct determined destination. Virtue's path was hard – steep, thorny, stony, winding, tiring. The way for the carnal man of weak character, Mr Worldly Wiseman, was easy, a 'primrose path', as Macbeth puts it, but leading to an 'everlasting bonfire' and 'sulphurous pit'. Virtue required steadfastness of belief. Stephen Bateman's engraving *Of Faith* depicts a knight, fully armoured in the Elizabethan style. He bears a shield with the cross of St George on it and has a lance and a sword. He stands on the body of the Devil sprawled on his back and looks out across a bay where a ship is sailing and over which the clouds have opened to reveal, in Hebrew, the words of God. The accompanying signification reads, 'The man in armour signifieth all stedfast beleuers [believers] of the veritie being armed with constant zeale of Christianitie, and weaponed with the shielde of liuely faith, the spere of continuance and the sworde of the word of God: the Deuil vnder him is temptation being ouercome by faith in Christ Iesus'. In *Of Justice*, Justice carries the scales of equity, a sword to 'cut off all rebellious persons and offenders' and has one eye in the middle of her forehead representing 'vpright iudgement'.

Because *Dream* is not designed as a tragedy, the potential for sins to take hold and destroy is persistently turned aside, thwarted, marginalized or resolved. Sinful behaviour holds our attention because it is intriguing and potentially dangerous, but virtues are evident and engage actively with sins. The anger of Egeus and the demand for death is a real danger that needs to be pre-empted. The elopement is intended to do just that, but generates other sins and is a sin in itself. Theseus's delaying intervention in the opening scene may be intended to give the lovers a chance to elope or simply a calming tactic giving everyone a chance to look at the problem less confrontationally. Oberon's good intention (to make Demetrius love Helena as much as she loves him) similarly goes awry and Puck's mistake causes a potentially life-threatening situation. But again the men's determination to fight is blunted and danger averted. The repressed negative thoughts Lysander has of Hermia and the same submerged criticisms and jealousies the two young women harbour about each other surface in their argument in the woods, threatening to rupture their relationships. All is, however, forgotten when the couples wake next morning, confused by the rags and shreds of the dream they think they have had. The sins that emerge – wrath, jealousy, vengefulness, covetousness, discourtesy, disobedience, disrespect – are all transgressions of both expected Christian and courtly conduct. They provoke questions that hold our attention for they create tension and drama between the characters and for the audience, but the simple nature of the storyline, the persistent comic treatment and mood make us suspect that all will be artificially worked out for the best.

The centrality of virtue to living the good life was not only recognized in Christian thought. Classical writings, particularly Plato's Socratic dialogue *Protagoras*, Aristotle's *Nichomachean Ethics*, Cicero's *De Officiis* (*On Duty* or *Obligation*), Seneca's *De Ira* (*On Anger*) and *De Clementia* (*On Mercy*) all extolled virtue. Each listed those qualities required to live the good (that is, virtuous and wise) life. Plato names wisdom, courage, justice, kindness, circumspection and holiness as essential components of excellence. Aristotle identifies courage, temperance, liberality, magnanimity, proper ambition, patience, truthfulness, friendliness, modesty and righteous indignation. Schoolboys studied Cicero's works particularly as models of good Latin style, elegant but direct. In an age when one's first public duty was to others and not to selfish individual desires, *De Officiis* became the key exemplum of good citizenship. Studied at university as an essential guide to the moral life and public conduct for young men who might later be active in national arenas, it advised how to discern false flattery from wise counsel and how to divert unreasonable, angry demands. Seneca too was studied and his essays were of particular relevance to the formation of a wise and just ruler.

The qualities identified evolved into the four virtues of Christian thinking, then extended to seven with the so-called theological virtues, faith, hope and charity, originating in Paul's letter (I Corinthians 13:13), with charity elevated as the greatest. Charity means not only the donation of alms to beggars or assistance to the poor but also the extension of love and sympathy to all fellow living beings. In Epistle to the Galatians 5:22–3, Paul also said, 'The fruit of the Spirit is love, joy, peace, longsuffering, gentleness, goodness, faith, meekness, temperance'. Such characteristics are part of the moral excellence that constitutes a person's virtue. The Christian fathers, St Ambrose, St Augustine and St Thomas Aquinas (*Summa Theologica*, II (I). 61), reacting to and refining St Paul, discussed and detailed what became the seven key characteristics of the pious Christian and incorporated them into the main body of church teaching. By the Renaissance their meanings had proliferated into an extensive didactic and mentoring literature aimed not just at individual Christians but also at any sort of leader or governor.

Temperance was a crucial characteristic for a prince. Theseus shows it in handling Egeus and Hermia both at the start of the play and toward the end. For James I temperance meant not only the opposite to gluttony but moderation in all things, particularly in the exercise of justice, power and anger. However, temperance was not something he actually followed himself, being an intemperate drinker and given, like Queen Elizabeth, to immoderate anger when thwarted. To Thomas Elyot self-control and emotional balance were crucial qualities in someone with the immense potential for punishment available to a king.

Along with prudence or circumspection, moderation (a synonym for temperance) was fundamental to queenly rule. Not jumping to conclusions but considering options and outcomes carefully is a vital skill for any civic leader whose actions and judgements have widespread consequences. Within the fiction of the play, it is as well to remember that potentially Theseus's power allows him to make unilateral executive decisions. He could thus overrule Egeus. He prefers rather to talk to him and let matters take a natural course. This soft-touch management does not work, so in 4.1.178 he overbears Egeus, but not tyrannically. Round the time when *Dream* was first performed, few would have known of James I's contribution to the discussion of princely duty in the anonymous *Basilikon Doron*. Only seven copies were printed and privately circulated. However, *The Trew Law of Free Monarchies*, published anonymously in 1598 as well, was generally known to be by the king. Both works promulgated absolutism and shared many of the basic concepts of princely conduct already currently accepted under Elizabeth's rule. There was already broad agreement by most writers on the subject and the power of monarchs and the subject's duty of obedience are already clearly established in *An Homily against Disobedience and Wylful Rebellion* (1570). If Elizabeth watched the play, she might have acknowledged the wise proceedings of Theseus, but squirmed a little in her royal seat at recognizing the standard regal virtues transgressed on stage in the bullying, autocratic and spiteful behaviour of Oberon. Perhaps the gender difference would have been enough to blind her to his failings being like her own. Then again, she had acute perception and was no fool. Patience, perseverance, courage (the bravery to do the right thing and to face evil), fairness (justice for all who deserve it), tolerance, truthfulness and honesty, respect for others, kindness, generosity and forgiveness were key to right conduct, but not always displayed by the queen. In his favour, be it admitted, Oberon's spitefulness is only aimed at his recalcitrant wife and is swiftly terminated when he has achieved his goal. He also is very quick to see a good he can do in helping Helena regain the love of Demetrius. The domestic conflict of the fairy rulers is not something that should be allowed to spill over into the public domain. It does and this is not acceptable regal or courtly conduct. The recriminations that surface are, like those of the lovers, deep-seated psycho-emotional problems that demand either silence in public or private resolution. The opposites of the princely virtues are presented in *Dream* – pride, intemperance (in the form of excessive bad temper), greed, sexual licence, envy, indulgence, irreverence, dishonour, violence, deceit – but are marginal and, because this is a comedy, thwarted or diverted.

Prudence is the patience of the circumspect ruler who does not react impulsively, but weighs up options, considers possible outcomes and makes decisions calmly and with the advice of trustworthy counsellors. Theseus has no wise adviser but is prudent enough himself. He talks privately to Egeus and Demetrius, giving them a chance to reconsider their positions.

Justice (along with appropriate mercy) was a key quality in a king, for in those days a monarch had absolute power and could act outside the law. That might be a good thing if it meant showing fairness and merciful pardon for all who deserved it, but absolutism, authoritarianism and arbitrary whim in the hands of bad monarchs litters the pages of the chronicles. Shakespeare's history plays alone demonstrate the all-too-human spitefulness, pettiness and brutality of kings, queens and overmighty noblemen. Recent experience of the Tudors made it clear that God's representatives on earth were often no better than their lowliest subjects. Mercy, thought to be a major attribute of God, was certainly within the scope of a monarch, but needed to be exercised carefully so as not to encourage further crime. In *Measure for Measure* Escalus, co-governor of Vienna comments that 'Pardon is still the nurse of second woe' (2.1.281). It must be shown where deserved, but if easily available it becomes abused and a let-out for the unscrupulous. Perseverance, courage (the bravery to do the right thing and to face evil), tolerance, truthfulness and honesty, respect for others, kindness, generosity and forgiveness were key to right conduct, but not always displayed by Elizabeth. Only Egeus is overmighty. He fails to prudently consider the possible side effects of his either/or ultimatum to his daughter.

Fortitude is strength in the face of hardships. It is inner strength that helps a person persevere through negative situations by striving to resolve them or enduring that which cannot be changed. Bottom exhibits an admirable degree of imperturbable positivity. Whatever odd incidents happen to him, he remains upbeat and grounded.

Faith, Hope and **Charity** are all religious characteristics thought to be absolutely vital for a Christian prince. No ruler could govern justly and properly unless he was a committed follower of Christ and could reasonably hope for salvation at the end of life. Charity was largely interpreted as the sort of generous largesse traditionally expected of any prince figure. But it had a more than material dimension relating to a general love of a ruler for his people. Caritas was expressed in the protection a shepherd gave his flock and the care a father took to look after his family. 'Shepherd' and 'father' were terms used to describe a governor's concern for his people.

The black cynicism in plays from 1600 onwards reflects a sense of spiritual and moral decline. The spirit of *Dream* is more positive. It warns and hints at the potential for dark outcomes, but offers a happy ending. For an age believing everyone was a sinner to greater or lesser degrees, the corruption of man was a basic given. Pessimism about individual probity (personal goodness, honesty, openness) is seen to extend into the wider workings of society and government. Individuals from all ranks are regularly shown as morally corrupt in different ways, but the supposed leaders of society – the titled governing elite – who were the expected exemplars of good practice, are persistently shown as selfish, indifferent and morally bankrupt. Deadly sins parade through the contemporary drama, but in this play they are relegated to passing temptations and man's benevolence is allowed to triumph. His folly is evident and there are brief displays of his pettiness and jealousy, but they pass quickly and good wins through.

Three other moral schemas had become part of the automatic thinking about how men should behave toward each other.

The Seven Corporal Works of Mercy

1. To tend the sick
2. To feed the hungry
3. To give drink to the thirsty

4. To clothe the naked
5. To harbour the stranger
6. To minister to prisoners
7. To bury the dead

Bateman's gloss to the engraving *Of Charitie* is virtually a verbatim repetition of the Corporal Works. Charity is

> to fede the hungry, to clothe the naked, to harbour the harbourless, & lodge the stranger, to visite the sicke, and to relieve the prisoners and poor afflicted members of Christe, this is the dueties of all faithfull people.

Cesare Ripa's allegorical personification of *Carita* is less socially oriented. It portrays family love, a woman, a mother, leading two children and suckling a third. His personification of Largess or Generosity (the readiness of the rich man to 'shake the superflux', that is, give liberally from his excess to the poor) is labelled *Liberalita* and shows a woman bearing two large cornucopias. The horn of plenty in her left hand is full of fruits, while that in her left is inverted in order to spill out its gifts. Tucked into the right hand is a pair of dividers symbolizing the idea of apportioning her liberality so that each needy person receives a due and equitable share.

The Seven Spiritual Works of Mercy

1. To convert the sinner
2. To instruct the ignorant
3. To counsel those in doubt
4. To comfort those in sorrow
5. To bear wrongs patiently
6. To forgive injuries
7. To pray for the living and the dead

The Seven Gifts of the Holy Ghost

1. Counsel
2. Fear of the Lord
3. Fortitude
4. Piety
5. Understanding
6. Wisdom
7. Knowledge

Bateman's depiction *Of Wisdome* shows two houses, one solidly built on rock the other a rickety hovel about to collapse. The former represents 'the stedfaste belief of the faythfull'. The house built on sand is 'the church of Antichrist and all popishe preaching'.

These schemas officially disappeared at the Reformation, rejected as part of Catholic doctrine, but were still in people's heads and hearts. They became absorbed into Protestant thinking, particularly in relation to social responsibilities. These are the positives by which the actors on stage would be judged by the contemporary audience. Though fun and the desire to see how the intriguing complications of the plot would work out are probably the dominant feelings the audience had in watching the play, the moral values of the time would still be operative.

Chapter 5

KINGSHIP

Savage and relentless anger is unbecoming in a king [...]

(Seneca, 193)

Now what shall I say about the courtiers? For the most part they are the most obsequious, servile, stupid and worthless creatures, and yet they're bent on appearing foremost in everything.

(Erasmus, 176)

[...] the aim of the courtier is to make his prince virtuous.

(Castiglione, 320)

They do abuse the king that flatter him:
For flattery is the bellows blows up sin.

(*Pericles*, 1.2.39–40)

Rule is a matter of some concern in *Dream*. There are four active rulers of people – Theseus, Egeus, Oberon, Titania. Hippolyta is an ex-ruler of the Amazons but is about to be transformed into a consort who will have some rule within the court and perhaps co-rule the state with her new husband. She has been conquered and annexed by Theseus. Though she still has her own voice and views, expressed in a narrow range within the relatively tiny scope she is given in the text, her exact role and its extent after her marriage are not yet negotiated and do not fall within the scope of the play. Oberon and Titania's relationship is disintegrating when we first see them but seems, by the end of the play, like that of Theseus and Hippolyta, to have reached a peaceful stasis, but one still to be renegotiated. The king of the fairies appears to have conquered his wife, but it is not clear whether that relationship is now fully resolved. Most of the cast misrule themselves, but in this chapter it is those who rule (or misrule) others who are the focus.

Erasmus's *The Education of a Christian Prince* (published 1516) had great influence throughout Europe. In England concern over training men for public office and social leadership had a history going back at least to King Alfred's translation of Pope Gregory the Great's *Pastoral Care* which comments on the duties and responsibilities of those in governing roles. More contemporary with Shakespeare are Sir Thomas Elyot's *The Boke Named the Governour*, the successive editions of *The Mirrour for Magistrates* (1574, 1578, 1587, 1610) and James I's *The True Law of Free Monarchies* and *Basilikon Doron* (both 1598). Though James I's works post-date the writing and performance of *Dream*, they reflect the common thinking on ruling and rulers. Relevant too as a handbook for the development of refined accomplishments and manners in courtiers is Baldassare Castiglione's *Il Cortegiano* (*Book of the Courtier*, 1528, translated by Thomas Hoby, 1561). These, and many sermons and pamphlets on the subject, indicate contemporary anxiety about what was suitable educational material, what was a workable stepped programme and above all how to properly train the minds and conduct of young men of rank. The education debate was not just about assimilating facts or developing skills. It was set within a basic belief that upbringing should be moral and the aim should be the production of a virtuous Christian prince. The term 'prince' applied to any ruler of a state (be they a duke, count, bishop and so forth) and all the way down the governing hierarchy to minor gentry acting as the 'prince' or leader of their community (comprising their household, estate and surrounding villages). It applied as well to fathers and heads of commercial enterprises. The alternative word used was 'governor' and comprised anyone in a governing, controlling role. Essential to the argument about what children should learn and how they learn, is the belief that nurture will not work if a person's nature is against it and that some types of personality resisted learning how to behave according to the Renaissance idea of the cultured civilized gentleman.

The little we see of Theseus suggests there is an aura of loftiness and dignity about him. He appears at first to handle the Hermia problem weakly, postponing a decision and taking Egeus and Demetrius off to talk to them. Like a schoolmaster/father/mentor he calls this 'private schooling' for both of them (1.1.116). Why both of them together? He had heard of Helena being jilted and 'with Demetrius thought to have spoken thereof' (1.1.112), but why should Egeus also be there? It seems possible he wishes to withdraw them from the public arena of his court, remonstrate with them, counsel them about their behaviour and advise how they should proceed – but without embarrassing them publicly. He has also quietly informed Hermia of the convent option which her father neglected to mention. The loyalty he has evoked in his ordinary subjects is very evident in the readiness of the mechanicals to trespass into a sphere not generally part of their world. Acting in mummers' plays by amateurs was a rarity confined to seasonal events like Christmas or to special occasions like the birthday of their lord of the manor or the marriage of one of his children. Such performances were informal and local, a community celebration, and though often rather poor in quality it was the thought that mattered and the thought was of loyalty and love. At the end of the play, Theseus overrules Egeus and arranges to share his own wedding day and celebration with the lovers, an act of comradeship and bonding. During the 'Pyramus' play, though he mocks some aspects of the acting, he is largely a sympathetic voice, mature enough to see that the love that drives the putting on of the play is worth more than any reservations about the skill of the performance. The lovers, by contrast, are snobbish, immature and reveal their detachment from those of lower rank.

Egeus, as a paternal ruler, is clearly to be condemned. Many in the audience would support fatherly dominance, but might disapprove of his manner of doing it. He is too prescriptive, too punitive, too excessive. Any social unit needs a leader, but he should lead with humanity. Egeus is a wrathful dictator. His approach to Hermia's marriage is autocratic and death dealing. Where is his love, his affection, his respect? There was an ongoing tension between the old, patriarchal view of fatherly behaviour vis-à-vis arranging a marriage and the new affective approach (see chapter 6). Egeus is no different in his demands and expectations in act 4 and it is significant that he is not at the postnuptial celebration where the 'Pyramus' play celebrates a famous story of unsympathetic parents, filial transgression and accidental deaths. The lovers (Hermia and so on) have been saved from the continuing stigma of transgression by the guidance and protection of Theseus.

Oberon, the third ruler figure, is even guiltier of misconduct than Egeus. He is dogmatic in his demand for the changeling boy, unsympathetic to how Titania might feel at losing a votaress and friend, and vindictive in his reaction to her opposition. He can only see the situation in terms of his will and authority being thwarted. In this he parallels Egeus in the human world. There is some ambiguity about the status of the boy and legitimate ownership of him. Puck states that the changeling is 'stol'n from an Indian king' (2.1.22), but Titania claims he is the son of a 'votress of my order' [follower of her cult] and that she has adopted the child to 'rear up'. He is one of her attendants, so clearly is past infancy, though perhaps still young. Who is telling the truth? Or are both defending their sex's claims: Oberon standing up for male precedence by law and custom, Titania standing up for female bonds of friendship and loyalty? Oberon's claim is based on his authority as her husband. He offers no evidence to substantiate his right on any other grounds. Titania does explain the emotional background to her claim to the child. Orphaned son of a priestess who worshipped Titania, the boy has been 'stol'n from an Indian king' (2.1.22) and is now the fairy queen's attendant. He is thus a changeling. It was a long-established belief that fairies (like gypsies) did steal children. Just who was the 'Indian king' who had 'ownership' of him is not made clear. He was possibly perhaps the father, and the boy the illegitimate offspring of a liaison with the priestess. The king may simply be the master of him as a young attendant follower. Either way, the situation focuses on how the law of that time gave preference to the father over the mother when it came to custody of children. In law fathers owned their children.

Alternatively, it represents how a master was thought to 'own' his servants, and Titania (in the name of feminine sentiment) has liberated him in memory of her dead friend, his mother. But there are wider issues here. Deborah Baker Wyrick claims it is a gender contest about the boy being of age to leave the female zone of upbringing and move into the male sphere.[1] Customarily, in titled families, this happened at seven. There is more to their tussle than this, however. A deal of sexual jealousy is aired. Oberon has an inclination to be lured by attractive females. Titania refers to this:

> I know
> When thou has stol'n away from fairy land,
> And in the shape of Corin, sat all day
> Playing on pipes of corn, and versing love
> To amorous Phillida. (2.1.64–8)

She asserts that Hippolyta ('the bouncing Amazon') is his 'mistress' and that he has come from India to be present at her marriage and 'to give their bed joy and prosperity'. That seems entirely appropriate. In classical literature there are many instances of deities who favour a particular mortal, protect them and take a keen interest in how their lives pan out. Oberon seems to have a special interest in Hipployta; she is his 'mistress' in the sense that concern for her dominates his thoughts. He is spontaneously sympathetic toward the unhappy plight of Helena and appears to have a soft heart for a pretty face. Oberon retaliates with accusations of how his wife has favoured Theseus ('I know thy love to Theseus') and how she has assisted him in his various amorous escapades. The conflict is not only for custody of the child, with a surrogate mother wanting to keep control for reasons of sentimental attachment to her erstwhile friend and companion, and a 'father' claiming the boy is now ready to enter the male sphere. Such collisions must have often happened in aristocratic households when a boy, reaching breeching age, would expect to

---

1 Deborah Baker Wyrick, 'The Ass Motif in *The Comedy of Errors* and *A Midsummer Night's Dream*', *Shakespeare Quarterly* 33, 1982.

leave off his childhood dresses and don male attire.[2] Many mothers no doubt tried to hang on to their 'baby' and fight his move into the world of schooling, riding, hunting and coming under the influence of his father. This is an out-come of the separate lifestyles of many upper-rank husbands and wives. The disharmony of the fairy rulers has negative effects on the human population just as conflicts between the powerful affected the people of England, either nationally or locally. Personal, domestic squabbles between a ruler and spouse should not affect their subjects, but in reality they did, just as servants and family members suffered when a titled master and mistress fell out. The fairy subjects are in disarray and the squabble of these deities is spilling into the human world. *Basilikon's* Book the First opens with an orthodox declaration that immediately places Oberon in the wrong:

> he cannot bee thought worthie to rule and commaund others, that cannot rule […] his owne proper affections and unreasonable appetites, […] Neither can […] his Government succeed well with him […] as coming from a filthie spring, if his person be unsanctified. (1)

Titania too is wrong in her outspoken and obdurate attitude. Neither was thought acceptable for a wife.

The matter of government – of people, of self – is common to all Shakespeare's work. Kingship is inevitably an explicit theme in the history plays. Popular audiences seemed insatiable for dramas revisiting the English past, displaying the fortunes of heroes and villains, plotters arrested and executed, monarchs succeeding or failing. The stories of Henry V, King John, Richard III and Richard II were popular subjects that Shakespeare was to rework in his own way. The fall of kings was endlessly fascinating and the history genre continued popular at the Swan and Rose theatres even into the 1600s when other venues and other writers, doubtful and discontented about the running of public affairs and the direction in which society seemed to be going, turned to topical satire to voice their anxieties. Reading or watching the many chronicle plays infesting the stage, leads inevitably to the conclusion that though kings are theoretically honoured as God's vice-regents on earth, in practice history shows them as persistently opposed, plotted against, harried from battle to battle, disrespected, often removed from the throne and violently disposed of. The vicissitudes inciting the drama in *Dream* are not of a public nature but are made public – they are all personal, but public virtue originated at the private individual level. The

---

2 Infant males wore female-style dresses while under school age. At seven they went into breeches.

ruler who organized his or her private life according to the prescriptions of the Bible and classical models and applied those values in public life had a good chance of ruling well. Oberon has made a prime mistake for a governor – putting his own selfish ends before his duty. Egeus puts his own will before the demands of Christianity. Good kings can be undermined by evil men. Weak kings, however virtuous, can be misled by devious lords. Theseus has the strength to counter Egeus's heavy-handed approach. Bad kings have nasty ends, being shown as unworthy of their role, either on personal or political grounds. But such an ending would be out of keeping with a play aiming to celebrate love, harmony, marriage and happiness – if that is what *Dream* was intended to do. Charismatic rulers generated powerful displays of patriotic loyalty and provoked a similar response in audiences when their stories were dramatized, but by the end of Elizabeth's life a general cynicism seemed to attach to real-life leaders (nobles and monarch). A strong leader's decline provokes consideration of failings that would be diplomatically ignored while the ruler's strength was feared. Elizabeth's death precipitated many long-repressed fears. The chronicle plays crowding the early public stage reflected not just an interest in rethinking the nation's past. They also sublimated contemporary anxieties about stability, masked and made palatable by dead personae and long-gone events. The approaching end of the century released many superstitious fears of apocalypse and gloomy anticipation of the new era inexorably coming. These fears transferred into negative representations of magistrate figures. Ben Jonson's *Sejanus* and the numerous revenge tragedies do not portray leaders as divine or their courts and advisers as anything other than basely human, grasping and unscrupulous. Roman history and recent Italian city-state politics afforded a useful means of dealing with current English concerns under the mask of foreign settings. The question of government is not confined to the history plays. It is present too in the four great tragedies with a focus on the qualities that may enable proper or improper governorship of self or polis.[3] Be that polis a household, a city or a nation, the control of emotions, appetites and vices (and the consequences of not doing so) is always at the heart of Shakespearean drama. Such serious concerns and outcomes are only minimally relevant here but as the comic complexities proliferate and the laughter mounts there are niggling questions that keep looming in the shadows. Shakespeare's mature dramas and late plays are similarly focused on the personal politics of small courts and individual relationships. With restrictions on what aspects of contemporary life could be presented and with portrayal of the monarch prohibited, indirection was the only means. *Dream*,

---

3   City-state (Greek). In theology, morality and political theory a person was seen as a
    state, governed well or ill.

while not a history play, is a study of faulty governorship (Oberon), faulty self-governorship (the lovers and Egeus), faulty parenthood and an exposure of the flawed personal dynamics of a group of young courtiers.

5.1 Preparation for Rule

In order to understand how people in the 1590s thought about princely conduct, the work of two writers on the subject is worth considering. They implicitly precipitate comparisons with the state rule and personal misrule of the characters in the play. Tudor conceptions of preparation for rule were dominated by Sir Thomas Elyot's *The Boke Named the Governour* (1531). The next generation would also have James I's *The True Law* and *Basilikon Doron*. They post-date *Dream* by two or three years, but the thinking is in line with orthodox political philosophy and indeed echo Elyot in many ways. Elyot asserts the need of 'one souerayne gouernour [...] in a publike weale', but acknowledges the need for councillors and a nationwide group of 'inferior governours called magistratis'.[4] Egeus seems not to occupy such a role. Indeed, he seems to have no specific role at court. Was he thought unfit? Possibly.

The basis for rule at any level is the proper upbringing of 'the chylde of a gentilman which is to have auctorite in the publike weale'. Elyot discusses lengthily the curriculum for this education because 'gentyllmen in this present time be not equall in doctrine to th'ancient noble men', due to 'the pride, avarice, and negligence of parentes', snobbery and a lack of teachers. Elyot complains that gentlemen believe 'it is a notable reproche to be well lerned'. The better sort of families pay high wages for skilled cooks or falconers, but not for a tutor to educate their child and inculcate virtue. The lovers all have the standard classical knowledge of gods and goddesses, so it is not their education that is at fault but the application of it in daily conduct. They have not seen that the Ovidian loves of the deities, represented in *Metamorphoses*, are not a model to follow. It is to be doubted whether Hermia (though not educated to govern) has been brought up properly. She does not govern herself and seems rather a wild, free spirit. Aristocratic society, the very society that might well have been the play's first audience, would not have approved of such wilful, independent behaviour. It could lead to inappropriate liaisons, secret assignations, pregnancy and loss of personal and familial reputation. Patriarchal strictness had its downsides, but it could act as a form of moral control of those ever-troublesome sexual urges. Girls were, by and large, chaperoned. Sons, away at university or roaming free in London, were an altogether more difficult problem.

---

4 All quotes from Elyot come from the 1970 Scolar Press unpaginated facsimile reprint.

The general qualities needed by any man who was to govern at any level were prudence, industry, circumspection and modesty. Monarchs required comeliness in language and gesture, dignity in deportment and behaviour, honourable and sober demeanour, affability, mercifulness, placability, humanity, benevolence and liberality, well-selected friends, sharp discernment of the 'diversity of flatterers', a sense of justice, personal fortitude and 'the faire vertu pacience'. Theseus seems not to have gathered round him courtiers who were well-selected friends and would alert him to problems, but he was aware that Demetrius had behaved inappropriately for a gentleman. Presumably if he knew this he would also have known of the growing love of Lysander for Hermia and expected a problem with Egeus.

Elyot sees obstinacy as 'a familiare vice' among men with power (both Egeus and Hermia display obstinacy) and recommends a set of passion-controlling virtues – abstinence, continence, temperance, moderation, sobriety, sapience (wisdom) and understanding. These requirements, echoing the Seven Virtues and the Works of Mercy, are very demanding. Theseus's past was not entirely moderate or restrained as regards sexual liaisons. He is a 'renowned duke' (in the words of Egeus – unless this is merely flattery) and has been a successful conqueror. He appears now to have matured and be ready to settle into marriage having sown his wild oats like many young gentlemen in Elizabeth's court. Privilege, power and the money that comes with them, brought responsibilities and responsibilities mean sacrifice – the spending of time administering a government, man management, keeping calm when angered. Theseus has what Elyot calls 'the exposition of maiestie' (an air of dignity that sets him apart), generates loyalty and love. The ability to inspire subjects with loyalty is crucial to kingship. It was one Elizabeth had pre-eminently.

It is the governor's role to keep just harmony between the 'comunaltie' ('the base and vulgare') and those with honour and dignities (titles and responsibilities). Maintaining order is vital. The 'discrepance of degrees' (differences of ranks) is part of 'the incomprehensible maiestie of God'. 'Take away ordre [...] what shulde then remayne? [...] Chaos. [...] perpeyuall [perpetual] conflicte [...] vniuersall dissolution'. This has an ideological affinity with Ulysses's degree speech in *Troilus and Cressida*. Elyot asserts that the hierarchies of Heaven are reflected on earth – the elements have their 'spheris' and men do not all have the same gifts from God. Potters cannot administer justice, and ploughmen and carters 'shall make but an feble answere to an ambassadour'. One might add that weavers and carpenters make poor actors.

With Oberon and Theseus we have something of the two unacceptable faces of rule as defined by James I in *Basilikon*: 'extreame tyrannie [...] and extreame slacknesse of punishment' (64–5). Though neither ruler falls completely into all these categories, they exhibit minor similarities. Oberon's judgement is suspect and his behaviour peremptory and demanding. Theseus appears to be too lenient in dealing with Egeus, Hermia and Demetrius in 1.1. The event proves him gently decisive and effective. He is lucky to be given a second chance to address the problem when he meets the lovers in the woods. Central to the situation as viewed by most orthodox Englishmen is that a ruler who subverted normative hierarchy, God's order, brings disruption to the whole chain of being. Oberon and Titania have caused such a subversion. This disorder is metaphorically reflected in the human dissensions with which the play starts and its scope is shown in the extreme weather and the proliferation of problems in the natural and human world (fogs, flooding rivers, rotting corn, drowned fields, sheep diseases) to which Titania refers.

Key to the infant education of men destined to authority is that their early years be lived in a milieu of virtue, that the language and behaviour of mothers, nurses and maids be irreproachable. At seven boys should be removed from 'the company of women' and tutored by 'an auncient & worshipfull man' with grave demeanour, gentle manners and impeccable morality. (This may be part of the conflict between Oberon and his wife: a tussle over control of their substitute child.) Then began a classics course that would develop rhetorical skills and perfect their Latin and the fluency and accuracy of their English. (Theseus speaks always in measured tones, fluently and confidently.) Elyot does not exclude physical exercise from his regimen, recommending hunting, hawking, dancing, wrestling, running, swimming and weapons training – in moderation.[5] This is standard Renaissance elite male education. Elyot deplores the tendency of noble families to halt their children's education at 14 and 'sufre them to live in idelnes'. He believes education is a lifelong process and is essential for the production of governors if they are to resemble Plato's philosopher-king. James I deprecated the tyrannical distortion of the state to suit the monarch, though both he and Elizabeth regularly did just that. Gentlemen should be 'trayned in the way of vertue' as Elyot recommended, and avoid the usual high-end lures of gluttony, avarice, lechery, swearing and dicing. Elyot exhorts young men to 'lerne wisdom & fal nat' [do not fall into sin] and abide by Christian precepts of behaviour, for 'from god only procedeth all honour' and God 'shal examine your dedes & serch your thoughtes'.

---

5 Demetrius has hounds, a gentlemanly marker, but is happy to leave Helena darkling in the woods to the mercy of wild beasts. This is most ungentlemanly. He has therefore the superficial signs of being a gentleman, the outward flourishes, but is discourteous in other respects. Theseus is out hunting with his entourage (4.1.) and is an experienced hunter.

Since no one man can know all that is happening in a realm, kings need reliable deputies to act as their eyes, ears, hands and legs. The body image was often invoked. The nation was 'the body politic': the head was the monarch; the major organs were the nobility; and the hands, legs and muscles were the labouring part of society. All had a job to do and if one part did not work properly the whole became less effective. Such subsidiary governors (courtiers, councillors/counsellors, magistrates) should be men 'superiour in condition or haviour [...] [and] vertue'. Elyot demands they have 'their owne reuenues certeine, wherby they have competent substance to lyve without taking rewardes: it is likely that they wyll not be so desirous of lucre' [lucre = money]. This defence against bribery had disappeared by the time Shakespeare wrote *Dream*, but the jobbery, corruption and greed that were standard at court are not explored. The play's focus is not in the court and its mood is festive rather than satirical. Outside the play's fiction, in real life, two generations of luxurious living and extravagance had left many high-status families financially embarrassed. An unseemly scrabble for lucrative posts, the lobbying for monopolies, cringing subservience to the queen (or anyone who could advance your fortunes) and a readiness to accept bribes were ways to help recoup family fortunes. Another was a profitable marriage such as Demetrius is possibly seeking. In the sixteenth century, marriage for mainly monetary reasons stood at 20 per cent among titled families rising to 34 per cent by 1660.[6]

5.2 A King's View of His Office

Theseus's calm control and Oberon's angry misrule are contextualized by a real king's contribution to conduct literature on the role and nature of kingship. *Basilikon Doron*, was structured as an advice book to his son, Henry, Prince of Wales. It is in three books: 'Of a King's Christian Duty towards God', 'Of a King's Duty in his Office' and 'Of a King's Behaviour in Indifferent Things'. ('Indifferent' means matters relating to private time.) The first section, about a king's duty to follow the tenets of Christianity, establishes strongly the idea of kings as God's representatives. This becomes a running motif throughout. Many ideas parallel Elyot and there are verbal echoes of the earlier work. Marginal notes indicate how much the book owes to Plato's *Republic* and Cicero's seminal work, *De Officiis*, the common source for books on the perpetual need to remind the governing ranks what their function in society was.

---

6 Stone, *The Crisis...*, 617.

The play's lightness and relative brevity mean that the criteria for ideal rule are less prominent than in plays like *Antony and Cleopatra*, *Measure for Measure* or *King Lear*, but the characters' conduct and the portrait of humanity emerging reflect some of the critical remarks made by James I.

Basilikon begins with an abstract of the 'Argument' in sonnet form:

GOD giues not Kings the stile of Gods in vaine,
For on his throne his sceptre doe they swey:
And as their subjects ought them to obey,
So Kings should feare and serue their God againe.
If then ye would enjoy a happy raigne,
Obserue the statutes of your heauenly King,
And from his Law, make all your Lawes to spring:
Since his Lieutenant here ye should remaine,
Reward the iust, be steadfast, true, and plaine,
Represse the proud, maintaining aye the right,
Walk always so, as euer in his sight,
Who guards the godly, plaguing the prophane:
And so ye shall in Princely vertue shine,
Resembling right your mightie King Diuine.

Overlapping the belief that kingship was divinely sanctioned with the image of God's 'Lieutenant here', the king almost becomes divine. Few Elizabethans or Jacobeans questioned that rule should be monarchical or doubted the continuing English system should have one-person government, but more and more they questioned kingship's divinity, the relationship between ruler and ruled and what should be the limits to princely authority. Increasingly as Elizabeth's reign reached its end such questions were asked more urgently. It is usually assumed divine right was universally accepted. It was and was not. The unthinking mass accepted that the king – a distant figure of power and awe to them – was like a god on earth. Largely they were voiceless, but others spoke for traditional beliefs. Robert Filmer formalized these in *Patriarcha*. Written in the 1620s (published posthumously in1680), it summarizes the accumulated ideology of divine right. Filmer believes the model monarchical state is founded on the idea of familial patriarchy and asserts Adamic dominion established by God (in Genesis) as the origin of patriarchy and kingship. As fathers rule the domestic polis, so do kings rule the nation state. Elizabeth's death was shortly to foreground discussions focused on the complex concept of divine right and how kings should govern. The justificatory line of argument went as follows: God made Adam lord of all creation, with dominion over his wife, family and the fruits of the earth. Male rule, therefore, was divinely sanctioned. Kings had similar incontrovertible, unopposable rule, reigning like the king of Heaven – autocratic and unquestionable. Disagreement was a sin against God, against nature. Thus bulwarked against opposition, monarchy and patriarchy became firmly embedded in society and their power developed. Kings had absolute power over life and property, could have people imprisoned, executed or pardoned, declare war, make peace, levy taxes, regulate trade, charter markets, issue licenses for manufacture, legitimize bastards and send people to the Tower. Their will was law and the law bent to their will. Regal proclamations were made with the mantra 'The king wills it' or 'The queen wills it'. Laws were only passed if similarly authenticated. The monarch nominated government officers, bishops, judges and peers. His or her power was absolute, his or her favour vital. James I declared of kings and queens that 'even by God himself they are called gods'. Theseus clearly has some of the aura of a god or hero on earth. His exploits and military successes prior to the timeline of the play are briefly mentioned and, from their education, many of the audience would know something of him before seeing this theatrical projection of him. It is only lightly presented, but he has a dignity and quiet authority that speaks of the potency of a king who claims godlike supremacy.

Basilikon's Book the First opens with an orthodox declaration that immediately places Oberon in the wrong:

> he cannot bee thought worthie to rule and commaund others, that cannot rule [...] his owne proper affections and unreasonable appetites, so can he not be thought worthie to governe a Christian People [...] that [...] feareth not and loveth not the Divine Majestie. Neither can [...] his Government succeed well with him [...] as coming from a filthie spring, if his person be unsanctified. (1)

It may be argued that Oberon is a fairy king and is therefore not to be judged by Christian values and that it is irrelevant to judge at all a play that was essentially written for fun and entertainment. This fails to take account of the probability that not even the most light-hearted, lightweight play could be watched without the exercise of some degree of moral judgement. This was an age much concerned with sin/virtue and right/wrong conduct. Comedy as a genre was particularly open to criticism as presenting immoral behaviour without sufficiently disapproving that behaviour. However, a tendency to judge would have been more insistent in the minds of an Elizabethan audience than today. To make moral judgements of the actions of the play is not to diminish the humour of it. To consider those serious issues that shadow its action is rather to enhance it and increase its underlying seriousness.

Book the First stresses the need for kingly piety and a life lived (as an example
to his court and people) according to the demands of Christianity: virtue,
self-control, respect for and obedience to scripture, conscience and faith ('the
Golden Chaine that linketh the Faithfull Soule to Christ' 9). The series of
guiding precepts are the following: 'wrest not the World to your owne appetite'
(4); 'The summe of the Law is the Tenne Commandements' (6); 'wisely [...]
discerne [...] betwixt the expres Commaundment and Will of God in his
Word and the invention and ordinance of Man' (15); and 'kythe [show] more
by your deedes then by your wordes the love of Vertue and hatred of Vice' (16).
Despite his colourful past Theseus seems to exude a sense of personal virtue
that would be a suitable role model for his people. He has certainly made
a strong, positive impression on his common subjects. A public profile built
through public appearance was an important aspect of Elizabeth's image and
Theseus's too has not shied away from meeting his people (see 5.1.93–105).

Book the Second, 'A King's Duty in his Office', links the lesson of being a
good Christian to the prince's second calling – being a good king. This office
is discharged through 'justice and equitie' (fairness), achieved by 'establishing
and executing good lawes' and 'by your behaviour in your own person, and
with your servants, to teach your people by your example: for people are
naturally inclined to counterfaite (like Apes) their Princes manners' (17–18).
The masterful but gentle manner of Theseus is a good example to his people
and may be part of why the mechanicals express such loyalty to him.

James I defines the difference between a true king ('ordained for his
people') and a tyrant (who 'thinketh his people ordained for him, a pray to
his passions and inordinate appetites' 18). A good king 'employeth all his
studie and paines, to procure and maintaine [...] the well-fare and peace of his
people [...] as their naturall father and kindly maister [...] subjecting his owne
private affections and appetites to the weale and standing of his subjects' (18–
19). We see too little of Theseus to be able to complete a profile of him.
Readers of Plutarch would have known that he had an immense reputation
not only for his adventures and conquests (military and amatory) but also
for his energy in drawing the scattered settlements into a conglomeration of
dwellings and civic institutions that established Athens as a strong city that
dominated the area of Attica. He was not a tyrant (and Renaissance Italian
history provided plenty of examples) and has a thoughtful calmness and
knowledge of humanity that emerges in his comments about lunatic, lovers
and poets.

James I warns that good new laws are always being needed to deal with 'new
rising corruptions' (20) and that 'a Parliament is the honourablest and highest
judgement [...] as being the Kings heade Courte' (21). He constantly called
Parliament when he needed it to vote him money and regularly left the country

in the charge of his Privy Council while he gallivanted off hunting for days on end. James I did not deal with the old or new corruptions that surrounded him, did not settle the country 'by the severitie of justice' (22), but left in place the institutional corruption of many judges and lawyers. He did not 'embrace the quarrel of the poore and distressed' (26). Neither did he live up to the precept that you should 'governe your subjects, by knowing what vices they are naturally most inclined to, as a good Physician' (27). Elizabeth often went on long, meandering progresses, neglecting her political duties and avoiding addressing difficult problems. She had a similar contempt for Parliament as a threat to her absolutism. She did little to alleviate the hardships of the poor, but did make herself visible to her people. Her readiness to meet them, while she never relinquished her view that she was a lofty, divinely ordained being, nevertheless encouraged great love and loyalty. The fictional ruler Theseus is a deal more human and sympathetic than the real ruler Elizabeth. Shakespeare cannot say this, of course. The comparison is there for the audience to make. The writer simply makes the complimentary allusion to a 'fair vestal, throned by the west' and an 'imperial votress' who passes on untouched by Cupid's dart (2.1.155–64). This has been taken by critics to refer to Elizabeth. When he came to power James I simply found the English situation too complex and deeply ingrained, gave up trying to reform either court or country on the lines of *Basilikon* (if he had ever intended to) and, hypnotized by the immensely increased disposable income the English crown gave him, stopped bothering to be a good king and enjoyed the ritual, the status and the luxury. The failure to see that privilege, power and luxury come with responsibilities would lead James I's other son, Charles, into civil war.

James I never got to grips with any of the underlying social problems he inherited from Elizabeth, seeming to let the nobility act as they pleased, despite his admonitions in *Basilikon* about repressing aristocratic pride and supporting the poor. Elizabeth, in contrast, kept her nobility well in hand. Echoing Elyot, James I advises, 'Acquaint your selfe [...] with all the honest men of your Barrones and Gentlemen' (34) for 'vertue followeth oftest noble bloud' (35) and such men 'must be your armes and executers of your lawes' (35). These words express the common belief that the nobility are born innately virtuous. This view, promulgated by the nobility, ignores both original sin (the belief that all men are born sinful) and the daily evidence of aristo-gentry misconduct. Theseus certainly seems to understand Egeus and Demetrius: one guilty of excessive punitiveness in exercising his power as a father and the other guilty of ungentlemanly behaviour and breaking the law by breaching his troth.

James I's recommendation 'bee well acquainted with the nature and humours of all your subjects [...] once in the yeare to visit the principall parts of the country' (40) was not something he did. Both Elizabeth and Theseus did visit their people. After reading Polydore Vergil's *Anglica historia* James I agrees that a king's actions determined his country's fate.[7] The image of a 'filthie spring' polluting the stream (a ruler's corruption corrupting the country) occurs frequently in contemporary drama. Oberon, though not personally evil, has corrupted good government by allowing a personal problem to overwhelm and distract him from maintaining a harmony in nature. He causes disruption and a split among the fairy folk and harmful consequences in the mortal world. The gap between precept and practice is made wider and more ironic when James I discusses a prince and his court as exemplars:

It is not enough to a good King, by the sceptre of good lawes well excute to governe, and by force of armes to protect his people; if he joyne not therewith his virtuous life in his owne person, and in the person of his Court and companie: by good example alluring his subjects to the love of vertue, and hatred of vice. [...] all people are naturally inclined to followe their Princes example [...] let your owne life be a law-book and a mirrour to your people. (45)

This was achieved 'in the governement of your Court and followers' and 'in having your minde decked and enriched so with all virtuous qualities, that there-with yr [sic] may worthilie rule your people. For it is not enough that yr [sic] have and retaine [...] within your selfe never so many good qualities and virtues, except ye imploy them, and set them on worke, for the weale of them that are committed to your charge' (45). Care was crucial when appointing public officers who had responsibility for 'the weale of your people' (50). They should be men 'of knowne wisdome, honestie, and good conference [...] free of all factions and partialities: but specially free of that filthy vice of Flattery, the pest of all Princes' (51). We see little of the Athenian court in action and no individual courtiers of power speak apart from Egeus (not a worthy exemplar) and Philostrate. The latter comments only on the entertainment choices available. If they are his selection of the best, they are less than impressive, but that may be due to a dearth of material on offer rather than a comment on the taste of the Master of the Revels or on the cultural quality of the court. In any case, the dull stuff listed: 'The battle with the Centaurs', 'The riot of the tipsy Bacchanals ...', 'The thrice three Muses mourning for the death/Of learning' are only there to mock the moral earnestness of contemporary Elizabethan

---

7 A History of England, cited in *Basilikon*, 62.

writing and make 'a tedious brief scene [...] very tragical mirth' of Pyramus and Thisbe seem more attractive.

As regards personal kingly virtues, James I echoes many of Elyot's recommendations. A prince should follow the four cardinal virtues with 'Temperance, Queene of all the rest' (62). The synonym for temperance used by both Elyot and James I is 'moderation'. A king needs the quality of 'wise moderation [...] first commanding your selfe [...] in all your affections and passions, [...] even in your most virtuous actions, [so you] make ever moderation to bee the chief ruler' (63). If civility, education and cultured behaviour are to be part of social-civic interaction, moderation is vital in assisting the repression of those aspects of man's nature that are disruptive to the moral profile of a state. Incivility, anger and the workings of youthful passion and jealousy, inevitable within small, inward-looking groups, threaten the peace of the court and threaten the harmonious run-up to the duke's marriage, so they are banished to the wild wood and the storm allowed to blow itself out. The mayhem in the woods is a metaphor for how dangerous, disruptive and antisocial human instincts are. The closed, hothouse atmosphere of Elizabeth's court encouraged liaisons to be formed, but also permitted changes of alliance and jealousies to grow. Only when the heat of passion has cooled is a return to the Athenian court possible. After temperance comes justice: 'the greatest vertue, that properly belongeth to a Kings office' (63). 'Use Justice [...] with such moderation as it turne not in Tyrannie' (63). Shakespeare would explore the 'difference [...] betwixt extreame tyrannie [...] and extreame slacknesse of punishment' (64–5) – the former in *Lear*, the latter through Duke Vincentio in *Measure*. Theseus seems to rule with soft government though his belligerent past may suggest he can be firm when needed. This perhaps shows when he overrules Egeus in act 4. Even then there is no sense of brutal autocracy and his firmness is gently applied without threat or violence. Orthodox paternalist belief favoured firm authoritarianism. James I specifies 'Clemencie, Magnanimitie, Liberalitie, Constancie, Humilitie, and all other Princely vertues' (64) as essential.

Dream was perhaps chosen for performance on a specific occasion and as an entertainment. This does not mean it has to be lightweight, meaningless and ephemeral. Darker issues and important matters are embedded in the text, but not allowed to overshadow the fun. The important second book of *Basilikon Doron* finishes with a series of pertinent precepts: 'Embrace true Magnanimitie [...] thinking your offender not worthie your wrath, empyring over your owne passion, and triumphing in the commanding your selfe to forgive' (71): 'Foster true Humility [...] banishing pride' (71) (relevant to the overconfident and wilful lovers): 'Beginne not, like the young Lords and Lairds, your first warres upon your Mother [...] O invert not the order of nature, by judging your superiours' (72). The inversion of nature is caused by the superior powers of those who appear to have control of nature – the fairy king and queen. The humans express their own arrogance, but it is humbled and they are made to suffer, even though the turmoil of minds and the bodily discomforts of their night in the woods are diminished by afterwards seeming like a dream, 'like far-off mountains turned into clouds' (4.1.187). This is what Oberon predicted:

> When they next awake, all this derision
> Shall seem a dream and fruitless vision;
> And back to Athens shall the lovers wend,
> With league whose date till death shall never end. (3.2.370–3)

So, was it all for nothing, other than the delight of the audience? Not at all. The lovers may have forgotten what happened to them as we forget a dream when we wake, but the audience has been entertained and observed the folly of their kind (especially over matters of love) and the realigned relationships have led to a 'league' [a union] that it is assumed will last. Nature is perverted/ inverted, the world turned upside down, with a weaver turned half ass and becoming the ostensible lover of a queen and the upper-rank courtier/govern- ing class governed, wandering distracted, confused, muddy and briar torn, controlled by forces they cannot see. Most crucially, James I concludes with the admonition 'exercise true Wisedome; in discerning wisely betwixt true and false reports' (74), reminiscent of Michel de Montaigne's comments on the misuse of words. Montaigne deplored the art of fine speaking as 'deceiving not our eyes but our judgement, bastardizing and corrupting things in their very essence' so that feelings are 'inflated with rich and magnificent words'.[8] The flowery duets of the different pairings of the young courtiers (Hermia with Lysander, Hermia with Helena, Helena solo, Helena with Demetrius, Lysander with Helena) display the intricacy and unreality of words, ideas and emotions that inflate feeling and distort reality by creating a new pseudoreal- ity of rhetoric. The long interchanges of these different pairs are artificial con- structs that sound beautiful and poetic, but drive the emotions to extremes. Having worked themselves into heightened states in act 1, scene 1, the disori- entation of the woods and the interference of Puck induce a dream/nightmare state where all sorts of oddities happen. Their experience in the woods has the unexpected, surreal quality of a dream where unconscious, repressed thoughts and desires emerge in unusual combinations. James I's final dictum resonates with the ironies of the failings of Egeus and the lovers: 'Consider that God is

---

8 'On the vanity of words', 343.

the author of all vertue, having imprinted in men's mindes by the very light of
nature, the love of all morall virtues […] preasse then to shine as farre before
your people, in all vertue and honestie; as in greatnesse of ranke […] as by
their hearing of your lawes, both their eyes and their eares, may leade […]
them to the love of vertue, and hatred of vice' (75). Egeus has been driven
by anger and determination to have his will. The lovers have been similarly
carried away by will and determination to leave home, break with family and
break the law.

5.3 Theseus and Queen Elizabeth

The duke is not a fictional representation of the queen. He is a ruler, minimally presented at the opening and closing of the piece and on the whole
handling matters effectively. Overt identification of fictional ruler with the
real ruler watching the play (if she did) would not be allowed. All plays
were licensed by the Revels Office and registered at the Stationers' Office
only once the government officials were sure the work contained nothing treasonable or heretical. The meaning of treasonable was elastically
expanded to mean any criticism of the monarch. Direct representation of
or critical reference to a reigning monarch was prohibited and removed
from the script. The author could face imprisonment. The delicate compliment to 'the imperial votress' is kept suitably vague. Shakespeare knew how
to cloak his concerns by indirection, smuggling in themes and presenting
them in such a way as not to appear overtly critical of particular persons.
As a leading writer, actor and sharer in the Lord Chamberlain's Men, he
could ill afford to upset his employer. Flawed leadership and satire of the
ruling classes become very evident in all his post-1600 plays. But they are
often removed from immediate identification with contemporary England,
its court or its monarch, by time and setting. *Measure* is set in Vienna,
Lear in pagan times, *Macbeth* in the medieval past (but showing the restoration of a legitimate line from which James I was descended), *Antony
and Cleopatra* in the Roman era, *Timon of Athens* in Athens, *Coriolanus*
in Rome, *Cymbeline* in pre-Christian Britain, *The Winter's Tale* in Sicily
and Bohemia, and *The Tempest* on a Mediterranean island. His early comedies are similarly set abroad – Ephesus, Navarre, Padua, Verona. Whatever
the locational or time-frame indirection, the themes were resonantly of
contemporary relevance. Theseus is merely an idealized ruler displaying
his qualities in a minor arena. Any ruler on stage invited automatic mental comparison with the current monarch. The critique of styles of rule
aims at provoking thought and a possible adjustment of values. It effects
this indirectly. Greek background, classical names, a male ruler – nothing

treasonable there. Theseus, what little we see, seems not to be a micro-manager. He stands back, allows people to deal with their own problems, may advise and then only step back in if a solution does not emerge naturally. This differs considerably from Elizabeth's style. As a counter to the uncertainties of her early life she created an appearance of supreme confidence, decisive, implacable and determined to keep power. Her motto was *Semper Eadem* (Always the same). This suggests firmness and steadfastness, but also obstinacy. In reality she was often uncertain and afraid, but hid it behind a mask of assurance. By implication, and distantly, Theseus offers an alternative style, but one that conformed to the agreed myth of Elizabeth as confident, just and adored. No one dared say otherwise, whatever they might think.

Chapter 6

PATRIARCHY, FAMILY AUTHORITY AND GENDER RELATIONSHIPS

6.1 Patriarchy and a Woman's Place

> Yet will not I forget what I should be
> And what I am, a husband: in that name
> Is hid divinity.
>
> ('*Tis Pity*, 4.3.135–7)

The matter of gender relationships is full of ambiguities, contradictions and inconsistencies. Each gender brings its own unacknowledged prejudices to the discourse and there is a persistent discrepancy between theory and practice. For Elizabethan times two features are definite: theoretically men ruled, and in practice women often subverted male domination. Custom, doctrine and law made fathers heads of families. God ruled creation, kings ruled nations and fathers ruled the home. God punished sin, kings punished earthly crime and a man could beat his wife, his children, his servants. Custom recommended moderation in corporal punishment, advocating its avoidance if possible, but its support in law meant it could happen. Beating causing bodily harm was not allowed. There were abusive and violent men who caused serious injury, but they could be protected in individual cases by an all-male legal system. A husband was an authoritarian figure whose word was law and the law supported men. St Paul authorized male dominance in the New Testament, *the* primary conduct book.

> Wives, submit yourselves unto your own husbands, as unto the Lord.
> For the husband is the head of the wife, even as Christ is the head of
> the church.[1]

---

1 Ephesians 5:22–3. See also I Corinthians: 11:3.

Theoretically then, husbands were dominant and wives supposedly subordinate in all things – in legal status, physical strength, intelligence, virtue.

Patriarchy originates in Genesis when God makes man first, gives Adam dominion over all animals, then makes Eve out of Adam's rib and gives him rule over her. She is designed as 'an help meet' (Genesis 2:18) – a companion and assistant. When Adam is tempted by Eve to eat the apple God upbraids him for listening to his wife and acting according to her encouragement rather than God's command against eating the forbidden fruit. This story shows how easily influenced men were by women and is the unacknowledged counterbalance to all the complaints about male domination. In reality, women wielded much greater influence than is usually admitted – and they wielded it by the ancient means – their sexual power.

The story of the Fall, written by men, while partially displaying male weakness was also used to endorse male superiority and the need for male rule. It reflects too the hierarchy of the chain of creation, justified how society was organized and re-enforced by a misogynistic Catholic Church deeply suspicious of women. To the fallen Eve God says,

> I will greatly multiply thy sorrow [...] in sorrow thou shalt bring forth children: and thy desire shall be to thy husband, and he shall rule over thee.[2]

Thus the pains of childbirth are annexed as punishment for Eve's sin and misogyny given divine authority.

The sixteenth century saw female inferiority as predating the Fall. Made after Adam, Eve was always secondary. So were all women. The poet-satirist George Wither summed this up: 'The woman for the man was made/And not the man for her'.[3] Advising his son about marriage, James I quoted Genesis 2:23 (where Adam claims Eve is 'bone of my bone, and flesh of my flesh'), commenting on the institution as 'the greatest earthly felicite or miserie, that can come to a man, according as it pleaseth God to blesse or cursse the same'.[4] His advice is largely orthodox. Henry should 'marrie one [...] of your own Religion; her ranke and other qualities being agreeable to your estate'.[5] There is awareness of the partnership aspect of marriage but it is patriarchal:

---

2 Genesis 3:16.
3 *Hallelujah* (1641). This echoes I Corinthians 11:8–9: 'For the man is not of the woman; but the woman of the man. Neither was the man created for the woman; but the woman for the man'.
4 *Basilikon*, 54.
5 *Basilikon*, 58.

Treate her as your owne flesh, commaund her as her Lord, cherish her as
your helper, rule her as your pupil, and please her in all things reasonable […] Ye are the head, as she is your body: […] your office to commaund, […] hers to obey; but yet with such a sweete harmonie, as shee
should be as readie to obey, as yee to commaunde […] suffer her never
to medle with the politick government of the common-weale, but hold
her at the Oeconomick rule of the house; […] yet all to be subject to
your direction: keepe carefullie good and chaste companie about her;
for women are the frailest sexe.[6]

Publicly, it was a man's world, but whatever the theory, whatever the
biblical and legal support, the reality varied greatly. In defining gender roles
and attitudes it is always important to remember, whatever the stereotypes, in
practice matters could be different and women subverted patriarchy in many
ways and in a variety of arenas. There had been some liberalizing of opinion
under the new Anglican Church and as a result of humanism. There was a
lively discourse about the nature and role of women, but while the bulk of
orthodox thinking conformed to the old-established view of male superiority
and dominance, what happened within doors, inside the privacy of each
domestic polity was very different. The queen's own experience brought her
into contact with some very strong-minded, independent, difficult women.

The traditional medieval position on women still persisted, despite some
changes. Orthodoxy saw women as the origin of sin, the source of temptation.
This 'man's world' took its authority from the Bible. Paul told wives to submit
to their husbands and keep silent in church (Colossians 3:18). He wrote,

I will therefore that the men pray […] Let the women learn in silence
with all subjection. I permit not a woman to teach, neither to usurp
authority over the man, but to be in silence.[7]

The Bible's good women, the Virgin Mary and the church's array of female saints,
were outweighed by evil women from scripture and history and the diatribes
of the Church Fathers. The biased selection of biased texts built up formidable
prejudice against the sex. Tertullian (c. 160–c. 225 AD), saw women as 'the devil's gateway'.[8] St John Chrysostom (c. 347–407 AD) claimed, 'from beholding
a woman [we] suffer a thousand evils […] The beauty of woman is the greatest
snare'. Clement of Alexandria (c.150–c. 215), went further: 'Every woman should

6 *Basilikon*, 60–1.
7 I Timothy (2:8–12).
8 *De Cultu Feminarum*.

be ashamed that she is a woman' for they are 'the confusion of men, an insatiable animal [...] an eternal ruin'.[9] Male mistrust of female sexuality underlies much of the patriarchal system. It was a factor in the intermittent waves of witch trials and executions. The *Malleus Maleficarum* (*The Hammer of Witches*, 1496) declared, 'All witchcraft comes from carnal lust, which in women is insatiable'.[10] Behind this perspective lies the sense that the female world was a mystery to men, a shadowy and frightening world, full of unknowns. Menstruation, pregnancy, childbirth, the confederacy of gossips and married women were all part of network of emotionally charged situations from which men were barred, failed to understand and were therefore regarded with suspicion.

Women's main role was keeping the house and largely keeping to the house. In rural areas women helped in the fields (particularly at harvest time), but many of their tasks were home based – cooking, feeding poultry, tending vegetable gardens, cleaning, making clothes, child minding. A shopkeeper's wife or daughter might occasionally help behind the counter, but saleable products (pastry, clothes, crafted items) were made by men (apprentices, journeymen, masters) and shop assistants were largely men. Women were barred from the professions, public life and higher education. The standard view was that women were intellectually feeble, unreliable, irrational, shrewish gossips unable to keep a secret, bad tempered, sexually voracious, endlessly demanding, never satisfied and would interrupt and take over any public/social meeting. A common image in medieval comic writing was that while the man worked and the servants kept the house, the wife gossiped with friends, entertained her lover or gallivanted wasting money shopping. This view persisted. It was generally believed women were overemotional and easily overheated sexually. Belief in the insatiability of the female sex drive reflects male insecurity and uncertainty over whether the child he is bringing up is indeed his own, fears related to questions of inheritance and keeping the family bloodline pure. It explains the obsession with the chastity of daughters and wives. A tainted daughter shamed the family, had little value in the marriage market and remained a drain on family finances. A wife who was 'loose i'the hilts' degraded the husband's public reputation and honour, wounded his personal esteem, cast doubt on his children's legitimacy and made him the butt of jokes about cuckolds and horns.[11] Proverbs 12:4 put it thus, 'A virtuous woman is a crown to her husband: but she that maketh ashamed is as rottenness in his bones'. Patriarchy's dominance perpetuated

---

9 Clement also advocated equality of the sexes and women being admitted to leading roles in the church.
10 Kramer and Sprenger, *Malleus Maleficarum*, sec. 1.
11 The words of the incestuously obsessed Duke Ferdinand in *The Duchess of Malfi*, 2.5.6.

stereotypes and explains why so many men had low opinions of women and treated them unsympathetically and as sex objects. But so too did the actual behaviour of some women. Some women did behave badly. Misogynistic, derogatory views are voiced frequently among the rakish male characters crowding Elizabethan-Jacobean comedies, though Hamlet and Iago are misogynistic too. This loose-living, loose-tongued, bawdy, joking brotherhood stretches from Lucio (*Measure for Measure*, 1604) through Willmore (Aphra Behn's *The Rover*, 1677) to innumerable libertines in later drama and novels. A counterbalancing philosophy offers the *gentils domna* (gentle and genteel lady) of courtly love, the beautiful but virtuous woman whose example civilizes brutish men. Her self-effacing quietness is courtesy and confidence, not the silence of submission. She has the self-effacing quiet of the self-assured but restrained woman. Her silence is not that of a downtrodden creature. Hermia and Helena are not modest, retiring females. They have plenty to say. Though Lysander and Demetrius spout reams of the standard adoring rhetoric poets traditionally addressed to their mistress, it is a ritualized, artificial recitation of cliché images of praise for their beauty, and the females too are equally voluble and in the same style. Noticeably eyes are commonly mentioned. This is ironic as it is the myopia of love and the impaired vision induced by the magic flower, applied to the eyes, that is the source of the lovers' desperation and the audience's amusement. Numbers of references are made to vision: 'I would my father look'd but with my eyes' (1.1.56); 'O hell! To choose love by another's eyes' (1.1.140); 'Your eyes are lode-stars [...] My ear should catch your voice, my eye your eye' (1.1.183, 188); 'he errs, doting on Hermia's eyes [...] Love looks not with the eyes' (1.1.230, 234); 'ere Demetrius look'd on Hermia's eyne [...] to have his sight thither and back again' (1.1.242, 251). Among the many eyesight references are others relating to madness and being lost. They counterbalance images of moderation and calmness and emphasize the misperceptions that are common to love and essential to comedy.

Neither Hermia nor Helena are quiet or restrained in the way a sophisticated, cultured Renaissance lady was expected to be. They have much to say for themselves and, not backward in coming forward, stand up for their views. At times they sound like viragos or shrews. Their aggressive independence of thought, accepted nowadays (though not necessarily acceptable), would have been regarded by many in Elizabethan times as pushy, out of place and sinful. Humility and modesty were regarded as virtues required of both sexes. The orthodox expectation of a daughter was that she should be a *pia filia* (dutiful daughter), modest, speak when spoken to and defer to adult views. The same was expected of young men. There are few female characters in Shakespeare who conform to this model. Hermia's opposition to her father is transgressive of the commandment to honour your father. To some degree it transgresses the boundaries of genteel and courtly behaviour as does her acceptance of Lysander's presents, serenadings and poems. She has permitted all the courtship tokens her father lists. That would be thought unseemly and morally dangerous. She goes even further, agreeing to the illegality of contemplating marriage without parental consent. This too would have been regarded as an immoral move, putting herself into the hands of a man without the support and protection of her family and without the protection of a communally sanctioned marriage. It was not acceptable that a pair should unilaterally decide on their union. A wedding, in those days, was agreed to by the families of the couple, acknowledged by a betrothal in front of witnesses (*sponsalia de presenti*), formalized by lawyers, announced to the community through the calling of the banns in church on three consecutive Sundays and then finally sealed by the priest. The proposed elopement is the instinctive, age-old reaction of youthful passion obstructed. It is the romantic thing to do, but it is still inadvisable and potentially dangerous. Helena, like Beatrice (*Much Ado*), Viola (*Twelfth Night*) and Rosalind (*As You Like It*), has no male parent or adult male relative to guide her. She too puts herself in the hands of a man, putting her trust in his 'virtue'. It is a great risk. An audience of the time might well regard her as foolish. Shakespeare's comedies often use the device of the orphaned youth or maiden making misguided choices. The underlying message seems to be that however self-reliant, resilient and confident you are you can still make mistakes – particularly if judgement is distorted by passion. With or without adult advice, the Bible should always have been the source of guidance. Will and appetite are what guide Hermia and Helena. Neither is a reliable means of judgement and neither is supported by the Bible.

The 1571 *Book of Homilies* sermon on the state of matrimony declared woman was 'a weak creature, prone to all weak affections and dispositions of the mind', indicating that the Anglican Church was essentially little different from Rome. Greater respect for women, though still wary, emerged among the Puritans, who demanded abstinence from both men and women, but Puritanism was a minority sect.

Theatre commonly reverted to stock types of females for their humour or dramatic value. The garrulous nurse in *Romeo and Juliet*, the witty but overwhelming Beatrice in *Much Ado* and the scheming unscrupulousness of Lady Macbeth follow stereotypical lines. Another stock character from drama, the widow – either rampantly free and easy or easily victimized – reflects the standard view of predatory female sexuality and echoes anxieties about overhasty second marriage for women. Dynastic and financial concerns are involved. Family fortunes could quickly be lost to a spendthrift second husband and the children of the first union disposed of in marriage or simply sent to a faraway estate and neglected. The 'merry widow' was not just a comic figure. *Hamlet* and *The Duchess of Malfi* present tragic examples of the difficulties a second marriage could bring. In practice second, third and fourth marriages were common among both sexes and all classes. Moralists admitted that humankind was inordinately lustful, but since most moralists were male they tended to be more tolerant of male libidinousness and more critical of female failings. Neither the wildfire spread of syphilis nor the widespread ecclesiastical condemnation of intercourse outside marriage as a deadly sin for both sexes curbed the natural lustfulness of either. With the blatant hypocrisy, chauvinism and prejudice that each sex brings to stereotyping the other, there was, on the male side, a double standard accepting young men fornicating indiscriminately, regarding possession of a mistress as a sign of manhood, while demanding chaste behaviour among their women. Both female heroines in *Dream* trust themselves to young men at night in a wood. Neither expresses any awareness of the danger of this except for Hermia's refusal to let Lysander sleep by her side. She appeals to his 'courtesy' and cites her 'modesty' when he 'riddles very prettily' (2.2.52) in explaining he only wants to protect her and will not take advantage. By a nice irony, this very modesty causes Puck to think that the gap between them indicates this is the arguing pair Oberon saw. No good deed goes unpunished and Puck's mistaken identification (while showing that even such a clever sprite cannot always understand reality and has not God's omniscience) sets in train the madcap errors of the night.

Young women in Shakespeare's time were not allowed much freedom of access to young men. They were kept at home much of the time and chaperoned in public. Fiction and real life showed how predatory youths could be. The church was abundantly clear about the ubiquity of the temptations of lust. Though neither Hermia nor Helena seems likely to give way to sexual longing and neither young man seems likely to take advantage of them, they would nevertheless be regarded by the audience as putting themselves in a situation that was morally indefensible, would provoke gossip and tarnish their reputation.

The orthodox husband-wife relationship is defined in Shakespeare's early sex-war comedy *The Taming of the Shrew* (1593–4).[12] Petruchio, seeking a wife in order to refill his coffers (as many did), announces to the assembled wedding guests,

> I will be master of what is mine own.
> She is my goods, my chattels: she is my house,
> My household stuff, my field, my barn,
> My horse, my ox, my ass, my anything. (3.2.229–32)

---

12 A similarly orthodox view is voiced by the unmarried Luciana in *The Comedy of Errors* (1588–93) 2.1.

At the end of the play Kate supposedly defines the theoretically submissive role of the wife:

> Thy husband is thy lord, thy life, thy keeper,
> Thy head, thy sovereign – one that cares for thee,
> And for thy maintenance commits his body
> To painful labour both by sea and land,
> To watch the night in storms, the day in cold,
> Whilst thou li'st warm at home, secure and safe. (5.2.146–51)

She sees 'love, fair looks, and true obedience' as a duty a wife owes like that 'the subject owes the prince' and deprecates the rebellious wife seeking 'rule, supremacy, and sway'. Is this sincere or has she, like women before and since, discovered she can get all she wants by appearing submissive while secretly gaining control of the household and of him? This is the comic discrepancy inherent in the gender relationship. Man plays the master and to all intents and purposes is so publicly, while the woman pulls his strings behind the scenes.

Manipulation, deviousness, sheer bloody-mindedness and simple evil (their weapons of mass subversion in the sex war) were attributed to women in the social comedies of the 1590s/1600s. In *Dream* we have two young women determined to do as they choose. There is no evidence to say just how young they are, but whether 16 or 26, they are being foolish. Helena's revelation of the planned elopement seems not well rationalized. It is a betrayal of a confidence, a betrayal of a friend. Did she hope the news would bring it home to Demetrius that he had no chance with Hermia? Did she hope it would trigger a return to her? Was she happy to be second best? Though such detailed motivation is not suitable or to be expected in a largely unbelievable plot where the aim is to make the audience laugh, such questions are unavoidable.

While female tenderness and sensitivity are acknowledged, misogyny is accurate in its definitions too. In Thomas Middleton's *A Mad World My Masters* the superior cleverness of the courtesan Frank (Frances) Gullman is openly admitted by the country gentleman surreally named Penitent Brothel:

> The wit of man wanes and decreases soon,
> But women's wit is ever at full moon. (3.2.159–60)

and

> When plots are e'en past hope and hang their head,
> Set with a woman's hand, they thrive and spread. (3.2.246–7)

He is right. The aptly named Gullman (man fooler) lures into marriage Follywit, the heir of Sir Bounteous Progress.[13] Shakespeare's comic heroines – Beatrice, Rosalind, Viola, Portia – are similarly clever, inventive, resourceful women, but their virtue prevents them intending or doing evil. Lady Macbeth, Goneril and Regan (Lear) are prime examples of devious women whose ambitions are ruthless and destructive. In the real world theory and practice diverge once again and diversify into a variety of relationships. Every marriage was unique – some paralleled the orthodox model, in some the woman ruled unopposed, in most a compromise was negotiated or appropriated. There were happy marriages, arranged or not. Many men and women married only for fiscal or dynastic reasons and found love grew between them later – or not. Slowly a shift was taking place that saw marriage as a partnership of companions, physically and spiritually. Lord Montagu advised his son, 'In your marriage looke after goodness rather than goodes'.[14] Traditionally men sought love and sexual relief outside marriage. This was the negative aspect of arranged marriages where there was no initial attraction and none developed afterwards. The Earl of Northumberland advised his son, 'As you must love, love a mistress for her flesh and a wife for her virtues'.[15] This outlook adopts the traditional stance of marrying for breeding while taking a mistress for one's pleasure. Some women took lovers (usually less openly, though not always) and others sublimated their emotional needs through running estates and raising children, while their husbands attended court or parliament, joined the army or spent their time in usual male activities – hunting, gambling, drinking, theatregoing, whoring. Many marriages were based on separate lives, but many thrived on the love and respect that formed the new companionate marriage. Puritan pamphlet/sermon input to the marriage debate promoted the development of the helpmeet/companion element.

A play marking the emergence of the strong, independent woman is John Fletcher's The Woman's Prize, or The Tamer Tamed (1610). Appropriating Shakespeare's Petruchio, the shrew tamer, Fletcher has him tamed (or humanized) by his second wife, Maria. She outwits the standard chauvinistic male. She, no longer 'gentle' or 'tame,' her 'new soul' is

Made of a north wind, nothing but tempest,
And like a tempest shall it make all ruins
Till I have run my will out. (1.2.77–9)

---

13 A gull was a fool, someone gullible.
14 Cited in Stone, The Crisis ..., 615.
15 Stone, 614.

Her sister advises abandoning her plan and accepting her expected sexual destiny. Maria is implacable:

> To bed? No, Livia, there be comets yet hang
> Prodigious over that yet. There is a fellow (Petruchio)
> Must yet before I know that heat – ne'er start wench –
> Be made a man, for yet he is a monster;
> Here must his head be. (1.2.101–5)

Where does she point? To herself as his head, her breast where his head must rest lovingly, or under her foot? She is being transgressive, though expressing something of the rebalancing of the gender roles of the time. Her cousin, Bianca, contextualizes Maria's stand:

> All the several wrongs
> Done by imperious husbands to their wives
> These thousand years and upwards strengthen thee!
> Thou hast a brave cause. (1.2.122–5)

To her this is an opportunity for extreme gender revenge. Maria's apparent goal is less extreme though radical enough at the time – equality in marriage. She declares

> that childish woman
> That lives a prisoner to her husband's pleasure
> Has lost her making and becomes a beast
> Created for his use, not fellowship. (1.2.137–40)

This play contributes to the lively late sixteenth-/early seventeenth-century debate about just what women were like and what their place/role in society should be. *Dream* does too in a different way. It displays the crazy vagaries of love and presents two young women who wilfully, naively disregard all caution. To Baldassare Castiglione 'the emotions of love provide excuse for every kind of fault'.[16] Robert Burton has much to say of the dangers of love, especially the blurred line between love and lust:

> if it rage, it is no more Love, but burning Lust, a Disease, Phrensy, Madness, Hell. 'Tis death, 'tis an immedicable calamity, 'tis a raging madness 'tis no virtuous habit this, but a vehement perturbation of the mind, a monster of nature, wit, and art.[17]

---

16 *The Book of the Courtier*, 198.
17 *Anatomy of Melancholy*, part 3, sect. 2, memb. 1, subs. 2, 650–1.

Some of the language of the lovers looks like raging. It is a verbal sublimation of the natural hotness of youth and, though it falls short of actual physical sin, it could get out of control and does in act 3, scene 2. Allowing too much freedom to young people was as dangerous as overstrict repression. Opinion was mounting against arranged marriages forced for dynastic and material reasons (characteristic of royal and aristocratic unions) where there was no attraction or love. Arranged royal marriages were traditionally a facade only, sometimes fruitful, sometimes not, often becoming a union of separateness. There were exceptions, but the recent example of Henry VIII shows how personal choice too could be mistaken, especially when driven by an absolute will. And the word 'will' at this time meant not only determination to do something but also the sex drive. It was difficult to navigate safely between the Scylla of loveless arranged unions and the Charybdis of the uncertain and potentially unworkable choices freely made by emotionally unstable and changeable young people. We see how unreliable Demetrius's decisions are. Shakespeare's comedies in general explore the vagaries of emotion. In *Measure for Measure* the danger of giving the young 'too much liberty' is focused; in *Much Ado* the acute hero and heroine fail to intuit who is their right partner; and in *Twelfth Night* Orsino is a prey to overblown emotion. Thomas Becon, in his *Golden Boke of Christen Matrimonie* (1542), describes couples trapped unhappily in arranged/forced marriages cursing 'their parents even unto the pit of hell for coupling them together', though there were also many who coped or even found happiness. Egeus is immune to moderation or reason. Anger distorts his thinking or he would take time to verify Lysander's character and honesty and find proof he was not a suitable partner or accept that he was. By his intransigence he alienates his daughter's love and pushes her to take extreme action. Egeus fails to make allowance for instinct and appetite. After all the sex drive is one of the strongest primal impulses. As the usually coy Ophelia sings in her liberated and unrepressed madness,

> By Gis and by Saint Charity,
> Alack and fie for shame,
> Young men will do't if they come to't –
> By Cock they are to blame. (*Hamlet*, 4.5.58–61)

She might have added that young women will 'do't' too, if they get the chance. Blinded by his anger Egeus does not believe (or does not want to believe) that they really do love each other. Lysander has 'bewitch'd the bosom of my child' (1.1.27) and 'stol'n the impression of her fantasy' (1.1.32) with all the paraphernalia of young love ('bracelets of thy hair, rings, gauds, conceits,/Knacks, trifles, nosegays' 1.1.33–4). If he does believe they are in love and persists in having his way, then he shows himself as an altogether unfit father. But then parents are often dubious about just what allures a young man to their daughter and how honourable his intentions are. Fathers were once young men themselves. Love at first sight is a recurrent device in romances and comedies. It is part of the fiction that the reader/viewer believes the impulse is genuine, the instinct true. But we know in real life that instant attraction can be false, a sexual feeling that will fade once satisfied or once the other person displays aspects of themselves we do not find agreeable. Shakespeare presents a whole host of mutual fallings in love at first sight. Antipholus of Syracuse falls for Luciana (*The Comedy of Errors*), Romeo for Juliet, Rosalind for Orlando (*As You Like It*), Viola for Orsino and Olivia for Viola (*Twelfth Night*), Florizel for Perdita (*The Winter's Tale*) and Miranda for Ferdinand (*The Tempest*). Romeo and Juliet, of course, are the famous prime example, but all the others turn out to be reactions to genuine, continued and viable attraction. Whether Lysander and Hermia fell for each other instantly we are not told, but the relationship has been established for something over a month and a half, for Lysander refers to meeting Hermia once in the wood with Helena in order to 'do observance to a morn of May' (1.1.167).[18] The word 'once' suggests it was not recent. If it had existed longer than that, then Egeus has certainly been remiss in not stepping in sooner to supervise, assess and agree to it or to stop it. Lysander also hints that he is to inherit from his aunt, 'a dowager/Of great revenue' (1.1.7–8). Has he told Egeus his relative is rich and of rank? It might have carried weight. Has he even approached Egeus for permission to court Hermia? That was the customary procedure. He refers to being as of as good a family as Demetrius and of 'fortunes [...] as fairly rank'd' (1.1.101). It seems the father ignores this because he simply wants to have his own way. We may also ask why Egeus, if he has observed so closely the progress of the relationship, has not stepped in before? Theseus knew of Demetrius's previous liaison with Helena. Did Egeus not?

Gender politics underlie, indeed begin, the play. Theseus and Hippolyta met as opponents, fought, and now vanquished and victor have formed a new relationship. They parallel the sex war with a real war, but reach a compromise in which conflict is defeated by love, the conquered Amazon becomes a winner gaining new status and the conquering male is in some measure mastered and tamed by emotion and commitment. A new phase is about to begin for both of them. This process suggests that man and woman are like animals; they are in natural opposition, will fight to establish dominance and then settle more or less peacefully to mating and rearing a family. Some critics see Hippolyta

---

18 If the May Day and Midsummer Day are in the same year then the relationship has only lasted from 1 May to 24 June. This brief time is nevertheless long enough for Lysander to have given all the gifts Egeus refers to.

as suffering residual resentment at being tamed and made conformable. Her reaction to Theseus's impatience at having to wait four days may, however, be seen as calming and positive:

Four days will quickly steep themselves in night;
Four nights will quickly dream away the time;
And then the moon, like to a silver bow
New bent in heaven, shall behold the night
Of our solemnities. (1.1.7–11)

Not only does she introduce the idea of a dream passing the time or time passing like a dream but also gives no hint of not looking forward to the marriage. At the end of 1.1. she may be somewhat downcast at the disruptive and life-threatening situation of Hermia casting a shadow over her forthcoming nuptials. Is there evidence for her and Titania striving for 'Amazonian autonomy'?[19] There are grounds for seeing the two women as being 'firmly brought back into line under male husband-rulers', but both seem happy to accept the resultant reassertion of harmony.[20] Perhaps they realize they can achieve private rule by avoiding public confrontation.

Gender conflict between a parent and child is clearly there, evoking the ongoing problem of how to mitigate strict patriarchy with more affective family relationships over the matter of marriage, while still preserving female safety in a male-dominated, predatory world. Overstern patriarchy is a plot feature in *The Taming of the Shrew, Romeo and Juliet, King Lear* and in the late romance *The Tempest*, with very different outcomes. Standard gender conflict is blatantly there in the struggle for dominance between a husband and wife in the Oberon and Titania story.

The increasing vocal presence of women in society and at court, combined with their increased presence in print, ratcheted up the gender discourse. Though women were beginning to record their lives in private journals and letters, few are represented in print, but that was changing rapidly. Gender issues are addressed mainly through male dramatists. The public dimension of theatre and the growth in the practice of printing play texts for commercial sale foregrounded this age-old concern, made it a public domain. But in privately circulated manuscripts and in occasional printed texts, women were emerging as authors and were raising gender issues on their own account.[21] *The Memorandum of Martha Moulsworth, Widow* (1632) offers a touching

---

19 The view of Helen Hackett (Introduction, Penguin edition, xlvii).
20 Hackett, xlvii.
21 See Louise Schleiner for discussion of the small coteries of women authors.

verse account of her life and three happy marriages. A loving father brought her up 'in godlie pietie [...] In modest chearfullnes & sad sobrietie'. Unusually, for her sex and rank (rural gentry), she was taught Latin, but lamented 'two universities we have of men/O that we had but one of women then!' (lines 33–4).[22] Martha married at 21 (quite late), was widowed after five years, mourned a year and then remarried. Ten years later she was widowed again. After nearly four years she married for the third time. Of this last relationship she writes,

> The third I tooke a lovely man, & kind
> such comlines in age we seldom find
> [...]
> was never man so Buxome to his wife
> with him I led an easie darlings life
> I had my will in house, in purse in Store
> what would a women old or yong have more?

She declares she loved all her partners, was very happy with them and enjoyed domestic responsibility: 'I had my will in house, in purse, in Store' (lines 67–8). She completes her autobiography with a neat and witty couplet in keeping with her sense of satisfaction in marriage:

> the Virgins life is gold, as Clarks us tell
> the Widowes silvar, I love silvar well.

Martha is a positive example of a woman living in the provinces. There is insufficient evidence to form a distinct pattern or profile showing how widespread such education for girls was or how common such happiness in marriage.[23] Both Hermia and Helena have been educated ('She was a vixen when she went to school' 3.2.324) and display some classical learning. Martha's education makes her an exception. She is not unique, but the bulk of women (and men) had little learning. How much love they found within arranged unions is impossible to tell.

If working, running the estate or living a life of pleasure and leisure was a man's life in aristo-gentry circles, family tended to be the major part of

---

22 Greenblatt, ed., *Norton Anthology* 1553–5.

23 The letters between the gentry couple Sir John and Margaret Winthrop evidence both a loving marriage and a highly articulate woman (see in Bibliography under Winthrop). They relate to the second decade of the seventeenth century. There is correspondence too between Bess of Hardwick and her husbands, testifying to affective relationships (see Lovell).

the female sphere, along with overseeing the household economy (though responsible to her husband for expenditure in both areas).

Traditionally women were thought more naturally inclined to be loving and nurturing. Many fathers were distant, even when at home. James I warned his son that when he had 'succession' (children) he should 'bee carefull for their virtuous education: love them as yee ought', but 'contayning them ever in a reverent love and feare of you'. Some mothers too were distant (especially court ladies), so that noble offspring were often reared by nurses and maids. Fathers tended to be strict, concerned to discipline children to conform to society's expectations of their gender role and attitudes. Formality and ritual deference were more common among the elite. In their parents' presence children stood in silence, speaking only when spoken to. In very strict aristocratic families they knelt. Even a citizen's children asked father's permission and blessing before beginning any undertaking – making a journey, going to university, leaving home to marry, leaving the table, going to bed. The addressing of a father or mother could be very formal – using their title or calling them 'Sir' and 'Madam'. Similar formality could apply between husband and wife. That said, in many families there was affectionate informality. In the exchange of views and demands relative to the Egeus/Hermia conflict, neither shows any affection for the other. Egeus refers only to 'my daughter' and Hermia to 'my father'. Neither speaks directly to the other, uses any affectionate form of address or makes any rational plea for the other to understand or compromise. Arbitration will be difficult. Neither side is willing to give way and neither is very tactful.

The unsubmissiveness of Hermia is transgressive and inappropriate in a young woman untried in the ways of the world and dependent on her father. Humility (valued in men too) was not merely a device for keeping women quietly deferential. Overwhelming, garrulous adults were unacceptable whatever their sex. Knowing when to give your opinion and how to give it least offensively and most courteously was a social skill prized among courtly people. The idea that a young woman or man had the right to speak up independently and freely was centuries away. Deference, humility and self-effacing silence were expected, but human nature being what it is, were not always displayed. Talkative, gossipy adults, always butting in, were unacceptable whatever their sex. There are blabbermouth males in Shakespeare and other dramatists, but at least since the rise of medieval misogyny there was a belief that, given their head, many women would talk ceaselessly. The terms gossip, flibbertigibbet, scold and shrew range through the types of more ready female verbalizing. If women stereotype men as talking too little, men stereotype women as talking too much. The implication is that much female vocalization is silly, pointless, idle gossip and verbal diarrhoea. As the saying had it, 'Every ass loves to hear himself bray' – or herself. Gratiano (*The Merchant of Venice*) and Lady Would-Be (*Volpone*) are a male and female example of the comic figure of the incessant chatterer who makes little sense. Benedick, fairly vocal himself, expresses frustration at Beatrice being 'possessed with a fury' (*Much Ado*, 1.1.160) and 'huddling jest upon jest' (2.1.214), nominating her 'my Lady Tongue' (2.1.240). Dusinberre, discussing what she regards as female repression, asserts, 'A woman suffers continually from the impotence which is exceptional in a man'.[24] Shakespeare's 'impotent' women are far outnumbered by his articulate, resourceful and independent ones, reflecting perhaps his perception that despite patriarchy, despite the public limitations of their horizons, women did achieve a deal more of their own way than might be assumed if theory and orthodoxy alone are considered. And were a good deal more audible.

Legal and biblical authority made man the head of the woman and the family. His wife's money and property became his, his claim to custody of the children took precedence over hers and theoretically he had the final say in all things. In practice many different arrangements were negotiated by individual couples. Some women were independent, bossy termagants. Some efficiently ran households with the power of decision over menus, furnishings, the hiring and firing of servants, the education of the younger children. Some were docile shadows. There was an immense range of different male familial profiles too, from the ultrachauvinistic father (like Egeus), through the liberal, kindly, affectionate and caring father, to the weak henpecked nonentity or the man who lived his own life and took no interest in his family.

There was considerable debate about how fathers should behave to their children and how best children could be brought up. Mostly it focused on boys. Michel de Montaigne and Francis Bacon have much to say on the subject. Largely, fathers were stern, distant and formal, partly because high infant/teenage mortality discouraged too close and affectionate a relationship developing, partly because strict fathers were thought better teachers of respect and discipline. Mothers were thought too lax. Fathers reflected the loving sternness of God. Children were thought to be like wild creatures needing taming and training if they were to be self-disciplined in later life and cope with the customs and practices of a highly stratified, ritual conscious, traditionalist society. The traditional suspicions men had of female irrationality, unreliability and emotional instability transferred to their attitude toward a mother's relationships with her children. In elite families boys were removed from female control at seven, were breeched

---

24 Juliet Dusinberre, *Shakespeare and the Nature of Women*, 278.

and were put under a tutor until ready to be sent away to complete their education.

Affective family relations did exist, of course, as did companionate marriages. Not all was male chauvinism or female submission and not all marriages were perpetual conflict. Many wives were joint rulers of the married estate, being given back their dowry and allowed to keep their landed property. In her husband's absence a titled lady might well manage the estate. Widows were accepted as managers of estates and businesses and did so very effectively. It was an accepted thing and quite common. There were many more such women than one might think since men tended to marry later than women and die earlier. It was not unusual or unexpected for a woman to remarry. In business a widow commonly married a partner or one of the journeymen or a senior apprentice. A journeyman had completed his seven-year apprenticeship. Not yet master of his craft, he was sufficiently skilled and experienced for it to be a practical union keeping the business going and money coming in. Among elite families marriage and family relationships were often thought of not as loving supports which developed a child's personality within a sheltered environment with people who cared about him or her, but as units of child production that would enable the family title, status, money and property to be kept together and handed on. It is a chilling fact that one-third of marriages did not last longer than 15 years, many women dying in childbirth (as Titania's votaress does) and old husbands dying first. Remarriage was common and often swiftly followed the funeral. These dynastic concerns may seem inhumanly disagreeable to modern minds, but in an age when death was a constantly imminent possibility such severe considerations were crucial at every level of society where property (however minor) was held. At stake might be the tenure of thousands of acres, a title and a place at court, a commercial enterprise or simply the hedging tools of a farm labourer and the lease on his cottage. Apart from biblical authority for patriarchy there were practical reasons for it. Among the aristo-gentry, who remembered the violent precariousness of the Wars of the Roses, men bred large families hoping at least one male would survive. This required a wife who was fertile and would be home based in order to rear the offspring. Lawrence Stone puts it thus,

> Among the landed classes in pre-Reformation England [...] (the) objectives of family planning were the continuity of the male line, the preservation intact of the inherited property, and the acquisition of further property or useful political alliances.[25]

25 Stone, *The Family, Sex and Marriage in England, 1500–1800*, 37.

Such objectives persisted through the sixteenth and into the seventeenth century.

Feminist historians and literary critics have drawn attention to the marginalized role and restricted potential of women throughout the ages.[26] This useful counterbalance to the male-dominated view of history and sociology has, simultaneously, overemphasized the negative aspects of male domination, overstated the repression of women and underemphasized the forms of overt and covert petticoat power. The behind-the-scenes and in-the-bedroom influence of women at court is an acknowledged but underexplored factor. As Hugh Bicheno asserts, in discussing the constant manoeuvrings and bloodlettings of Renaissance Italian politics: 'No one should doubt that women were [...] as able, ambitious and even more devious than men, and that although sexual dimorphism ruled them out of actual combat in the era of muscle power they were probably braver as a sex and certainly no more gentle and peace-loving than men'.[27] The assumption has been that because male dominance was legally institutionalized it was the overwhelming norm. Archival evidence shows women more politically engaged than hitherto claimed. The most material sign of male dominance was the husband's appropriation of his wife's property and money to do with as he wished. Where the husband was a cash-strapped, in debt, thriftless wastrel (whether the eldest son or a younger son) this led to the dowry being swallowed up, provoking resentment and tension. Liberal, less chauvinistic men often left their wife's money and/or property in her hands.[28] Less well advertised was the jointure arranged by a groom's parents and lawyers. This was an agreed annuity payable by the husband's family if he predeceased his wife. It could represent a considerable sum if paid over a long period of time.[29] Also, all debts accumulated by a wife were legally payable by the husband and extravagant female spending, a traditional feature of satire, is frequently referenced in Jacobean drama and particularly targeted at women of the better sort and citizens' wives. The rise of extravagant ostentatious consumerism among the better sort (particularly the female members) was a persistent cause of comment, satire and disapproval.

It has to be recognized that materially and emotionally every arranged union had two potential victims. Men too could be trapped unhappily inside an arranged marriage. The patriarch keeping family property intact through

---

26 See Dusinberre.

27 Bicheno, *Vendetta*, 6.

28 Mothers often bequeathed money or property to a younger son to ensure he was not left destitute when his father died and the eldest inherited all.

29 For an example of the difficulties a jointure could pose, see Lovell, 302.

primogeniture may himself have been forced into marriage with a wealthy but old, ugly, ill-tempered or extravagant woman. Until younger offspring had been found appropriate marriages they were an expense to keep in a style suitable to their status. Sons were a problem, tending to drift into similarly cash-short homosocial groups in London, unsupervised, uncivilized and antisocial. They were increasingly pushed into high-status professions – the church, law, government service, the army – but often dropped out. Many young high-status women remained unmarried, without a vocation, without the chance to work other than at relatively trivial domestic and social accomplishments (sewing, embroidery, music). They could be a considerable drain on the family's resources, with novelty and fashionable buying acting as an emotional placebo for their dull lives. Those who married had to be found dowries and that could be a financially crippling requirement.

While parental wishes, much influenced by financial, hierarchical or political interests, were dominant in choosing a partner, increasingly the child's consent was sought. This approach was particularly evident in the wealthy upper-middle ranks. If a child did not like and was not attracted to a possible partner, that could put an end to negotiations. In 'Tis Pity Florio tells a fellow citizen who is seeking Florio's daughter as wife for his booby fop of a nephew,

> My care is how to match her to her liking:
> I would not have her marry wealth, but love;
> And if she like your nephew, let him have her. (1.3.10–12)

Ironically, this liberal approach is voiced while Annabella is in bed with her chosen lover – her brother.[30] Drama presents a mass of different conflicts over courtship and marriage because it offers excitement and more plot possibilities than demure agreement. Largely, however, in real life, it seemed that parents commonly chose a suitor or bride when they saw there was already attraction. In the case of a candidate picked by the parents but unknown to the prospective bride/groom or self-presented by a free bachelor, again the son/daughter's response was taken into account. But, if a candidate was strongly preferred by the parents on material/political/dynastic grounds and rejected by the son or daughter, then parental pressure and patriarchal weight (threats of disinheritance, home imprisonment and other punishments) would be applied. Marriage without parental consent was illegal, putting the archetypal romantic lovers, Romeo and Juliet, outside the law. Lear, in his anger, disposes of

---

30 The early 1600s were a time of punitive action by various authorities against fornication, adultery, incest, homosexuality and prostitution. See Dabhoiwala, ch. 1.

Cordelia to the lowest bidder without her say. Prospero is more caring. Egeus is not.

Though the odds might appear against it, there is evidence of loving marriages and happy families 'long before the eighteenth century'.[31] Studies show that

> [p]atriarchal authority applied in theory to this period, but could be modified in practice, by illustrating the range of experiences of married couples in which much depended upon factors such as the personality and relative status of the husband and wife.[32]

More importantly, counterbalancing the idea of women being universally dominated,

> [f]ar from being passive subordinates, some women developed strategies to modify or resist patriarchal authority, including marshalling support through friends, neighbours and kin to circumvent their putative subordination to their husbands.[33]

Deep-seated institutional misogyny was in place and persisted through the 1600s. Though the Catholic Church held no sway in England, its ideas had bitten deep into the male psyche, and suspicion of women was endemic in masculine thinking. The Church of Rome, systemically anti-female in its doctrines, saw women's secondary role as part of God's plan. The Church of England was more of the mind that men and women should respect one another, that husbands and wives should work in harmony, but was also clear that ultimately the man was in charge. Women, as Eve's descendants, were thought more inclined to sin. Men too were sinners but a neat argument mitigated that:

> though an husband in regard of evil qualities may carry the image of the devil, yet in regard to his place and office, he beareth the image of God.[34]

Male commentators tended to disregard the argument that while men were supposedly more rational and controlled than women they were also very obviously and rather easily susceptible to sexual impulses and generally weak when attracted by a woman.

---

31 Berry and Foyster, *The Family in Early Modern England*, 3.
32 Berry and Foyster, 3.
33 Berry and Foyster, 3.
34 Gouge, *Of Domesticall Duties*, 1622.

No one statement or view can be universally true of the complexities of male-female relationships, but in general a woman's place was subordinate to that of the males within her family and social sphere. There were, of course, numbers of strong-minded women who would not be dominated within their family or in any situation. Women did have status. Being married gave a woman greater status within her community. Being a mother boosted that status. A mother had authority over her children (in the father's absence). A housewife had authority over her servants (in the master's absence). The wife of a guild master, a titled lady or a shop owner's wife was superior to anyone of an inferior station (male or female), but within her own rank was secondary to any adult male, even to a son of age if he had inherited from a dead father and was head of the family, though respect for her as a woman, as mother, as dowager (widow of a titled/propertied man) would partially mitigate his authority. However, irrepressible women dominated all these situations. It is clear that Lear regards his daughters as very much his property. As father and king he disposes of them as he sees fit. But once free of him, with his power diminished to a level where only affection might work in his favour, the two older daughters display a barbaric cruelty transgressing custom and civilized behaviour. Egeus too thinks of Hermia as a commodity, his property, and he will decide whom she will marry. She outmanoeuvres him by an age-old ploy.

The subordination of women was part of an unfair hierarchical system and accepted within a social structure that designated a place for everyone and in which most people (men included) were subordinate to someone. It was unjust but most of the social and legal structure was unfairly organized in favour of the rich over the poor and men over women.

In 1558, the most strident statement of female inferiority was made by the Scottish radical Protestant John Knox, from his exile in Geneva:

> To promote a woman to bear rule, superiority, dominion or empire above any realm, nation or city is repugnant to nature, contumely to God, a thing most contrarious to his revealed will and approved ordinance, and finally it is the subversion of good order, of all equity and justice.[35]

He added that 'woman in her greatest perfection was made to serve and obey man'.[36] Knox's views resonate with fear that transgressing the social, familial or gender order would herald anarchy and collapse. Montaigne, usually liberal and fair, declares that

35 *The First Blast of the Trumpet against the Monstrous Regiment of Women*, 1558.
36 Cited in Borman, 63.

women should have no mastery over men save only the natural one of motherhood [...] It is dangerous to leave the superintendence of our succession to the judgement of our wives and to their choice between our sons, which over and over again is iniquitous and fantastic. For those unruly tastes and physical cravings which they experience during pregnancy are ever-present in their souls.[37]

This fails to take account of the general tendency of women (1) to oppose by a variety of means all attempts by males to repress them, and (2) to achieve some independence for themselves by negotiation, by clandestine action or by default. Some women failed to win any area of domination. Some ruled every area of family life or a limited area. Some said, 'Yes, dear, no, dear' and then secretly did as they wished. Some men could not be bothered about household matters or child-rearing, so the wife/mother ruled by default. Some women gained rule of estates or businesses through their husband's decease, while some administered their own property during their husband's lifetime, but largely Heaven's hierarchy persisted on earth and religion backed it. Thus, 'by marriage, the husband and wife became one person in law – and that person was the husband'.[38]

Just where women were placed in the day-to-day reality is problematic. The bulk of ordinary people were voiceless. Women provide even less evidence of their existence than men. Printed documents enabling the profiling of actual relationships are scarce and differ between court and country and between the aristo-gentry and other ranks. The lower down the social scale the less material is available. Archives hold a few personal diaries and letters by women and probably more await discovery. It was a period in which few people committed personal feelings to paper, but that was changing. Cost of materials was one factor but the culture was only slowly coming to accept that an individual's thoughts and feelings were of value. The various intersecting sixteenth-/seventeenth-century conflicts (religious, political, national, social) did push more people to express their views. The expanding print culture enabled many individuals to publish pamphlets that contributed to a war of words on religion, politics, gender and a multitude of topics. Urban trading families needed literate heirs and from the mid-seventeenth century dissenting groups began establishing academies that provided excellent broad education, more liberal, practical and extensive than the limited classical studies of high-end families. In Elizabeth's time education was much more narrowly focused. It was available to aristo-gentry boys and was rigidly classical

---

37 'On the affection of fathers for their children', 448.
38 Stone, *The Family...*, 136.

in its curriculum. There were many grammar schools and these often had endowments, bursaries and scholarships that enabled talented boys from poor families to gain formal education. Little formal schooling was given to girls, even from high-status families (apart from the royal family and a few cultured aristocratic households). Literacy and numeracy, taught at home, was about the scope of it for girls. There were some formal institutions for girls set up by Puritans, but these are the exception not the rule.

It was common (among Dissenters particularly) for Christians to make personal daily examination of their lives. In time this was written down in a spiritual journal and from then on more material is available. The decade prior to the Civil War saw many pamphlets (many by women) offering opinions on everything from politics to horoscopes (and religion particularly). By the Restoration (1660) there was a slightly higher proportion of female-to-male professional writers, reflecting some easing of male repressiveness, but as a demographic percentage figures for female writing are small. There are more questions than evidence to answer them. Did women write but not publish? Often. Did women just not write much? Some did. Could they access reading material that triggered their own writing? Increasingly. Was female literacy just too low to make a showing? Yes, except among small pockets of highly literate upper-rank women. Much female-authored fictional work circulated in manuscript among social networks like the court, London-based writers and literate and literary families and their friends. A number of literate all-female groups wrote, read out and published poetry or closet dramas. These were the coteries of waiting gentlewomen serving an aristocratic lady.[39] Prohibited from acting women seem not to have written for the public stage until Aphra Behn.[40] Any assessment of women from 1600 to 1620 can largely only be constructed from male perspectives. The general picture seems to be that private individuals (male and female) were increasingly writing about their lives, opinions and personal struggles. This accelerated in the Civil War and afterwards. But most of this manuscript material is locked away in scattered archives, public and private.

The later Stuart period provides many spiritual autobiographies, but an interesting early example of personal writing, giving insight into provincial life, comes from Lady Margaret Hoby's 1599–1605 diary. A Yorkshire heiress, educated in a Puritan school for gentlewomen which was run by the Countess of Huntingdon, she married three times, making alliances with high-profile court dynasties (the Devereux, Sydneys and Hobys). Her life was spent near

39 See Schleiner.
40 Her first play was *The Forced Marriage* (1670). Some privately performed masques and dramas for private reading were female-authored before this.

Scarborough, with a few visits to London. Her diary, the earliest known to have been written by an English woman, records local charity work and the running of the household and estate, details domestic activities – managing servants and paying them – describes mundane activities like gardening, arranging the washing and ironing and preparing medicines, and discusses her contacts with neighbours and estate tenants. It recounts the outer structures of her spiritual life – organizing household prayers and her personal devotions and reading – but does not delve into her inner feelings.

At every stage of life a woman was expected to be deferential, submissive and constantly aware of her different and separate expectations. Among the upper and middling sort her infant education (if any) would be at home and limited to letters and figures, while her brothers attended school (or were home tutored), and once literate and numerate, moved on to Greek, Latin, mathematics, history and geography, followed by university. In a lower rank a school leaver might be apprenticed or simply join his father in the family business. A girl stayed at home and learned housecraft and needlework skills. Farmers' daughters joined the women in planting, tending animals, spinning, cooking and nursing younger siblings, but brothers ploughed, reaped, herded animals, made and used tools, went to market and met the world. Once of marriageable age, whatever her rank, she might be contracted to a man of her father's choosing if it was profitable to the family or she might remain at home unmarried as general help, that is, an unpaid servant. If lucky she might be sent away into service. While exposing her to innumerable risks, this event opened better prospects. She might climb the ladder of service from housemaid to housekeeper. A prime fantasy was that she would attract her master's eldest son and they would marry. In practice parents reacted in horror at their heir wishing to unite himself to a maid. Often the allure was sexual only and claims of love merely the bait set out by a predatory young man. Once satisfied and bored the male would dump her.[41] Girls from the governing ranks and bourgeoisie had fewer opportunities for going into society, and largely waited to be courted. Numbers from all ranks simply never got married. The tediousness of such limited horizons is well detailed in the eighteenth and nineteenth centuries, but the bored girls of the Renaissance England are relatively silent. Like their brothers, they had virtues to cultivate – piety, chastity, discretion, modesty, gentleness, decorum, prudence, diligence, industry. If a girl was from a comfortably off family, she was expected to join her mother in charity visits to the poor and other almsgiving. Lower down the social ladder things were

---

41 The classic version of this is found in the early part of Daniel Defoe's novel *Moll Flanders* (1722), which is partially based on the life of Mary Frith, a seventeenth-century pickpocket.

better as regards active occupation, for you were expected to work and earn money to contribute to the family income. Middle- and upper-rank girls had to do much sewing and embroidery, cutting out and assembling clothes for younger siblings or for charity children. Often their only projection of identity was in the samplers they embroidered with their name on it. These acted as samples of patterns that might be later stitched onto cushion covers or quilts. They also acted as a measure of a girl's needlework skill to be shown off to a would-be courter who might never come calling. Thousands on thousands must have let their father marry them off to the first man who offered, simply to escape to another life and a home of their own to run.

There were differences between how the court treated women and how they were expected to behave elsewhere. Outwardly there was decorum and the punctilious etiquette of public politeness. Privately court women were perceived (often correctly) to be promiscuous, flattering and fawning gold-diggers (therefore manipulative and devious hypocrites), overly interested in clothes and show, given to gossip and rumour-mongering, jealous of their position and generally flirtatious and frivolous. There were differences in how men regarded and treated women and what was expected of them according to their rank. Common girls were regarded as skivvies and sexual prey, and middling ones as sexual prey and sources of fortune. A girl from a titled family could not easily be predated sexually if she had kinsmen to take revenge, but she could be courted for her money, married and then left to nurture the offspring. Girls in the two upper tiers did get some education. A degree of learning was an announcement of status. Ignorance of reading and writing was a marker of the commoners. But the extent of intellectual skill depended as always on parental attitudes (the father particularly) and there was a swing toward humanist ideals that saw female education as essential for the next generation of wives and mothers.

6.2 Renaissance Improvements

Richard Mulcaster, first headmaster of Merchant Taylors' School, then High Master of St Paul's School, strongly favoured female education. His book, *Positions* (1581), declares that as 'our' closest 'companions', women should be 'well furnished in mind' and 'well strengthened in body'. Fathers have a 'duty' to educate their daughters. God 'require[s] an account for natural talents of both the parties, us for directing them; them for performance of our direction'. Mulcaster believed women's education should be selectively targeted toward strengthening virtue. He emphasized four essential skills – 'reading well, writing faire, singing sweet, playing fine', plus languages and drawing. Maths, science and divinity were less useful, but not excluded. Women, he felt, were weak by nature, but education could strengthen intellect and soul. Men should be educated 'without restraint for either matter or manner'. Countering the stereotypical view that women's education was neglected he asks,

> Do we not see in our country some of that sex so excellently well trained and so rarely qualified in regard both to the tongues themselves and to the subject matter contained in them, that they may be placed along with, or even above, the most vaunted paragons of Greece or Rome?[42]

But it is only 'some of that sex'. How broadly spread female education in the upper and middling ranks was, is unquantifiable. We know that masses of boys went to grammar school, then university, and that scholarships, bursaries and endowments enabled poor scholars to get an education otherwise beyond their reach. Such institutional learning was generally unavailable to girls, and such home tutoring as was provided has left few examples of its existence.

Whatever sort of school Hermia attended and whatever reading she undertook, she and Helena make a wide range of classical references and speak with some degree of rhetorical skill. It must be remembered, however, that again it is a male dramatist who composed their lines.

Henry VIII's daughters, Mary and Elizabeth, were, unsurprisingly, very well taught. Elizabeth, with Latin, Greek, Hebrew, Italian and French, was one of the most learned rulers in Europe. Her speeches use rhetorical devices displaying her classical learning, but she insisted that a prince's education should be useful to ruling the nation. The princesses were tutored by leading scholars, including Juan Vives, the Spanish humanist. Vives, conservative, wary of providing a classical education because some political-historical material was unsuitable and the poetry of Ovid and Catullus immoral, based their curriculum on his own *Instruction of a Christian Woman*, broadened to include Erasmus's *Paraphrases* and Sir Thomas More's *Utopia*. He believed 'most of the vices of women [...] are the products of ignorance, whence they never read nor heard those excellent sayings and monitions of the Holy Fathers about chastity, about obedience, about silence, women's adornments and treasures'. Women had to be obedient to their duties and needed their morals shaped and their virtues developed – as did men. Only 'a little learning is required of women' while 'men must do many things in the world and must be broadly educated'.[43] Women should confine their reading to works on chastity. This outlook betrays the orthodox anxiety about female sexuality. Men felt that independent female sexuality would lead to increased illegitimacy thus

---

42 Mulcaster citations in the *Norton Anthology* (Stephen Greenblatt, ed.).
43 Vives, cited in *Norton Anthology*.

obscuring the fatherhood of any child and confusing matters of inheritance, the central concern of patriarchally controlled marriage. Erasmus, friend of More and a key figure in the development of Renaissance ideas, suggests (*The Institution of Marriage*, 1526) education is more effective than needlework in chasing away idleness, preserving virginity and enhancing matrimonial relationships.

It should not be assumed that humanist ideas greatly influenced the court or spread very far beyond it. Young women attending court would already be past the education stage. Their personalities and tastes already formed, they usually had more worldly matters on their minds. Away from court there was a huge variety of attitudes among the country aristocracy and gentry as regards rearing and educating daughters. Learned education (Greek and Latin) was briefly fashionable for aristocratic girls from 1520–60. Thereafter it waned. Other positive influences did emerge, though again it is impossible to chart their influence. One was Castiglione's *Il Cortegiano*. This important handbook suggested a little knowledge of 'letters' (classics, modern languages, history, literature) was acceptable for women, but that the social graces – playing music, singing, dancing, drawing/painting, doing needlework – were more civilized and made a woman more marriageable. Thomas Hoby claimed the book was 'to Ladies and Gentlewomen, a mirrour to decke and trimme themselves with vertuous conditions, comeley behaviours and honest entertainment toward all men'.[44] Castiglione also acknowledged, in some detail, that cultured education should be more than a mere social ornament for women. He strongly endorses their potential for virtue and their potential for positive influence in a court. This new courtly ideal promoted the self-effacing but agreeable woman, witty, cultured, but chaste. Renaissance courts could be centres of high culture but were also deathtraps of intrigue, of plotting, of power struggles, assassinations, political coups, rape and seduction. Court history exemplified that double-sidedness – culture and killing, music and murder, poetry and poisoning. Executions, torture, the rise and fall of favourites, hothouse animosities and sexual intrigue made English courts (from Henry VIII to James I) like the set of a bloody play.

As evidence of some shift in attitudes to women, Thomas Campion (1567–1620) explores how women's restricted social opportunities encourage a vigorous inner life, while men are easily distracted by the world's superficialities:

women are confined to silence,
Loosing wisht occasion.
Yet our tongues then theirs, men,

---

44 Thomas Hoby, *The Courtyer of Baldessar Castilio*, from 'The epystle of the translatuor'.

Are apter to be moving,
Women are more dumbe then they,
But in their thoughts more roving.[45]

Female-authored literature was beginning to emerge. Lady Mary Wroth (1586?–1651?) from the high-status, literary Sidney family, wrote a sonnet sequence and the first known prose romance by an English woman. Both texts contribute to the on-going gender discourse.

Elizabeth Cary (1585–1639), the first woman to write a history, also wrote the first female-authored tragedy. *The Tragedy of Mariam* (written 1602–4, published 1613), intended as a 'closet drama' to be read in domestic surroundings, contributes to the gender debate in contrasting honest, principled Queen Mariam with devious, promiscuous Princess Salome and presenting the absolutist and violent patriarch King Herod. Another contributor to the man-woman question was Rachel Speght (1597?–?). A Calvinist minister's daughter, she entered the literary world with panache, stepping straight into gender-discourse controversy. Aged 19, with her name boldly attached, she published *A Mouzell for Melastomus* (A Muzzle for Blackmouth, 1617), an articulate, spirited, clearly and logically argued attack on the bigoted misogyny of Joseph Swetnam's *Araignment of Lewde, Idle, Froward, and Unconstant Women* (1615). Biblical and classical references reveal her religious background and education. Living at the centre of London commerce and clerical debate, she understood the current polemical climate and had seen many examples of husband-wife cooperation among merchant families. She claims respect is due to women as children of God and sees the possibilities for companionate relationships between men and women. A lively style, often akin to the acerbic, insulting, combative language of male pamphlet polemics, makes her work readable, while her ideas make it convincingly sympathetic and reasonable. Marriage is a true union: 'as yoake-fellowes [married couples] are to sustayne part of each others cares, griefs, and calamities'. 'Marriage is a merri-age, and this worlds Paradise, where there is mutuall love [...] husbands should not account their wives as vassals, but as those that are heires together of the grace of life'. As 'Head' of his wife, the husband must protect her and lead her to Christ. To 'exclaime against Woman' is to show ingratitude to God.[46] Swetnam focuses female vanity and lechery, and Speght voices a new mood of companionship, shared piety and compromise between gender egotisms.

---

45 See Campion, in Greenblatt, ed., *Norton Anthology*.
46 Greenblatt, ed., *Norton Anthology*, 1036–9. For the texts of Speght, Swetnam and others, see Butler.

The entrenched history and literature of Catholic misogyny, with its horror of the filthiness of women (menstruation and childbirth were repulsive mysteries to men, a view encouraged by women's group secretiveness and exclusiveness, particularly during confinement) and their sinfulness (insatiable lustfulness and vanity mainly) passed into male thinking and persisted after the Reformation. In religious thought the body (a temporary house for the soul) was considered corrupt and its sinful needs and dirty functions were to be minimized so the spirit could be kept pure and nourished. Subject to fleshly temptations and the vagaries of emotion, human beings were a comic treasure. One of Castiglione's disputants says, 'In each one of us there is some seed of folly which, once it is stirred, can grow indefinitely'. Another remarks, 'Our bodily senses are so untrustworthy that they often confuse our judgement as well.[47] Folly, the senses, unreliable judgement – in these are the sources of tragedy and, notably, of comedy too.

The virtue/sin, duty/desire conflict produced a body of 'sex war' literature focusing the persistent hostility between men and women – men as bullying, lascivious brutes (or gullible fools), women as devious, unreliable and bullying (shrewish) in their own way (or innocent victims). Shakespeare addresses the virago-virgin polarity in *The Comedy of Errors* (Adriana and Luciana), *The Taming of the Shrew* (Katherine and Bianca) and *Much Ado* (Beatrice and Hero). The trickiness of women is often a source of comedy while their evil is fitting for tragedy. Contrast the polarities of the kite/tiger/wolf/monster sisters in *Lear* and the gentle sensitivity of Cordelia. *Lear* has little to say of women directly, but many negative implications resonate round the words and actions of Goneril and Regan. Both sisters are white devils – a common metaphor for hypocrites who disguised their evil. The sisters are a study in the evil that females can perform. Shakespeare had often presented the failings of women, but deep evil had only been explored through Queen Tamora's cruelty (*Titus Andronicus*, c. 1588–93), and in *Henry VI* with Queen Margaret, a 'she-wolf' with a 'tiger's heart wrapp'd in a woman's hide'. His other great study of female evil is Lady Macbeth. The middle period plays also exhibit demure and humble women (Ophelia, Desdemona, Cordelia, Lady Macduff) and highly articulate, irrepressibly independent ones (Viola, Rosalind, Beatrice). The last plays, however, project positive images of articulate but self-effacing women through Hermione, Paulina, Perdita (*The Winter's Tale*), Imogen (*Cymbeline*), Thaisa, Marina (*Pericles*) and Miranda. The sinfulness of women, indeed sinfulness altogether, is only hinted at in *Dream*. There is a little of the virago-virgin polarity in Hermia and Helena, but it is ambiguously mixed. Both girls are

---

47 Castiglione, *The Book of the Courtier*, 47, 108.

aggressive and gentle but either polarity is a temporary comic device creating conflict in the woodland encounters. It is there largely for its amusement, but does reflect peripherally the darker issues that are implied in the play, suggesting that young females can be both vixenish and soppy.

Men had ambivalent, contradictory views of women. As the source of human sin they needed controlling in order to repress their opportunities for tempting men. A multiplicity of pejorative terms – virago, termagent, shrew, Whore of Babylon, hussy, wagtail, punk and more – provides lexical markers of male suspicion. In opposition to the Eve/Delilah/Jezebel/whore image, twelfth-century medieval courtly love projected an idealized woman of beauty, intelligence, elegance, chastity, while Mariolatry raised the Virgin Mary to an archetype of gentle, sympathetic womanhood and loving, nurturing motherhood that partially redeemed women. Mary became a key human intercessor in approaching Jesus or God, and an icon of the respect men should have for women. In loving a woman you re-expressed your love and respect for your mother, showing the love you first learned from her. Martin Luther asserted Mary was 'the highest woman' and 'we can never honour her enough' and 'the veneration of Mary is inscribed in the very depths of the human heart'.[48] While lauding Mary's model status, Luther also made very derogatory remarks about ordinary women in general.[49] Despite some easing of extreme patriarchy and improvements in the status of women, negative views persisted and progress was slow.

Medieval hagiographies (lives of saints) celebrated the virtues of women martyrs. This was problematic for Protestantism had banned statues, days, prayers, relics and oaths associated with saints. This hampered the assimilation into church dogma of any ideology applauding women, though veneration of Mary persisted in people's private faith.[50] A small amount of literature iconized particularly virtuous women and applauded romantic, affectionate relationships as long as they remained rational. There is a scattering of references to courageous, faithful women in the Bible. There are Geoffrey Chaucer's 'Legend of Good Women' and 'The Book of the Duchesse' and more recently Sir Thomas Elyot's *The Defence of Good Women* (1540) and Edmund Spenser's *The Faerie Queene* (1590 and 1596). Notable continental contributions include Giovanni Boccaccio's *De Mulieribus Claris* (Of famous

---

48 Sermon 1 September 1522.
49 'The word and works of God is quite clear, that women were made either to be wives or prostitutes' (*Works*, vol. 12, p. 94). 'God created Adam master and lord of living creatures, but Eve spoilt all, when she persuaded him to set himself above God's will. 'Tis you women, with your tricks and artifices, that lead men into error' (*Table Talk*).
50 See Rubin, *Mother of God*, part 6.

women, 1374) and Castiglione's *Il Cortegiano* (Third Book), where, despite sharp misogynistic interruptions, Guiliano de Medici constructs the idealized court lady, ably acknowledges female capacity for virtue and illustrates his case with classical and contemporary examples. But generally all churches were suspicious of sex and passion, encouraged men to control their own and female appetites and warned against women as the ready provokers of lust. Men were supposedly more rational, while women were more emotional and vulnerable to fleshly temptations. Polemic writing tended to highlight female failings. Literature uses the constant interplay of tension between the positive aspects (affection and love) of the appetites and the dangers of following them excessively. Men, supposedly superior and rational, were susceptible to female charms, and love was seen as a madness, an illness caught from women. Theseus describes love's insanity:

> Lovers and madmen have such seething brains,
> Such shaping fantasies, that apprehend
> More than cool reason ever comprehends. (5.1.4–5)

The Church of England's second *Book of Homilies* (1571), which vicars used for sermons, includes 'On the State of Matrimony', defining the church's views on women and how fathers and husbands, being in authority over them and being more rational beings, should approach them:

> The woman is a weak creature not endued with like strength and con-
> stancy of mind; therefore, they be the sooner disquieted, and they be the
> more prone to all weak affections and dispositions of mind, more than men
> be; and lighter they be, and more vain in their fantasies and opinions. (503)

They were 'the weaker vessell, of a frail heart, inconstant, and with a word soon stirred to wrath'. A commentary in Matthew's Bible (1537) says that men, being intellectually stronger and in authority, had a duty to ensure their women conformed to the demand for chastity and modest behaviour. If she was 'not obedient and helpful to him, [he may] beat the fear of God into her head, and that thereby she may be compelled to learn her duty and do it'. Corporal punishment was common in the Renaissance. Whores and criminals were publicly whipped, children caned at home and school, and servants beaten.[51] Legally a wife too could be beaten.

---

51 Resentful, beaten servants could not legally run away and leave the parish. That was to become a masterless man/woman and carried a prison sentence. This implication that a servant was the property of the master was yet another of the ancient practices that restricted the liberties of English people.

The Bible exhorts wives to be in subjection to their husband, counterbalancing this by requiring that the husband should honour the wife and that they should have 'compassion one of another' (I Peter 3:8). Bishop Aylmer gave a sermon before Queen Elizabeth, outlining the best and worst aspects of women, in polarities evident in Shakespeare and most other dramatists:

> Women are of two sorts: some of them are wiser, better learned, discreeter, and more constant than a number of men; but another and worse sort of them are fond [simple], foolish, wanton, flibbergibs [silly chatterer], tattlers, triflers, wavering, witless, without council, feeble, careless, rash, proud, dainty [fussy], tale-bearers, eavesdroppers, rumour-raisers, evil-tongued, worse-minded, and in every way doltified [made foolish] with the dregs of the devil's dunghill.[52]

Legally women had few rights. Neither did most ordinary men, but they had the key ones. There were some shifts in behaviour, but how far they penetrated society as a whole is unclear. There had been a sixteenth-century increase in stern patriarchy as regards marital and parental relations. In the seventeenth century there were countermovements against both.

Imperceptibly slowly the stern, patriarchal, authoritarian father became more affectionate and considerate. Stone's comment suggests the gradual emergence of the more companionate marriage and more affective family relations:

> For a considerable period, two conflicting trends were at work at the same time, and the growing authority of the husband can only be seen in a relatively pure form during the first half of the sixteenth century.[53]

Playwrights hint at the hope for harmonious, loving marriages at the end of comedies, but within the piece tend to use the dramatic possibilities of conflict between the sexes. Offering more opportunities for humour, tension and the exploration of violent emotions, it is better theatre. Stone captures the essence of this in quoting a character in a play by George Wilkins:

> Women are the purgatory of men's purses, the paradise of their bodies, and the hell of their minds: marry none of them.[54]

52 Stone, *The Family...*, 137.
53 Stone, 137.
54 Stone, 136.

One might briefly pity Demetrius for the irritation of Helena stalking him. In John Marston's *The Dutch Courtesan* (1604), Malheureux says, 'The most odious spectacle the earth can present is an immodest, vulgar woman' (1.1.154–5) and Helena's 'accompanying' Demetrius to the woods is an immodest act. Marston, a member of Shakespeare's circle, worked in the same areas of problematic moral ambivalence central to *Measure for Measure* and touched on in *Dream* and *King Lear*. Freevill (his name conflating evil/freedom/free will), a libertine trying to terminate his relationship with the courtesan Franceschina so he can marry Beatrice, a respectable and wealthy heiress, passes on the whore to his friend Malheureux (the unhappy or misfortunate one), who tries to repress his powerful sexual feelings. Freevill and Malheureux represent two significant forces in contemporary society – traditional male unfettered sexuality and the newer moral code of Puritanism attempting to control the sex impulse. Franceschina admits, 'Woman corrupted is the worst of devils' (2.2.201). Her remark has relevance wider than London's sex trade and applies to the conduct of some of the court ladies. Today we might applaud the romantic gesture of Hermia and Helena running away for love and sticking by their men, but at the time *Dream* was written the older members of the audience, in line with orthodox thought, would condemn both as rather forward, courting temptation and disaster and certainly sinners and transgressors.

Shakespeare presents the counterargument when the hitherto chaste Angelo, feeling the prickings of lust, asks, 'The tempter, or the tempted, who sins most, ha?' (*Measure*, 2.2.164). This acknowledges partial male responsibility for lust. Lysander it was who suggested the elopement and Demetrius encouraged Helena in loving him, so they too bear some responsibility. King Lear makes sharp comments on lust and female lust in particular. His strictures sound as condemnatory as those of any Puritan preacher:

> Down from the waist they are Centaurs,
> Though women all above:
> But to the girdle do the Gods inherit,
> Beneath is all the fiends: there's hell, there's darkness,
> There is the sulphurous pit – burning, scalding,
> Stench, consumption; fie, fie fie! pah, pah! (4.6.126–131)

In different ways Marston, Jonson, Shakespeare and others explored the difficulties of trying to keep to virtue's path. While others mocked the pretensions and greed of contemporary London through their theatrical satires, Shakespeare dives deep into human depravity and cruelty, into self-delusion and folly, in settings that are universal, removed from readily identifiable topical references, but still with targets that prompt resemblances to his time and audience. Happiness and a celebration of love are at the root of *Dream*, but the moral dangers, though not allowed to develop into misery and disaster, are acknowledged too. Hermia's anger against her long-time friend is a reminder that Miss Prim-and-Proper can turn into a vixen if moved to jealousy, and that the demure exterior may harbour a turbulent temper.

While Elizabethan-Jacobean dramatists display considerable sympathy for women in a male-dominated world and present their wit, virtue and sprightliness, they are also alert to women's fierce brutality and display how disturbingly similar it is to men's.

Chapter 7

MAN IN HIS PLACE

First walk in thy vocation,
And do not seek thy lot to change.[1]

By God's will you were born into a particular rank (your lot in life). You were expected to know your place, keep it and work at whatever calling came within the scope of your family's position. Each family might rise, through hard work and God's grace. Small status rises were not too disturbing for one's neighbours. However, great success provoked envy, jealousy and suspicion of overreaching ambition. Doubts about the means by which you rose might arouse accusations of magic and devilish assistance. People would be all too ready to credit the Bible's view: 'he that maketh haste to be rich shall not be innocent' (Proverbs 28:20). The industrious, careful man, slowly improving his position, was safe from negative gossip, for 'wealth gotten by vanity shall be diminished: but he that gathereth by labour shall increase' (Proverbs 13:11). The rapid increase in bourgeois wealth created an interplay between envy, condemnation of luxury, suspicion of avarice and dishonesty, and fears of an upstart, ambitiously aspirational group rivalling the traditional ruling class.

The Elizabethans and Jacobeans were suspicious about social movement. If God made the world, putting each man in his place, was it not counter to God's will to change your social status? A poor man becoming poorer was thought punished for some unnamed sin, but a man going up in the world was usually not thought of as being rewarded for virtue, but rather guilty of sinful means. Some argued that God gave men abilities or talents, expected them to be used and rewarded hard work. If that meant you could climb out of your birth rank and better yourself then you could be said to be doing

---

1 Robert Crowley, *Voice of the Last Trumpet* (1550). The idea echoes St Paul in 1 Corinthians 7:20: 'Let every mad abide in the same calling wherein he was called'.

God's will and worshipping him by developing the talents he gave you. This was a popular view among Non-Conformists for whom the work ethic was central. They believed in industry, thrift and found the idea of making money acceptable. A rise in fortunes, place and public status should not, however, be accompanied by a complacent attitude to making money at any cost. The means had to be ethical and the amounts within reason. Excessive gains should be redistributed through charities, and the money-maker and his family should avoid arrogance, ostentation and snobbery – in theory.[2] A hard-working shop assistant might marry the shopkeeper's daughter or his widow, might rise to wealth, become a guild master or a town councillor, but was expected to give thanks by making charitable donations and remaining humble. Education could help a poor man's son to a government clerkship. Talented, active men could rise, particularly if they earned the patronage someone of note and power. They could fall too if they followed a favourite who fell from favour. The court was a roller coaster of fortune where many people rose by intrigues, plots, lies, favouritism and ruthless opportunism, and could fall by the same means.

Sometimes men rose by honest service. Even the relatively simple-living, humble mechanicals imagine Bottom's acting might earn him a special reward from the duke in the form of a daily pension payment of sixpence a day. Such regal largesse was not unknown. Generosity and magnanimity were leadership qualities. But they needed to be awarded to the honest and worthy. All too often it was the flattering sycophant who gained rich pickings. Bribery too was a means of rising. Stephen Bateman's engraving for covetousness shows a man on a throne with a man on either side. He has four hands and four arms: 'two to deliuer & two to receaue'. The giving hands hold papers – the official notice of appointment to a place ('preferment for small gaine'). The receiving hands are outstretched for the money the placemen are donating to his private fortune. The transaction is a 'deceit' and is done 'priuily' (privily = secretly).

The many new men rising to prominence caused conservative thinking unease about social mobility. Extreme reversals or improvements in rank portrayed on stage were seen as omens warning of impending disaster and social implosion that might engulf everyone. Subversion of any sort was disturbing and threatening to the orderliness of society. In *Eastward Ho!* the goldsmith's daughter, Gertrude, obsessed with becoming a knight's wife, contemplates the pleasure of having gained superiority over her father:

---

2 For attitudes to commercial enterprise, Max Weber (*The Protestant Ethic and the Spirit of Capitalism*, 1904–5) and R. H. Tawney (*Religion and the Rise of Capitalism*, 1926) are still relevant. So too is L. C. Knights, *Drama and Society in the Age of Jonson* (1937), chap. 1–4.

he must call me daughter no more now; but 'Madam', and, 'please you Madam', and, 'please your worship, Madam', indeed. (3.2.63–5)

Gertrude is suitably punished, marries Sir Petronel Flash for title and prop-erty, but finds he is like his name, all show, no substance, no castle, no money. He (claiming he loves her) marries her for her inheritance, while she (claim-ing she loves him) marries him for his status and wealth. Each is cheated by the other and their pride is humbled. Additional to pride and ambition, Gertrude shows extreme disrespect to her father, thus striking at the very root of social order by breaking a commandment. *Lear* demonstrates even worse subversion of family values and many city comedies show disturbing threats to the fundamental basis of social life – the family. In *Dream* the father-daughter bond is exposed as a conflict of wills. Tension between the ranks is not an issue, but the assumed superiority of the better sort is shown to be precari-ous, petty and in bad taste. All the laughter evoked by the confusions in the wood has a cruel undertone as it shows the lovers as little more than spoiled, vindictive brats. Their courtly manners are stripped away as Fate/Fortune and mischance play with them and put them through an emotional and physical ordeal.

Movement was not always upward. A third to a half of the sixteenth-century population existed at subsistence level and suffered acute unemployment. The majority of the lower or baser sort suffered their hardship fairly stoically, but the urban underclass was always a worrying barrel of gunpowder. It took little to ignite it and regular outbreaks of riot occurred – in London particularly. At the other end of the scale increasing numbers of merchants, financiers, manufacturers and industrialists were making huge fortunes, becoming wealthier than established aristo-gentry families. They copied elite cultural habits, seeking titles, estates and political power. This latter aspiration frightened the ruling ranks. The bourgeois elite was well educated, 2.5 per cent of males aged 14–20 receiving university training. With male literacy improving (80 per cent in London), clearly life-enhancement possibilities were expanding. The middling sort was unstoppably on the move. Though the very poorest remained poor and their numbers increased due to enclosures, unemployment and inflation, those able to struggle upwards to literacy, and thereby to effective commercial activity, were also increasing. This widened the divide between those succeeding and the failing underclass with no means of reversing their downward spiral. The growth of capitalism created many different levels of sophistication and increased the need for minutely observed differentiations to distinguish between people. When a merchant's wife could afford to dress as well and in the same fashions as a lady at court, it was the normal response of human nature to seek finer status identifiers to enable those with established rank to mark themselves apart from those newly arrived.

In the 1600s voices were beginning to speak for the lower orders. The need to do so indicates growing tensions between the ranks. At the end of his progress south in 1603 James I arrived at Theobalds, Robert Cecil's magnificent palace north of London. He was handed the 'Poor Man's Petition'. Like other such appeals it demanded the new king promise religious uniformity and the purifying of public life, particularly attacking the legal profession: 'A pox take the proud covetous Attorney and merciless lawyer! [...] fye upon all close biting knaverie!'[3] The very existence of the petition indicates how social tensions had grown toward the end of Elizabeth's reign. Social divisions showed in other more public ways. Luxury clattered by on the streets in fine coaches. Successful men, their wives and families displayed their new-found luxury. Conspicuous consumption and ostentatious showing off through carriages, horses, houses, furniture, clothes and expensive banquets were all forms of vanity. The many mocking stage representations of the purse-proud nouveau riche and the wasteful excess of the aristocracy had little effect. Sumptuary Laws controlling expenditure and regulating the types of clothing worn and the amounts/types of food consumed by the different ranks were ignored.

Established in the Middle Ages, updated by Henry VIII and extended by Elizabeth, these laws officially claimed to restrain vain, wasteful habits and protect English trade, but were really the elite's attempt at maintaining the visual differences of rank. As everywhere else, there was hierarchy – in the fur trimming permitted for your level in society, the fabric you could wear, the headgear, the jewellery. To dress 'above your station' looked like pride. The laws were designed to discourage someone from one rank imitating the manners and appearance of another, but were frankly a form of social control and a means of identifying a person's standing and reinforcing the distinctions between the nobility and the up-and-coming entrepreneurial groups. Attempts to regulate extravagant expenditure on clothes by aspiring, fashion- and status-conscious bourgeois women were put in moral terms stressing restraint and humility. Elizabeth's 1574 law declared the craze for fine show led to

> the wasting and undoing of a great number of young gentlemen, other-
> wise serviceable, and others seeking by show of apparel to be esteemed
> as gentlemen, who, allured by the vain show of those things, do not
> only consume themselves, their goods, and lands which their parents

3 Quoted in De Lisle, 195.

left unto them, but also run into such debts and shifts as they cannot live out of danger of laws without attempting unlawful acts. [4]

The words 'show', 'vain', 'consume' and 'debts' suggest disapproval based on medieval ideas of moderation, evoking the deadly sins and stereotypes linking suitability of behaviour to rank. Rank, income and gender were the criteria that decided what you could wear. Thus dress signifiers supposedly identified social rank and preserved 'degree'. Though there were harsh punishments for sumptuary infringements they were largely ignored and the laws were repealed in 1603–4 as simply unenforceable. To some this was opening the floodgates that would swamp distinction between the orders and herald social collapse. In 1583 Philip Stubbes had remarked on

> such a confused mingle mangle of apparel [...] that is verie hard to know who is noble, who is worshipful, who is a gentleman, who is not; for you shall have those [...] go daylie in silkes, velvets, satens, dam-asks, taffeties and suchlike, notwithstanding that they be both base by byrthe, meane by estate & servile by calling. This is a great confusion & a general disorder, God be mercifull unto us.[5]

High-end fashion became more lavish and impractical; it was saying 'I don't need to work, so my clothes are for show only'. The real audience for *Dream* and the fictional one for *Pyramus and Thisbe* would without doubt be wear-ing silks, velvets and satins.[6] Bottom and Co. would be wearing plain work clothes (until they dress up for their play). Puck, spying on their midnight rehearsal, calls them 'hempen homespuns' (3.1.73). It is a precise indica-tion of their relative poverty. Home-woven clothing made of hemp was the sign of low status and creates a visual contrast with the rich cloths worn by the courtly characters. Snobbery drove people to seek minute markers to show their superiority and courtiers' clothes became more and more lavish. Shakespeare's drama from 1600 onward is much concerned with how cloth-ing disguises what people really are, how the discrepancy between appear-ance and reality relates to clothes and office and inner probity and how fine robes suggest rank and rank implies virtue, while exposing how clothes hide sin, gold covers it and office (or authority) does not mean the man occupying

---

4 The wording of the 1574 Statute.
5 *Abuses*, 33.
6 Though nominally inhabitants of ancient Athens, the characters would have worn Elizabethan costume. Little concern was shown in the Elizabethan theatre for replicating period clothing.

it is there by merit. Brachiano in *The White Devil* suggests that the Duke of Florence is all show:

> all his reverend wit
> Lies in his wardrobe; he's a discreet fellow
> When he's made up in his robes of state. (2.1.189–91)

This reminds us of Lear's remark on 'the great image of Authority': 'A dog's obey'd in office' (4.6.). People perceive and treat you according to your robes and accoutrements of office, regardless of the fool or knave you might actually be. 'Robes and furr'd gowns hide all' (*Lear*, 4.6.). Fine silks paraded in public simply emphasized the fact that some were rising fabulously while most were in the mire. In *Dream* there would be clothing differences evident in how Theseus and the courtly characters are dressed and the costume of Bottom and his companions. These differences are reversed when it comes to conduct. The mechanicals are much nicer people, more honest and straightforward. The lovers, as already hinted, betray that a high, privileged background does not always translate into characters being decent, reliable or admirable.

Each man was guardian of his own soul, his own virtues and responsible for his own sins. But he had other associations to which he owed loyalty and responsibility – his family, his village, his trade or craft, his county, nation, his church, humanity, the whole of creation.

Family and community were the strongest bonds, though faith might take precedence and separate a man from these commitments. Each man occupied a place in the detailed stratification of society, from king to pauper. The theory of the natural order was based on harmony. Each rank, high or low, had its part to play if concord and perfect working were to be achieved.

> This is the true ordering of the state of a well-fashioned commonwealth, that every part do obey one head, or governor, one law, as all parts of the body obey the head, agree among themselves, and one not to eat up the other through greediness, but that we see order, moderation, and reason, bridle the affections.[7]

This theory of order and orderliness was conceived by those who governed and wished to preserve degree. Rulers were the brains and heart, and the nobles the important organs. The others – the limbs – had little else to do but obey. This often-voiced analogy is false. Society is not a body. If you cut off

---

7 From 'King Edward's Remains. A Discourse about the Reformation of Many Abuses', *History of the Reformation*, Bishop Burnet.

the head the body dies, but if you cut off the king's head or remove the aristocracy, society will continue with a new political settlement. The Civil War would show that. If the lavishly bedecked audience thought the play would be a light-hearted romance with sophisticated witticisms and a little clowning to make them laugh outright, they were wrong. It carried in its texture warnings to the frivolous and the self-satisfied. It provokes questions about loyalty in friendship, the nature of love, education and parenting. Shakespeare never wrote a light-weight play. His romances and comedies have dark undertones. In 1631 his colleague Ben Jonson wrote,

> All Repraesentations, [...] eyther have bene, or ought to be the mirrors
> of man's life, whose ends, [...] ought always to carry a mixture of profit,
> with them, no less then delight. (Preface to *Love's Triumph*)[8]

Jonson was not just referring to court masques. A classicist by education and inclination he is alluding to Horace's maxim 'He has gained every point who has mixed profit with pleasure, by delighting the reader at the same time as instructing him'.[9] Laughter often diffuses and loses the underlying message. How much profit and instruction would the courtly audience take from this representation? History suggests not much.

8 Jonson, *Ben Jonson: Works*, 7, 735.
9 *Ars Poetica* (*The Art of Poetry*), 1.351.

Chapter 8

IMAGES OF DISORDER: THE RELIGIOUS CONTEXT

The lay people know the Scriptures better than many of us.[1]

The sixteenth century was undeniably a religious age. Religion impacted all lives to varying degrees. The church, present in everyone's life, was an arm of the established power that ruled England. The church, often in the heart of the village, was visible from the fields as you worked. Its bells punctuated your day. The city parish church was likewise nearby. The priest would be visible haggling in the market like anyone else, perhaps occupying a corner of the local tavern. He was part of the civic power structure as well as sitting in judgement over your spiritual life. He reported your civil and moral mis- demeanours, convened and presided over the church court, arranged poor relief and preached. One form of socio-moral reinforcement was the homily the priest was obliged by his superiors to read out every Sunday. The *Book of Homilies* (the first 1547; the second in 1571) had 33 homilies, intended to bed in the ideas of the new reformed Church of England, to educate the masses and assist conformity. They covered doctrinal and liturgical subjects but included moral sermons: 'Against peril of Idolatry', 'Against gluttony and drunkenness', 'Against excess of apparel', 'Of alms [charity] deeds', 'Of the state of Matrimony', 'Against Idleness', 'Against disobedience and wilful rebellion'.

Religion meant much to the Elizabethans. It was central to many of the age's controversies, but not all those who attended church did so in a spirit of devotion. Many went simply to avoid the punishments meted out for non- attendance, but 'there was no escaping the rhythms of the Prayer Book or the

1 Bishop Edward Fox, 1537. Cited in Dickens, 108.

barrage of catechisms and sermons'.[2] Though a largely churchgoing society, there had always been those who claimed (and believed) they needed no church or priest to intercede between them and God. Increasingly Dissenters would assert they could worship in the field, the workshop, their home. Enforced church attendance was increasingly resisted. One sailor expressed the view in 1581 that 'it was never merry England since we were impressed to come to church'.[3] The pursuit and prosecution of non-attenders depended on the zeal of the vicar. Sunday worship was theoretically a time of communal affirmation of shared beliefs and values. That excludes those parishioners with rather different thoughts in their heads while the parson exhorted them to virtue. There would always be some who were doctrinally opposed to Anglicanism, but kept quiet. Though everyone was nominally Church of England, some in the congregation would be Catholics conforming to the law, others Puritans passively conforming while having more radical and aggressive beliefs about which they were mostly, but not always, quiet. Increasingly there were hostile interactions in the church that created simmering grievances in the outside community. For some congregations their vicars were too zealously reformist, for others they were too lazily traditionalist.[4] Some Dissenters separated from the official church and formed their own unofficial congregations. These were illegal and the congregants subject to dispersal or arrest.[5] There were those who, indifferent to religion, called themselves Christian, but did not allow faith to interfere with life more than they could help. Atheists tended to keep their views to themselves (or share them only with like-minded others); denial of God was punishable by arrest, interrogation, torture, imprisonment.[6] There were always those more concerned with the pint of ale in the inn after the boredom of the sermon was over. Some chatted, snoozed, made mocking comments on the priest and his sermon, laughed aloud, flirted or transacted business.[7] Others would be more preoccupied with the members of the opposite sex seated across the aisle. The parish church was a place where the community's social and religious differences were reinforced as much as the shared Christianity. Finally, there were those who had genuine faith in the Anglican Church and lived in as holy and virtuous a way as possible. It

---

2 Cressy, *Agnes Bowker's Cat. Travesties and Transgressions in Tudor and Stuart England*, 139.
3 Thomas, 179.
4 Cressy, chap. 9.
5 Ten years after *Dream* was first staged, separatists exiled themselves to Leiden before sailing to America, fleeing increasing persecution. See Bunker, *Making Haste from Babylon*, part 2.
6 Cressy, chap. 10.
7 Falling asleep during the sermon and disrespecting the vicar were fining offences.

is impossible to say what proportion of the population at any one time fell into these categories; there was much genuine piety and much irreligion. The service was intended as a celebration of solidarity and a reminder of the demands and sacrifices faith and virtue required. The overarching zeitgeist was religious, though like a rainbow it was of many colours, and despite the various forms of internal, external, silent and vocal opposition to imposed worship, most English men and women were regular churchgoers and those who were not, those who moved away from their village community to the anonymity of the city, would nevertheless have the vestiges of religious upbringing and the remnants of biblical teachings still in their memories.

Another aspect of this structure, that all faiths agreed on, was that the orderliness of the cosmos and the natural world was fantastically varied and complex, yet each part of the system worked and did its allotted job, and that all this is God's doing: 'The heavens declare the Glory of God and the firmament showeth his handiwork' (Psalm 19).

8.1 Unsettling Questions

Astronomers contributed to the gradual dismantling of the Ptolemaic system, but plays too could unsettle. Audiences watching the Admiral's Men perform Christopher Marlowe's *Tamburlaine the Great* (1587) at the Rose would have heard Edward Alleyne declaim,

> Our souls, whose faculties can comprehend
> The wondrous architecture of the world
> And measure every wand'ring planet's course,
> Still climbing after knowledge infinite
> And always moving as the restless spheres,
> Wills us to wear ourselves and never rest
> Until we reach the ripest fruit of all,
> That perfect bliss and sole felicity,
> The sweet fruition of an earthly crown. (part I, 2.7.21–9)

This combines traditional views – man's distinguishing faculties of under-standing that separate him from the animals and the glory of God's creation (the 'always moving [...] restless spheres') – with progressive, dangerously blas-phemous views on man's restless seeking for knowledge that trespassed into the secrets of the divine. The final idea is unusual, for instead of 'perfect bliss and sole felicity' being spiritual, a heavenly crown, Tamburlaine's goal is the 'earthly crown' of supreme material power – a very Renaissance ambition. This work, by a restless, enquiring, turbulent young university man, was intended for an audience with some fairly sophisticated members in it. But 80 per cent plus of England's population was rural: landless farmworkers and small sub-sistence farmers with beliefs still primitive, basic, medieval. Many large-scale landholders, farmers and nobles were similar. Centuries of Catholicism could not be erased overnight. Changes in thinking take several generations when few are literate, have no access to academic research and have closed minds. Nationwide instant communication just did not happen and the church always stood in the way of the free sharing of intellectual ideas, especially if they were unorthodox. There was no organized dissemination of news, regular newspapers appearing first during the Civil War. There was also the normal monumental public resistance to change. The majority of the population was exceptionally conservative. Ignorance, fear and simple intellectual inertia played their parts as always. The Reformation changed the official outer world, but the private inner world of daily life and its cluster of beliefs lagged far behind. The Reformation had many fervent supporters, but was grafted onto a residue of long-ingrained beliefs and practices. Individuals, devoted to the new faith, might conform to the new rites and liturgy of Anglicanism while still performing little acts of superstition like crossing themselves automatically or calling on a favourite saint. The lines between magic and acceptable doc-trine remained as blurred as they ever had been, but, given the growing print culture and the spreading knowledge of what the Bible said, huge numbers of controversial debates sprang up as to what was orthodox, what heresy, icono-clasm, superstition, idolatry, papist mumbo jumbo or diabolic magic. Services in English made doctrine more accessible and as Anglicanism settled, versions of the translated Bible became more readily available and individuals could read for themselves the words that were the basis of a priest's hitherto unique quasi-mystical interaction with his congregation. This new-found capacity for personal interpretation allowed many doctrinally divergent views to spring up and this worried the Anglican hierarchy. In response bishops became more repressive, demanding greater conformity from vicars and parishioners. This encouraged stronger opposition though Puritanism's rise was slow. The Puritan sectaries' drive to change religious thinking was regarded with irrita-tion and new ideas in medicine, politics and science always provoked opposi-tion. Puritans are almost always figures of fun and derided as hypocrites in plays. Their ostentatious overpiety provoked mistrust and mockery. The mass of people just wanted to continue living as they had always done. But, regard-less of this conservatism, seismic shifts were rumbling in many aspects of life. John Donne's 'An Anatomy of the World' (1611) declares,

New Philosophy calls all in doubt,
The Element of fire is quite put out;

The Sun is lost, and th'earth, and no man's wit
Can well direct him where to look for it.
And freely men confess that this world's spent,
When in the Planets, and the Firmament
They seek so many new; then see that this
Is crumbled out again to his Atomies.
'Tis all in pieces, all coherence gone;
All just supply, and all Relation:
Prince, Subject, Father, Son, are things forgot.

The Ptolemaic system represented God's order, a divine harmony, a coherence that reassured. To hear it questioned, to hear of old beliefs discarded by new science, was destabilizing, forcing doubts into people's heads in an age already full of changes, with a new religion, new worlds being discovered, new economic practices, new towns growing (and creating new problems) and old feudal relationships breaking down. Family was the commonest, closest bond for everyone. Family history, family honour and family loyalty were central to the audience's thinking and feeling. It would be painful for people to see taken-for-granted relationships called into question, especially if the answers suggested family love is a thin veneer of pretence. The Egeus/Hermia relationship is at breaking point. It does not show any signs of affection. It remains unresolved at the end of the play, but Egeus's absence from the wedding banquet suggests he has not yet accepted the duke's diktat or his daughter's marrying against his wishes. He is, additionally, transgressive in not accepting the ruling of his liege lord.

But familial and societal disassembly is averted by a restoration of the Oberon/Titania relationship and by Theseus's intervention in overruling Egeus and setting aside the 'ancient privilege of Athens' (1.1.41). In late-Elizabethan England there were growing fears that the family was faltering as a societal unit based on instinctive parent-child affection. The essays of Francis Bacon and Michel de Montaigne alone witness concerns.

Shakespeare's history plays amply displayed the natural desire for order and peace. Political vacuums were dangerous and so was illegitimate rule. Both usually led to bloody struggles, generating uneasiness and repression, putting into perspective the desperate anxieties surrounding a queen's pregnancy and the nervous wait for a hoped-for male heir. The audience had experienced the traumas of the Tudor continuities and discontinuities. Change was disturbing and dissension at the monarchical level was very frightening. Familial rupture in Athens, marital rupture in fairyland and the disturbance of nature's rhythms provide an uneasy atmosphere running in the background of the play. Like *The Comedy of Errors*, the threat of a death sentence hangs over the action, but is forgotten as the carnival of chaos builds up. From God to earth's dust, everything had its place. Man, man's communities and states were part of that orderliness. The fast-changing, apparently disintegrating, world disorientated the Elizabethans and a court-based drama was commonly the source of that threat to order, whether a history play, a revenge tragedy or a comedy. In this play that drama is outdone by the subverted order of nature and the fairy court where the consequences are much more widespread. Titania's speech (2.1.81–117) shows dissension in the fairy court affecting human life down to the village level.

The disorderliness of courtiers was regularly condemned. Concern about unprofessional conduct among judges and justices of the peace was similarly and regularly voiced. On 11 July 1604 Sir Philip Gawdy MP (Member of Parliament) describes the Commons Speaker addressing the problem of

> Justices of Peace of wch ther wer two kyndes he founde great fault withal, the one wer such as go downe into the country, and presently fall to hawking, and other sportes, and yf any man comme about Justice, they sende him to their next neybur Justice; the others be suche as put downe one alehouse, and set vp two for it, set up one constable, and put down an other, and yf any matter be stirring whatsoeuer he must haue an ore in it.[8]

The double standard of the apparently virtuous public man whose apparent probity masked private corruption recurs in drama, in the court and in real life, though Egeus would no doubt see himself as the injured party and not the villain. Part of the play's development is in stripping back appearances and exposing the realities hidden beneath. The declarations of love that so amuse and charm in act 1 are put to the test in the woods. Disturbing things emerge in the unsettling dark as they do in dreams. Thomas Middleton's 1605 city comedy *A Mad World* has the mother of the courtesan Frank Gullman declare in a neat epigram,

> Who gets th'opinion for a virtuous name,
> May sin at pleasure and ne'er think of shame. (1.1.164–5)

All not being what it seems is a recurrent image and theme in both Shakespeare's tragedies and comedies. The audience may have moments of doubt about whether this dream play will truly be a comedy as it turns into an unsettling nightmare.

8 Gawdy, 148.

PART II

THE ELIZABETHAN PRESENT

Chapter 9

THE CONTEXT OF COMEDY

Life does not cease to be funny when people die
any more than it ceases to be serious when people laugh.
(George Bernard Shaw, *Doctor's Dilemma*, act 5)

Tragedy is as old as human misery and comedy is its almost-but-not-quite-identical twin, for laughter is as old as tears. It is suitable that Greek tragic performances were followed by satyr plays and Elizabethan dramas by a jig; laughter as an antidote to overwhelming sorrow or as a counterbalance reminding the audience that tragedy is a temporary interruption to or distraction from the need to laugh and mock at a world that was a joke.[1] Viewed through the teachings of religion, most aspects of this mortal life were not to be taken seriously. Pride in your status, obsession with fine clothes, the struggle for power and vanity about your looks were all transient fripperies. All flesh was as insubstantial as grass, as a flower, cut down by death. The next life was the important one. This life was just a preparation for Heaven or Hell. The church promulgated the view that people are endlessly foolish, that folly leads to sin, that the wages of sin were death and that death was the portal to Hell if you died an unrepentant sinner. Tragedy portrayed how folly could lead to sin and disaster. Comedy too deals in the portrayal of folly, but presents it in such a way as invites laughter, exposes and eradicates folly (temporarily) and leads to a happy outcome. Comedy generally depicts folly of a type that shames and humiliates but does not kill. It may drive characters to the edge of madness, however. In *The Comedy of Errors*, *Twelfth Night* and

---

1 A jig here does not just mean a lively folk dance, but a mixture of dancing, singing, music with a comic sketch or farcical routine. In Tudor times these end pieces developed from short, knockabout sketches, often satirizing topical events, into full-length comic dramas in their own right. They often kept songs and music in them, but the dialogue and the outcome of the action became the main vehicle for instruction.

certainly in *Dream*, mistaken perceptions spiral out of control until characters are near to frenzy, even madness, as they lose control of their lives and their grip on reality.

Tragedy has a set of terms used to define key aspects of how its story is structured dramatically. These were derived from Aristotle's series of lectures on Greek tragedy, *The Poetics*. The tragic hero/heroine has a tragic flaw of personality (*hamartia*) that makes them blind to how their confidence in their control of their life and fortune is ill-founded. This overconfidence is called hubris. At some point in the narrative the hero/heroine experiences a reversal of fortune (*peripeteia*) and a recognition of their mistake (*anagnorisis*). It is not generally recognized by critics that these terms apply in many comedies also, but Egeus and the lovers all have personality defects that render them foolish and thus objects of amusement. They suffer a reverse of fortune and some limited recognition of their mistakes. All exhibit a degree of hubris. Sixteenth-century commentaries on Aristotle, who laid down the criteria for assessing the structure, development and success of tragedy, have some digressions into consideration of comedy. A developing plot must reveal character, character must be believable (even if exaggerated) and the story must reflect realistically the manners of the time frame of the play's setting. The plot must not be episodic, but pursue a single story. The characters should represent flaws and follies. Lodovico Castelvetro identified four areas of imitative representation relevant and essential to comedy and the triggering of laughter: (1) 'everything that becomes ours after we have desired it long or ardently'; (2) deceptions that make characters say or do what they would not otherwise do or say if they were not deceived; (3) the portrayal of physical or spiritual deformity (that is, conduct that is counter to reason or ethical custom); and (4) anything to do with sex and lewdness.[2] Area one is evident in the exaggerated longings expressed by Hermia, Lysander, Helena, Bottom and Titania. Area two, deceptions distorting conduct, are rife in many aspects of the narrative. Physical deformity is clearly present in Puck's transforming of Bottom and the overacting and amateurish devices in the Pyramus play. Spiritual deformity is evident in Egeus, Oberon and Demetrius. Area four is, for an Elizabethan play, curiously absent. This perhaps reflects the probability that the piece was written for a high-status wedding, and vulgar or sexual remarks would be unacceptable.

---

2 Lodovico Castelvetro, *Poetica d'Aristotele Vulgarizzata et Sposta* (1570), from *Castelvetro on the Art of Poetry* (trans. Andrew Bongiorno), cited in *The Cambridge Companion to Shakespearean Comedy*, 13.

The business of comedy was more important and serious than simply raising a laugh. It has always served a much graver purpose than mere humorous entertainment, but has also been regarded by religious, moral and cultural guardians as a lesser form than tragedy and a morally questionable one. In a world where society was strictly stratified even the arts had hierarchies. In painting devotional studies (annunciations, nativities, crucifixions) were thought to be the highest endeavour, and historical subjects were thought superior to landscape and portraiture. Grotesque topics of common life (card playing, village dances, tavern scenes) were thought of as very low art. In literature the epic poem, tragic drama, religious poetry, history plays, even lyrics and love verses were thought of as higher forms than mere comedy. Though the plays of Terence and Plautus were studied, translated and performed by schoolboys and undergraduates, and the satires of Juvenal and Horace similarly appeared on educational syllabuses, comedy was regarded with suspicion. It was thought to be a too vulgar form, too associated with the bourgeoisie and the commoners, too concerned with trickery, knavery and sex. Comic sketches performed at fairs commonly dwelled on the cuckolding of husbands by promiscuous wives and lustful young men. Other trickery stories figured too. The fairground performances were a low form, but comedy, properly handled, could use laughter to draw attention to personal or societal failings that need correcting.

Comedy could therefore be morally instructive. To the Elizabethans the didactic aim was the justification for literature, but church and state remained uneasy about comic forms. They were thought (correctly) to encourage disrespect for the governing elite and the clergy because they debunked and exposed their moral failings and generally portrayed morally unacceptable situations. Comedies might expose corruption, but the fear was that the laughter blurred the moral lesson, that delight in lewdness and the irreverent pleasure of laughter distracted from driving home the ethical point. Philip Stubbes expressed the ambiguous status of comic drama when he has one of his speakers, Philoponus, assert, 'Of comedies the matter and ground is love, bawdry, cozening, flattery, whoredom, adultery. The persons or agents whores, queens [vulgar, base young women], bawds [prostitutes or pimps], scullions [kitchen servant], knaves, courtesans, lecherous old men, amorous young men with suchlike of infinite variety'. The other aspect is expressed by the second interlocutor, Spudeus, who says, 'But notwithstanding, I have heard some hold opinion that they be as good as sermons, and that many a good example may be learned out of them'. Pholoponus becomes incandescent in his response, condemning 'filthy plays and bawdy interludes' for spreading 'bawdry, heathenry, paganry, scurrility, and devilry itself'.[3] He deprecates how

---

3 *The Anatomie of Abuses* (1583), cited in King, *Voices of the English Reformation*, 224–5.

play-going encourages idleness given the numbers thronging the theatres and how plays display too many forms of flirting and promiscuous conduct and how audiences too indulge in similarly unseemly behaviour. The ranting nature of the condemnation of different worldly vanities is typical of the Puritan stand on an increasingly wealthy and decadent society and specifically of their opposition to the theatres.

Love and the foolish things it makes people do was a traditional subject for comedy. Robert Burton devotes his Third Partition of *The Anatomy of Melancholy* to 'Love-Melancholy', prefacing the discourse by asserting that some will 'discommend' his focusing love at all for it is

> too Comical a subject [...] too phantastical, and fit alone for a wan-
> ton Poet, a feeling young love-sick gallant, an effeminate Courtier, or
> some such idle person. And 'tis true, they say: for by the naughtiness of
> men it is so come to pass, [...] that the very name of Love is odious to
> chaster ears.[4]

He largely anatomizes the psychological consequences of love – jealousy, obsession, melancholy, madness and suicide – but opens the section by acknowledging the positives: the attraction to what is beautiful, good and fair and how love can 'sweeten our life'.[5] What makes him anxious (he was a cler-gyman) is the tendency of the emotion to turn into excess of lust or to become distorted into various forms of negative psychological or physical reaction – maddening jealousy or bloody revenge. During the Renaissance comedy was expected to instruct, to teach a lesson, fully as much as tragedy, but moralists were as uneasy with the genre as they had been in the Middle Ages. The growth of public theatres and the concomitant increased accessibility of many plays to many more people made the censoring authorities and the church (both Catholic and English) ludicrously sensitive to the downsides of comedy. They feared that laughter often obscured what was serious underneath the situation being laughed at and that the content and subject of comedy were often immoral and handled distastefully, that serious matters were too readily mocked, that lofty people were treated with contempt. They suspected that the display of immorality, the basic human fascination with the rude and the lewd, was the real intent of the writers and actors and the real interest of the audience.

This uneasy suspicion is reflected in Sir Philip Sidney's *Defence of Poetry* (probably written 1581, published 1595). He examines in detail and at length

---

4 Burton, part 3, sec. 1, 611.
5 Burton, part 3, sec. 1, 612.

the potential of tragedy to delight and instruct and does not look at comedy at all as a separate genre. He does consider the inappropriate mingling of comic elements with serious tragic subjects in that 'mongrel tragicomedy'. He deplores how dramatists 'thrust in the clown by head and shoulders to play a part in majestical matters with neither decency nor discretion'.[6] His attitude is aristocratic, superior, purist and elitist. He speaks for high poetry and tragedy as a cultural preserve of the privileged and learned.

> Having indeed no right comedy, in that comical part of our tragedy, we have nothing but scurrility, unworthy of any chaste ears, or some extreme show of doltishness, indeed fit to lift up a loud laughter, and nothing else: where the whole tract of a comedy should be full of delight, as the tragedy should be still maintained in a well- raised admiration.[7]

His ideal comedy would be the witty, elegant complications of courtly characters, such as we find in the plays of John Lyly. He regards delight as the outcome of genteel comedy and distinguishes between delight (quiet pleasure) and the belly laugh. Delight derives from that which is natural while

> laughter almost ever cometh of things most disproportionate to ourselves and nature. Delight hath a joy in it, either permanent or present. Laughter hath only a scornful tickling.
>
> [...] we laugh at deformed creatures, wherein certainly we cannot delight. We delight in good chances, we laugh at mischances [...] the representing of so strange a power in love procureth delight, and the scornfulness of the action stirreth laughter. [...] the great fault [...] is that they [comic writers] stir laughter in sinful things [...] or in miserable, which are rather to be pitied than scorned. For what is it to make folks gape at a wretched beggar and a beggarly clown?[8]

For Sidney comedy's proper targets are 'a busy loving courtier [...] a heartless threatening Thraso; a self-wise-seeming schoolmaster; an awry-transformed traveller'.[9] The problem here is that Sidney's targets are narrowly exclusive stock types, whereas Shakespeare's are all-inclusive. Shakespeare mocks the failings of types from all ranks and sees how comedy can happen in moments of tragedy and that life is a complex mingling of what makes us cry and laugh.

---

6 *Defence of Poetry*, 67.
7 *Defence of Poetry*, 67.
8 *Defence of Poetry*, 68–9.
9 *Defence of Poetry*, 69. Thraso is the braggart soldier in Terence's comedy *Eunuchus*.

In discussing the tragic playwright Seneca, Francis Meres linked the Roman with the rising star of English theatre: 'As Plautus and Seneca are accounted the best for Comedy and Tragedy among the Latins, so Shakespeare among the English is the most excellent in both kinds for the stage'.[10] Among the Shakespeare comedies listed as 'accounted best' is *Dream*. Even thus early in its life the play had made a mark. It has always been a favourite, regularly staged by professionals and amateurs.

The impulse to correct mistaken or morally reprehensible conduct through mockery, parody and deflation is as natural as breathing. Children from a very young age tend to imitate and are quick to see what is funny and deserves drawing attention to. The comic spirit's domain is man's endless folly. Disproportion, affectation, pomposity, overfussiness, hypocrisy, self-delusion, being tricked, plain stupidity, obsession, vanity, false vanity, simple-mindedness and naivety all evoke various forms of humorous response from the wry smile to uncontrollable gales of laughter. Laughter becomes possible whenever reason is offended, whenever someone says or does something that is silly, outrageous or irrational. Comedy aims to cleanse irrationality by mocking the perpetrator into humiliation. It is revenge against those who offend common sense and balance. Any form of excess was seen as contrary to reason, whether it was being overdressed, spending too much on ostentatious display, thinking too much of yourself, being obsessed with money, being overly infatuated with another person, being a snob, being caught out in a deception you were trying to work on others or just being rather stupid.

As tragedy can have its grimly humorous aspect so too comedy can be black. The most serious happenings (death, love) often trigger jokes as if laughter were a way of dealing with matters that are so grave and hurtful they cannot be addressed easily by serious discussion. Laughter acts as a safety valve to take away the pressure of something that affects us deeply but cannot easily be expressed. A serious situation made fun of has a shock effect, making us laugh involuntarily in response to its inappropriateness. The shock of Bottom re-entering the stage with his head transformed into an ass's head shocks and elicits a snort of laughter because it is hideous, a surprise and because it is so ludicrous. For some Elizabethans it might also have had a frightening effect, for it borders on the devilish and is visually unnatural. A common feature of what makes us laugh, seen in the punchlines of jokes, is the unusual, unexpected juxtaposing of items that are normally not brought together – like playing the 'Dead March' at a wedding instead of 'Here Comes the Bride', or a man with an ass's head.

---

10 *Palladis Tamia* (1598), subtitled *Wit's Treasury*.

Dream offers a wide range of humour. There is Egeus as the stock angry father excessive in both his wrath and his demand for death. How pompous and high-handed he is, so sure he is right, so dismissive of any opposition. He is ripe for a fall and comedy often displays overmighty characters brought down. His anger alone is funny because most people losing their temper splutter, fall over their words (catachresis), make outrageous or silly claims, get red in the face.

There is the elegant and carefully arranged duet of Hermia and Lysander reciting the traditional obstacles to young love. The very artificiality of it is amusing. How naive they are, how soppily romantic, how breathlessly they express their feelings in an almost self-consciously stylized manner. Their complacent certainty of how right their love is may prompt us to cynically and nastily want to see them suffer. Comedy is often expressive of a cruel streak in us. The boisterous confidence of Bottom showing off his self-assumed ability to act, his enthusiasm to play all the parts, his tendency to take over the conversation and deliver his opinion on everything and his misprision of words are all amusing. Someone imitating is always funny and Bottom offers a range of caricature types – the ranting tyrant, the cooing lover, a romantic female, a lion rampant and a lion all cuddly and domesticated. He is a grotesque, a larger than life, good-hearted fool, a lovable buffoon.

From the list of past pranks he and the fairy mention (2.1.44–57), we are prepared for Puck's being a source of humour. At the mention of the flower's ability to make people fall in love we anticipate the enjoyment of watching Puck stage-manage the mistakes and look forward to whatever it might be that Titania will inappropriately dote on. Puck's recitation of simple tricks and his shape-changing imitations remind us of the precariousness of our control of the physical world, how we mistake what we see or hear, how we spill things, bump into things, trip and fall. He is a metamorphosed version of the witty and tricky servants of Roman comedy that we see in the Dromios, Tranio, Grumio, Lancelot Gobbo and others in Shakespeare alone. Jan Kott views him as an evil '*commedia dell'arte* Harlequin', asserting,

> Puck is not a clown. He is not even an actor. It is he who, like Har-
> lequin, pulls all the characters on strings. He liberates instincts and
> puts the mechanisms of this world in motion. He puts it in motion and
> mocks it at the same time. Harlequin is the stage manager and pro-
> ducer; just as Puck and Ariel are.[11]

11 Kott, *Shakespeare Our Contemporary*, 174.

The spluttering rows of the lover are cruel fun. There is the brilliant device of having Puck mistake the 'disdainful youth' Oberon saw and making Lysander fall for Helena, and then extending the confusion by making Demetrius fall for Helena too, while all the time none of the lovers knows that the two men are under the influence of magic. Hermia's complacent certainty that their love is true and eternal is destabilized when she suddenly finds herself rejected by the man she was so sure of. Cruelly amusing too is the vicious series of mutual accusations as the long-time friends fall out. Hermia isolated is a reverse of the situation at the beginning when Helena was alone and the girls' catty comments are a verbal parallel to the two youths squaring up to fight. We have just enough nastiness in us to enjoy watching a public row and hearing the abusive epithets thrown back and forth. Considered calmly the situation is disturbing. Neither girl knows of the magic act that has forced both youths to fall for Helena, so the whole row is based on lack of knowledge (as quarrels so often are). More worrying is the way the situation releases long-repressed criticisms of each other, just as Lysander under the effect of the love juice says some very nasty and hurtful things about Hermia that he has kept silent about. But neither young woman is under the mind-disturbing influence of magic. A further unsettling feature is that these negative comments coming out into the open remind us that family, friendship and love relationships contain similar views that we do not express until we are angry enough. Such open expression threatens to destroy society. Hearing them reminds us how much of social life is based on the agreement to pretend we like people or to keep silent about the negative aspects of those we genuinely like.

The vicious row between Titania and Oberon is an even more extreme and upsetting situation. Their selfish, irrational quarrel (trivially provoked over the ownership of the changeling, who could be amicably shared as a foster son), with neither side admitting they are in the wrong, exposes something of the visceral, instinctive hatred that can exist between the sexes and particularly between a husband and wife, where proximity encourages territoriality and power within the relationship to become extreme. There were, no doubt, couples in the audience, watching a play performed probably at a wedding celebration, who disliked each other intensely. In an age when arranged marriages were the norm, there would have been some partners who abhorred each other. The love-hate sex war of married couples was an ancient theme, sometimes treated in tragedy but rather more commonly the subject of comedy.

Titania's blind, unknowing, magic-induced obsession with the ugly monstrosity of Bottom with his ass's head is ludicrous and yet it reminds us of the many odd pairings love creates. It is another mistake or misperception caused by magic, but represents how the fiction of love, the impression, the perception, the conviction that the attraction we feel is love can lead us into an absurd pairing. How often may what we think is love have all sorts of other origins: desperation, loneliness, lust, pursuit of an unattainable dream. How often have we, observing an unusual couple, said, 'What on earth does she see in him?' or 'How on earth could he fall for her?'

The saving grace of the coming of daylight is that the lovers remain in the dark about what has happened. It all seems a dream and, like many dreams, they forget its details as soon as they awake. It is nevertheless amusing to see their confused, bemused state as they try to explain to Theseus what they think might have happened to them. As observers, we know precisely what has happened and have that sense of superiority that is inherent in comedy.

The climax of the comedy is the metadrama of the appallingly bad acting of the play-within-a-play. Metadrama is the self-conscious referencing within a play of the fictional nature of the play as a pretence, yet one which the actors pretend to take seriously and which audiences take for real while it is being staged. They do this for the sake of the truths about human life buried within the fiction. The French novelist/philosopher Albert Camus put it thus to a creative writing class: 'Fiction is the lie through which we tell the truth'. We know it is all pretend, but there are messages embedded in the story, messages that teach us or re-emphasize what we already knew but needed reminding of or confirming.

From the moment Quince introduces the idea of putting on a play, Shakespeare toys with the conventions of staging and what Samuel Taylor Coleridge called the 'willing suspension of disbelief'.[12] He suggested that if a writer could create 'human interest and a semblance of truth' in a fantastic and unbelievable story, the reader would suspend judgment of the incredibility of the narrative however implausible it might be. We know all the time that the lion is not a lion but a man playing a man playing a lion. But we laugh at the innocence of the mechanicals worrying that the courtly audience might be frightened by the appearance of the beast. They similarly agonize over how to represent moonlight and a wall. Part of the joke is that, while they worry about insignificant matters, like the range of different coloured beards Pyramus could wear, they pay no attention to how badly written the piece is and how Bottom overacts. Somewhat cruelly, the courtly characters make rather snooty comments on the performances, but then real audiences had become quite sophisticated and were very ready to make vocal criticisms during what they regarded as a substandard production. Another amusing feature of the metadrama aspect is the way Bottom interacts with the audience, stepping in

12 *Biographia Literaria* (1817).

and out of character at will. The outer play as a whole has shown how what appears to be reality is often a misleading misperception and the inner play blurs the boundaries between fiction and reality too. Finally, of course, there is the inflated language of Pyramus and Thisbe, parodying how the lovers expressed themselves (and that itself is a mockery of over-romantic expressions of feeling by lovers in traditional literature and in real life). Pyramus and Thisbe's unreal rhetoric is a satire on the love language of the court literature of the time. That court literature was in turn inherited from the love poetry of Petrarch and Dante and a host of Renaissance romances in prose or poetry.

The central comic scenario is the various vagaries of love and jealousy, starting in the court and spirally upwards into inextricable complexity and madness in the woods, before dying down in sleep and evaporating like a dream. Taking four characters, two male and two female, and playing with the permutations of attraction and repulsion, allows for mistakes to be made, declarations, denials and all the madness of what we do and say in the name of love. The wise ass, Bottom, sums it up suitably: 'reason and love keep little company together nowadays' (3.1.138–9). Even this is undercut by Titania's rejoinder, reflecting her partially wrong, magic-distorted vision: 'Thou art as wise as thou art beautiful'.

The intermix of social ranks and types of humour in *Dream* might have horrified Sidney, but Shakespeare notoriously disregarded hard and fast theoretical definitions of what was allowed and what was not. He not only introduces a mingling of fairies, courtly types and artisans but also mixes comedy styles as well. There is witty banter, carefully constructed couplets, broad caricature, physical mischances, grotesquerie and some element of the comedy of humours. This latter is founded on the theory of the four bodily humours and the idea that some people have a dominant humour that rules their life and behaviour – jealousy, greed, lust and anger are common personality traits that are made fun of. *Dream* displays the dominating anger of Egeus and Oberon, the all-consuming, overblown trust in love of the young people and the persistent brash self-confidence of Bottom. Language styles too are mixed. The courtly characters speak in decasyllabic blank verse, suitable to serious discussion. After Theseus exits with Hippolyta, Egeus and Demetrius, the poetic form changes to rhyming couplets as Lysander and Hermia lament the lot of lovers. Helena's speeches are in the same form, which is maintained for the discussions and arguments in the woods. The entry of Bottom and Co. signals the usual switch into prose for the common sort. With the fairies, the language reverts to poetry, but it is again mixed – couplets for Puck and the fairy he meets (with some moves into different, shorter metre, sometimes of six, seven or eight syllables), but blank verse for Oberon and Titania. Later there are songs with very varied metre and uncertain scansion. There are rhymed charms too set by Oberon and Puck in seven-syllabled rhyming couplets. The metrical pattern of the 'Pyramus' play is as varied and uneven as the writing itself. All work together, however, to evoke different types of laughter. The intricacy of the lovers' lines works to amuse by its elegance, artifice, cleverness, balance – and naivety. With Puck and the 'Pyramus' text we laugh at the sheer cheeky awkwardness of the metaphors and rhymes. The hybrid lexis and hybrid versification are suited to a play that is meant to be playful and serious, that addresses important issues but then undercuts them. If the 'Pyramus' play can be described in Philostrate's brief as 'tragical mirth', then the play as a whole is similarly paradoxical – comical seriousness or serious comedy.

Chapter 10

THESEUS AND THE SETTING

Shakespeare commonly mixes timelines and cultures. This does not matter. It is the underlying meaning that is important. Anachronisms are rampant in *Dream*. Midsummer Eve and Midsummer Day are 23 and 24 June, but in act 4 Theseus appears to think the lovers have come to the woods to observe May Day (1 May). This is such a glaring discrepancy it seems hardly credible Shakespeare did not notice it. It may be, however, that Theseus is speaking ironically, mocking the apparently reconciled lovers. It is like someone receiving a present and quipping, 'Oh, is it Christmas?' Theseus is perhaps joking that as they are all paired up it must be the May celebration of spring and birds mating. He refers to Valentine's Day having passed. Valentine's, May Day and Midsummer were all festivals connected with love.

Bottom and his companions are recognizable artisans from the shops of London or Stratford – a weaver, a carpenter, a bellows-mender, a tinker, a joiner and a tailor. Such tradesmen serviced domestic needs everywhere. They are also universal characters such as may have been found in any town or city in any age – even a mythological ancient Athens. But their names are a stark contrast to the Greek names of Theseus and Hippolyta and the other court characters. The names establish the difference between gentlefolk and ordinary citizens. The counterpointing of court and city was a common structural and thematic device. So too was the binary opposition of court and country. Here all three are locked together. The court and the city (the lovers and the artisans) are transported into the woodland world of the fairies. Yet, though set in the woods, the fairy element represents another court location, a mobile one that can move from the Indies to Greece. The two trains of fairy followers are each obedient to their head. Titania's are very much at her beck and call, to play music, sing, dance, guard her while she sleeps, serve her ass-headed guest and be discreetly absent when she orders them away. Even Bottom knows how to mitigate his rough and domineering ways and is courteous in talking to the fairy courtiers and giving them his orders. This third element of the characters – the fairies – are notably English. Apart from Oberon and Titania, the fairies have names that link them to rural life – Moth, Mustardseed, Peaseblossom, Cobweb. Puck is a version of the Old English word *puckle*, a mischief-making wood sprite in pagan folk lore. He is found in Irish, Swedish, Welsh and Cornish folklore too. The word 'pixie', a small fairy, may also be a variant of Puck. His pranks are often located in woods at night leading travellers astray and he is linked to the hobgoblin figure Robin Goodfellow (very much an English figure), to whom were attributed many of the things that went wrong on farms or in dairies. In the fairies, creatures of the countryside, of ancient English pagan religion and folklore and of the sometimes dark mindset of most of the English population meet the new and very different worlds of court and city. The fairies in general are identifiable creatures of rural legend and are not ancient Greek at all. Shakespeare combines his memories of a Warwickshire childhood with more recent literary emanations. Reginald Scot (*Discovery of Witchcraft*, 1584) and Thomas Nashe (*Terrors of the Night*, 1594) both derided and dismissed the lingering but diminishing belief in elves and goblins. Edmund Spenser, a poet whose work Shakespeare seems to have known, is alluded to, echoed and quoted from in a wide range of plays. His *Epithalamion* (1595), celebrating his own wedding, ends with an invocation to luck and a plea for protection for the new union and the nuptial bed. The piece as a whole has that familiar mix of classical gods and goddesses with very English features, much as *Dream* does:

> Let no lamenting cryes, nor doleful tears,
> Be heard all night within nor yet without:
> Ne let no false whispers, breeding hidden feares,
> Break gentle sleepe, with misconceiued dout.
> *Let no deluding dreames, nor dreadful sights*
> *Make sudden sad affrights;*
> Ne let no housefyres, nor lightnings helplesse harmes,
> *Ne let the Pouke, nor other euill sprights,*
> Ne let no mischiuous witches, with theyr charmes,
> Ne let hob Goblins, names whose sense we see not,
> *Fray* [frighten] *vs with things that be not.*
> Let not *the shriech Oule*, nor the Storke be heard,
> Nor the night Rauen that still deadly yels,
> Nor damned ghosts cald vp with mighty spels,
> Nor grisely vultures make vs once affeard:
> Ne let th'unpleasant Quyre of Frogs still croking
> Make vs to wish theyr choking.

Let none of these theyr drery accents sing;
Ne let the *woods* them answer, nor ther echo ring. (334–52)

My italics highlight terms associated with the play. If the play was originally performed for a courtly audience then Shakespeare is presenting his sophisticated gathering with fairy figures to be mocked as something the common folk once credited. But then the piece would be moved on into the public theatre where the range of credibility would be wider. Regardless of the social origins of individual audience members, the fairies work as a source of fun, mayhem and mischief, disorienting and deflating the posh folk.

The middling sort of both Elizabethan and Athenian society are omitted. We see only the idle, privileged rich and the 'hard-handed' workers, skilled artisans who topped the bottom portion of the hierarchical pyramid. In the woods the regulated artificiality of court life and the indolence of the spoiled darlings of fortune are completely nullified. Their elegance is useless. Indeed they and their clothes are scratched, torn and muddied, just as their suave assumption of superiority is erased as they become disoriented, hectic, angry and confused.

However skilled the artisans may be, that counts for nothing. They are out of their depth as actors and out of their comfort zone in the eerie alternation of moonlight and dark in the woods. They, like the lovers, are denizens of the city. All are used as playthings, none is superior and all are fooled and behave as fools. The audience laughs at their discomforts.

Bottom, Quince and Co. are clearly English, common and their names related to their trade in the English manner.[1] The Athens of the setting is a fantasy of the classical city and merely presents an imagined exotic location that may trigger multiple echoes from the audience's reading.

The duke too is a figure from mythology, but in a different register from Puck and the fairies. Actor of many brave feats, killer of the Minotaur, abandoner of Ariadne and seducer of numerous other young women, he was later a legendary ruler, having cleared Attica of various brigands and monsters. Shakespeare has resurrected a figure he came across in Thomas North's translation of Plutarch and in Geoffrey Chaucer's 'Knight's Tale'. This character is not to be taken as a factual representation. The mythological Theseus's father, Egeus, has also been resurrected and realigned, for in the legend he commits suicide thinking his son has died in Crete. Not only has Shakespeare brought him to life again

---

1 Bottom was the name for the wooden core on which skeins of wool were wound. Quines/quoins (Quince) are the wedges carpenters insert into joints. Snug is how a joiner describes a good fit. Tailors were proverbially thin and starveling in appearance. A snout is part of the kettle tinkers would often have to men and a flute is part of a church organ pipe filled by air from the bellows.

but he has also transformed him into the father of Hermia. This is not the only 'translation' in a play crammed with metamorphoses. Plutarch provided the list of women Theseus had previously been involved with (as mentioned by Oberon – 2.1.74–80 – in his argument with Titania) and Chaucer's 'The Knight's Tale' provided both the duke and Ippolita and a situation where two young men fall in love with the same woman. Shakespeare's Theseus is no more an Athenian ruler than the lovers are Athenian youth. He seems more like the ruler of a small Italian state with a court like that of the Duke of Urbino, whose cultured coterie was the subject of Baldassare Castiglione's influential conduct manual, *The Book of the Courtier*. Though referencing Theseus's profligate and colourful past, Shakespeare makes no mention of his greatest claim to fame – the killing of the Minotaur. However, Plutarch's 'Life of Theseus', in mentioning the monster, quotes Euripides's description:

> A mingled form where two strange shapes combined,
> And different natures, bull and man, were joined.

That Shakespeare knew North's translation is well attested. The mix-species creature – the bull/man Minotaur – may just have given him the idea of Bottom's translation, combined with Apuleius's well-known fantasy *The Golden Ass* (where a man is transformed into an ass) and the many folk stories of humans turned into animals by assorted witches, wizards and fairies. Another important contribution from Plutarch comes in the last paragraph:

> His tomb is a sanctuary and refuge for slaves, and all those of mean condition that fly from the persecution of men of power, in memory that Theseus while he lived was an assister and protector of the distressed, and never refused the petitions of the afflicted that fled to him.[2]

Of the many good and bad characteristics of the legendary Theseus it is this merciful and caring aspect that Shakespeare chooses to display. Hermia addresses him as 'your Grace', the correct term, though of course 'duke' is not a Greek word. It derives from the Latin *dux*, a leader. During the Middle Ages the title was held by a number of German and Italian rulers of small states with virtually monarchical powers. In Theseus then we have a feudal governor with Renaissance characteristics. More resonantly, the epithet indicates that this ruler does have some degree of grace, that breadth of sympathetic understanding, goodness and gentleness that Jesus had. In his small way, for his part in the play is verbally quite limited, he provides a calming, moderate, humanist, rational and gracious input to counter the extreme anger of Egeus,

---

2 Both quotations from *Plutarch's Lives* (Everyman translation) 9, 27.

the potentially dangerous conflict between Demetrius and Lysander and the possibility that the fire of love will get out of control. It seems clear too that the lovers are Renaissance courtiers and their story a courtly entanglement shifted into a rural setting. But this will be a farcical pastoral with some bitter undertones.

Chaucer's Theseus is 'worthy' and renowned for 'wisedome, and [...] chevalry'.[3] This is Shakespeare's starting point. His duke is situated as a wise ruler and is the framing orthodoxy of the play. His name gives authority and dignity, while the Greek names of the lovers lend a courtly and aristocratic air to the central drama. This is essentially a play focused on upper-rank love tangles, with a strict patriarchal father like the stock angry parent/old man (*senex iratus*) of Greek and Roman comedy who opposed young lovers marrying.[4] What Shakespeare does though is move his courtly characters out of the court and into the woods, from the protected, supposedly civilized world of ducal control into the wildness of nature. This shift is typical of many contemporary comedies, a way of testing affected, cossetted aristocratic types in a location to which they are not used. Shakespeare does this again in *As You Like It* (1599–1600) and *The Tempest* (1612). The language in which they express their love comes from a similarly hybrid background: courtly love (from twelfth-century France), Petrarchan love sonnets (fourteenth-century Italy) and the balanced euphuism and graceful, witty lyricism of John Lyly's Elizabethan comedies. The locational shift signifies the limits of ducal control as a correlative for how ineffective reason and moderation are in combatting the powerful insistence of appetites, specifically the passion of love. In other words, Theseus tries to control and restrict both Egeus and Hermia, but finds instinct is stronger than reason. Two young people are prepared to thwart paternal demands and ducal law in order to be together. Another young woman is prepared to contravene the loyalty of friendship and the requirements of modest virginity and reveal Hermia's plan while also endangering her own virtue by venturing into the woods at night with a man who claims to hate her. The ethical framework relates very much to the thinking of Castiglione and the Elizabethans. In pleading Lysander's case Hermia asserts that he is as worthy a gentleman as Demetrius. The Duke states the orthodox, hierarchical view:

> In himself he is;
> But in this kind, wanting your father's voice,
> The other must be held the worthier. (1.1.53–5)

---

3 Stow's edition of *The Woorkes of Geffrey Chaucer*, 1561.
4 There were other forms. The *senex* could be a wise old counsellor. The *senex amans* was an old man foolishly in love with a much younger woman.

Wanting perhaps to settle matters simply, Theseus appeals to the standard view that patriarchal wishes should dominate. He tries to blunt the wilfulness of young love, but fails. At the same time, though he has theory, custom and practice on his side, it is clear that Egeus is not taking child consent into account. He insists that his choice will predominate and hers be annulled, ignored. Hermia's defence of her choice is transgressive; it dishonours a parent, is publicly too pushy and privately puts her virtue to the question in her ready acceptance of Lysander's love gifts and her ready agreement to run away and marry without consent. So much for the orthodox view. Her situation, of course, is meant to touch us with sympathy.

She is caught, like so many young people in romantic comedies, between duty and desire. She is led by her heart, that uncertain, changeable, but influential organ. Helena too is trapped by her ungovernable feelings and endangers her virtue. In the excess of her infatuation she betrays her friend, but then such an act is inevitable for she has, in the extent of her obsession with Demetrius, stepped over the boundary between reason and folly and will do anything in the attempt to win back his affection.

The framework of reason is established as a basic value at the start of the play and is reasserted at the end, but it is the fairies, bringing magic and chaos, who rule the whole middle of the piece and have the last word. In the final moments of the play Theseus thinks he is closing the mortal fiction by telling everyone to go to bed. Oberon thinks he is then closing the story by blessing the house and inhabitants and wishing luck for the future. He represents the unseen power of Fate that brings good fortune to some and not to others. But it is Puck, the spirit of mischief, mayhem, magic and anarchy who closes the entire proceedings of the theatrical fiction for the audience by addressing them and soliciting applause. Human reason does what it can to resolve problems, exercising virtue, controlling irrationality or extremes, but in the end common sense is always assailed by superstition, irrational beliefs, uncontrolled emotions and an imperturbable tendency at betrothals and marriages to wish for good luck. It is a case of blind hope overcoming our awareness that humans have a great capacity to foul up. Theseus does what he can to arrange for happiness to take place, but the audience knows that the best arrangements are easily derailed and in the end a blind belief in luck is all we can cling to.

Regardless of the mistakes the lovers make during the course of the drama and may make in their future married lives, Theseus represents a ruler, like a father (and a far better one than Egeus) trying to guide the young ones into the paths of calmness and positiveness. He first tries to shepherd Hermia into the expected path of conformity, then appears to be about to talk to her father and her unwanted prospective groom while giving the lovers a chance to plan an escape. In act 4 he quickly perceives that 'these wood-birds' have begun 'to couple now' (4.1.139) and that a workable solution has evolved. He then hears Demetrius's apologia for his second switch of affection and firmly but gently overrules Egeus's persisting anger. It is the sort of compromise wise rulers make. It takes account of the changed situation and forces Egeus to face the inevitable. Theseus represents reason, decency and hope, but he is not God and cannot control all human action or feeling. Nor can he control Fate. He represents the limits of human power and reminds us that hope and good luck ultimately affect the outcomes of our lives, especially if we step into the labyrinth of love.

Chapter 11

PUCK'S PERMUTATIONS: THE CONTEXT OF LOVE

> The stage is more beholding to love than the life of man. For as to the stage, love is ever the matter of comedies and now and then of tragedies; but in life doth much mischief, sometimes like a siren, sometimes like a fury.[1]

The stock plot line of comedy is the complication of relationships through mischances and mistakes. What begins as a relatively simple situation (or several situations) is steadily made more entangled until denouement seems impossible. Simple physical mistakes can be funny, but are somewhat limited in their scope for humour. What adds to the comedy is the emotions experienced, the disappointments, the misplaced feelings, the misunderstandings caused by the distortion of understanding stemming from excessive feeling overriding reason. These features are focused through characters and their individual behaviour emerges as mildly funny or grotesquely caricatured or anywhere in between. Greed, ambition and vanity may be the principal target, or indeed any of the many failings of humanity, but the subject most commonly focused in comedy is love and its various stages, permutations and guises.

With good reason Alexander Leggatt called his study of Shakespeare's contribution to the genre *Shakespeare's Comedy of Love*, for, from *The Comedy of Errors* (1588?) to *Twelfth Night* (1599?), love and its multiple misperceptions is the driving impulse of all his comic pieces. Robert Burton alludes to Plato calling love 'the great Devil, for its vehemency, and sovereignty over all other

1 Bacon, 'Of Love', 88.

passions' and defining it as 'an appetite'.[2] To Francis Bacon love is 'the child of folly'. In an echo of Bottom's comment that 'reason and love keep little company together nowadays' (3.1.138–9), he comments, 'Whosoever esteemth too much of amorous affection quitteth both riches and wisdom'.[3] That puts love into the category of a dangerous emotion, liable to excess and therefore potentially sinful.

> They do best who, if they cannot but admit love, yet make it keep quarter [keep its proper place], and sever it wholly from their serious affairs and actions of life; for if it check [interfere] once with business, it troubleth men's fortunes, and maketh men that they can no ways be true to their ends.[4]

Unless it is divine love. But even love for God could be pushed too far, become a monomaniac mental state, a religious obsession and thus a target for comedy. As with conduct literature there was a long history of writings – philosophical, theological, imaginative – dissecting the nature of love and its dangers. From classical times the most famous is Plato's *The Symposium* which posits the idea of true lovers being twin halved souls that have found each other and become whole again. The dialogue differentiates between erotic love with all its psychological entanglements and a purer love that incorporates charity, sympathy and selflessness. More racy is Ovid's practical, instructional manual *Ars Amatoria*, paralleled in the twelfth century by the *De Amore* of Andreas Cappellanus and the French *Roman de la Rose*. The process of attraction, flirting and all the tactics of love are compelling. Every spectator has a vested interest – wants to know the signs, recognizes what he or she has been through, wants to learn where they went wrong perhaps, wants to laugh at others making fools of themselves. The emotion invested in falling in love and maintaining a relationship is of universal concern. It is one of the most important events in life, which is why getting it right is so crucial and getting it wrong so devastating. All the ways of getting it wrong will be amusing to the spectators. It may be heartbreaking for the victim(s), but a laugh for the audience. To see what may have been our own folly enacted before us, with someone else as the figure of fun, is a humorous experience. We may feel shame or embarrassment inside to be reminded of our own stupidity, but on the outside we grin and chuckle, for looked at objectively our follies are pathetically laughable. In protesting to Lysander that she will meet him and

---

2 *The Anatomy of Melancholy*, 618.
3 Bacon, 89.
4 Bacon, 89.

run away, instead of simply saying, 'Yes, I will meet you, I promise', Hermia makes a typically overblown declaration:

> I swear to thee by Cupid's strongest bow,
> By his best arrow with the golden head,
> By the simplicity of Venus' doves,
> By that which knitteth souls and prospers loves,
> And by that fire which burn'd the Carthage queen
> When the false Trojan under sail was seen. (1.1.169–74)

This is a comic circumlocution, a long-winded way of saying something that could have been expressed very briefly. It is amusingly naive and artificially structured. But it also carries within it moral warnings. Comedy is always moral; either the author intends to preach a lesson or independently the audience draws its own conclusions. To trust in Cupid is a dangerous mistake. The mischievous god, portrayed by writers and painters as blind, was notoriously unreliable, making people fall in and out of love arbitrarily ('Cupid is a knavish lad/Thus to make poor females mad!').[5] This symbolizes the inconstant, vacillating nature of human attraction. The reference to Venus's doves is no more sensible, for though doves can symbolize peace and hope, here they have a different iconography, representing unrestrained sexuality, referencing the fact that doves do not have a single annual mating, but may breed several times during spring and summer. The allusion to Dido and Aeneas is an unhappy one too, for though the Carthaginian queen was an emblem of love's strength, the outcome of her story is a tragic one. Abandoned by Aeneas she commits suicide. Hermia seems unaware that her promise to meet is laden with doom and morally culpable, but the speech acts as a proleptic hint by Shakespeare, foreshadowing the dramas to come. Her interchange with Helena seals her fate, for everything she says only emphasizes that she attracts Demetrius more than Helena does. This is testing friendship to the breaking point and may go some way to encouraging Helena to betray the planned elopement.

What is taken for love and feels like the thing itself, may be lust, a passing fancy, a temporary fixation, a fiery passion or a desperate need to feel wanted. These misperceptions can be a part of a love comedy and help, by contrast, to define a true love. Indeed, contrasting and comparative parallels are often paraded before the audience in order for them to see whether they can tell the genuine from the false, the true and deep from the shallow. This play presents,

---

5 Renaissance thought posited the idea of two Cupids to go along with the two kinds of love – *Amor Coelestis* (heavenly love) and *Amor vulgaris* (earthly, that is, fleshly, love).

explores and resolves a series of less than harmonious relationships – Egeus/
Hermia, Lysander/Hermia, Hermia/Demetrius, Helena/Demetrius, Lysander/
Helena/Demetrius, Titania/Oberon. The imminent marriage of Theseus and
Hippoltya has already emerged out of an unpromising first contact between
prospective bride and groom. He had embarked on a campaign to defeat her
Amazon tribe by force of arms, had conquered and captured her and then fell
in love. The Amazon part of the Duke's previous life Shakespeare would have
found in Thomas North's translation of Plutarch's 'Life of Theseus', but the
marriage with Hippolyta is not there. He seems to have got that from Geoffrey
Chaucer's 'Knight's Tale'. Wooing her with his sword and winning her love
'doing thee injuries' (1.1.17) symbolizes the aggression/affection polarity of
human mating. The sword represents the phallus and male aggression, but
the image of winning a woman's love by doing her injury reflects the common
phases of animal mating. Phallic penetration and the breaking of the hymen
are the physiological 'hurt' and 'injury' necessary to achieve congress and are
part of the 'pleasing punishment that women bear' in the drive to have sex and
children.[6] The female animal attracts a male by giving off naturally produced
pheromones indicating her fertile state. She does not consciously set out to
attract and may initially fight him off, run away, then be caught and submit
(willingly or not) to mating. In human society matters are more complicated and
motivations less easy to discern clearly and accurately. A woman might have
good looks and possess sexually exciting secondary assets which she enhances
with attractive dress, perfume, make-up and hair styling. Enhancing her
advantages may not be for attracting a mate, but simply to stimulate attention
that pleasingly reinforces her self-esteem. Unmarried Elizabethan girls, usually
still under the guardianship of parents and a variety of other protectors, would
not be allowed out unchaperoned or allowed to wear provocative clothing,
though they did dress with their bosom uncovered. This does not mean that
their breasts were bare and visible, simply that the area from the neck to the
top of the dress did not have a covering. On marriage a kerchief of linen
or lawn was placed over the cleavage. It was a visual way of marking her
status as a married woman and that she was off the marriage market and
was no longer sexually available. Though a wife was seen as secondary to her
husband, she did also gain in hierarchical power on marrying. For both men
and women marriage changed how they were perceived. The marriage service
was a rite of passage and an entry into the adult world. They gained cachet
and respect in the community and had new rights and responsibilities. If a girl
was being put on the marriage market her social dress might be designed to

---

6 *The Comedy of Errors*, 1.1.46.

attract a partner, usually chosen by her parents, but it would strive for elegance and taste rather than be sexually provocative. Her clothing was a sign too of the wealth of her parents – a family status statement. If she lived a less protected life (as court gentlewomen did) she would then dress to please not just herself. If she were aroused sexually or wished to attract a mate (for sex or for marriage) her body language would indicate her readiness and her clothing might encourage attention. The means by which this might be signalled could range from very demure, petty ploys – glances, smiles, blushes, the fluttering of eyelashes – through a range of increasingly immodest behaviours. Throughout the sixteenth and seventeenth centuries more and more of the bosom was progressively shown among court ladies until the areolae and nipples (their 'roseate buds') were partially visible. Thomas Nashe describes how court ladies

> stand practising half a day with their looking-glass how to pierce and to glance and to look alluringly amiable. [...] Their breasts they embusk up on high, and their round roseate buds immodestly lay forth, to show at their hands there is fruit to be hoped.

He warns that it is not such ploys and all the fashionable 'puffings up' of fashion that are offensive to God, but 'the puffings up of your souls' and 'the pride of your hearts'.

> Nothing else is garish apparel but Pride's ulcer broken forth. How will you attire yourselves, what gown, what head-tire will you put on, when you shall live in hell amongst hags and devils?[7]

Customarily, a virtuous female presented outwardly an emotionally uncommitted appearance (whatever she might feel within). She physically repelled any advances until she was sure of the man's genuine attraction and readiness to marry and support her and was sure of her parents' consent. Then she gave her emotional consent verbally and the pair declared their love and permitted the legal and religious bonds to be arranged. One phase of this, prior to marriage, was the betrothal ceremony where, in front of witnesses, the couple made their declaration of love and their promise to marry. Betrothal or handfasting was a legally binding contract. Helena, betrothed to Demetrius (4.1.171), has created her relationship outside all these customary practices. The betrothal was probably a private agreement made between just the two of them. Among those ranks of society where girls were less closely chaperoned,

---

7 *Christ's Tears Over Jerusalem* (1593).

betrothal was often the signal for prenuptial sex, but a virtuous lady, particularly of the upper and the middling sort, did not yield herself until the bridal night. The penetration of a virgin bride, the breaking of the hymen, was a pain linked with pleasure, like Theseus's image of winning Hippolyta doing her injury. Hermia declares quite clearly that she would rather die a virgin nun

> [e]re I will yield my virgin patent up
> Unto his lordship [Demetrius] whose unwished yoke
> My soul consents not to give sovereignty. (1.1.80–3)

She refuses to let Lysander cuddle her for warmth when they are exhausted and lost in the wood and decide to sleep it out until dawn. So, however feverish and breathless their expressions of love may be, and however ardently they long to be married, they appear not to have sex or intend to do so prior to the official sanction given by the wedding – even if that takes place without parental consent on Hermia's part and in exile from their homes. Nevertheless, her virgin status is tarnished somewhat by her acceptance of Lysander's tokens of love and her transgressive immodesty in pursuing a relationship not sanctioned by her father. Her reputation would finally be lost by the elopement. However we today may applaud her independence and feel empathy for the romantic stance she takes, it is unlikely many in the original audience would feel she has behaved properly, particularly if the spectators were high status. Among the titled and wealthy dynasties marriage was very much an economic union with political dimensions. High-end unions were strictly monitored by parents and only celebrated with parental approval.

Helena is warned by Demetrius that she has taken a great risk with 'the rich worth of your virginity' (2.1.219) by coming to the wood with him. Virginity was highly prized. No girl of any virtue would allow herself to lose it just because a man happened to please her. Both girls in the play have behaved with immodesty in risking their reputation by coming to the wood with a man. Though not intending to lose their virginity, they are playing a dangerous game. They display the symptoms of 'wanton love'. Bacon had delineated clearly that 'nuptial love maketh mankind; friendly love perfecteth it; but wanton love corrupteth and embaseth [debases] it'.[8] Burton warns of the passions that could be aroused and could get out of control:

> Naughty love, to what dost thou not compel our mortal hearts? How it
> tickles the hearts of mortal men, I am almost afraid to relate, amazed,
> and ashamed, it hath wrought such stipend and prodigious effects, such

8 'Of Love', 89.

foul offences. [...] but if it rage, it is no more Love, but burning Lust, a Disease, Phrensy, Madness, Hell. 'Tis death, 'tis an immedicable calamity, 'tis a raging madness 'tis no virtuous habit this, but a vehement perturbation of the mind, a monster of nature, wit, and art.[9]

'Vehement perturbation of the mind' and 'raging madness' are what we see in the arguments between the lovers in the woods. The rage of love is particularly evident in Hermia's suspicions that Helena has stolen her lover. The physical and verbal ferocity of Hermia is a prime example of what love jealousy can do to a well-brought-up young woman. It would also be a chastening warning to Lysander of what his sweetheart can be like – if he were able to remember it afterwards.

The delaying tactics – flirting, arousing interest, yet keeping sex at bay – are part of the theory of virtuous love. The idea of courtly love is that physical passion is by and large sublimated through words, through flowery and intricate language (such as we hear between Lysander and Hermia). It is an overflow of breathless sexuality diverted into the images of classical allusion to lovers from mythology, to metaphors of fire and burning, Cupid's arrows, hearts, sparkling eyes and 'Venus's doves'. It is meant to act as a safety valve, though it may be suspected as encouraging and increasing longing, and takes no account of the possibility of rape or seduction (with or without alcohol) or the ready consent by the female. The power of the petticoat to initiate and drive sexual activity should not be discounted or underestimated. Despite all the parental and clerical pressure on young women to be chaste, the libido when repressed will, like a rampant weed cut back, reassert itself. Elizabethan-Jacobean comedies are full of wilful daughters determined to pursue their man. The tragedies too display determined women. In real life, many girls acted independently of parents. Nature was often stronger than faith, morality or self-control. Queen Elizabeth used to become irrationally angry when her waiting gentlewomen got themselves entangled in liaisons at court. And they did, regularly. Boxed ears and verbal assault were normal. A pregnancy outside marriage meant banishment from the queen's service – even imprisonment, as in the case of Sir Walter Raleigh when he married Bess Throckmorton without the queen's consent. For all her Virgin Queen image, the queen's own sexuality was strong and her life strewn with ambiguous relationships in which lust bubbles under the surface.

Theseus and Hippolyta have been through the attraction-rejection-consent stage and are on the brink of marriage and seem to happily anticipate it.

9 Burton, part 3, sect. 2, memb. 1, subs. 2, 650–1.

The duke sends his master of revels to organize 'the pert and nimble spirit of mirth' and promises his bride-to-be to wed her in a different mode from their belligerent meeting: 'With pomp, with triumph, and with revelling' (1.1.13, 19). The aggression of the warrior has been blunted or diverted by the oldest instinct (sexual attraction) and turns to another ancient impulse – to pair and mate under the official umbrella of the sacrament of marriage. The relationship, born in violent opposition, now more affectionate, reflects the polar love-hate coupling of the male-female sex war which is both the reality of life and the staple of comedy. But the happy anticipation of a joyous wedding is clouded, the mood spoiled, by the eruption onstage of Egeus and the nasty little problem he initiates: either his daughter will marry his choice or he will invoke Athenian law that can put her to death. Another supposed love situation, that of parent for child and child for parent, shows its hateful aspect. His greeting on entering, 'Happy be Theseus ...', is ironic since he is about to give the 'renowned duke' a conundrum to solve that could well lead to anything but happiness. This situation initiates the permutations of love and change that are at the heart of the play's plot and themes and are part of its attraction and humour as a perennially popular piece. The ups and downs and the perversity of emotion are a reflection of the general clerical view that human life is inconstant, always changing, and that nothing is permanent. It is fitting that Puck presides over the mayhem in the woods, for the changeability of emotions suits well with his love of mischief. We do not know the ages of the four lovers, but can recognize the dramas that happen and the interchanges of partners that may ensue in any group of young people. In his magic-induced love of Helena Lysander gives voice to the subconscious feelings of attraction he may have had for Helena but repressed because he was in love with Hermia. Because you love one person does not mean you cannot see the attractiveness of others. It is a wonderful comic moment when Helena wakes him and he instantly declares, 'And run through fire I will for thy sweet sake!' (2.2.102). While in his conscious mind he genuinely loves Egeus's daughter, he could still, nevertheless, consciously and unconsciously acknowledge that Helena is worthy of his love, that she is fair, that she has attractions. That is now allowed to spill out.

> Content with Hermia? No. I do repent
> The tedious minutes I with her have spent.
> Not Hermia, but Helena do I love:
> Who will not change a raven for a dove? (2.2.110–13)

Symbolic of peace and purity, the white dove contrasts with the black, croaking and cawing raven associated with witchcraft. There is perhaps here a sub-conscious sense that Hermia talks too much and that her dark colouring is not entirely to his liking. He later calls her an Ethiop and remarks on her smallness. He has sometimes, perhaps, felt she was a bossy, bad-tempered little thing and that a tall, cool, calm blonde might suit him better. He rationalizes his change of heart:

> The will of man is by his reason sway'd,
> And reasons says you are the worthier maid.
> Things growing are not ripe until their season:
> So I, being young, till now ripe not to reason;
> And, touching now the point of human skill,
> Reason becomes the marshal to my will,
> And leads me to your eyes, where I o'erlook
> Love's stories, written in love's richest book. (2.2.110–21)

He is wrong. The 'will' or appetite too often overrules reason. Demetrius uses a similar argument to explain his attraction to Hermia. How many times have young men used immaturity as the reason for loving one girl and growing up as the excuse for a transfer of interest? The other excuse is, 'I wasn't myself, I was sick, I was out of my mind, I wasn't thinking straight'. It is neatly argued like a syllogism in logic. This is the perversity of love that can make a young man, established firmly in love with one girl, suddenly and inexplicably fall for another and endanger his relationship. There is a subtle joke in his claiming he has found reason and can now see clearly: his eyes have been the means of this distorted vision which appears so real and his vision is anyway fabricated and artificially affected by the magic juice. In real life magic juice is not required. Throughout the play the idea of seeing true, of right perception, is played on – and it is often when the speaker is not seeing correctly that they claim they are now seeing truly. The word 'eyes' and associated sight lexis recurs multiple times. The appearance/reality dichotomy is recurrent throughout Shakespeare's work and is particularly evident in the comedies where love is the subject.

In Egeus we have the stock angry parent, the dictatorial father of Roman comedy, verse ballads and folk song, but also a contemporary figure representing a current issue. He is an old-fashioned patriarch insisting his will be obeyed whatever the consequences and without considering that Demetrius might not be to his daughter's liking. Paternal love has become distorted. Egeus is 'full of vexation'. His wrath makes him a sinner and anger distorts judgement. His daughter, in opposing the paternal wish, contravenes the commandment to 'honour thy father …' and is thus a sinner too and will suffer her penance through the 'fierce vexation of a dream'. She has, somewhat immodestly, embarked on a quite hot and hectic love affair. She has not given in to lust, is holding back the scorpion, but the relationship is quite advanced, appears mutually genuine and is exercising a powerful effect on both her and Lysander.[10] But now the collision has taken place between her choice and her father's. This is an old story, universal, the conflict between youth and age, parent and child over the choice of marriage partner. It is an inevitable and common plot line. Underlying it is, of course, the primal impulse, the animal urge to have sex, which is often stronger than moral teaching or parental disapproval. The girl has chosen her lover and her father does not approve. The situation goes to the heart of animal attraction or the so-called chemistry of love. The young girl, repressed physically and emotionally, is now ready to become sexually active. She has become attracted to and is infatuated with her young man. Her father disapproves and is unwilling to give up his role as protector and decider. It is right that a father should be protective and concerned, but Egeus has crossed the border into authoritarianism that is less concerned for his daughter's happiness than about getting his own way. *Dream* is a comic counterpiece to *Romeo and Juliet* – the comic and tragic masks of love. Like Juliet's father, Egeus has made a choice for his daughter and the drama comes from their disagreement. It is one of the oldest stories in the world and beneath it is the drive toward sexual satisfaction that impels all young people and the worry of all parents that the child has chosen badly, will give in to nature and become pregnant. Fathers know what young men are like. They have been there. It was a theme Shakespeare would revisit with Polonius's reaction to Ophelia's claim that Hamlet had made 'tenders' of 'affection' to her:

> *Polonius.* Affection? Pooh! You speak like a green girl,
> Unsifted in such perilous circumstance.
> Do you believe his tenders, as you call them?
> *Ophelia.* I do not know, my lord, what I should think,
> *Polonius.* Marry, I will teach you! Think yourself a baby
> That you have ta'en these tenders for true pay,
> Which are not sterling. Tender yourself more dearly,
> Or (not to crack the wind of the poor phrase,
> Running it thus) you'll tender me a fool. (*Hamlet*, 1.3.589–96)

There would have been fathers in the audience who would recognize the situation, some remembering their own domestic conflicts, some fearfully

---

10 Ripa's engraved allegorical emblem of 'Libidine' (Lust) shows a seated beautiful young girl, with luxuriant black hair. One hand rests on the head of a goat standing beside her (goats symbolize lust) and her raised right hand holds a scorpion. The zodiac sign of Scorpio is thought to represent sex and death – the alpha and omega of life.

anticipating the behaviour of their own daughter. Some would sympathize with Egeus, some might not. Some might feel that Egeus has been too lax in protecting his daughter. She has after all developed a detailed, close love situation with a young man about whom Egeus seems fully aware. Or has he only discovered this moments before he erupts onto the stage? The father has allowed the daughter too much freedom and is now facing a problem partly of his own making. Young people were closely supervised in those days, though they were just as devious in eluding watchful eyes as in any age. Servants were (as we see often in drama) useful messengers and easily bribed. But a close watch seems to have been absent in Hermia's case. Unmarried girls were kept at home much of the time and chaperoned when out in public. Where is Hermia's mother? No mention is made of her so we may assume she is dead. There seem to be no other female relatives or a nurse or governess. Helena too seems to have no parental support. Her father, 'old Nedar', is mentioned twice but makes no appearance. He too is perhaps dead or too old to be able to keep an eye on his child. Thus we have two young women of rank, beauty and presumably some wealth, at liberty to fall deeply in love. Many in the audience would be waiting to see what sort of honour the males display. Young men, especially those of gentry background, were not often inclined to conduct themselves with decorum, moderation or decency, particularly where young women were concerned, and neither Lysander nor Demetrius are shown to have any adult male monitoring their behaviour. In their favour it must be said that they do not appear to be sexually predatory, but the liberty all the young people have is a fertile ground for mistakes to be made and for drama to be developed.

Applying orthodox beliefs to the uncontrolled conduct of the lovers introduces a slightly different approach to the play. Instead of the carefree humour of a light-hearted comedy emerging out of the love tangles of bright young things, it suggests that the experiences in the woods are the 'fierce vexation' they deserve for their freethinking attitudes. They transgress, behave badly and are punished. Shakespeare would revisit this problem in *Measure for Measure* where Claudio faces execution for getting his girlfriend pregnant. Escorted through the streets to prison he meets his friend Lucio, who asks, 'Whence comes this restraint?' Claudio replies, 'From too much liberty, my Lucio' (1.2.116–17). There is an interesting pun here for 'restraint' refers most obviously to the fetters Claudio has, but references also the moral quality so prioritized in clerical and secular discourses on kingship and personal ethics. Moderation, temperance, self-control and restraint are all variants on the same concept. 'Nothing in excess' has already been discussed. The context of this is the church's concern at increasing immorality and its crusade to improve manners and expand the readiness of the law to punish fornication.

While sexual indulgence may not yet be a factor in *Dream*, the freedom these young people have had would most certainly be a matter of concern to some in the audience.

An audience might laugh at the discord between the lovers, delighting in the mistakes they make and the pacy, witty language of their rows, while disapproving of their lack of courtesy, their betrayals and intemperance of language. They might be seen as suitably punished for their various transgressions. Samuel Taylor Coleridge sees the 'ungrateful treachery in Helena' as a 'very natural' reflection of female moral laxness.[11] It is certainly a mark of her infatuation with Demetrius that she will so materially betray her childhood friend by revealing the elopement plan. Did she seriously believe it would so emphasize Hermia's alliance with Lysander that it would end Demetrius's interest in Egeus's daughter and trigger a return to loving her?

The artificial, but elegant rhyming verse in which Hermia and Lysander express their love and the standard obstacles to it (no comedy permits love to run smoothly – there is no drama in that) is nevertheless bubbling with scarcely suppressed passion. Their exchanges are typical of the balanced euphuism of comedy. Such witty alternation of ideas (called flyting in Shakespeare's time and stichomythia in modern criticism) can be made between friends (as with Mercutio and Romeo), but is a very common feature of love comedies and focus on the hero and heroine. The classic examples in Shakespeare are Berowne and Rosaline (*Love's Labours Lost*), Beatrice and Benedick (*Much Ado*), and Rosalind and Orlando (*As You Like It*).

The control and artificial neatness of the interchanges is at ironic odds with the uncontrolled, unpredictable messiness of real life and real love. It also contrasts with the mess they get into in the woods. How right Lysander is to declare, 'The course of true love never did run smooth' (1.1.133). He has no idea how rough its course will become when he takes the transgressive path to the woods.

In 23 lines Egeus succinctly expresses his state of mind, posits the conflict situation, describes Lysander's ploys to win his daughter (suggesting he has used magic, sent her poems, exchanged love tokens, serenaded her) and makes his demand for resolution – marriage to Demetrius or death. The speech instantly reverses the hopeful mood introduced by Theseus and instead of life-enhancing marriage (with offspring), unhappiness and possible death sour the atmosphere. Hermia's position, caught between her own instinctive, natural, animal attraction and her father's different choice of partner, neatly encapsulates the contemporary problem of the potential wrongfulness of a

---

11 *Coleridge's Shakespearian Criticism*, 1, 90.

non-consensual, forced, arranged marriage and the ever-present danger of a wrong choice made by an immature son or daughter. As previously asserted, it is the age-old problem of the conflict between the old and the young, the impulsive and wilful girl sure that she is in love and cannot live without her man, the old parent anxious she should not make a mistake, determined to enforce her obedience, perhaps sensing she is moving beyond his control. Here it is dramatically complicated because the father is proposing another mate and threatening death. The headstrong girl wishes her father 'look'd but with my eyes' and Theseus asserts the orthodox view: 'Rather your eyes must with his judgement look' (1.1.56–7). As we have seen in chapter 6 the custom of patriarchal choice overriding other considerations was under attack and slowly yielding to some degree of child input in the decision-making. Egeus has been thwarted already by Hermia's choice and will be fobbed off by Theseus's tactics in giving the girl 'time to pause' and consider her position. With the mix of mercy and calm moderation expected of a wise ruler, Theseus introduces a third way to resolve the conflict. In addition to the options of giving in to the paternal demand or facing death, he offers the possibility of her retreating into a convent. It is hardly an attractive option, but better than death. Egeus had not mentioned this, presumably hoping the possible death sentence would frighten the girl into accepting Demetrius. Theseus then tactfully (perhaps deviously) commands Egeus and Demetrius to accompany him to discuss some of the marriage arrangements and to confer 'of something nearly that concerns yourselves' (1.1.126). This and the four-day postponement of a decision until the next new moon looks like a trick to give the lovers time to hatch a plan.

Perhaps he foresees they might elope. Putting off his judicial decision until 'the sealing-day betwixt my love and me' (1.1.85) seems odd. It would sort ill with a wedding if Hermia chose to disobey her father and face death or the convent. If Theseus is not planning to try and dissuade Egeus and/or give the lovers a chance to run away, then he is being a weak leader, procrastinating over a difficult decision. In 4.1. when the lovers are discovered asleep in the woods, Egeus is still angry and now vengeful. Far from being relieved to find his daughter safe he bursts out against Lysander, 'I beg the law, the law upon his head!' (4.1.154). His priority concern is that Lysander has tried to defeat his consent. In fact it is Demetrius who thwarts Egeus's will by having returned to loving his previous sweetheart, thus undercutting Egeus's position. Theseus closes the matter with

> Egeus, I will overbear your will;
> For in the temple, by and by, with us,
> These couples shall eternally be knit. (4.1.178–80)

Events have overborn Egeus. Demetrius has withdrawn his candidacy as Hermia's husband. Like the traditional deus ex machina (the god in the machine) descending on a throne or in a chariot, to arbitrate a human difficulty, Theseus, as a literally down-to-earth mortal conflict manager and problem-solver, has cut through the complicated claims focused in the dispute about Hermia's marriage partner. He does this by exercising his right as absolute ruler to set aside a cruel law and a cruel father. Demetrius's new position in any case nullifies Egeus's will, though the father could still have technically and legally refused a marriage with Lysander. That would have been petty and vindictive, and Theseus's will fortunately predominates. In this he shows the fortitude to make a difficult executive decision. His action marks the return to normality, order and hierarchy. Before this though the lovers go through a world of unsettling changes.

Theseus provides a framework for the play structurally and ideologically. The piece begins in his court with his marriage anticipated and ends there with his union solemnized and the two pairs of courtly lovers happily joined. The two other strands – mechanicals and fairies – are there too, completing the social mix, making a happy unity that echoes the mood created by three marriages. Bottom and his crew perform their parody of a tragic love drama. That it proves comic in its inept acting reflects how life often derails the serious and ceremonious, making mockery of our pretensions. The mechanicals close the human story with a rustic dance as a rough blessing for future happiness. Dancing is a feature of weddings and is a traditional adjunct to the idea of hopefulness and new happiness beginning, a communal activity expressing the supposed unity of the family, guests and the village community.

Dancing symbolically represents harmony, but harmony that comes out of disharmony. A dance begins with everyone in their place, goes through a series of changes with all the moves interwoven and complicated, the starting order completely broken, yet ending with everyone back in their place and with or opposite their initial partner. Such is the nature of the fiction of comedy that it should be seen to display in its actions the mess and mistakes of life, but end with a restoration of order and happiness. In real life we know that neat resolution is rarely achieved, but in fiction we see it as reflecting our hope that life will work out happily. We know it is an artificial fabrication, but we accept its positive hopefulness.

Such are Puck's permutations that the situation in the wood at one point represents a mirror image reverse of how the characters were paired at the beginning. When order is restored the fairies close the whole proceedings by setting a charm of blessing on the newly paired couples. Most of the play is a progressively messier muddle that, though it appears to be resolved by Theseus meeting the lovers in the wood in the clarity of daylight, is actually sorted out by magic. The happy ending is made possible by reversing the effect of the love juice on Lysander's eyes so that he returns to his original love for Hermia and by leaving the magic on Demetrius's eyes so that he returns to his old love of Helena. It is a way of saying that good luck, a touch of magic, is what all unions need in order to succeed. The restoration of harmony is delightful, but the real attraction of the play, the source of immense amusement, is the muddle.

Chapter 12

'SWEET MOON': THE WOODS AND THE CONTEXT OF MAGIC

Pyramus. Sweet Moon, I thank thee for thy sunny beams;
I thank thee, Moon, for shining now so bright;
For by thy gracious, golden, glittering gleams,
I trust to take of truest Thisbe sight.

(5.1.261)

12.1 Moonlight and Madness

The absurdity of describing shafts of moonlight as sunny beams and the light itself as golden is in keeping with the confusions, reversals and mad misperceptions that are integral to the play's texture. Pyramus *will* see his truest Thisbe. He appears to be perhaps the only lover who sees accurately until we remember that this is only pretend, that Thisbe is actually a man playing a man playing a woman. But Pyramus too misperceives in seeing the blood-stained mantle as a sign Thisbe has been mauled to death by a lion. Nothing is what it seems and constantly changes like the content of a dream. And it is all illuminated by the eerie light of the moon that helps create the atmosphere of unreality and other-worldliness that fills the play and is a presiding symbol of the many changes portrayed. Its phases, its ability to bathe a scene with magic or with edgy mystery reflects the many changes or transformations threaded through the texture of the piece: Theseus and Hippolyta going from enemies to lovers to married couple, Egeus from rational to raging, Hermia from obedient to transgressive, Lysander from gentleman to abductor and would-be illicit husband, Demetrius from lover to jilter, Helena from friend to betrayer, both young women from upper-rank ladies to screeching cats, workmen to actors, fairy king and queen rowing indecorously, a changeling boy,

Puck's many shape-changing forms, Bottom turned ass-head, night to dawn, antipathetic lovers to harmonious couples. And the moon presides over all.

It would not be amiss to retitle the play A *Midsummer Night's Nightmare*, for, though matters in Athens are complicated and tense enough, the escape to the woods releases all manner of dark things and makes the entanglements even worse. The piece can be acted in two ways. The traditional approach has been to display it as a fast-moving, action-packed, farcical romp; a carnival of silliness; a light-hearted celebration of human foolishness, full of mistakes and misperceptions, nonsense and laughter, but turning out all right in the end, not to be taken seriously as it is only a playful entertainment. It may also be seen as a play where oppressiveness, manipulation, misplaced love, hatred and menace dominate and the inconstancy of the human heart is disturbingly exposed. Hermia escapes from Egeus's dictatorial threats only to find herself (and her complacent assumption of happiness to come in exile) at the mercy of forces she cannot control and does not understand. What happens in the woods is unsettling and represents the more frightening fears that lurk in the psyche and emerge in dreams. It is the woods that provoke the dream/ nightmare element.

To the Elizabethans woods and forests were places of ancient forces, connected with mystery, the spirit world, magic, evil and the misperceptions that can come in the dark. They also provided refuge for vagabonds, bandits, thieves hiding from the law and all sorts of other unsavoury characters. They provided fuel and food and a location for numerous rural customs mostly to do with happiness and celebration, with love/lust and with the pairing off of young people. The Greenwood, the Wild Wood, was a potent reality for most country-dwelling Englishmen, but its power penetrated the subconscious too through the many stories about fairies and sprites, ghosts and monsters that were associated with the forests and woods that were within easy reach of most rural villages and towns. The problem is deciding how much the threatening nature of the woods and its fairy denizens influence the mood of the play. To Jan Kott the shadows in *Dream* loom so large they overshadow happiness and stifle laughter. He brings a Freudian interpretation, laced with an Eastern European post-Nazi existential angst, to his essay 'Titania and the Ass's Head'.[1] He raises some stimulating and interesting points but goes too far.

Dream is suffused with magical/folkloric beliefs and descriptions of country life. Many of these relate to the activities of the fairies and especially the record of Puck's activities. There are multiple references to the moon, mentions of May Day, St Valentine's Day, animals (not all native to the British Isles),

---

1 Kott lets the idea of dark elements run away with his imagination. For a useful corrective, see Bevington's essay in A *Midsummer Night's Dream, New Casebook* series.

flowers, herbs, birds and the activities of the farming world. These are situated firmly within a rural framework such as surrounded the young Shakespeare. The countryside was not physically far away from Stratford. Shottery, where Ann Hathaway (his wife-to-be) lived and Wilmcote (where his mother, Mary Arden, had lived as a girl) were a walkable distance from his Henley Street birthplace. The nearness of the woods to Athens, 'a league without the town' (1.1.165), was similar for many towns.[2] Even Londoners only had to walk out through the city gates to be in a country setting and Waltham Forest (now called Epping Forest) was on the north-east edge of the city. The relatively tiny size of Stratford meant that the rural surroundings were easily accessed and the country came into town every market day. Anyway, the customs and beliefs of rural England were part of everyone's thinking and upbringing. Many at court had estates established in the shires and many in the audience were country-born like the writer. A huge array of superstitions, medical and weather lore and beliefs in fairies and elves was in the substrata of the audience's conscious and subconscious. So this is familiar terrain, though given a novel, funny and slightly frightening twist.

The moon is the presiding influence of the play. Like the sun, it had an important influence on human life. In astrological readings the ascendancy of the moon was taken into account. Its position always had a bearing on the horoscope cast. In its growing or waxing phase it was thought to affect the germination of seeds and increase the chances of fertility when putting a male animal to the female stock for breeding. The waning phase (the dark of the moon) was a time of passivity or low energy. Astrologers and farmers prioritized the moon's influence and some plants picked or planted by moonlight were thought to have greater potency. Moon is the sixteenth word in the text and is mentioned 21 times (as moonlight, moon, moonshine) from 1.1. to 3.2. It recedes once the dawn comes and the lovers' night of chaos and nightmare is over, but during the wedding celebrations it returns in a virtual form as Starveling's representation of Moonshine and is used another 21 times (including Puck's reference to 'the triple Hecate's team' 5.1.370, Hecate being a form of the moon goddess). Even the calm, commanding Theseus refers to the moon's passage as a measure of his impatient anticipation of his wedding, for a waning moon was not thought to be lucky for solemnizing marriages. He is impatient for a new moon, but his emotions are as nothing to that injected suddenly by the eruption onstage of Hermia, her father, her lover and his rival. In keeping with astrological beliefs, which would have been part of most of the audience's value system, existing illogically and often uneasily with their

---

2 A league is equivalent to three miles.

Christian ethics, the moon is the play's ascendant planet. Its long folkloric history of association with change, with chastity, with love and with lunacy and magic makes it the most appropriate symbol and image for a mad play about the vagaries of love.

As well as the word 'moon' and its variants creating, by repetition, a dominant verbal and imaginative pattern, this emphasis is reinforced by a variety of references to the forms by which the moon's presiding deity was known – Phoebe, Lucina, Hecate and Diana are all mentioned. Like so many classical deities the moon goddess has different names and sometimes opposing characteristics. In the heavens she was Luna or Lucina, on earth Diana and in the underworld Hecate or Proserpina. Diana, the virgin huntress and presiding divinity of chastity, was also, paradoxically, related to fertility and childbirth. Roaming the woodlands wild she is accompanied by a train of nymphs, her handmaidens. In this respect she is like Titania. There is another similarity from Greek myth. Actaeon, discovering Diana bathing, is punished for seeing her nakedness by being turned into a stag and being hunted by his own dogs. Bottom's transformation is less dangerous. Being turned into an ass-headed man is appropriate, for in some respects, despite his harmlessness and good nature, he is an ass. The ass was a symbol of stupidity and sexuality.

The latter aspect is minimalized by Shakespeare, reduced to some cuddling by a somewhat aroused and amorous Titania accompanied perhaps by some lewd facial expressions made by Bottom to the audience. The trouble-making flower, Love-in-Idleness, also has a doubleness; once white and pure, it is metamorphosed to being purple with lust. Its antidote, the plant Artemisia, references Diana in her chaste emanation. Artemis was the Greek goddess of chastity, the parallel to the Roman goddess Diana. The power of purity over lust (or its preference at least) is encapsulated in Oberon's accompanying spell as he releases Titania from her enchantment:

Dian's bud oe'r Cupid's flower
Hath such force and blessed power. (4.1.72–3)

This represents a return to balance, to normality after the volatilities of infatuation, the spell of love and the mad things it makes people do and say. The interchangeability of these deities reflects the vacillating state of everything and everyone in the play. Women particularly were thought much influenced by the moon. Their monthly cycle, their unpredictable mood swings seemed to corroborate that.

There are resonances attached to the idea of love-in-idleness. Medieval and Renaissance moralists regarded idleness (Sloth, the deadly sin) as a force tempting people toward love liaisons. The idea that the Devil makes work for idle hands applied to those who had nothing to do and so involved themselves in casual seductions. Many an idle gentleman, in real life and onstage, passed his time in flirtations and affairs. It is difficult to conceive today that in Tudor times there were large numbers of people in society who simply did not work because they had land, money, title and rank, and did not need to earn a living. In the late seventeenth century Gregory King claimed there were 16,586 families in this aristo-gentry category.[3] Each of these families might have a son or two or more, plus idle daughters. The court and City were filled with such so-called gentlemen, idling around and getting into a variety of mischiefs that make Puck look like an angelic exemplar of good conduct. But the connection of love and idleness goes back to Ovid. In *Remedia Amoris* (Love's remedy) he asserts, 'Otia tollas, periere Cupidinis arcus' (Take leisure away and Cupid's bow loses its power). In other words, if you keep busy, you have no time for love (or lust). Hermia and her companions are, of course, idle, rich, young gentry. Other cures offered by Ovid are trying to stop loving before it becomes too important (too late for the lovers in the play), contemplating the negative aspects of the other person (this emerges in the arguments in the woods) and having other affairs. For the purposes of the moral context of *Dream*, the level of emotional entanglement of the Hermia/Lysander and Helena/Demetrius relationships is an example of love pushed to extremes and across the boundary of restraint. By becoming excessive, the feelings expressed put the lovers into the danger zone of sin. Lysander is shown attempting (though unaware) to cure his love of Hermia by switching his affections to Helena and expressing his feelings in equally extreme language. Demetrius is cured of his fascination with Hermia by a return to loving Helena. But both actions are achieved under the influence of the flower and not as exercises of personal willpower. In the influential medieval allegory of love, *Le Roman de la Rose*, Idleness is the gatekeeper of the garden where Love resides. In John Lyly's influential romance *Euphues* (1578), the author asserts that 'idleness is the onely nourse [nurse] and nourisher of sensual appetite'. In the equally influential *The Faerie Queene* (1590), Edmund Spenser calls idleness the 'nourse of sin' and says it leads the pageant of the vices.[4] Contemporaries would agree that having little to do did encourage people into vice and that only those who lived according to reason were truly civilized and human. The others were closer to the animal world.

The magic flower is picked by moonlight and it was a common belief that natural medicines had most efficacy if picked then, an efficacy inevitably

3 Perkin, 20.
4 The Ovid, Lyly and Spenser references appear in Paul Olson's 'A *Midsummer Night's Dream* and the Meaning of Court Marriage', *English Literary History*, 1957.

connected to magic properties by association with the moon. Charms and spells too were thought to be more powerful and likely to succeed if cast in moonlight. The moon had many superstitions associated with it. Lunatics were thought to be particularly unstable and reactive during the full moon phase. It was a dominant mood maker for romantic meetings and was traditionally addressed and emblematized in poetry. Its changing appearance became a symbol for the vicissitudes of life and the inconstancy of women. In the famous balcony scene in *Romeo and Juliet*, the newly enamoured hero vows his love by the moon as it shines on them. Juliet interrupts with the warning

> O, swear not by the moon, the inconstant moon,
> That monthly changes in her circled orb,
> Lest that thy love prove likewise variable. (2.2.109–11)

Theseus's comments likening the lunatic to the lover and poet focus on the effects of imagination in distorting or creating perception (or misperception). The moon and the imagination combined make a powerful and dangerous mix. The imagination, making something out of nothing, is particularly excited by the effects of moonlight. Love can be triggered by the romantic glow of the moon, but it can be strained to breaking by the negative working of the imagination. Theseus shows he has understood the events in the woods when he concludes his meditation

> in the night, imagining some fear,
> How easy is a bush supposed a bear! (5.1.21–2)

The effects of light and shade in a wood at night play tricks as the audience has seen. Love too distorts accurate perception and 'sees Helen's beauty in a brow of Egypt' (5.1.11). A similar view is expressed by Helena:

> Things base and vile, holding no quantity,
> Love can transpose to form and dignity (1.1.232–3)

From the beginning of the play love is represented as affecting how the characters think and see. Helena is as beautiful as Hermia:

> But what of that? Demetrius thinks not so;
> He will not know what all but he do know (1.1.228–9)

The problem is complicated by the use of the word 'love'. It is all too easily used without precision and as an easy catch-all term. Physical attraction alone, out-and-out lust, passing fancy, temporary sympathy, affection, friendship and needful loneliness can all be called love by those in whom emotion has taken over and reason retired defeated.

In setting the most exciting action in the woods, releasing chaos and misunderstanding, Shakespeare is injecting an antipastoral element into the mood of the play.[5] These woods are not the sweet sylvan glades of a pastoral romance, where idyllic lives are led in harmony with each other and nature. These woods are not an idealized state where all is good and no one intends harm. Pastoral was an artificial courtly literary construct to please urban and court-based aristo-gentry figures who knew nothing of the hardships of country life, but liked the idea that it was a relaxing vernal idyll of simplicity far removed from the unreal rituals and hypocrisies of politics in the prince's court. The woods of *Dream* are the woods of an ancient, pagan time. In Neolithic Britain most of the country was covered by dense forest, but the New Stone Age saw the beginning of a long, accelerating process of clearance in order to provide new land for farming. By the time the Romans arrived half of Britain had lost its woodland. By 1086 Domesday Book recorded that tree cover had seriously declined. This was a relative assessment for vast swathes still presented unpassable and sometimes dangerous forest. Outlaws made it necessary for travellers to group together and arm themselves to traverse the woodlands. Ballads, fairy tales and other story forms tell repeatedly of strange meetings located in the forests. Some are based on repeated retellings and gradual transformations of travellers' stories of encounters with ghostly hounds, headless horsemen, ogres, wood spirits, witches and wizards. Many are remains of beliefs in pagan vegetation deities. The Celtic inhabitants of ancient Britain believed, as did the Greeks and Romans, that all nature had a spirit essence in it. This anthropomorphism required a placatory prayer to the spirit of every tree when you cut it down and a prayer for permission to every stream you crossed. Every grove, every outcrop of rocks, every cave had its genius loci, its spirit of the place. Innumerable rituals (like those of Midsummer Eve) were designed to appease the crop deities that guarded your orchards or cornfields. Ploughing, planting, growing and harvesting all required devotional acts dedicated to the Earth Mother if success was to follow. Most of the population of England until 1851 was living in the country and working on the land, and a bad harvest meant famine and famine meant death.[6] Just as the balance between urban and rural population was slowly changing, so too was that between arable farmland and woodland. Both supported large

---

5 Pastoral was a literary form that used the countryside as its location. It was a romanticized and idealized genre (poetic, dramatic and in prose) designed to appeal to metropolitan-based, court-centred readers longing, or thinking they longed, for a quiet time in a rural setting. It included love stories and visions of the simple life.

6 The 1851 Census revealed that 51 per cent of UK inhabitants lived in towns and cities. The process of urban living was increasing in Shakespeare's time, but 80–85 per cent were still country dwellers.

numbers of crafts and livelihoods and both were situated within a complex of festivals and beliefs both pagan and Christian. The religious year was packed with dates when the communal life and its connection with the land were celebrated. Intermixed were vestiges of pagan superstitions. A key nature figure is the Green Man, sometimes called Green George or Jack in the Green. Carved versions of this vegetation spirit are found in a number of churches, indicating how the pagan became assimilated into the Christian. The conclusion to the medieval romance *Gawayne and the Green Knight* suggests the defeat of pagan savagery by Christian virtue. Other emanations of this nature force are to be found in songs about John Barleycorn, and stories of Puck or Robin Goodfellow and Robin Hood. Robin Hood alone spawned a whole literature of songs, poems and stories. Arthurian romances also use forest locations for various types of incident. The wild man or man of the woods was a stock character in pageants and folk plays in the Renaissance period. This figure, an emblem of our savage prehistoric self, became conflated with the Green Man, who continued to be venerated through medieval times, despite church opposition. In book 6, canto 4 of *The Faerie Queene*, Spenser introduces a 'Salvage Man', a wild man of the woods (a *wodwo*). Bremo in *Mucedorus*, a 1598 romance drama, is nominated 'a wild man' in the cast list. He lives in the woods, is brutal and captures the heroine with the intention of forcing her to be his bride. Puck has something of the wild woodland spirit. Shakespeare was to create another mischievous spirit in Ariel (*The Tempest*), who can be seen as the benign corollary of the savage Caliban's evil. In Puck, similar in many ways to Ariel, he has created a fairy spirit with some hints of a wood and agriculture deity, who, though quite definitely a servant of the king of the fairies, acts independently at times. Any malevolent hobgoblin characteristics have been discarded to leave a playful prankster who is given the role of closing the piece. Jan Kott opens his chapter on the play with an out-of-date definition:

> Puck has simply been one of the names for the devil. His name was invoked to frighten women and children together with the ogre and the incubus.[7]

Reginald Scot had already (1584) pointed out that the diabolic connections of Puck had been diminished from what they had been earlier. The malice had been turned into devilment, which is only reckless mischief. Kott is unable to detach the 'devilish origin' from the character, and fails to see

---

7 Kott, *Shakespeare Our Contemporary*, 171

that the aim of the Devil was not to thwart farmers' wives making cheese or mislead benighted travellers, but to lure people into sin and set them on the road to perdition. The Devil was an altogether more terrifying and danger-ous idea than a fairy japester. The fairy who meets Puck at the beginning of act 2 identifies him as 'that shrewd and knavish sprite' Robin Goodfellow. The Arden editor asserts that in Middle English 'the Shrew' meant the Devil, but that the meaning was weakening into 'mischievous'. It could also simply mean 'astute' so that the epithet defines Puck as clever and vulgarly naughty. Shakespeare has diminished the wickedness of the fairies (Puck included), making them more like naughty children, spiteful and full of tricks, but not malign. In medieval times belief in fairies was a strong feature in folklore, but in the Elizabethan period it had diminished considerably though had not disappeared entirely. In sophisticated circles it was an amusing example of past superstition and rustic simplicity and useful as a comic device in writing. Owen Davies puts it thus:

> In England there are numerous accounts from both early modern and modern periods of people claiming they had taken part in nocturnal fairy revels […] English meetings with the fairies […] were usually con-ducted corporally and not spiritually. Yet while the notion of fairy frater-nising was certainly a vibrant aspect of English popular *belief*, it was not integrated into the world of popular magic as elsewhere. Whereas in Ireland the problem of fairy-inspired illness and fairy changelings con-tinued until the last century, In England it had largely disappeared by the mid sixteenth century.[8]

The common belief that fairies stole human children and often substituted a fairy child for the mortal one is transformed in *Dream* to a changeling boy adopted by Titania when one of her priestesses, the boy's mother, dies. What had traditionally been an act of mischief and malice has become one of loving-kindness. Owen Davies claims literacy wrought the change in attitude to fairy lore:

> There is certainly strong evidence to confirm that literacy was more widespread in Protestant regions during the early modern period. In this sense, the cautious growth if literacy did not banish the fairy but rather reduced the potency of fairy power.[9]

8 Davies, *Popular Magic: Cunning-folk in English History*, 182–3.
9 Davies, 184.

This did not stop James I referring to 'these kinde of spirites that are called vulgarlie the Fayrie'.[10] He later makes the conflation of Diana, the woodland huntress goddess and emanation of the moon, and a leader of the fairies, a version of Titania.[11] He goes on to describe,

> There was a King and Queene of *Phairie*, of such a jolly court & train as they had, how they had a teynd, & dutie, as it were, of all goods: how they naturallie rode and went, eate and drank, and did all other actiones like natural men and women.[12]

This sounds very much like the presentation of Titania and Oberon. James I wrote *Demonologie* while still living in Scotland and it has the context of what Davies identified as a vestigial feature of the Celtic areas (that is, Wales, Ireland and Scotland) 'where fairy lore remained an established strand of belief well into the nineteenth century'.[13] Puck too has been 'sanitized' and agrees with the fairy's definition of him, but puts a slightly more positive gloss on himself as a 'merry wanderer of the night'. From here onwards Puck becomes a 'merry director' of the play, inciting chaos, but always seeing it as a good jest.

Another inaccurate perceiver. When exhausted and unhappy Helena cannot take any more wandering in the wood and lies down to sleep (which she does instantly), he comments,

> Cupid is a knavish lad
> Thus to make poor females mad (3.2.40–1).

Love has certainly destabilized Helena's rational judgement, as it does the other lovers, but Puck has made the situation worse and has the nerve to accuse Cupid alone. It is significant that he uses the adjective 'knavish' that was applied to him. Like those who enjoy playing practical jokes, he does not blame himself at all and does not think of the victims. Yet it is clear from act 2 onwards, when the magic elements enter the action, that Shakespeare is not condemning the activities of Oberon and Puck. They may be questionable as to their advisability and taste, but are not evil in intent. Oberon's trick on Titania is vindictive, as lovers can be when rowing, but ends as soon as he gets his way. But his planned trick on Demetrius is aimed at doing Helena a

10 *Demonologie*, 57
11 'That fourth kinde of spirites, which by the Gentiles [that is, pre-Christian pagans] was called Diana, and her wandering court, and amongst vs was called the *Phairie*' (*Demonologie*, 73).
12 *Demonologie*, 74.
13 Davies, 184.

good turn. The tricks and mistakes represent the inherent tendency of mortal plans to go awry and the mess to be attributed to gremlins. Mistaken perceptions and opportunities missed (by moments only or by misunderstandings) are essential and traditional in comedy.

Shakespeare's intentions are obvious in the role he gives the fairies at the close of the piece. While Oberon and Titania (in harmony once again) cast their all-important hymeneal good luck charm on the futures of the newly married mortals, Puck is given the role of appealing to the audience for their approbation as a good luck blessing on the actors. These positive actions suggest that the writer does not want the fairy figures seen in a negative light. They are not to be linked to the diabolic witchcraft aspect of magic. They suggest that there are black aspects to life, that the subconscious harbours unsettling nightmarish fears and repressed desires, that actions can have unintended consequences, but after the world is turned upside down in the central acts and the lovers (and the audience) get a glimpse of how fragile their happiness is, all is returned to normal and life begins again after those who were 'full of hateful fantasies' have been tormented and cleansed through suffering 'the fierce vexation' of the 'dream'.

12.2 The Ambiguous Status of Magic

John Bainbridge, a London physician, was also an enthusiastic astronomer and mathematician. In the predawn dark of 28 November 1618 he peered through his telescope, charted the path of a comet, recorded its appearance, calculated speed and altitude, then wrote his findings and conclusions in a book. Oddly, among the scientific data, algebraic equations, verse and flattering dedication to the king, Bainbridge claimed the trajectory between New Guinea and the Arctic, crossing Britain, was a sign that God would reveal to his chosen English race the long-sought location of the north-west passage to the Indies.[14] This bizarre mix of scientific method and belief in revelation highlights the uneasy coexistence in the seventeenth century of the growing body of natural philosophy (the name then for the sciences) with religious superstition and the vestiges of magic. It also indicates the indeterminate terrains a doctor inhabited as part-magician, part-scientist in a godly society. The blurred boundaries between magic and science are evident too in Isaac Newton's dabbling in alchemy while also authoring the severely rational and methodical *Philosophiae Naturalis Principia Mathematica* (The mathematical principles of natural philosophy). In 1687, when Newton published his work,

14 See Bunker, *Making Haste from Babylon*, 18–19.

magic's status was still unclear. The same blurred status of magic had existed at the time *Dream* was written.

The church disapproved of magic strongly yet it was a continuing part of general life. Surviving from pagan times into post-Reformation England, magic persisted in its hold on the popular imagination and in affecting many practical activities. Superstition is an innate constituent of the human psyche – a way of explaining or at least dealing with the inexplicable, an instinctive attempt to annex good luck to our side. You never know, it might just work. Religion was beginning to be dismissed by some as institutionalized superstition and the church itself was undecided doctrinally whether witches and ghosts could be authenticated and officially believed in or not. Both were thought of as evil emanations linked to diabolism. Exodus 22:18 asserted, 'Thou shalt not suffer a witch to live'. The majority of ordinary people believed in religion *and* magic and witches. So too did the higher ranks, visiting high-end, high-profile, high-price 'wizards' and astrologers like John Dee, Simon Forman and William Lilly. The village wise woman or cunning man persisted into the nineteenth century, exercising white magic, much of it herbal and medicinal, based on centuries-old country lore, some efficacious, much superstitious nonsense, but satisfying people's beliefs in and need to believe in the predictability of the future and the effectiveness of charms, amulets and talismans related to preserving good health (yours, your family's and animals'), finding lost items, discovering who would marry you or making someone fall in love with you.[15] Along with spells and predictions about personal luck were charms to outdo or harm rivals in business or love. These activities edge dangerously close to black magic and witchcraft or wizardry. That often depended on whether the goal of the magic was good or harmful and whether the local climate was vehemently anti-magic. That in turn would depend on the zeal of the vicar and the attitudes of neighbours. Localities that were strongly Puritan were more likely to be obsessively alert to signs of magic activity. The story of the Salem witch trials, though set in Massachusetts, is a prime example of how accusations of witchcraft could be symptoms of revenge in isolated communities where there were grievances about landholding, personal relationships, inheritance, boundary demarcation and any of the many niggling squabbles that break out between neighbours.[16]

Among the various words for men with power over the forces of the world – magician, conjuror, charmer, wizard, necromancer, sorcerer – the last two carry occult implications. A necromancer learned of future events by communing with or calling up the spirits of the dead – an act in itself that was interpreted

---

15 'Cunning' is a corruption of 'conning' [knowing] suggesting they had knowledge beyond the normal.
16 See Frances Hill, *A Delusion of Satan: The Full Story of the Salem Witch Trials.*

by some as occult. The name 'sorcerer', derived from Old French *sorcier/sorcière* (wizard/witch), implied the use of black arts and therefore devilish activities. Whatever title you used, you could be subject to accusations of witchcraft depending on the climate of the time. Outbreaks of witchcraft accusations rose if the local vicar or the diocesan authorities were active and if the register of communal fear was high, with anxieties about epidemics (among humans or animals), extreme weather, the activities of Catholics. All were thought to originate in the malign activities of witches. Prejudice in the locality was often stoked by the vicar if he was personally vehement against witchcraft, but individual laypeople might also be activated against a specific old man or woman who practised the cunning arts and was thought responsible for illness among animals or bad luck in the family. People are always quick to point the finger of blame at others and not too fussy about evidence, logic or proper cause and effect. There were intermittent outbreaks of zeal against such shadowy characters as the cunning folk. The clerical and legal authorities were particularly active in prosecuting theft magic. The spell to discover who had stolen your goods was often found to accuse innocent people and opened the question whether the accusation was motivated by malice, vindictiveness, profit or just incompetence. But, depending on the current local climate, anyone divining the future or performing treasure magic, lost magic or love magic might be unlucky enough to be taken up as dealing in black arts, tried and burned. The flower Oberon gives to Puck to affect love skirts dangerously close to witchcraft.[17] Unusual birth deformities ('the blots of Nature's hand' 5.1.395) could provoke a charge that the unfortunate mother had had dealings with the Devil. Oberon's blessing at the end of the play wishes the married couples should have children free of 'mark prodigious' like moles, hare lips or scars. Such blemishes could be taken as marks that the Devil owned the child. Renaissance man was still pretty primitive in his thinking. The presence in a locality of anyone claiming they could identify witches tended to produce a spike in accusations. These would dwindle once he left the area. This seems to be due to (a) the general suggestibility of people (if you tell them there is witchcraft in the village they will soon find a culprit), and (b) specific factors in the region (existing tensions in religion, commerce, farming, landholding, personal rivalries). Particular regions seemed to be more prone to 'discovering' witchcraft. Scotland had more trials and burnings than England. The Holy Roman Empire (largely Catholic) was subject to periodic witch hysteria and mass trials while England was largely free of such extreme outbursts.[18]

---

17 Of witches and love magic James I says, 'They can make men or women to loue or hate each other, which may be verie possible to the Deuil to effectuate' (*Demonologie*, 45).

18 Oldridge, *The Devil in Tudor and Stuart England*, 162.

Fanatical Protestant demonologists made no distinction between white and black magic, associating all magical practices with diabolism. Despite the official stance on all forms of magic, ranging from suspicion and disapproval to drastic punishment, plays seemed a permitted medium for its portrayal, sometimes for didactic condemnation (as in *Faustus*), sometimes as a vehicle of satirical comment on the corruption and follies of society (as in *The Devil Is an Ass*, 1616 and *The Witch of Edmonton*, 1621) or more commonly just for its comic possibilities (producing mayhem and mistakes) and its visual sensationalism (as in *Friar Bacon and Friar Bungay*, 1598?). Representing onstage the mistakes or spectacular effects magic could generate was a way of saying this is the dangerous chaos released if you dabble in magic.

The magic in *Dream* is riotously humorous in its effects and no one is ultimately hurt. The sufferings of Hermia and Helena are nullified by amnesia, for what they can remember is taken for a dream only. Titania too seems unaffected by the 'visions' she had, and in her waking state loathes the ass-headed monster hybrid. The play inhabits a strange no-man's-land between the fleshly world of men and the airy world of spirits. It is suffused with an atmosphere of magic, enchantment, tricks, illusions and fairy music, and yet is embedded in Christian values. The mad, inexplicable enchantment of love at first sight is there in the Titania-Bottom storyline, a symbol of the sometimes unusual pairings manufactured by the capriciousness of the human heart. The magic in no way endorses diabolism. It is for fun only and is harmless – in the end – for under its spell some nasty emotions are released. It is part of the spellbinding effect of theatre, illusion masquerading as reality and, sometimes comically, sometimes chillingly and potentially tragically, reflecting the actions and outcomes of real life. Puck describes the other aspect of magic: those 'damned spirits' who must 'for aye consort with black-brow'd night'. They are explicitly allied to evil for 'they wilfully themselves exil'd from light' (3.2.382, 387, 386). Oberon corroborates this, distancing his court from evil, when he claims 'we are spirits of another sort' (3.3.388) and allies himself with the light (that is, good): 'I with the Morning's love have oft made sport'. Given that Midsummer Eve and Midsummer Day, like many of the year's festivals, were a sometimes uneasy mix of pagan ritual, Christian annexation and superstitious folklore, an audience would have some anticipation of what to expect, and Shakespeare keeps on the safe side of the law by making it clear the fairies are not purveyors of malefic magic.

What magic does the play display? There is the natural enchantment that turned Theseus and Hippolyta from enemies to lovers, and the chemistry that drew Hermia and Lysander together. Helena and Demetrius were similarly spellbound with each other, but then Demetrius experienced a reverse that changed his affections. If this reverse is not motivated by mercenary/property motives, then his change of heart represents, perhaps, the inconsistency of our feelings whereby one day we suddenly experience a loss of love for one person and a shift to loving another. Put another way, it demonstrates how emotion and appetite (that is, unrestrained passions) exercise a spell over reason. Feelings can take us over – sometimes for the good but often for the bad. And feelings of love act like a spell and take away conscious control of what we do. Apart from the human magic, the love chemistry, there is the artificially applied 'interference' by Puck and Oberon that affects the mortals by realigning their pairings. Puck not only applies and misapplies the love juice, but he also thickens the darkness and imitates the voices of the male lovers to mislead them. His invisibility and his making of the dark darker are attributes of the Devil according to James I.[19] He induces sleep so that he can apply the antidote to Lysander and return him to his original love of Hermia. He is able also to lead the frightened mechanicals 'through bog, through bush, through brake, through briar' (3.1.102), while adding to their fear by appearing as a horse, a hound, a pig, a headless bear or a fire. These are the sorts of appearances that travellers claimed to have seen when travelling alone at night. They are the sorts of imaginings that many drunken men claimed to have seen, but they also remind us how in the dark familiar objects can take on frightening other shapes, through imagination and physical misperception – combining the mental aberration with a physical failure of our eyes to see accurately. This pushes us into the world of childhood's nightmares, but speaks also of a world where such apparitions were believed to be real, to be the work of the Devil or goblins. The lovers, apart from fallings out and misunderstandings, are subjected to dispersal and distraction, being misled around the woods, getting separated and lost. As Puck draws them all back to the same spot, each unaware the others are there, the stage manager of their mishaps induces sleep. Hermia's last words before her nightmare ends, depict the physical discomfort she has experienced:

Never so weary, never so in woe,
Bedabbled with the dew, and torn with briars,
I can no further crawl, no further go;
My legs can keep no pace with my desires.
Here will I rest me till the break of day, [Lies down.]
Heavens shield Lysander, if they mean a fray! [Sleeps.] (4.2.442–7)

19 'If the deuil may forme what kinde of impressions he pleases in the air, why may he not far easilier thicken & obscure the air, that is next about them by contracting it strait together, that the beames of any other mans eyes, cannot pearce thorow the same, to see them?' (Demonologie, 39).

It is touching that after all the upset she has experienced, rejected by her lover and her friend, she still thinks of Lysander's safety. Similar physical discomforts are meted out by Ariel in *The Tempest*. Physical discomforts symbolize how precarious is our control of our life and how easily we are destabilized. If physical discomfort can so break us, how much more vulnerable is our emotional stability. It is a staple of comedy that human pretension, complacency and dignity should be degraded and mocked physically as well as verbally and ideologically. Underlying comedy, just as it does tragedy, there are images of man's fragility and folly. The pinnacle of God's creation is vulnerable mentally and physically, easily destabilized from his assumed supremacy of spirit and bodily control.

The most serious, critical and questionable magic is transforming Bottom's head to that of an ass. His appearance is a shock that might make an Elizabethan audience laugh but feel unsettled too, for this looks like the work of the Devil. Puck also reports his common tricks: neighing like a young female horse to attract and mislead a sexually excitable stallion, becoming a crab apple to bob against a gobby woman's mouth as she drinks and so make her spill the drink, appearing as a stool that disappears when the wise aunt (self-satisfied and full of advice) goes to sit down. These are trivial japes, common slapstick, as are the reports of the fairy about Puck frightening village girls, making the milk fail to clot into cheese, preventing the beer from fermenting, leading astray night-time travellers. These traditional attributes of Robin Goodfellow and other assorted goblins and fairies are remembered perhaps from tales of Shakespeare's childhood, but again are petty and harmless. The tricks he plays on the lovers do not necessitate any onstage sleight of hand conjuring by the actor, but can create amusement if performed with good timing by the victims. These tricks are done at the behest of his master, but left to the improvisatory inventiveness of Puck, as is the decision to give Bottom the ass's head rather than any other creature. An ass does not figure among the animals Oberon imagines Titania falling for, but Puck's invention is much funnier, more suitable and at the same time much more horrific. The ounce, cat, leopard, bear or boar the king imagines are at least all natural, but the species mix of man and ass has shock value. It is grotesque and echoes mythological hybrid monsters and the grotesque story of Pasiphae and the bull and more recent reports of monstrous birth defects.[20] Puck sees it as appropriate for the strangeness of a blunt and vulgar weaver playing the

---

20 Sensationalist pamphlets reporting unusual birth defects were popular. In February 1606 the pamphlet *Strange News from Carlstadt* reported a blood-like sun, a woman bearing three children – one a blackamoor, one like death, the third with four heads – each speaking bizarre prophecies (Harrison, *Jacobean Journal*, 280).

part of a courtly lover (as Pyramus) to be mirrored by such a man becoming a half-ass. To some, Bottom would appear a metaphorical ass and they would immediately think of the iconography of Renaissance satirical engravings that used the image usually as an anticlerical attack on those who were fools but thought much of themselves.[21] Jonson refers to this in *Volpone* ('Acted in the yeere 1605 by the K. Maiesties servants') when Mosca remarks,

> Hood an ass with reverend purple,
> So you can hide his two ambitious ears,
> And he shall pass for a cathedral doctor. (1.2.112–14)

In *The Tempest* the ousted Duke of Milan, who has made himself a magician of great power, claims much more serious magic achievements:

> I have bedimm'd
> The noontide sun, call'd forth the mutinous winds,
> And 'twixt the green sea and the azur'd vault
> Set roaring war; to the dread rattling thunder
> Have I given fire, and rifted Jove's stout oak
> With his own bolt; the strong-bas'd promontory
> Have I made shake, and by the spurs pluck'd up
> The pine and cedar: graves at my command
> Have wak'd their sleepers, op'd, and let them forth
> By my so potent Art. (5.1.41–50)

These illusions all relate to command of the elements, except for the necromantic calling up of the dead. This is the most morally questionable magic, closest to black magic – divining the future by contact with the dead – and is a form of spiritualism. Raising the dead, even if they did not then return to normal living, is blasphemously near to imitating Christ – but to no apparent good or ill. This was not like calling Lazarus back to life. Titania and Oberon's rift affects the elements, though they do not appear to initiate such reversals of normality other than by being the union that, if harmonious, makes nature work as it should, but which, being dissonant, causes upsets. They are faulty as rulers in that, being aware that they have caused nature to behave abnormally, they do nothing to immediately restabilize nature. It is their duty to do so and they should not put personal problems before the restoration of smooth running in the world. Apart from calling down fog or making the night darker

---

21 Hans Holbein engraved a doctor of divinity with large ass's ears as an illustration to Erasmus' satire *Praise of Folly*. The ears connote those who appear wise, present themselves as such, but are in fact fools and cannot hide it.

Puck does not appear to have control of nature, but can create temporary impressions or illusions of things. The really potent magic is that of the juice of the flower that makes people fall for whatever living thing they first see after its application. This ties to the widespread belief in natural magic related to the effects of flowers and herbs and other natural remedies. It is significant that the flower is called Love-in-Idleness (the wild pansy) for it suggests that the love that has sprung up between the two pairs of mortals may be the result of being wealthy and privileged and having nothing to do. Such a state often leads to casual liaisons, especially in the court.

The experiences in the woods will test how genuine and strong the feelings expressed actually are. It does this by a reverse symmetry; the love relationships of act 1 are turned around so that instead of Helena being alone and unloved, it is Hermia. The whole is a mirror image with two different isolated, rejected characters. This is simply resolved by reversing Lysander's artificially induced love for Helena back to Hermia. Leaving Demetrius under the influence of the magic flower enables the neat pairing of all four back in the alliances they had prior to the play.

A final type of magic at play is the enchantment of drama itself. If love is an artificial feeling, entrancing and enchanting us, masking what is in reality an animal urge for mating (developing, with luck, into a supportive, caring relationship), so too a play is an artificial construct that tricks audiences into spending two hours plus watching pretended actions and listening to words purportedly meant to be genuine spoken by unreal people being played by real people pretending to be them. And laughing at them and being concerned that their misadventures should end and end happily. If it holds us in its charm that is a spell of some potency.

Shakespeare was not concerned to create a credible magician in Puck. The magic of the flower is a laughably simple, fairy-tale trick that makes us laugh by its daring, bare-faced effrontery. The nerve of Shakespeare expecting us to believe it. The absurdity of the flower's effects is sufficient to create a simple, useful and flexible device, complicating the alliances between the lovers, like the steps of a dance, before all is put right and the happy ending is wheeled on with its obligatory blessings and good wishes for the married life of the couples. When harmony has been restored the couples are reunited with a community tradition of which the next stage is the birth of children and family life. Attempting to logically analyse credibility, motive and character is out of place. None of the characters is deeply conceived as a psychologically consistent entity. They are simple stereotypes to be manipulated for the purposes of laughter and instruction. The play touches on some serious issues, but is not a comprehensive exploration of them. We are supposed to accept what Puck has done in the past and what he does in the play, without looking too closely into it. The audience would have accepted that such magic was possible and be too lost in the fiction of the illusions of the play to dwell on such questions. They would also have been fascinated to know the outcome. This is inherent in the telling of any story. 'What is going to happen next?' and 'Where will it lead?' are more impelling than logically dissecting everything minutely to see if it holds together and is convincing.

Magic and religion are central to the atmosphere of the piece. Magic is essential to most of its action developing and religion central to its ethical framework, which is why Oberon asserts the essential goodness of these 'spirits of another sort'. Neither he nor Puck performs the sort of sorcery involving devils that Friar Bacon does in Robert Greene's play *Friar Bacon and Friar Bungay* (performed c. 1590–1). Bacon transports two characters through space. This is achieved by simple theatre means (they exit one scene and reappear onstage at a location meant to be elsewhere). The first event involves Bacon (in Oxford) striking dumb Bungay (in Suffolk) so that he cannot marry the hero and heroine, then '*Enter a* devil, *and carry off* Bungay *on his back*' (2.3.; italics in original). The stage direction does not have the devil appear through the trap as was normal practice, but as he carries Bungay on his back perhaps it was easier for a simple stage-level entrance and a piggyback exit through one of the doors at the back. The second act of transportation occurs when a German magician, who challenges Bacon to a contest of skill, calls up the spirit of Hercules and is then, at Bacon's command, carried away to Hapsburg by the spirit. Stage business becomes more spectacular when Bungay, safely delivered to Oxford, conjures the tree of the Hesperides '*with the Dragon shooting fire*'.

These props might be kept in the inner room and the curtain drawn back to reveal them. The spirit of Hercules when summoned could use the trapdoor to rise from the underworld. But the danger of magic is addressed when Bacon is persuaded to renounce his art by what may be seen as a warning from God. He has made a huge bronze head that will speak. Giving life to an inanimate object is an act of blasphemy. In appropriating the prerogative of the Divine, Bacon transgresses unacceptably the boundaries of nature. The head speaks three times gnomically: 'Time is […] Time was […] Time is past'. Then '*a lightning flasheth forth, and a hand appears that breaketh down the* Head *with a hammer*' (4.1.; italics in original). This is dramatic and could be frightening if realized effectively. The hammer represents retribution, God's vengeance. Bacon predicts bad luck is coming. Two scholars ask him to show them their fathers back home. In his 'prospective glass' (crystal ball) they describe seeing the two men fight and kill each other. The sons then argue about who was to blame and they stab each other too. This convinces Bacon his skills are dangerous and he breaks the glass. He fears damnation for 'using devils to countervail his God' (4.3.98), regrets 'the hours I have spent in pyromantic spells/[...] papers full of necromantic charms,/Conjuring and adjuring devils and fiends [...]' (4.3.88–91) and 'wresting of the holy name of God' (4.3.93). But he seeks forgiveness:

> Sins have their salves, repentance can do much:
> Think Mercy sits where Justice holds her seat,
> And from those wounds those bloody Jews did pierce,
> Which by thy magic of did bleed afresh,
> From thence for thee the dew of mercy drops,
> To wash the wrath of high Jehovah's ire,
> And make thee as a new-born babe from sin. (4.3.157)

Bacon admits,

> I have dived into hell,
> And sought the darkest palaces of fiends;
> That with my magic spells great Belcephon
> Hath left his lodge and kneeled at my cell;
> The rafters of the earth rent from the poles,
> And three-formed Luna hid her silver looks,
> Trembling upon her concave continent,
> When Bacon read upon his magic book. (4.1.8–13)

Spectacular effects would not be needed in *Dream*. The transformation of Bottom during the moonlit rehearsal is accomplished simply. As Bottom/ Pyramus he exits to 'the wings' (or through one of the entrances to the stage), Puck follows him and offstage Bottom puts on the ass head, tucking the base under his shirt and doublet, and re-enters. Hey, presto! The transformation is accomplished.

Is magic itself suspect? Leading Puritan William Perkins, for whom all magic was diabolic, would condemn Puck and all the fairy band. The church certainly saw all attempts by humans to claim or affect harnessing more than human powers as dangerous, possibly diabolic, probably heretical, definitely to be discouraged. Divination (using supernatural means to ascertain the future), selling magic talismans, casting love spells, writing spells on paper notes worn in a pouch hung about the neck, making love potions and making astrological predictions all came under the heading magic, but were less seriously opposed by the church than the summoning of devils, selling your soul to Satan, demonic possession, putting pins into wax effigies to affect people from a distance, causing disease and death or calling up the dead. These were satanic works. The church was unhappy with both white and black magic, but intermittently more tolerant of white magic. This explains the uneasy and sometimes punitive reaction to scientific advance; it often looked magical, diabolic or like trespassing into God's domain. The church was desperately trying to consolidate its hold on England's faith. It was besieged, by those Catholics who never gave up their religion and wanted to restore papal power in England, by the inertia of those who did not much conform to any religion devoutly but tended to cling on to semi-superstitious vestiges of old pagan lore, and by the general reluctance of even Protestant believers to give up belief in magic. In 1584 it was claimed, 'Three parts at least of the people' remained 'wedded to their old superstition still'.[22] Black and white magic were delicate matters at this time. All occult or diabolic dealings were punishable by death. Astrological predicting and all those forms of 'magic' relating to medical, amatory, monetary needs and a host of personal matters were open to suspicion, however benign they might be. For the purposes of theatre the make-believe display of magic was acceptable, but the whole subject was controversial. The representation of spirits, elves and fairies was part of many comedies. The Devil, goblins and demons were brought on stage, but it had to be made clear that they were condemned doctrinally and represented evil, which is why Shakespeare is at pains to emphasize Oberon and the rest are not diabolic creatures. The supernatural in general conflicted with church doctrine and with the growing knowledge of science. Magic was in decline, but eradicating the superstition attached to it was very slow.

The Church of England had officially banished all papistical superstitious beliefs – in the miraculous powers of saints' statues or the thousands of relics held in churches and cathedrals all over the country at the time of the Reformation. Holy shrines like those at Canterbury and Walsingham were destroyed. Holy wells and other sacred places like springs and grottoes were prohibited (though secretly still visited). Non-Christian superstitions were regarded as dangerous, as were all beliefs deviating from prescribed orthodoxy. In 1600 the Italian intellectual Giordano Bruno, who had met with Dr John Dee's circle during a stay in England, was burnt by the Catholic Church for various heresies, including interest in the occult and questioning church doctrine about the Trinity, Christ and the Incarnation, whether Jesus was Christ, whether Mary was a virgin, whether bread and wine turned to Christ's flesh and blood during communion. Satanic allegiance was a handy label to put on anyone who raised awkward questions about doctrinal inconsistencies. The English Church was just as intolerant of intellectual freedom of thought.

22 Cited in Thomas, 84.

The good (that is, white) magician was, like the good prince, expected to be an example, expected to aim at the bettering of people. He should cleanse himself of appetites and passions: those 'disturbances experienced by [...] intemperate souls [...] afflicted [...] by the stupor of ignorance, and [...] by the turmoil caused by their blind and perverse desires'.[23] The magic in *Dream* may be seen as representing the random and unpredictable way matters work in life, the obstacles to plans, the minute mistimings or mechanical breakdowns that wreck the smooth running of our projects. Though supposedly educated and cultivated sons and daughters of privilege, the lovers display what Baldassare Castiglione had warned about and are intemperate even before the challenges of the woods. Hermia displays anger against her father, Lysander against Demetrius, Demetrius against Lysander. Helena too is excessive in her fixation on Demetrius and betrays the confidence of her friend. All will be punished. Not excessively, for this is a comedy, but they will be put through a period of torment, a form of shock treatment, testing and cleansing them.

There would be sceptics who saw the minor magic done as merely part of the fiction and spectacle of theatre. They had seen actors as devils (and other supernatural effects) in *Faustus*, which had been performed by the Admiral's Men in 1594. In *Macbeth* (1606) they would 'see' witches, the goddess Hecate, ghosts and speaking oracles. It was all part of the fiction, illusion and fun of plays. Sometimes witchcraft was shown as evil and leading to the damnation of a soul, but often it was playful hokum, unbelievable nonsense and therefore not a danger. In books of merry tales the Devil was often portrayed as a foolish, gullible figure easily hoodwinked by clever humans. The evil evident in *Dream* comes from humans, though it is kept minimal. The runaway lovers do not end as Romeo and Juliet do. Though the play is designed as entertainment it is not without its didactic elements, but they are lightly presented, faults lightly punished and entanglements easily resolved. Though produced to look like magic the woodland scenes were the sort of comic episodes found traditionally in commedia dell'arte and other populist drama. This early form of comedy, coming from Italy in the sixteenth century, presented short improvised sketches or scenes with masked actors playing stock characters like the angry father, a foolish old man, devious servants, lovers, the braggart soldier, doctor and drunken clowns. Though there were a number of common basic storylines involving adultery, love and jealousy, with sex, cheating and trickery as staple features of the plots, the custom of introducing improvisation allowed the set stories to be adapted and updated with topical satirical political or personal references. Song and dance were integral components and though most of the

---

23 Castiglione, 300.

scenari were comic some incorporated more serious plot strands. The I Gelosi troupe, formed in Milan in 1569 by Flamineo Scala, toured Europe and helped spread the form to England. In 1611, he published 50 scenarios and roles in Italian. This is too late for Elizabethan-Jacobean writers to have pillaged them for stories and ideas, which suggests strongly that a troupe visited England at some time during the period, triggering copying of subject and style by the various types of playing companies.[24] There are records of sixteenth-century tours. However, so many elements appear in English plays and then in court masques that some direct viewing of an Italian company performing must have taken place or returning tourists recounted pieces they had seen abroad.

Accumulatively the onstage illusion of illusions reminds us of the essential fictional nature of all stage representation. It is mimetic – not reality but an imitation of it. The magic also serves to remind us that sometimes it takes luck, magic, leaps of faith or unexpected acts of forgiving and forgetting to solve the otherwise irresolvable. In some respects too, the magician is like God or a king: he can make things happen that otherwise would not. In *Dream* the maze of love needs Puck's mischievous magic to make all come right and then Theseus's firmness to enforce it. *The* achievement of the play, the *real* magic, is the pleasure of seeing the desperate entanglements the lovers get themselves into while the audience knows (or suspects) no lasting harm will come to them. It is the magic of laughter evoked in the audience as they watch to see if the lovers emerge from their test better – chastened and enlightened.

James I was unsympathetic to the discussions of how the wonders of science were colonizing much that had once been considered supernatural. Elizabeth had been happy for the astrologer and astronomer John Dee to predict the best day for her coronation and to teach her sea captains navigational skills using the stars and maps. Telescopes and microscopes opened up a world beyond sight, but the dark psychic corners opened up by belief in black magic, remind us that most men were still primitive in their thinking. James I was wholly unsympathetic to witchcraft and before he became king of England had published his book on the subject (*Demonologie*, 1597). It combatively announced in its preface,

The fearefull aboundinge at this time in this countrie, of these detestable slaves of the Devill, the Witches or enchanters, hath moved me (beloved reader) to dispatch in post, this following treatise of mine, not in any way (as I protest) to serve for a shew of my learning and ingine, but onely (mooved of conscience) to preasse thereby, so farre as I can, to

24 The view of Chambers, 1, 494.

resolve the doubting harts of many; both that such assaultes of Sathan are most certainly practiced, and that the instrumentes thereof, merits most severely to be punished: against the damnable opinions of two principally in our age, whereof the one called SCOT an Englishman, is not ashamed in publike print to deny, that ther can be such a thing as Witch-craft: and so mainteines the old error of the Sadducees, in denying of spirits. The other called WIERUS, a German Phisition, sets out a publick apologie for all these crafts-folks, wherby, procuring for their impunitie, he plainely bewrayes himselfe to have bene one of that profession.[25]

It was written to counter Reginald Scot's *The Discovery of Witchcraft* (1584) that attempted to persuade readers that witchcraft was a hoax, that most instances of so-called witchcraft were illusion, conjuring, mistaken perception, ignorant prejudice, criminal scams or hoaxes staged by Catholics to destabilize society.[26] Puck's illusions are clearly distinct from the diabolic evil of the witches in *Macbeth* or Sycorax in *The Tempest*. While black magic was prohibited and could be punished severely when discovered, many apparently 'natural magic' spells, potions, salves and other remedies were shown to be the outcome of scientifically explicable processes though manufactured and administered with the ritual mumbo jumbo of age-old white magic. Though intellectuals and scientists were beginning to develop rational, chemical, biological and physiological explanations of supposed magic they still faced a highly critical conservative opposition backed by the immense power of the Roman and Anglican Churches.

12.3 John Dee

Ben Jonson's play *The Alchemist* (performed October 1610) focuses its satire on the greed and gullibility of men, but also targets the long-held belief of alchemy that base metals could be turned into gold by means of the *lapis philosophorum* (the philosopher's stone). "Tis said that Jonson had his hint of the Alchemist from Dr. John Dee'.[27] Dee was a high-profile celebrity. An internationally renowned scholar and astronomer, astrological and navigational consultant to Elizabeth I and supporter of imperial ventures into the

25 *Demonologie*, xi.
26 Scot refers to the 'the illusion and knaverie of Robin good-fellow' being once believed
    in as strongly 'as hags and witches be now' (bk. 7, chap. 2). See Arden edition (1979),
    Appendix I, sec. 6.
27 Harrison, *Second Jacobean Journal*, 227.

Americas, he would be charged with necromancy under James I, after living most of his adult life under the shadow of rumours of wizardry. Shakespeare would certainly have known of him and may have used him as a model on which to loosely base his main character in *The Tempest*. Though folk tales are full of stories of wizards, real life had its practitioners too. The fantasy of a man with more than natural power, able to control the elements, able to marshal spirits and manipulate people is potent.[28] It would have been intensely attractive to Elizabethans considering the sea and land storms, floods, bad harvests and eclipses that litter the weather calendar of the 1590s. Titania's description of the appalling weather and its effects, resulting from her conflict with Oberon, would have triggered memories of such events, though most would have considered they were punishments sent by God rather than the results of a row in fairyland. Few ordinary people could have explained the meteorological causes of such happenings. Extreme magic is not shown in *Dream*, though presumably Oberon could perform such feats had he needed to. Christians regarded hurricanes, floods, earthquakes, eclipses and storms as signs of God's anger and as part of his secret plans. Astrologers predicting weather events by reading the stars and planet positions, were regarded as little different from astronomers who predicted eclipses, comets and astral events. Both inhabited a suspect terrain between God and the Devil. The church denounced the impiety of predictive divination as distracting people from seeing divine providence at work in all things.

Foretelling the future by reading the alignment of stars and planets (called judicial astrology) was regarded as occult and heretical. Yet it is certain that a number of the first-night audience would have resorted to astrologists. All sorts of subliminal angst reverberate in *Dream*, echoing the complex and ambiguous coexistence of inner pagan beliefs in woodland spirits, belief in the authenticity of magic and the outer world of Christian faith and support for the Anglican Church. What was just about tolerated was natural astrology that dealt with medical problems and meteorological astrology that predicted the weather. Both were suspect but accepted as part of natural sciences, using the forces and cross-connections existing in nature. From the cunning woman in the village to the queen's physicians at court much medical knowledge and practice rested on herbal and other natural remedies handed down the ages and semi-mystical correspondences like believing the stomach was the organ influencing courage and the liver ruling love, that certain foodstuffs affected certain organs, that dandelion petals increased one's martial ferocity.

---

28 See *Friar Bacon and Friar Bungay*, *Faustus*, *The Merry Devil of Edmonton*.

Where the unacceptable boundary was crossed was when the Devil, malign intentions to cause death, anti-Christian ritual and the pursuit of power became involved.

John Dee (1527–1608/1609) was a highly skilled mathematician and astronomer who knew Tycho Brahe and was conversant with Copernican theories (though not a heliocentrist).[29] Such was his knowledge of these fields he became a mentor/trainer of numerous navigators and a committed supporter of England's colonial expansion. His studies and obsession with gaining knowledge and discovering the intricate truths of the universe would eventually, like Faustus, take him across the dangerous border between science and magic, and into astrology and occultism. He often faced charges of divination. Though he acquitted himself successfully these constant accusations show how fine was the line between science and prejudice and indicate the precariousness and unpredictability of such borderline studies. Like Newton he was drawn to alchemical experiments and dabbled in predicting the future, especially by means of scrying (looking into a glass). This was thought very close to occult magic.

Aged 15 he entered St John's College, Cambridge. Graduating in 1544 he lectured in Greek studies and was made a fellow of the newly founded Trinity College in 1546. He created the stage effects for a performance of Aristophanes's comedy *Peace*, the most spectacular of which was a beetle-shaped machine or chariot that flew up to the heavens carrying a man. At this time stage machinery was rare and simple. Though the deus ex machina device, lowering a god from 'the heavens' to earth, had been used in classical theatre and, along with the stage-floor trapdoor, would become a standard feature in the London public theatres from the 1570s, in mid-century they would appear to be the results of magic. Dee's stage effects gained him a reputation for extranatural powers that would stay with him for the rest of his life. His arrest for casting horoscopes for the princesses Mary and Elizabeth led to a treason charge investigated in Star Chamber (yet he was later allowed to predict the best day for Elizabeth's coronation). Acquitted he began building a career and reputation as a scholar and adviser to the Crown especially on matters astronomical related to voyages of discovery. In *General and Rare Memorials Pertayning to the Perfect Arte of Navigation* (1577) Dee formulated a justification for colonial claims in the New World that became the guiding light of imperial expansion. Then, like Faustus, becoming discontented with his status and the limits of earthly knowledge, he turned to wilder supernatural ventures, including alchemy, reading the

---

29 Internationally renowned Danish astronomer and alchemist.

future and seeking to talk to angels through a crystal-gazing scryer.[30] He also began to make fantastic, invented assertions about England's claim to America predating that of Spain. Like most people of the time, though more notoriously, Dee lived in two worlds – the day-to-day world of Christian faith and that of the semi-magical, semi-scientific. Along with his practical skills in navigation and mathematics he pursued alchemy, astrology and the Hermetic philosophy that had got Marsilio Ficino and Giordano Bruno into trouble in Italy.[31] For Dee mathematics, navigation, astronomy, astrology, alchemy and speaking to angels were all part of an exploration to discover the 'pure verities' of the universe, the unifying spirit and the divine harmony with which God suffused creation and made everything part of everything else. At a time when much magical belief was metamorphosing into science his explorations often brought him into conflict with the authorities and with ordinary folk afraid of the rumours of his occultism and of the sometimes magical appearance of scientific phenomena. He died in 1604 shortly after petitioning James I for protection and planning to exile himself in Germany. His scholasticism had drawn him into the political elite and he mixed with William Cecil, Francis Walsingham, the Earl of Leicester, Sir Philip Sidney and the Privy Councillor Sir Christopher Hatton. His notoriety and the magic elements in *Dream* and other plays indicate the general interest in matters supernatural and the persistence of superstition.

How Puck and the fairies were costumed is not known. They would certainly not wear the flimsy, diaphanous costumes of Victorian imagining, but might have clothing coloured in various shades of green. This was traditionally thought to be the colour for fairy folk, linking them with the Green Man of pagan folklore. Whether the music accompanying their songs was played under the stage or backstage to create the effect of it being magically, eerily disembodied, we do not know. Such devices were practised and Shakespeare was to use them in *The Tempest*. It is also possible that Puck or any of the fairies might be wired up in a harness so as to 'fly' in. Such devices were being used more and more, especially for court performances. Nicholas Rowe's stage directions, 'Enter a fairy at one door, and Puck at another', are standard, but not necessarily how Puck did enter originally. He might have come up through the trapdoor or simply through one of two doors the Elizabethan open-air theatre had on either side at the back of the thrust stage. If the

30 A man called Kelly who claimed he could scry, that is, foretell the future through a crystal ball.
31 A form of mystic belief recently resurrected by Florentine intellectuals, combining the early philosophy of Plotinus and the even earlier mysticism of Hermes Trismegistus and the Jewish Kabbalah.

first performance was designed for a private house with a large refectory-style dining hall, such locations had screens masking the in and out doors for servants to bring in food and take out dirty plates. These would provide a similar entry possibility. The minstrel gallery above the servants' doors to the kitchens would provide a location for rigging up a flying wire. Rowe's directions were added in 1709 and do not preclude the use of a wire thus set up. Either way, the sudden appearance of these two supernatural creatures is unexpected. The recognizable world of the court has suddenly changed totally and the audience's mindset is propelled into a woodland world that is at once familiar and unfamiliar. It is unlikely that there would have been scenery representing the brakes, briars and trees of a wood. The language has to create the landscape, the darkness, the mood. For an indoor, private performance candelabra might be used to light the theatre and the stage. Their partial removal could be manipulated to create light/shade effects for the moonlit wood at midnight. Costume would help evoke the air of oddness if the fairies (and there would be two trains of them, each accompanying either the king or the queen) were quaintly dressed. They might all wear green or have green make-up. Some of the entourage might be the smallest of the boy players, for Puck talks of how Titania and Oberon's rows frighten 'all their elves' sufficiently for them to 'creep into acorn-cups' (2.1.32).

Old beliefs and new come face to face in *Dream*. Theseus represents the new humanist world of rationalism and protective paternalism, Puck the dark, pagan cults largely banned but not entirely banished from Europe. That the one has not completely expunged the other is evident in the combination of Theseus and Oberon's blessings at the close of the play. Some intellectuals, like Bruno and Henricus Cornelius Agrippa, were beginning to explore magic, superstitious and supernatural beliefs in a rational and scientific way.[32] It was a precarious line of study with the church on guard at every point to identify heresy and punish. Like the image of Dr Frankenstein, the mad scientist, Dee was drawn to push his studies further and further. For all his claims of serious scholarly research into unusual phenomena and the scientific bases for the workings of the world and nature, he often ran up against the church authorities for crossing boundaries into the occult and the frankly cranky.[33] Delving into the knowledge of God's designs and the workings of his creation was trespassing into prohibited territory.

---

32 Henricus Cornelius Agrippa. His *De Occulta Philosophia* (On occult knowledge, 1531) influenced Dee's thinking.
33 Though he defended his researches as non-occult and simply seeking to understand the Divine, he did get into some unusual areas, like his attempts to speak to angels.

Chapter 13

LITERARY CONTEXT

13.1 Genre

Indisputably *Dream* is a comedy. The problem is defining what sort of comedy it is – light or black? Is it mere froth and frolic, a mad mixture of courtly love, clownish buffoonery, charming fairies and the humorous mistakes and mischief Puck causes with his magic? Or is it all those things with a much darker edge always niggling at our consciousness? It can be played both ways. Traditionally it has been seen as the most delightful of Shakespeare's comedies, full of fun, nonsense, no more serious than a pantomime or farce – or a dream. It is commonly the first Shakespeare play schoolchildren study and is a popular choice for school productions. But, it is also a serious piece, grouped with *Much Ado, As You Like It* and *Twelfth Night* as mature comedies because they were written in a period when Shakespeare's artistry had matured both as to thought and stagecraft. It is one of the romantic comedies, what Dover Wilson called happy comedies, for, despite all the obstacles to love that make the plots fascinating and convoluted, the endings are happy and they largely exude a happy mood.[1] To William Hazlitt it was an 'ideal' play, and its realm was 'the regions of fancy'. To him, Bottom was 'the most romantic of mechanics'.[2] To a limited degree, Bottom's aspirations and dreams (not the one he has in the woods) are not what are to be expected of a simple weaver. There is something of the artist in him, creative, imaginative, with visions above his station (or out of it at least). He knows something of the drama, of 'Ercles' vein', imagines himself an actor, but has a bluffly realistic approach to stage effects that expose his limitations.[3] *Dream* has elements of pastoral fancy,

---

1 *Shakespeare's Happy Comedies*, 1962.
2 *The Examiner*, 21 January 1816.
3 His parody of 'a tyrant's vein' (2.1.36) is linked by Harold Brooks (Arden edition, 21) to Huanebango's ranting in George Peele's *Old Wive's Tale*, a play that similarly mixes genre types.

almost masque-like, with courtly characters with Greek names, a multiplicity of pastoral references, a woodland setting and love as its central theme and narrative impulse. Yet, despite the woodland setting, it is a strangely unpastoral play. The mechanicals supply the part of rustic clowns, but come from the city, and the fairies are a grotesque, sometimes conceivably threatening, version of the gods and goddesses who disport themselves in pastoral romances, whether in prose or dramatic form. In the romantic period (late eighteenth and early nineteenth centuries) darker interpretations were also being explicated in contrast to Hazlitt's sentimental view. Henry Fuseli's paintings and engravings of the play appeared in the 1780s and 1790s. He was drawn specifically to the Titania/Bottom theme and at the edges of these works, in the shadows, are some disturbingly ugly and evil-looking creatures, expressive of nightmare.[4] Even the fairies have unsettlingly overbright eyes and rictus smiles, like grinning gargoyle masks. This view of the play is given at its most extreme in Jan Kott's recent treatment. The 'amour' of Titania and Bottom becomes for him a suggestion of bestial sex, an echo of the man turned ass in Apuleius's *The Golden Ass* having sex with a depraved and phallus-obsessed patrician woman. Certainly Apuleius's work was well known enough to be a mental link some in the audience would have made. For Kott it is 'the most erotic of Shakespeare's plays', but that depends on how an auditor interprets Titania's lines. Looked at from Kott's point of view, stroking Bottom's 'fair large ears' becomes an act of arousing the male organ and caressing his 'amiable cheeks' a piece of foreplay. The post-Freudian approach will see sexuality and hidden motivations underlying everything and the title, with its use of the word 'dream' opens up a huge field of surreal, subconscious possibilities. The erotic interpretation breaks down when Bottom asks Peaseblossom to scratch his head and the queen readily accepts Bottom's desire to sleep and winds him in her arms. This makes the caressing of his ears into a piece of maternal tenderness, grotesque visually, but with an innocent gentleness about it. This is Titania cradling the child she does not have, but seems to want. The intended inexplicitness of drama a lot of the time, its ambiguity, means that the area between the actor's interpretation and the suggested innuendoes he might imply and how the audience understands it is ambiguous in the extreme. Anything becomes possible. The point that Shakespeare would avoid being too direct, too vulgar, too indelicate, with a private, aristocratic audience, is countered by the submission that Elizabethan drama was often exceptionally direct in its sexual references, that the age could be healthily direct about sex and that the imagination often inadvertently betrays ideas

---

4 See Tate Gallery's catalogue to the 1975 exhibition of Henry Fuseli, pp. 21, 60, 61, 62. His oil painting *Cobweb* (1785) has misshapen, ugly fairies.

and images without realizing their deeper significance. The imagination, like the mind freed of inhibitions by alcohol or drugs or dreams, is not embarrassed at expressing its more lewd interests. Whether we interpret the play as a black comedy or a light-hearted farce, *Dream* makes us laugh. It may be a hybrid of comic subgenres, but it is undeniably full of fun.

13.2 The Text Alone

Taken without its contexts the play is still comprehensible linguistically and still works theatrically. It works as a comedy of multiple situations and increasing confusion. It is the story of two pairs of lovers whose involvement with each other is both amusingly interchangeable and, to the audience, comically stressful. They are like any small group of teenagers or 20-year-olds who know each other well and spend much time together, falling out, making up, falling in and out of love with each other. Each new alliance is passionately felt and passionately expressed and oh-so-true and forever, until the transfer of affection to another, when the process of declaration begins over. There are recognizable tensions, grievances, rivalries and the inevitable changing round of partners. Their language is mannered and often highly structured, but in a style that Elizabethans already knew from the works of John Lyly with their witty stichomythic exchanges between entangled courtly lovers. Stichomythia is the quick repartee – sometimes abusive – between two characters arguing or discussing, with balanced alternating views delivered first by one speaker then by the other in a string of statements and replies. Often they will be lovers engaged in what Beatrice calls 'a sort of merry war' (*Much Ado*). Their speech is elegant, full of classical allusions, as signifiers of their educated and elevated status. Shakespeare adds to the courtly language and subjects of Lyly, typically mixing in vulgar characters whose demotic extends the lexical range and offers a different sort of liveliness full of slang, homely wit, lewd jokes and topical references. Bottom and Co. speak like men on the streets of London, but their rough style, though it seems at odds with the refined syntax of Hermia and her friends, was something Elizabethan playgoers were used to. Bottom works as a comic character without any context – he works as just a boastful blabbermouth, a larger-than-life figure, full of himself, never at a loss as to what to say, a bit irritating and overwhelming but ultimately not evil.

However, the contexts of the play add a new dimension. The narrative is comprehensible without them, but they add a more meaningful layer to the atmosphere of the piece. The moral framework in which the views and conduct of all the characters are set relates to the contemporary religious and ethical matrices within which all life was judged. It seems unlikely that any audience of the time, whether public or private, could watch the play without being aware of the transgressions committed onstage. Admittedly they are not as serious or sustained as in a history play or tragedy, but they are there. The excesses of Theseus are over before the play begins, but those of Egeus, the lovers, Bottom, Puck and the fairy monarchs create the plot and provide an ethical ambience that would lead the audience of the time to judge the characters even while laughing at their predicaments. Apart from the duke and Hippolyta every character offends Christian values and cultured behaviour. These values are not overwhelmingly dominant, are not heavily emphasized, but they do underscore what people say and do. The action is workable as an evoker of laughter, but the deviations from proper conduct give the instructive strand that was, in those days, thought necessary to all literature. Sin and man's endless capacity for folly provide the material for both tragedy and comedy. The Seven Deadly Sins are paraded throughout *Dream*, though not in the flood we find in the problem plays or major tragedies. However, being a comedy, excess is displayed from the moment Egeus enters until the overacting of the 'Pyramus' play. Punishment for losing rational balance is a standard feature of comedies, and unusual as this play is, with its dominating supernatural element, it too mocks behaviour that goes too far.

13.3 *A Midsummer Night's Dream* in Shakespeare's Oeuvre

Though commonly listed along with Shakespeare's mature comedies (*As You Like It, Much Ado, Twelfth Night*), for pace, narrative intricacy and an out-of-control madness, the play that *Dream* most resembles is *The Comedy of Errors*. It has a death threat hanging over it from the opening scene, has a central group of lovers (twin brothers and two sisters), is full of mistaken identity moments and their comic consequences, is about love, has a magic element (with Dr Pinch, the conjuror and exorcist), and moves at great speed, whirling into complexity and misunderstandings that become manic and look irresolvable. It too is a story of mayhem and fun, with no one hurt. *Love's Labours Lost* has contrasts between courtly types and clownish buffoons, but the key common feature that all the comedies share is the focus on the ravages of love's madness, what Robert Burton calls 'Love's Tyranny'.[5] The multipairing of lovers is a device Shakespeare uses elsewhere. *The Taming of the Shrew* has Petruchio/Kate, Lucentio/Bianca, and Hortensio/the Widow. *The Merchant of Venice* has Bassanio/Portia, Gratiano/Nerissa, and Lorenzo/Jessica. *Much Ado* has Benedick/Beatrice and Claudio/Hero. *As You Like It* has Orlando/Rosalind, Celia/Oliver, Silvius/Phebe, and Touchestone/Audrey.

---

5 The title of part 3, subsection 2 of *The Anatomy of Melancholy*.

Twelfth Night has Orsino/Viola, Sebastian/Olivia, and Sir Toby/Maria. In *The Two Gentlemen of Verona* there are two pairs of lovers, with one of the males switching his affections to his friend's beloved. The subsidiary pairs are contrasted with the central pair, so that a range of different attitudes to love can be explored, but here the pairs are interchanged and the pairings swapped to add to the comic complications of the plot and requiring a further stage of resolution to undo the interchange and restore Jack to Jill by the end.

Like all the comedies, questions of identity are raised. Mistaken identity where one person masquerades as someone else or is mistaken for another person, does not overtly occur. Bottom and the mechanicals make the apparent identity change involved in playing a part in a play, but it is uncertainty about self-identity (which plays a part in the other plays in the genre) that is integral to the woodland madness. This relates to the varied transformations or metamorphoses that take place. Even if these are only temporary, the matter of a night's fierce and vexing dreamlike state, they affect the mood and narrative, arouse amusement and release disturbing and destabilizing anxieties about just what love is and how we know the genuine from the false. As in the other comedies, any tendency toward evil and the possibility of evil triumphing is diverted and good appears to succeed. This is focused particularly in the multiple marriage ending, reinforcing the belief that love, when true, should lead to marriage and the hope of happiness ever after. The fairy blessings on the marriages with which the performance ends is the ritualistic, supernatural seal expressing the hope that luck or magic will indeed bring security, safety and happiness to the unions.

Though *Dream* comprises many of the features common to comedies in general and Shakespeare's in particular, the play has unique characteristics. The social mix in the final act, with courtly characters and commoners filling the stage, is unusual. By and large the comedies close with a resolution of the entanglements of the better sort (through marriage or the possibility of it). Here the high-profile presence of the mechanicals reminds an elite audience (both the fictional one and the real one) that they are part of a whole that includes others besides themselves. It is a political coalition. This apparent social harmony is only partial. While the loyalty and love of Bottom and Co. is undoubted, it is only really accepted by Theseus and then not without some belittling of the attempts of ordinary workmen at acting. The lovers remain somewhat sneering, unable to see that the 'Pyramus' play parodies their own overinflated expressions of their understanding of love as an emotion and their perception of the nature of their own loves. The other, more dominant unique feature is the degree to which the fairy element contributes to the narrative and the meaning. The fairies take over the narrative from 2.1., and are present through to the closing lines. Apart from the brief, farcical appearance of Dr Pinch, the conjuror in *The Comedy of Errors*, prior to *Dream*, magic, as expressed through characters like Puck, Oberon, Titania, and the tricks played by its means has no presence in any of the comedies. It appears later in its malign aspect in *Macbeth* and in Shakespeare's last solo-authored play *The Tempest*. The fairy element is part of the enduring attraction of the play and it is Puck and Oberon's playing with reality, manipulating the humans as if they were puppets, that forms a large part of the comedy.

13.4 The Literature of the Time

There is nothing quite like *Dream* in the literature of the time though there are some common features. It is a strange mix of other types of contemporary plays and has similarities to others of Shakespeare's comedies yet is at the same time unique in his oeuvre. While it contains many small elements that can be traced to other works by him and his contemporaries, none of these is sufficiently dominant to prove a major shaping influence. The idea of characters having the sensation that they have been in a dream, that their experiences while seeming real were in fact fantasy, is encountered in medieval vision poems like *Pearl* or William Langland's *Piers the Ploughman*. These have very much more religious and moral allegory integral to their content than *Dream*, but they do suggest that truth or truths can be revealed through dreams. The dream motif is present in some early Elizabethan comedies.

Elizabethan audiences would have drawn didactic lessons too from what they see in the play. These would largely be related to the conduct of the mortals and their deviations from religious and ethical norms. It is, however, an unusual play to an extreme degree. It starts looking like a typical court love entanglement story with A in love with B, B in love with C, C in love with D, D in love with C and C and D deciding to elope. The mechanicals introduced in 1.2. represent the usual low comedy light relief, the clown input, that is common in drama throughout the period. When we learn that the commoners are to congregate at midnight in the woods to rehearse (an unlikely enough plan), it looks as if the comedy might develop out of their meeting with the lovers in the dark and the subsequent misunderstandings the different groups experience. But then in act 2 the whole atmosphere changes and the audience is shocked by the injection of a supernatural scenario with fairies who have their own personal problems but interfere in the human plot in a very material way. Medieval popular, informal dramas had introduced mischievous devils occasionally. These were the sorts of short pieces performed at fairs or in inn yards, intent largely on entertaining the public, not necessarily to instruct them. They tended to take very human themes from everyday life – corrupt priests, cuckolds and promiscuous wives, miserly husbands, choleric fathers, romantic lovers, braggart soldiers. The more formal mystery cycles incorporated the Devil as part of a didactic experience, particularly those episodes that concern the fall of Lucifer and man's disobedience and fall. The mummers' plays or folk plays have some magic elements, with dragons, magicians, quack doctors and potions that revivify fallen knights.[6] Tudor interludes tend to have characters with allegorical or character-specific names: Honour, Reason, Good Fame, Virtuous Life, Pierce Pickpurse, Nichol Newfangle, Justice, Conscience, Manipulus, Haphazard, Subservus. Goblins, fairies and demons do appear in some of the early romantic comedies of the time. Most of these types of mixed genre, shifting between comedy and near tragedy, are no longer extant and are known only by their titles. But two texts of this type do still exist – *Mucedorus* (written some time in the 1590s) and *The Old Wives' Tale* (printed 1595). *Mucedorus* does not have fairies but does have a wild bear, a wild man of the woods and a typically convoluted romance plot. The lack of similar pieces alone makes *Dream* a fairly unusual play, a survivor that combines romance with folklore and magic. George Peele's *The Old Wives' Tale* offers some parallels too. This 'pleasant conceited Comedie' was 'played by the Queenes Maiesties players' probably some time after 1589, so either a stage production seen or the 1595 printed text may have had some influence on Shakespeare. The Queen's Players or Queen's Men was a company formed at Elizabeth's command in 1583, lasting until 1595. Its chief comic actor was Richard Tarlton, squint-eyed and flat-nosed, famous for his loose, wide, baggy breeches, his jigs and comic squibs (short sketches). He wrote for the company as well as acted and his mad mixtures of farce and slapstick made the company popular. Its most famous tragedian was Edward Alleyn who performed as Christopher Marlowe's towering heroes Tamburlaine and Faustus. The former may well be the sort of part 'to tear a cat in to make all split' (1.2.25–6) that Bottom refers to as 'a tyrant's vein'. Peele's play uses magic of many sorts and has the sorcerer Sacrapant, a ghost, a speaking head in a magic well, characters transformed (one into 'the White Bear of England's Wood'), a woman turned mad and amnesiac, two brothers carried off by the Furies, thunder and lightning, 'A Voice and flame of fire'. Such effects and the pantomime confection of incidents would have delighted the commoners in the audience and the satirical digs at the crowded mix of romance stereotypes would have amused the more sophisticated spectators. Romance here refers not just to a love story but also to the long verse or prose adventure/quest stories of chivalry that were a popular reading genre. Originating in medieval chivalric tales of Arthur and his knights, the romance persisted into the Renaissance.

---

6 For discussion of Robin Hood plays, St George plays and Plough plays, see www.folkplay. info/Texts.htm.

It recounted the improbable, sometimes fantastic, testing adventures of an idealized hero travelling to strange and remote lands (often arriving through a shipwreck), facing a variety of obstacles, some human, some monstrous and supernatural. Virtue's fortitude in the face of adversity and temptation was a theme running throughout and though the hero has strength, courage and military skill, the emphasis was on his personal chivalric qualities. Readily helping all sorts and conditions of people, he is decent, chaste, charitable, a Christian warrior fighting evil in whatever form encountered. Romances typically featured themes of sin, repentance and redemption that comprise loss and retrieval, exile and restoration. There is a love element and the hero's adventures may be in quest of rescuing a lady in distress or he may meet her during his journeys. In Peele's play the wandering knight Eumenides is in search of his love, Delia, kidnapped by the sorcerer. The amatory aspect is set within the courtly love tradition. This language and imagery of love is standardized and repeated in play after play between young lovers. The most famous romance is Ludovico Ariosto's *Orlando Furioso* (first part 1516, complete publication 1532: English translation, Sir John Harington, 1591).

Robert Greene's dramatization of *Orlando* was probably written in 1591 and performed at Christmas that year by the Queen's Men. Edmund Spenser's *The Faerie Queen* and Sir Philip Sidney's *Arcadia* are influential English romance spin-offs of the genre. When the customary features of a long romance are brought together and turned into the condensed form of a play the effect is ludicrous and draws attention to the fantastical and incredible aspects of such a concentration of events. Every page of *The Old Wives' Tale* has something astonishing, usually magical, and clearly parodies the sorts of romance plays that were popular, but which nowadays seem closest to pantomime. There is a series of broadly expressed moral lines in the play (the kindness of Clunch and Madge, the brotherly love of Thelea and Calypha seeking their sister, the courage and devotion of Eumenides seeking his abducted lady love, good versus evil) but they are not emphasized and are somewhat overwhelmed by a continual chain of astonishing incidents. *Dream* is similarly driven by surprises and astonishing changes of plot or character – and the magic element. A similar confection of love, obstacles, conflict and spectacular effects, wrapped in a framework of conjuring and pranks, is found in Greene's *Friar Bacon and Friar Bungay*. This play came after *Dream* and suggests there was a phase or fashion for such pieces. It was not entirely to die out even under the surge of satirical city comedies that focus strictly on the real world of contemporary London.

There are other similarities between *The Old Wives' Tale* and *Dream*. Both use the image of a wood as the precipitator of confusion. Peele also makes love a central motivation right from the opening lines. Three servants,

Antic, Frolic and Fantastic, are lost in the woods having accompanied their master in search of his lady love ('Cupid hath led our young master to the fair lady'). This achieved they have got separated and lost, 'like to wander with a sorrowful heigh-ho, among the owlets and hobgoblins of the forest'.[7] They hear a dog in the dark, 'Hush! A dog in the wood or a wooden dog!' 'Wooden' is a play on the Old English word *wod* meaning mad. This is perhaps echoed in Demetrius's claim that he is 'wood within this wood' (2.1.192), distracted because he cannot find Hermia. This is no mad dog or Devil's hound such as populated folk stories, but rather a 'trotting cur' belonging to a blacksmith on his way home. The three servants are taken into his cottage for the night and his wife Madge whiles away the evening by telling an old fairy tale. It is a story recognizable from ballads and folk songs: a lord has a fair daughter, she is stolen and he sends all his men in search of her. The abductor was a 'conjuror' who turned himself into a dragon, carries her off and imprisons her in his castle. At this point a real coup de théâtre (a very theatrical surprise event) occurs. Madge begins to tell how, after the lord's men had been searching unsuccessfully for some time, the lady's brothers set out to see if they could find her. At this moment the very brothers appear onstage. The smith's cottage recedes and the main acting area becomes the fairy story setting of Madge's tale. (In some respects Shakespeare does the same in *Dream* with the woods becoming a wholly new venue and both the human characters and the audience ejected into a completely different and alien world.) A range of new characters also enter, each pursuing the sorcerer for different reasons. This adds comic overload, confronting the audience with multiple plots and a quick succession of confusions. All this is backed up by the magical effects and by sound and lighting effects as well. As Shakespeare overlays incident and surprise on top of incident and surprise, so too does Peele. The language register is different. Peele's piece lacks the beauty and intricacy of the blank and decasyllabic rhymed verse and the accumulation of atmospheric animal and nature imagery found in *Dream*. Peele's piece is mostly in prose and has a large element of demotic slang. Both, however, use snatches of song and have clown types providing low humour.

Some sense that nature, normality and order have been reversed (an allegory strongly highlighted in *Dream*) emerges in the activities of the conjuror in general and in his particularly transforming Erestes (another cheated lover whose lady has been stolen). Part of the time Erestes is a white bear and the other part an old man: 'Seeming an old and miserable man:/ [...] yet [...] in April of my age'. The animal metamorphosis is an earlier echo

7 *Five Elizabethan Comedies*, 63.

of Bottom's comic predicament. Bears, headless or otherwise, are mentioned several times in *Dream*. Elizabethans only saw bears as captive entertainment dancing in the street or at fairs or chained to a stake and baited by dogs in the Bear Garden on the Bankside, but they appear also in heraldry and in spooky folk tales. Peele also has a braggart, self-confident character called Huanebango who asserts,

> it is a wonder to see what this love will make silly fellows adventure, even in the wane of their wits and infancy of their discretion.[8]

Voicing the traditional view of love's folly, his comments are not dissimilar to Bottom's remarks on reason and love not being seen together. Ironically, Huanebango then becomes besotted by a young woman whose attractive appearance is countered by her morose temper, nasty attitudes and sharp tongue. Like Shakespeare, Peele adeptly mixes the romantic with the ridiculous, fantasy with reality, the fantastically absurd with the serious.

Shakespeare used the idea of a play being a dream as part of the opening structural framework of *The Taming of the Shrew* (c. 1590–2). It is impossible to tell precisely whether Peele's play preceded *Shrew* or the other way round, but the similarities show how dramatists were influenced by each other in their continual desperate search to write new plays. In *Shrew*, a drunken tinker, Christopher Sly, falls asleep outside an alehouse, is carried off by a lord's servants to their master's house, dressed in fine clothes, woken and made to think he is a lord and is married (a page dresses as his lady). He is told he has been in a deep sleep for 15 years or more. A band of players then performs the *Shrew* play for him. Like Bottom, Sly is not fazed by his situation, but this framework is left unresolved at the end. The story of Petruchio and his shrew wife takes over and the Sly storyline forgotten. This means his 'dream' is not exposed as a trick. Bottom's 'dream' is not exposed as a trick either and only the audience is party to what happened.

Trickery and enchantment, love unrequited, love slighted and all the other labyrinthine entanglements of love occur in George Gascoigne's *Supposes* (performed 1566, printed 1573). This early Italian-style comedy has a master and servant exchange places so that the master may pursue an amorous adventure (as in *The Taming of the Shrew*). Gascoigne's prologue asserts what will be the simple basis for the subsequent generation of comedies: 'But understand, this our suppose is nothing else but a mistaking or imagination of one thing for another'. This aptly fits the comic genre in

---

8 *The Old Wive's Tale*, in *Five Elizabethan Comedies*, 71.

general and *Dream* in particular. Gascoigne's setting is Ferrara, and Italy (or the Mediterranean) was to become a common location for comic drama (Ephesus in *The Comedy of Errors*, Padua in *Shrew*, Venice for *Volpone* and *The Merchant of Venice*, Verona and Milan for The *Two Gentlemen of Verona*, Sicily for *Much Ado*, Illyria for *Twelfth* Night, Milan for The *Honest Whore*). The central characters are usually people of some status and wealth, sometimes courtiers, usually from the gentry or the upper bourgeoisie. Gascoigne's play exploits the confusions provoked by identity uncertainty and this will become a staple of comedy. In *Dream*, the lovers are unsure at times of the identity of their companions – Hermia confused by Lysander's behaviour, Helena confused by the conduct of both men, Lysander behaving counter to his previous courteous self, and Demetrius wavering in his desires. Titania makes an inaccurate assessment of the creature she falls for and inaccurately defines her feelings for him, while Oberon fails to see how his conduct subverts his role expectations as a king.

High-ranking characters occur too in Lyly's courtly comedy romance *Endymion* (1591). This, in broad terms, has something of the magic, love and fantasy features that crop up in *Dream*. Where Shakespeare introduces very English fairies and a king and queen of that strange world, Lyly populates his drama with goddesses and nymphs, but both works move easily in and out of the human and the supernatural dimensions. Lyly's play *Gallathea* also has much in common with *Dream* insofar as it uses love to drive the plot and deceptions and mistakes to complicate it toward a climax.[9] Lyly's *Campaspe* (1584), though ostensibly a dramatic entanglement with Alexander the Great in love with the same woman as Apelles the artist, is bland and tame as regards physical conflict and psychological tension. What it does offer are some standard views of the ability of love to derail reason. To his king's question 'Is love a vice?' the cynical Hephaestion answers, 'It is no virtue' (2.2.21–2). He further adds,

Ermines have fair skins but foul livers, sepulchres fresh colours but rotten bones, women fair faces but false hearts. Remember, Alexander, thou has a camp to govern, not a chamber; fall not from the armour of Mars to the arms of Venus. [...] There is no surfeit so dangerous as that of honey, nor any poison so deadly as that of love: in the one physic cannot prevail, nor in the other counsel. (2.2.93–5)[10]

---

9 Performed before the queen in 1588, recorded in the Stationer's Register on 4 October 1591, printed 1592. That year saw Lyly's plays *Endymion* and *Midas* also printed. Midas was another character with ass's ears.
10 *Campaspe* in *Five Elizabethan Comedies*.

This traditional opposition of the martial and the amatory (Mars and Venus), of man's role in the outer world and woman's focus on 'the maidenly skirmishes of love' does not translate into truly comic theatre. It remains almost a pamphlet-style dialogue on love. Shakespeare does at least engage with and present some of the mental and physical turmoil love brings and the Mars/Venus dichotomy is present in the transformation of Theseus from warrior to husband.

What both Gascoigne and Lyly lack is the brutally topical satire of everyday life that was shortly to emerge with Ben Jonson's first play, *Every Man in His Humour* (1598) and his development of the comedy of humours that mocked personality quirks (the humours) and used their distortions as the source of humour and instruction. Jonson also edges into the city comedy subgenre that takes contemporary London life as its target. *Dream*, for all it may have darker undertones, is a different sort of play altogether. That is partly due to its probably being an occasional piece specially written for a marriage. But it still has the common denominator of human folly. Puck's remark 'Lord what fools these mortals be' links the play with most comedies and certainly ties it to the values of the Elizabethan world. The sins that are exposed and punished in comedy are the sorts of follies preachers denounced from their pulpits in England from the Middle Ages to the Renaissance. Shakespeare's career was not far off from a change of tone, a shift into cynicism, and *Dream* is a transitional piece that mixes the traditional comic stereotypes – overstern father, overpassionate lovers, clownish buffoons – with blacker moments. Folly remains a target, but subsequent pieces develop an increasingly cynical mood. Even the other mature comedies (*As You Like It, Much Ado, Twelfth Night*) are not without their dark side, but the major tragedies and problem plays of the same period are distinctly topical, satirical and cynical. Their presentation of humankind is more pessimistic. There is folly and inconsistency in abundance in *Dream*, but, apart from Egeus, little ill will.

13.5 Sources

There is no overriding single source story for *Dream*. It is a mixture of different elements borrowed from a variety of origins (as indicated in the previous section), but none of them provides the central storyline of the lovers in the woods. The only feature that has a clear source, but that too is mixed, is the 'Pyramus' play. Theseus, as already mentioned, is partially developed from Plutarch and Geoffrey Chaucer. The two male rivals loving the same woman is perhaps an echo from 'The Knight's Tale', though the names are different. Also from Chaucer is the wedding of Theseus and Hippolyta, the anticipation and the actuality of which provides a handy framework for the play with a time pause between to allow love's caprices to be developed and then resolved. The name Philostrate appears in 'The Knight's Tale' but as that of a page. Chaucer is again the origin of echoes of the 'Pyramus and Thisbe' play. 'The Merchant's Tale' makes mention of them 'rowning [whispering] thurgh a wal' (918), but also refers to the king and queen of the underworld, Pluto and Proserpina. Pluto is referred to as 'king of Faierye' (1015) with 'many a lady in his compaignye,/Folwinge his wyf, the queene Proserpina' (1016–17).[11] So the classical figures who rule the world of the dead and live in Hades have become, in Chaucer, a fairy couple overlooking a human scenario in the garden of January, the central male figure and cuckolded husband in the tale. Rather than engage in a quarrel over a changeling, Pluto and his wife argue about how treacherous women are. Proserpina speaks up spiritedly for 'many a verray trewe wyf' in the Bible and 'the Romain geestes' [Roman tales]. This male versus female argument, quite emotional and powerfully felt on both sides, is ended by Pluto giving way, but insisting he restore the eyesight of a gullible, blind, cuckold husband at the climax of the plot. Proserina, conforming to medieval views of women, determines to have the last word ('I am a womman, nedes moot I speke') and insists on giving January's adulterous wife, May, the wit to wriggle out of the awkwardness of having been seen having sex with her lover.[12] Titania and the lovers also have their rational eyesight restored as harmony is reinstated. Chaucer thus provides the hints of supernatural beings influencing the human world, supporting opposing sides (as Theseus is supported by Titania and Oberon favours Hippolyta), while losing their own marital harmony. Shakespeare has turned the classical gods into fairies in keeping with the pagan traditions of Celtic Europe and medieval England, but has retained the sense of man in opposition to woman, that basic and visceral battle of the sexes. His fairy monarchs (conflating classical and folkloric figures) also share the same space as the human protagonists – in the woods first and later in the court. Chaucer has his supernatural figures share with the humans a garden that emblematizes and amalgamates a priapic haven (where husband and wife can have sex away from public eyes) with an ordinary domestic green place and the Garden of Love from the medieval poem *The Romance of the Rose*.

There is another more substantial Chaucer borrowing. The whole narrative of Pyramus and Thisbe appears in *The Legend of Good Women*. The prologue to the series of legends has Queen Alceste demanding the poet recount the lives of virtuous women to counter his misogynistic treatment of them in *The Canterbury Tales* and *Troilus and Criseyde* (a subject Shakespeare used in

---

11 *The Merchant's Tale* (ed. Maurice Hussey).
12 1072, 1073, 1093.

1601–2). She commands him to begin with Cleopatra, as a challenge to men, showing a woman who had 'doon so strong a peyne for love as she' (undergone such suffering for love). Cleopatra's story immediately precedes that of 'The Legend of Thisbe of Babylon'. It provides the whole narrative of Quince's play, with some verbal echoes.[13] The lovers, 'bothe in love y-lyke sore they brente' (both alike burning with love) curse the wall that separates them ['Thus wolde they seyn – allas! Thou wikked wal'] and describe 'thy lyme and eek thy stoon'. The unwitting bawdry of kissing the wall's stones (stones were slang for testicles) and kissing the wall's hole alluding to kissing the anus or the vagina) are a Shakespearean addition, reflecting the oblivious innocence and simplicity of whoever composed the 'Pyramus' play. Chaucer's Thisbe, about to kill herself in grief and love, addresses 'ye wrecched jelous fadres oure' (our fathers) asking they should bury the pair together as they were responsible for keeping them apart. This antipatriarchalism is echoed in the wretched tyranny of Egeus. The narrator closes the piece by re-emphasizing that he has found few men as true to his love as Pyramus, but that women too can be as faithful:

> For hit is deyntee to us men to finde
> A man that can in love be trewe and kinde,
> Heer may ye seen, what lover so he be,
> A woman dar and can as wel as he. (920–23)

That Shakespeare knew Chaucer's work is evident from numerous borrowings elsewhere.[14] He would resort to the *Legend of Good Women* again for an angle on Cleopatra when writing *Antony and Cleopatra*.

Chaucer was not the only source for the Pyramus story, for book 4 of Ovid's *Metamorphoses* tells it too. Shakespeare seems to have picked up a number of verbal and other echoes from Arthur Golding's translation, notably the word 'cranny' for the hole in the wall through which the lovers talk. Also, 'To steale out of their fathers house and eke the Citie gate' (line 40) is repeated in Lysander's line 'Through Athens' gates we have devis'd to steal' (1.1.213).[15]

---

13 It seems likely Quince authored the piece. Bottom immediately thinks of him to write the ballad of his 'Dream', which suggests he is thought capable of doing so. Someone among the group writes and inserts the prologue. Surely it must be Quince as director and speaker of it. The play is so bad – the style both inflated and deflating, the metre so uneven, the rhymes so awkward – it must be by the hand of someone among the mechanicals.

14 A number of sixteenth-century Chaucer editions were available: William Thynne's (1532 and 1532), John Stow's (1561) and Thomas Speght's (1598 and 1602).

15 All line references are to extracts from Golding in the Arden edition (1905), Appendix 4.

The plan to 'tarie underneath a tree [...] a faire high Mulberie' (lines 43–4) is picked up in Quince's prologue with 'And Thisbe, tarrying in mulberry shade' (5.1.147). Golding's rendering 'And as she fled away for hast she let her mantle fall' (line 59) is repeated in the prologue as 'And as she fled, her mantle did she fall' (5.1.141). Golding was the first to use the word 'mantle'. In Chaucer it is a wimple. In John Gower's version it is a scarf and a kerchief. These are minor borrowings such as poets use. What is more useful comedically is how Shakespeare builds on Ovid's and Golding's absurd treatment of the wall. In both the lovers absurdly thank the wall for providing the chink for them to use. In all three versions it is a bizarre piece of behaviour, but Shakespeare develops it by having Bottom go on to curse the wall because Thisbe is not there and to use the word 'wicked' which occurs in Chaucer's version. Altogether, Quince's play is comically over the top in its overblown, passionate language and awkwardly phrased as if written by a man not practised in versification or theatrical devices. Of course, it is meant to be bad writing. If it were only the acting that was bad the comic effect would be diminished. Though Shakespeare does not use the wonderfully inappropriate phrase 'did to hir heart it shove' (line 131) as Thisbe stabs herself, her lament over Pyramus's body is similarly sustained in its ludicrous humour.

Muir discusses some other possible small verbal echoes from minor verse of the time.[16] These may be rememberings or simply coincidental use of the same words. Overall, however, the whole 'Pyramus and Thisbe' play is a parody of amateur poeticizing, primitive drama and bad acting. Kenneth Muir puts it thus,

> It is possible [...] that all the versions of the Pyramus and Thisbe story, [...] read over the years, coalesced in his mind without his being aware [...] but it seems more likely that he consulted them all during the actual composition [...] One purpose [...] of the performance of Quince's company was to show that lovers cannot rely on the intervention of Oberon or Puck to save them from the consequences of their irrationality.[17]

Another borrowing/source for the mechanicals' play, and for some elements in the broader situations, is Shakespeare himself. He is parodying his own serious romantic love tragedy *Romeo and Juliet*. Written in the same period as *Dream*, it involves lovers whose parental attitudes prevent their open relationship, an illicit love affair, a secret marriage, an escape (on Romeo's part) from

16 Muir, *The Sources of Shakespeare's Plays*, 72 ff.
17 Muir, 77.

the city which is their home, a suicide that is unnecessary and based on a misunderstanding of the truth and an immediate second suicide in response. It also involves emotional death speeches. The handling of both pieces shows how similar situations can be differently treated and how language and action together can make or break the tone of a situation which is essentially moving but which can provoke laughter if not sensitively written or well acted. They both also show how the transgressive behaviour of young people can lead to tragedy. In this respect the Pyramus and Thisbe story acts as a reflective analogue for the situation into which Hermia and Lysander put themselves. When we consider Romeo's and Juliet's deaths as a tragic reverse of what happens in *Dream*, then the parallel doomed love story of Pyramus and Thisbe acts as a reminder to the lovers how lucky their own outcome has been. It is a comic relief too for the audience to mock the fiction of Pyramus and Thisbe's manner of speech and the manner and mood of their deaths. The fates of Lysander and Demetrius might not have been so dissimilar. Here laughter is the natural reaction for survivors who might so easily have been victims.

While the Thisbe story is an easily traceable source, other elements in the play have possible origins too, though nothing very substantial. Shakespeare changes the names of his king and queen of the fairies from Chaucer's Pluto and Proserpina. Oberon comes from a French romance entitled *Huon of Bordeaux* where we find this description of a wood:

> Full of the Fayryes and strange things [...] [and] in that wood abideth a King of the Fayryes named *Oberon*, he is of height but of three foote, and crooked shouldered, but yet he hath an Angell-like visage.[18]

Huon is the hero of this chanson de geste-cum-romance.[19] As punishment, expiation and reprieve for an accidental murder he is set a difficult quest (much as Hercules was forced to do) which requires him to achieve some apparently impossible and dangerous tasks. He seeks the aid of Oberon, the king of the fairies, meets him in an eerie forest and is able to recruit his help, achieve his mission and save his life – but not without multiple difficulties on the way.

Written in the thirteenth century *Huon* spawned some similar romances. One, *Le Roman d'Aubéron*, focused the fairy king. Another, *Huon Roi de Féérie*, turns Huon into the king of the fairies. In 1454 the story was changed into prose and then, circa 1549, translated into English by John Bourchier,

---

18 Bullough, *Narrative and Dramatic Sources of Shakespeare*, 389.
19 A chanson de geste is a short epic-type poem that told of the exploits of warriors. Literally 'a song of deeds'.

Lord Berners. Given the popularity of romance epics in sixteenth-century England it was inevitably used as the source for a play version, performed on 3 January 1593, and again on 11 January and 28 December 1593.[20] What Henslowe, in his usual poor spelling, notes as 'hewen of burdoche' and 'hewen of burdockes', is possibly a revival of the play that Thomas Nashe, prose writer and pamphleteer, makes mention of in 1589 as being about the king of the fairies.[21] The Henslowe reference places the Huon play just before Shakespeare wrote *Dream*. It was not uncommon for dramatists, constantly looking for new subjects, to remodel stories from other playhouses, using parts to tell a new tale or even simply writing their own version of someone else's work. Shakespeare did this with *Lear*, which was based on an earlier chronicle history play. In *Dream* he changes the warrior quest theme with its dangers into a comic tale of magic and mischief set largely in a wood. The questing hero has become the settling-down conqueror Theseus, but the device of a fairy king intervening in human affairs was dramatically promising, especially in a comedy. The character Oberon also occurs in the induction to Greene's play *James IV* (c. 1590). This too may have lodged in Shakespeare's memory as one of the impulses that helped form the play.

Huon of Bordeaux provides a number of recognizable features in *Dream*. My italics highlight the similar incidents. In self-defence Huon kills the Emperor Charlemagne's son. To expiate his offence and show his repentance the knight is sent on a mission impossible to kill the Bashaw (a pasha, a high official of the Ottoman Empire) of Baghdad, cut a lock from the Sultan's beard and remove four of his teeth. In addition to these trophies he is to kiss the Sultan's daughter, Rezia. In search of Oberon, to request his help, Huon gets *lost in a forest* 'haunted by *a goblin who could change men into beasts*'. There is an ominous feel 'in the very *silence of the dense shade*' with its 'gloomy recesses, where strange forms seemed to glide noiselessly about'.[22] Completely lost Huon sits under a 'mighty oak' in a glade when suddenly he sees 'the golden castle of Oberon, king of the fairies, and son of Julius Caesar and Morgana the fay' [fairy]. 'The glittering gates of the palace roll back as the king drove through them in a chariot of silver, drawn by leopards, himself appearing in the guise

---

20 See *Henslowe's Diary*, 20. Henslowe records takings of £3 10s on 28 December 1593, 14s on 3 January 1593 and 5s on 11 January 1593.

21 The connection is suggested in Muir (66), but seems tenuous. Nashe, commenting on the state of poetry remarks: 'Sundry other sweete Gentlemen [...] haue vaunted their pennes in priuate deuices, and tricked vp a company of taffaty fooles with their feathers, whose beauty if our Poets had not peecte [pieced] with the supply of their periwigs, they might haue antickt it vntill this time vp and downe the Country with the King of Fairies' (*Works*, ed. McKerrow, 3. 323–4).

22 H. A. Guerber, *Myths and Legends of the Middle Ages*, 219.

of the God of Love'.[23] Huon flees in fright and this arouses the anger of Oberon who brings down a ferocious storm. 'But *if the wrath of Oberon was easily roused it vanished as quickly*'. Aware of Huon's pure life and noble soul Oberon agrees to help him and gives him a golden beaker that will always be full of wine for the virtuous but would burn the lips of all evildoers. He also gives him a magic horn which sounded gently will distract hearers by making them dance. Blown loudly it will call Oberon to Huon's aid. After the king disappears it is only these gifts which convince Huon not to 'consider *the whole occurrence a dream*'.[24] After various incredible adventures, including a dream of Princess Rezia, Huon arrives in Baghdad. Both he and the princess dream that Oberon is 'their guardian spirit'. Huon kills the Saracen Bashaw but when he requests the Caliph donate a lock of beard and four teeth the angry ruler sets his guards on him. A blast on the horn brings Oberon who puts the Caliph and his men into a deep sleep while Huon and Rezia run away together. The tale turns now to their misadventures while journeying back to Charlemagne's court. As they await a ship at the port of Ascalon, Oberon appears and gives Huon the lock and the teeth he needed to fulfil his challenge. In return the king asks that Huon and Rezia go to Rome to have their marriage blessed. Though he readily agrees to this Huon forgets about it in the excitement of the voyage, with Rezia converting to Christianity and being baptized and renamed Amanda (meaning 'fit to be loved'). Oberon in his anger sends a tempest. The sailors organize a drawing of lots to choose who shall be sacrificed by being thrown overboard in order to allay the wrath of whichever god sent the storm. Huon draws the fateful lot but Amanda joins him in leaping into the sea. Both are washed ashore on an island where, searching for food, they come on a fertile valley which 'was the home of *Titania*, queen of the fairies, who had *quarrelled with Oberon*, and was waiting here until she should be recalled to Fairyland'.[25] Some months later Amanda, out walking, sits down in a lovely grotto and falls asleep. On waking she finds herself 'clasping her *new-born babe*, who during her slumbers had been cared for by the *elves* who owned Titania's sway' (were under the rule of Titania).[26] Anxious lest Oberon send new misfortunes on the family, *Titania takes the baby off to fairyland* for his protection. Pirates abduct Amanda and she is shipwrecked and washed ashore in Tunis where the Sultan falls in love with her. Oberon sends a messenger to tell Huon where she is and he arrives disguised as an Arab. The Sultan's daughter sees him and falls for him. Vengeful at his rejection of her she accuses him of a

---

23 Guerber, 219.
24 Guerber, 222.
25 Guerber, 232.
26 Guerber, 233.

heinous crime and he is condemned to be burned alive. Amanda refuses to save him by marrying the Sultan and is similarly condemned. As the flames are licking round them Oberon at last relents and carries them off to fairyland in his silver chariot. There is a happy reunion with their child and a happy *reconciliation between the two rulers of fairyland*. In this mood of joy Oberon transports Huon and his family to the gates of Paris, where he arrives 'just in time to win, at the point of his lance, his patrimony of Guienne, which Charlemagne had offered as prize at a tournament'.[27] Job done, happiness ever after. From this fairy story confection of amusing nonsense Shakespeare, whatever his source (Lord Berners's translation, the play Henslowe reported, or some other means) picked the elements he could use to embellish his own novel collage of similarly incredible events.

Titania occurs in book 3 of Ovid's *Metamorphoses*. She is not named Titania exactly but is called 'daughter of the Titans' and connected with Diana the huntress and moon goddess.[28] This links to the woods and to the influence of the moon, key motifs throughout the play. In the well-known metamorphosis story of Actaeon, the goddess Diana is surrounded by her nymphs. These nymphs are thought to be the originals of the fairy train that follows Titania. Then in book 14 the name 'daughter of the Titans' is used twice in connection with Circe, the witch-enchantress. Circe is used, by Shakespeare and other writers, as an archetype of the female evil sorceress. She is an obvious 'relative' of Titania, though the fairy queen does no malefic magic.

Puck in his form as Robin Goodfellow was a rural spirit of ancient reputation. The linking of the two, as already mentioned, is discussed in Reginald Scot's *Discoverie of Witchcraft* (1584). Robin and the fairies are folkloric figures, varying in size and characteristics according to requirement. Fairies creeping fearfully into acorn cups when Oberon and Titania quarrel are akin to the Victorian idea of the tiny winged creatures illustrated by Henry J. Ford for Andrew Lang's books of fairy tales or Arthur Rackham's famous series of fairy illustrations. Henry Fuseli, William Blake and Richard Dadd were renowned too for their various media representations of fairies, so that although Scot claimed the mainstream influence of and belief in the fairy-sprite world was diminishing by the late sixteenth century, the superstition continued to activate the imagination and linger in the psyche. Certainly Shakespeare has removed the frightening aspects of the fairies as being unsuitable in a comedy, not fitting with 'tragical mirth'.

---

27 Guerber, 237.
28 Book 3 also makes reference to Cadmus and hunting with dogs, some of whom are of the Spartan breed like those of Theseus. Hippolyta talks of hunting in 'a wood of Crete' with Hercules and Cadmus (4.1.111–25).

Man-into-animal transformations are found in many stories. Bottom's 'translation' may have come from an account in Scot where a man is turned into an ass, but has a more substantial possible origin in Apuleius's classic tale *The Golden Ass*. This was published in English by William Adlington in 1561. The other major magic, the love-inducing flower, is generally agreed to come from Jorge de Montemayor's Spanish pastoral romance *Diana*. *Los Siete Libros de la Diana* (The seven books of Diana) was published in 1559. The book became an international bestseller, influencing the fashion for pastoral tales, poems and plays. It is thought to have been a seminal influence on Sidney's *New Arcadia*. It is claimed that it was a source for the Proteus-Julia-Sylvia plot strand in Shakespeare's early romantic comedy *The Two Gentlemen of Verona* (1593–5). Had he been reading it in the early 1590s that would explain its influence in *Dream*, where the tiny flower has such immense and dramatic effects. Geoffrey Bullough cites the *Diana* as crucial to the atmosphere and incidents in Shakespeare's comedies.[29] This is particularly evident in the common theme, love – its entanglements, misunderstandings, intrigues – and in his pairing of heroines of differing personalities – strong/weak, witty/dull, confident/self-effacing. John Twyning suggests the central plot strand of the purgatory of the lovers in the woods was a variation on a medieval German poem called *Der Busant* (The Buzzard).[30] This fourteenth-century romance tells of the king of England's son eloping with the king of France's daughter to avoid an enforced diplomatic marriage being arranged for her. In a wood a Buzzard steals her ring. The prince tries to recover it, goes mad, lives as a wild man in the woods, is restored to sanity and marries his princess. Love obstructed, elopement, a wood, mental distraction and an eventual happy ending all fit the *Dream* plot loosely, but it seems unlikely Shakespeare knew of it and no translation is known to have been made.

The diversity of texts Shakespeare drew on provides him with the references, allusions and lexis to create the mood he wanted, but the bulk of the plot is his own imaginative, fantasy invention. Printed in 1600, described 'as it hath been sundry times publicly acted by the right honourable Lord Chamberlain his servants', the piece remains popular, though it has evoked a wide range of interpretations. Another edition of the text was printed in 1619 by Thomas Pavier and it is the eighth play in the 1623 First Folio that was the first 'collected works' edition of Shakespeare.

29 Bullough, 205. A point endorsed by Stuart Gillespie, 103–4.
30 John Twyning, *Forms of English History in Literature, Landscape, and Architecture*.

13.6 Some Critical Reactions

Samuel Pepys records in his diary on 29 September 1662,

> To the King's Theatre, where we saw *Midsummer nights dreame*, which
> I have never seen before, nor shall ever again, for it is the most insipid
> ridiculous play that ever I saw in my life. I saw, I confess, some good
> dancing and some handsome women, which was all my pleasure.[31]

A humourless and uncritical reaction. But many spectators have been unsure
how to interpret the piece. It is unsurprising that in the late seventeenth
century the fairy element was turned into a semi-opera. Henry Purcell's *Fairy
Queen* uses the Titania/Bottom strand as a form of antipastoral setting in
the background of a Thomas Betterton adaptation of the play. The fairies
were 'creatures of often sinister power and beauty' and 'the opening music is
full of menacing magic'.[32] Mixed with it are traditional pastoral characters –
Coridon and Mopsa (shepherd and shepherdess), a 'Dance for the haymakers',
singers personifying the seasons and a 'Dance for the Green Men'. The piece
is typical of the tendency of the period to hybridize genres, discarding those
elements that were not to the current taste. The integrity of Shakespeare's
texts was not yet established in performance and liberties of all sorts were
taken. John Downes reported of *Dream* that 'all the Singers and Dancers,
Scenes, Machines and decorations, all most profusely set off and excellently
performed [...] The Court and Town were wonderfully satisfy'd with it'.[33] In
1773 Samuel Johnson was to remark, with somewhat faint praise, that

> [w]ild and fantastical as this play is, all the parts in their various
> modes are well written and give the kind of pleasure which the author
> designed. Fairies in his time were much in fashion; common tradition
> had made them familiar.[34]

The much-maligned editor William Warburton had been more positive:

> *The Tempest* and *The Midsummer Night's Dream* are the noblest efforts
> of that sublime and amazing imagination peculiar to Shakespeare,
> which soars above the bounds of nature, without forsaking sense; or,

---

31 *Diary*, 3. 208.
32 Maureen Duffy, *Henry Purcell*, 199.
33 John Downes, *Roscius Anglicanus, or an Historical Review of the Stage from 1660 to 1706*
    (1708), 42–3.
34 Samuel Johnson, *A Midsummer Night's Dream* (1773), General Observations.

more properly, carries nature along with him beyond her established limits.[35]

The fairy aspect has been an obstacle to serious analysis. Because they are supernatural figures we have to come to terms with either accepting them as a playful part of a playful piece or rejecting them on the grounds that we do not believe in fairies. This latter approach automatically excludes the play from serious consideration. It is, of all Shakespeare's works, the closest to a children's fairy tale or a pantomime, and still has the power to charm. But, as with Kott's extreme interpretation, modern critics have seen much darker aspects to it. There is no doubt that for all its light-heartedness there are serious issues in it. These may be missed in the pace and pleasure of a rumbustious performance, but emerge more clearly during close reading. At a more obvious level the human entanglements of Hermia with her father and those of the lovers address a common set of predicaments of some importance.

It is generally the case that, from its composition until the late nineteenth century, the fairy element was seen merely as charming, amusing and increasingly an opportunity for lavish and colourful spectacle. The fairies offered costume designers, make-up artists, music arrangers, choreographers and lighting technicians a field day for extravagance and experiment. Stage sets too could be avant-garde and abstract like the Peter Brook white cube production (1970) with the actors on trapezes, or luxuriantly realistic with tree trunks, foliage, grassy banks and live rabbits.[36] In 1611 the court of James I was treated to Jonson's masque Oberon, with fantastical costumes designed by Inigo Jones, intricate sets, technical effects and music by Alfonso Ferrabosco. It bears no relation at all to his colleague Shakespeare's work, but was an opportunity for extravagance and imagination run wild.[37] Prince Henry played the part of Oberon and there is still extant Jones's design for his costume. It is a fanciful version of how Renaissance painters imagined Graeco-Roman armour – a lavishly plumed helmet, body-hugging breastplate, tight breeches, mid-calf-length boots with moulded lions' heads on them.[38] Rather than for combat it is a costume for show, for acting and dancing onstage.

35 Cited in the preface to The Tempest in Isaac Reed's The Plays of William Shakespeare (1809), 1, 154.

36 As in Beerbohm Tree's 1911 production.

37 One stage direction reads, 'There the whole palace opened, and the nation of Fays [fairies] were discovered, some with instruments, some bearing lights, others singing [...] At the further end of all, Oberon in a chariot, which to a loud triumphant music began to move forward, drawn by two white bears' (A Book of Masques, 59.)

38 See plates 1–9 of A Book of Masques, for set and costume designs. Plate 5 has three extravagant costumes for 'Three Fays'.

Criticism often tells the reader as much about the critic and his or her age as about the text criticized. There have been recent critics, like William J. Martz, who tended to idealize the piece as reflecting 'innocence, lyricism, poetic beauty, universal love' and Thomas McFarland, who rhapsodizes about it as an 'extended arabesque of hope and joy' and sees it as a celebration of pastoral innocence. John Dover Wilson declares the play is 'the happiest of Shakespeare's plays'. These views fail to take account of the varied transgressions displayed from Egeus's angry eruption onto the stage through to the discourtesy of the courtly 'drama critics'. That said, it is necessary to keep a balance, for though there are darker issues and some doubts whether romantic love is a delusion of hope over reality or just lust dressed nicely in fine verbal clothes. There is also a merriness about the piece suggesting laughter triumphs over pessimism and a persistently cynical view of life. Sigmund Freud's view of the ubiquity of sex and the nature of dreams as expressing hidden fears and desires, has something to offer in opening up the imaginative undertext of *Dream*, but should be seen as contributing to the meaning of the woodland scenes but not being the meaning of the whole play. The negative things said between the beginning of act 2 and the end of act 4 are no more real than what happens in dreams. It is, ultimately, what happens in real life that counts. For all Jacques Lacan's theory that 'it is the world of words that creates the world of things', the words of the lovers in the woods do not create lasting things; rather, they evaporate as if they had never been.[39] Shakespeare's plays are at best ambiguous. They tend not to offer simple black or white answers to the problems they address. Light always casts shadows and we get both in *Dream*, and critics vary in their interpretations as much as the changes displayed from scene to scene. Whether you see the black as dominating the white or vice versa is a matter of viewpoint. Both are there and the mistakes made in perception as the play slips from light to shadow to moonlight and back from moonlight to shadow to light, is where the comedy is generated. The Greek philosopher Heraclitus believed the world was in constant flux. Order to chaos and back, harmony to discord to order, attraction to repulsion to attraction, reality to dream to reality; these constantly shifting perspectives are the essence of *Dream*.

39 *Ecrits*, 65.

Chapter 14

PLAYING PARTS

> [...] every dream turns out to be a meaningful psychical formation which can be given an identifiable place in what goes on within us in our waking life.[1]

We all play parts: son, daughter, father, mother, husband, wife, lover, master of the household, shop owner, tailor's apprentice, friend. The roles are infinite and those we play may alter from moment to moment. Life is broken into stages and we play different parts at different ages. Then there are the parts we assume temporarily – angry father, rebellious daughter, jilted girl, passionate lover, fool, concerned friend, wise man, counsellor, actor, director.

Long before Pedro Caldéron de la Barca's 1635 play *La Vida es Sueño* (Life is a Dream) the image of life as an unreal experience was already current. To Christians life was a dreamlike, ephemeral, transient thing, soon over. We are born, we live, we die. Bede's *History of the English Church and People* (731 AD) describes the fleeting nature of life as being like 'the swift flight of a lone sparrow through the banqueting hall',

> in through one door of the hall, and out through another. While he is inside, he is safe from the winter storms; but after a few moments of comfort, he vanishes from sight into the darkness from whence he came. Similarly, man appears on earth for a little while, but we know nothing of what went before this life, and what follows.[2]

The afterlife – in Hell or Heaven – was what was real and most important. Mortal life only had value as a preparation for eternity, as a chance to live

1 Freud, *The Interpretation of Dreams*, 7.
2 Book 2, chap. 13, 125.

purely and devoutly, casting off all the fleshly burdens of sin and purifying your soul ready for union with God. Other metaphors for life were that it was a voyage, a pilgrimage, a play. All are forms of journey. Erasmus has Folly remark, 'What else is the whole life of man but a sort of play?'

> Actors come on wearing their different masks and all play their parts until the director orders them off the stage, and he can often tell the same man to appear in different costume, so that now he plays a king in purple and now a humble slave in rags. It's all a sort of pretence, but it's the only way to act out this farce.[3]

Shakespeare was to use the idea of life as a drama, full of changing scenes and acts, developing it fully in Jaques's speech 'All the world's a stage' in *As You Like It*. This simply divides a life into its component stages, the seven ages of man, and offers stereotypes of the type of part a person plays at different times of their life. Like the oddity of a dream a play offers a range of overlapping fictions and developing metamorphoses as the narratives become complicated and the characters evolve. It is from the start all a pretence, but a pretence that the actor pretends to take for reality. An actor is himself, but pretending to be someone else. The audience knows the character is not real, but someone pretending to be that person. It can happen that the fiction so possesses an actor that for a while he believes himself to be the character he plays and he identifies with that person. He can cry real tears when the character is sad, can work himself into a heart-pounding passion when the character is angry. Audiences too can identify with characters to such a level of intensity that they are moved to tears, laughter and relief for that character. Such is the fragility of the sense of self and the hold on reality that sometimes people believe they are another person. Jesus Christ and Napoleon are the joke stereotypes of personages that mentally ill people imagine themselves as being. At a less psychotic level, we all play parts when needed. Son or daughter, mother or father, husband or wife are long-term roles that we really play because they are us. Others are assumed for temporary purposes, like the stern disciplinarian when a child needs telling off, the jolly uncle for Christmas Day, the bored relative making concerned, sympathetic sounds as someone tells their troubles. Our jobs too require us to take on roles. Other parts we play according to customary expectations. Lovers buy chocolates and flowers, book tables for romantic dinners, give surprise presents, like all the love tokens Lysander has given Hermia. The actor playing Bottom has to assume different parts. First he is

---

3 *Praise of Folly*, 104.

the irrepressible weaver, then an actor rehearsing, then an ass-headed man, a lover and dreamer and finally Pyramus the lover. For all he plays so many parts, he is never not always Bottom. His sense of identity is strong. As an ass-headed man he is humiliated by a trick that reassigns him a status as a symbol of foolishness who loses control of his self's reality, is manipulated by a fairy but then is elevated to becoming the beloved of a beautiful lady, a queen and a queen of fairyland at that, but in all these roles he is never other than himself in character though changed in clothing, appearance and behaviour, however differently others treat him. His selfhood is firmly grounded. He is utterly unfazed by the appearance of Titania and her fairy attendants. He is always Bottom even when half ass. Once he wakes from his dream he is unsure what has happened. As he says,

> Man is but an ass, if he go about to expound this dream. [...] man is but a patched fool if he will offer to say what methought I had. The eye of man hath not heard, the ear of man hath not seen, man's hand is not able to taste, his tongue to conceive, nor his heart to report what my dream was. (4.1.205–12)

The misalignment of organs and senses, apart from being a standard Elizabethan misprision-of-words joke, is a reflection of the impossibility of being certain what has happened at any time. Different witnesses of an incident give differing statements. What would be exceptionally disconcerting, disorienting and frightening to one person is nothing very much to another. The physical confusions in the play are echoed by emotional and sensory misperceptions. Bottom, as Pyramus, repeats the same misalignment of senses when he declares,

> I see a voice; now will I to the chink,
> To spy and I can hear my Thisbe's face. (5.1.190–1).

The ethical-religious ground of the text is clinched by the readily recognizable verbal echoes of Paul's First Epistle to the Corinthians (2.7–10):

> 7. But we speak the wisdom of God in a mystery, *even* the hidden *wisdom*, which God ordained before the world unto our glory: [...]
> [...]
> 9. But as it is written, Eye hath not seen, nor ear heard, neither have entered into the heart of man, the things that God hath prepared for them that love him.

10. But God hath revealed *them* unto us by his Spirit: for the Spirit searcheth all things, yea, the deep things of God. (italics in original)

The Geneva Bible translation of this verse talks of the spirit searching to 'the bottom of God's secrets'. This was the Bible in all churches, prior to the King James Version, and the wordplays on these verses and putting the speech into the mouth of a character called Bottom would resonate with the audience. It suggests too, as the play does, that there are some mysteries in life that man's wisdom cannot fathom – they have no bottom, like Bottom's dream. Love and its crazy uncertainties are among those mysteries. Bottom, receiver of part of the mystery, and of the most bizarre part, is, like a child, completely baffled as to its meaning. The folly and blindness of man makes him unable to comprehend; man is the 'patched fool' Bottom describes. The lovers have only confused memories of what has happened to them.

But that does not matter for the audience observed it all and will draw its conclusions. This all fits with another possible allusive source. In his ironic satire on the corrupt practices and beliefs of the Catholic Church, *Praise of Folly*, Erasmus also drew on Corinthians, sensing how little man understood of God's purposes.[4] At one point he glosses how confused men are, particularly those enduring the madness and delirium of love:

> One moment they are excited, the next depressed, they weep and laugh and sigh by turns; in fact they truly are quite besides themselves. Then when they come to, they say they don't know where they have been, in the body or outside it, awake or asleep. They cannot remember what they have heard or seen or said or done, except in a mist, like a dream.[5]

This is exactly the case of the lovers and Bottom as dawn breaks. Bottom uses and confuses Corinthians with its reference to the mysteries of God that man simply cannot conceive or understand. He also talks of the dream he thinks he has had. The lovers talk of their experiences being like a dream. Demetrius says, 'I wot not by what power' his love for Hermia has melted and seems a childhood memory. The events of the past night 'seem small and undistinguishable/Like far-off mountains turned into clouds'. To Hermia 'everything seems double' and to Demetrius it seems 'we sleep, we dream' (4.1.166–201).

---

4 He alludes to Corinthians on page 207. Folly describes the Christian Church as 'founded on blood, strengthened by blood and increased in blood' (181) and far removed from understanding God's plans.

5 207–8. For Erasmus Folly was the daughter of riches and youth and nursed by drunkenness and ignorance (71–2).

Erasmus referenced Corinthians and in the next paragraph within the same penultimate section of *Praise of Folly* he alludes to the giddy nature of man, his unreliable perception and memory and how his life often resembles a dream. It is possible that Shakespeare knew the work. He may have studied the Dutch humanist's paraphrases of the Bible at school and almost certainly read further works by the influential reformist/satirist.[6]

Identity, who people are, who they think they are and who others think they are and how they treat them accordingly, are persistent matters of concern in the play, but often elusively slip out of the audience's understanding. Some men in the audience might have sympathized with Egeus's dilemma, but felt at the same time he was unbearably domineering. Some younger men might have been attracted by Hermia, but felt unsure as she emerges as a fierce vixen screeching at Helena. There is something grating in certain decibel levels and pitches of the female voice that aggravate the male ear like fingernails scratching down a hard surface. A pitch that can shatter glass is not an agreeable sound. We must not forget that Lysander is present as Hermia shows a less than cuddly side of her character. It would be a disturbing revelation if he could later remember it. But it seems to have faded from his memory.

In our dreams we are like actors. We play parts, but we are not the people we play. It is we who dream, but it is our brain that creates the fictions we imagine ourselves playing in. Conscious, rational choice is not involved. When the body sleeps the brain is free to imagine and construct dream stories as it wishes, reflecting perhaps our inner unacknowledged fantasies, fears and concerns. So too the lovers are manipulated. The two young men are put under the influence of the magic, while the young women are left untouched by the love juice, but very much affected by the workings of it in reaction to how the men behave.

It is a small, tight, friendship network, and they go through the manipulations of magic and changing permutations, like a four-hand dance. These are people of similar age and rank, spending their time together. The changing attractions and the complications that that creates are typical of court life or closed, exclusive groups. The relationships are knotted up, but like a dance the entanglement is unknotted at the end.[7] Loss of awareness of true self is what happens in the madness of the extremes of love. Not being themselves is what happens artificially when Puck uses the Love-in-Idleness

6 See Muir, 4. The *Encyclopedia Britannica* entry for Erasmus suggests some of Shakespeare's lines are direct reminiscences of Erasmus. *The Colloquies* was a Europe-wide influential collection of didactic-satirical pieces, popular in England because of its mockery of the Catholic Church.

7 The resolving of a plot's complications comes near the end of a play. It is called a denouement from the French for untying a knot.

flower. During the dream state each infected person thinks they are still within the real world, that what they see, say and feel is reality.

Hermia, totally confused by Lysander's apparent rejection of her, asks, 'Am not I thy Hermia? Are not you Lysander?' (3.2.273). She seeks affirmation of her own and his identities. When Oberon applies the antidote to Titania he chants a charm that will restore her real reality:

> Be as thou wast wont to be;
> See as thou wast wont to see (4.1.70–1)

She, in waking, immediately reclaims her relationship with him with the words 'My Oberon!' and he, after displaying the sleeping 'monster' she was 'in love' with, declares, 'Now thou and I are new in amity' (4.1.86). He says this after they have danced and he has announced that they will go to Theseus's court to dance as part of their blessing ritual after the marriage, the music and movement of their dance symbolizing harmony's return to them and to the mortal world. They dance as a replication of the dance that solemnized and sealed their marriage. It symbolizes the resumption of their marriage after its disruption. The music of the spheres and the circling dance of the stars symbolize the cosmological harmony of God's order, celestial harmony. This concord was reflected in the return of human orderliness. Puck speaks similarly in removing the ass head: 'Now when thou wak'st, with thine own fool's eyes peep' (4.1.83). During the wild night in the woods, in the thickened darkness Puck has created by magic, Demetrius and Lysander call to each other and think they hear the other reply when it is in fact Puck mimicking. So ears as well as eyes can be mistaken as to what is real and, all in all, our senses are unsure guides to what we experience. How certain then can we be of anything we assume we know?

Among the lexical patterns in the play eyes and seeing right is recurrent. How clearly does anyone see? Theseus first saw Hippolyta as an enemy to fight, but then as an attractive woman to pursue, and then as a lover and bride. In reply to Hermia's plea 'I would my father look'd but with my eyes', he warns, 'Rather your eyes must with his judgement look' (1.2.56–7). To see with your own eyes and judge by another's values is difficult. What is seen, how it is sifted and understood and the discrepancy between what is seen and what is actual will become the lexical and thematic basis of the play and its humour. Incongruity between perception and reality is resonantly evident in the difference between Bottom's idea of himself as an actor capable of playing a lover, a lady, a lion, a tyrant and his actual credibility in any of those parts. There is a crucial disconnect too between how he sees himself and how the audience assesses him. He is just an old ham actor, but does not know it. He and his companions think he is a fine actor, so they too are associated with not seeing clearly. But his misperception and the incongruity between what he thinks and what the audience sees is laughter's cue.

Eyes were crucial in Platonic philosophy's approach to perception, learning and the emotions. They were the major means by which the experience of the external world was assimilated into knowledge. Taste, sound, smell and touch contribute too, but the great proportion of what we know of the world is fed to the brain by the eyes. Thought and actual experiences were the other ways knowledge could be processed. But intellectualizing and imagining theoretically how things might be is not always matched by what our eyes tell us. At the same time what our eyes see may mislead us and our intuition be more accurate. As windows to the soul the eyes were the means by which humans show their emotions and others interpret them. Body language can tell a lot, but a person's eyes are the best giveaway. What was seen by the eyes was then processed by the brain. They are the means by which humans register interest in another and they figure much in the literature of love. It is a person's appearance that first attracts us. Subsequent acquaintanceship may confirm that their personality is attractive (or not). It is therefore, significant that the magic juice is applied to the eyes in order to misdirect, distort or manipulate perception. Titania is woken by Bottom's loud, rough singing and declares, 'What angel wakes me from my flowery bed?' (3.1.124), so the ears too can be misled. His voice is a common one, untutored for singing (and certainly not like an angel), and his song is not an elegant, intricately crafted piece (3.1.120–8), but a simple, alternately rhymed country ditty, listing a range of common birds. Her optical and aural misperception is clear in her comments:

> I pray thee, gentle mortal, sing again:
> Mine ear is much enamour'd of thy note;
> So is mine eye enthralled to thy shape;
> And thy fair virtue's force perforce doth move me
> On the first view to say, to swear, I love thee. (3.1.132–6)

Because of the effect of the magic flower her eyes and ears have misled her into several unfounded assumptions: that this stranger is gentle (of gentry status and genteel manner); that his sound his lovable, his shape is enthralling; that he has virtue; and that she feels love. He stands there in his commoner's clothes and with an ass's head! A fit lover for a queen!

In reference to Demetrius not knowing 'what all but he do know' (that is, that she is as fair as Hermia), Helena remarks that he dotes on 'Hermia's eyes'.

She goes on to theorize proleptically, for the same misperception will happen to Titania with Bottom:[8]

> Things base and vile, holding no quantity,
> Love can transpose to form and dignity:
> Love looks not with the eyes, but with the mind,
> And therefore is wing'd Cupid painted blind;
> Nor hath Love's mind of any judgement taste:
> Wings and no eyes, figure unheedy haste.
> And therefore is Love said to be a child,
> Because in choice he is so oft beguil'd. (1.1.232–9)

How wrong Helena is in practice. With the immature mind, love looks with the eyes and is attracted or repelled by appearances alone. This is precisely the cause of the mistakes in the wood and one source of Demetrius's disloyalty to Helena. It is the more mature mind that judges according to inner qualities rather than what is seen on the surface. This foreshadows much of what will happen in the centre of the play. If mentally we put inverted commas round the word 'love' every time it is used, it would suggest that the word needs questioning and that what is often talked of as love is actually an aberration – a temporary one in the case of Lysander and Titania who will have their impaired vision corrected by the antidote to the love juice. In Demetrius's case, like the child in Helena's analysis, he has been beguiled by choice: wanting Helena, getting betrothed, then changing his mind and choosing Hermia. He is left in an artificially induced 'in love' state in order to return him to the attraction he originally felt. It is as well, throughout the play, every time the word 'love' is used, to make a judgement whether the use is accurate and genuine. Love is an easily used word, commonly spoken without careful thought, casually applied, imprecisely understood and therefore capable of misuse, and in its misuse capable of creating misunderstandings that can have disastrous consequences. This makes it a potent field for comedy. Demetrius with the love juice on his eyes is as passionate in his expressed love for Helena as when he despised her. The audience would continually have been aware that what they are watching is the mayhem released when fleshly love is let loose without the control and restraint of divine love. While human love remains non-physical it is chaste and close to the spiritual. The pre-passion stage is innocent and charming. It is all smiles, and hesitations, and glances and stammerings. But once the appetites are aroused, lust,

---

8 Prolepsis is a verbal or situational device by which a development or outcome later in the narrative is anticipated, foreshadowed, hinted.

possessiveness, jealousy, rebelliousness and betrayal intrude. And yet, with comic irony, it is precisely when Hermia and Lysander are being chaste and restrained that Puck mistakes their lying apart as indicating this is the quarrelling couple Oberon told him of. Robert Burton's compendium of emotional states devotes many pages to 'Love-Melancholy'. As a churchman he naturally applauds divine love (God's love for man and man's love for God), but deprecates fleshly love: 'the one Love is the root of all mischief, the other of all good'.[9] He goes on to define the two loves:

> One love was born in the sea, which is as various and raging in young men's breasts as the sea itself, and causes burning lust: the other is the golden chain which was let down from heaven, and with a divine Fury ravisheth our souls, made to the image of God, and stirs us up to comprehend the innate and incorruptible beauty, to which we were once created.[10]

What worries him is the power of fleshly love to upset the balance of the humours (thus causing bodily illness) and to upset the rationality of the mind (causing emotional distress or even mental illness).

> The rational resides in the brain, the other in the Liver [...] the heart is affected of both, and carried a thousand ways by consent. The sensitive faculty most part over-rules the reason, the Soul is carried hood-winkt, and the understanding captive lie a beast.[11]

Love is emotionally unstable:

> The heart is variously inclined, sometimes they are merry, sometimes sad, and from Love arise Hope and Fear, Jealousy, Fury, Desperation. Now this love of men is diverse, and varies, as the object varies, by which they are enticed, as virtue, wisdom, eloquence, profit, wealth, money, fame, honour, or comeliness of person, &c.[12]

The problem is rooted in the tendency of the human mind to fixate its love attraction but then to turn the fixation of love to obsessional hate when things go wrong or another fixation replaces it, as we see with Demetrius's

---

9 *The Anatomy of Melancholy*, part 3, sec. 1, memb. 1, subs. 2, 620.
10 *The Anatomy of Melancholy*, 620.
11 *The Anatomy of Melancholy*, 624.
12 *The Anatomy of Melancholy*, 624.

change of attitude toward Helena. The obsessional aspect is well observed in Helena's fixation on Demetrius. Both monomaniac love and rejection are noted by Burton: 'They do dote on such a man, hate such again, and can give no reason for it'.[13] The irrational mood swings of love are represented and facilitated in the play by the introduction of the magic flower. The artificial nature of this renders it comic without being too disturbing. An audience will hoot with laughter when Lysander wakes to instant infatuation of Helena, declaring, 'And run though fire I will for thy sweet sake' (2.2.102). He had moments before said goodnight to Hermia and sworn his loyalty to her. There is an unexpected surprise in this twist. Often laughter is provoked involuntarily at unanticipated turns of events. The entanglement of Lysander's affections is not upsetting because we have already been prepared for the possibility of reversal. Before Oberon squeezes the juice on Titania's eyes to get his revenge, he announces he can 'take this charm from off her sight [...] with another herb' (2.1.183–4). Thus we can enjoy the subsequent complications knowing they can be reversed. They are artificially induced (in Lysander's and Demetrius's case) and can be turned around, but, more worrying are the deeply nasty recriminations and accusations voiced by Hermia and Helena. Neither is under the magic influence. Their sharp and personal criticisms are natural expressions, though admittedly uttered under stress and under misinterpreted circumstances. Hermia suspects Helena has stolen her lover and Helena thinks Hermia has joined with the men to mock her. Dreams are often forgotten as soon as we wake. Perhaps too the hysteria of the night is also dimmed like the morning after a drunken night when the catty things said are forgotten. A harmonious ending is required and it does seem as if all bitter recriminations and accusations have been deleted from the memory.

13 *The Anatomy of Melancholy*, 627.

Chapter 15

TRANSGRESSIONS AND TRANSLATIONS

Snout. O Bottom thou art changed! [...]
[...]
Quince. Bless thee, Bottom, bless thee! Thou art translated.

(3.1.9, 13–14)

In differing ways and to differing degrees the main characters are all trans-formed during the play. It is traditionally the business of comedy to encourage moral change. Its laughter is meant to shame, to instruct, to purify. It achieves this by the display of folly onstage in the hope that members of the audience will go away determined to mend their ways if they have seen their failings and sins represented or leave the theatre determined to avoid such pitfalls if they are innocent of them. So much for the *intended* effect of drama mediat-ing between writer and audience. It is common too that within comic drama foolish characters shown their failings will also be reformed, will see the errors of their ways, will be ashamed or humiliated and become better souls. Another aspect of this didacticism was the portrayal of public figures and power holders, shown up, mocked, humiliated and punished for their greed, cruelty, vanity and dishonesty. With the accelerating growth of the numbers of government employees, the expansion of society in general, of wealth and of poverty, such figures proliferated and the opportunities to objectify and vilify them expanded hugely in the late-Elizabethan theatre and even more so in Jacobean times. As the corruption of government, the governing ranks and the aspiring bourgeoisie worsened in the seventeenth century, so satirical writing increased.

The persistence of these problems, the failure of government to clean its own house and the increase of luxury and waste, would split society and turn written mockery to political action. In the 1590s, however, writers essayed the power of the pen to expose vice. Ben Jonson, in the induction to his early comedy *Every Man Out of His Humour* (1599), declared his aim to 'strip the ragged follies of the time'

> [n]aked as at their birth [...]
> And .... oppose a mirror
> As large as is the stage whereon we act;
> Where they [the audience] shall see the time's deformity
> Anatomised in every nerve.

The ever-present question with comedy was whether exposing vice and folly, making it the object of sneering laughter, was enough without showing the sinners severely punished and/or redeemed. In *Dream* the lovers are exposed as sinners and made to suffer during their nightmare dream though it is doubtful that they are reformed or repentant. They do not appear to be chastened during the last scene. Indeed their childish mockery of the 'Pyramus and Thisbe' performance suggests they are still as spoiled and complacent as they ever were.

Bottom too, displayed as having a rather inflated image of himself, is punished by the traditional fairy trick of 'abducting' him into a fairyland scene, ensconced in Titania's bower and surrounded by her attendants. But he too shows no contrition. Indeed the minute he is returned to his normal state he envisages Quince writing a ballad called 'Bottom's Dream' that he will sing at the end of the play. So, he intends to celebrate his experience and egotistically project himself in a public arena rather than learn by it to be more humble. In this he represents the irredeemability of some people. Whatever the warnings they ignore them, whatever the punishments they persist in their bad or aberrant behaviour. Bottom is completely unchanged by his experience.

Does the play teach anything? Or is it just a light-hearted romp? Shakespeare never wrote anything that did not convey numerous lessons, that did not carry a subtext of serious meaning however loud the laughter or absurd the situations. However madcap and funny, his comedies always address important issues. The fact that the lovers and Bottom are not transformed by their experiences does not mean the audience would not see their failings.

Helena is perhaps the only one to perceive her foolishness in doting so extremely on a man who seems no longer at all interested in her. But she 'devoutly' loves Demetrius to the point of 'idolatry'. Those two words alone indicate a love that has gone too far, is excessive. She has lost rational balance. To devote yourself to another human, to idolize them, was a sin. Devotion was for God alone. The first two commandments were quite clear: '1. Thou shalt have no other gods before me' and '2. Thou shalt not make unto thee any graven image'. At the end of the heart-wrenching rows in the woods, she announces, 'To Athens will I bear my folly back' (3.2.315). She may mean that while she still foolishly loves the unworthy Demetrius, she acknowledges that she is a fool for him, but will go back home as she has no chance of detaching him from his 'love' for Hermia. Or she may mean simply that she now sees what a fool she has been and will simply go home bearing the constant memory of her foolish naivety, but cleansed of the folly and cleansed by the memory of it. Readers and viewers are always the mediators of texts and the lessons displayed are manifestly evident to them in this play of changes and transgressions. While they may have laughed at many of the excesses and follies shown in the piece, they will at the same time have noted them for what they were and acknowledged their questionable moral status and emotional danger.

In the backstory Theseus was a belligerent warrior, fighting the Minotaur, battling with various tyrants. Hippolyta too has been an active fighter and huntress and there are references to the centaurs battling the Lapiths (in which Theseus was involved) and to hunting the Calydonian boar. Some in the audience would know even more of the martial exploits of these two. But they are now turned into lovers and shortly to be translated into husband and wife. Egeus too is transformed from a rational man into a ranting authoritarian. Presumably he had been a loving father at one time, but, though he knew of Hermia's being wooed by Lysander (and recounts it in some detail), yet has chosen someone else as her husband. Is this in order to assert his hierarchical superiority? It is not an act of affection. Hermia too changes, from a respectful daughter into a provocative and outspoken rebel against paternal authority and ducal control. Lysander too is drawn into subversion. He seems initially to be an intelligent, articulate young man who appears to be genuinely in love, but opposition to their love and the threat of losing Hermia turn him into a deceiver as he suggests the plan of elopement and secret marriage. He also transgresses the boundaries of respectfulness to an elder and a ruler. In his disloyalty and betrayal of Helena Demetrius has crossed the boundary of constancy and love before the play even begins. Like a child in a toyshop he changes his mind from one attraction to another. Because the characterization is so stylized and primitive the reasons for his change of mind are not given other than his later rationalization. He claims his temporary infatuation with Hermia was

[a]s the remembrance of an idle gaud
Which in my childhood I did dote upon. (4.1.166–7)

His rejection of Helena was like suddenly going off a food that you had liked very much but which you now loathe. Worse still, he admits he was betrothed to Helena. This was a serious, binding, publicly declared intention to marry, and he has broken his promise. No wonder Lysander calls him 'this spotted [tainted] and inconstant man' (1.1.110). He has not only transgressed the law but also has behaved dishonourably according to the requirements of courtly, gentlemanly conduct. Helena too does wrong in betraying her friend's confidence about the elopement. She does so in the name of a love that has become obsessive to the extent that she will betray the trust of a long-term friend.

The mechanicals transgress in so far as they step out of their allotted places as workmen and take on the unaccustomed role of players. This is a minor subversion of hierarchy and place and is committed in the name of loyalty and love and as a wedding gift, yet it is still technically a reversal or blurring of status and adds to the overall pattern of metamorphoses and reversals. The inappropriateness of their becoming something they are not shows admirably in the dreadful 'Pyramus and Thisbe' play. The script is badly written nonsense and their acting suitably bad.

The transgressions of the fairy king and queen are more serious. Each fails to respect the other as orthodoxy thought husband and wife should. Titania becomes wilfully obstructive, keeping the Indian boy partly because she knows her husband wants him. He is equally vindictive, claiming the boy even more vigorously because he knows how attached Titania is to him in memory of his mother. Oberon, however, pushes his wilfulness to an extreme in using the magic flower to embarrass and shame his wife. This is another situation where the underlying love is forgotten in the irrational exercise of will. Though Oberon's revenge provides the play with one of its most symbolically significant and hilarious transformations, it is never other than cruel. It must, however, not be forgotten how comic is the incongruous situation of a beautiful woman declaring her love for the vulgar monster that ass-headed Bottom has become. A more serious aspect of the transgressions among the fairy rulers is their effect on the human world. Their harmony keeps nature in its ordered, normal state.

Their disharmony turns upside down all the important processes of the farming world and of human societal activities. Titania, acknowledging as much when she admits 'we are their parents and original' (2.1.117), also opens up a whole range of fertility resonances. Oberon and she are parents of natural disorder, but not actual parents. Their fight over the changeling is symbolic of their lack of a child of their own. Titania's description of how her votaress companion's pregnant belly billowed like a ship's sails, provides an image of false pregnancy to parallel the real one. Her caressing Bottom has possible significance as a monstrous maternalism representing her desire for real maternity. These disorders, along with all the others (real and imagined), reflect images of distortion from how things ought to be that run throughout the verbal and visual texture of the play. It could also be argued that Puck takes practical jokes too far and in doing so suggests a malicious vestigial diabolism that lurks always beneath his playful mischief. He is, as Ernest Schanzer, suggests 'gross and earthy, boisterous, rough and boyish', in contrast to the 'aerial, timid, and courteous' fairies that follow Titania.[1] Laughter too can have its negative aspect. Mockery and humiliation pushed too far become counterproductive. This is an impulse Shakespeare introduces in his comedies and which edges toward excess. In *Twelfth Night*, the debunking of the pompous Malvolio drives him to a bitterness that shades toward madness. Puck's mischievousness has destructive capacity when we watch the falling out of the lovers and the threat of a duel. It is, however, the nature of comedy that it veers close to disaster and then swerves away. In tragedy the disaster is unavoidable.

Psychologically more interesting are the transformations that take place as the lovers change roles and status in the woods. They transgress all the rules of courteous, courtly conduct expected of gentle folks. Admittedly this is involuntarily and unwittingly done, as a result of Puck's application of the love juice. It makes for a humorous series of scenes full of misunderstandings and lively fallings out. Though the audience laughs at the release of reproaches and long-repressed grievances and the reversal of relationships and views, there may be some uneasiness at the nastiness. The veneer of politeness, the superficial courtesies that help society maintain a pretence of harmony, are easily discarded under pressure. Under the influence of the magic Lysander reveals a different side of his character, and under the influence of anger the two girls reveal their nasty side. He expresses those negative impressions of Hermia he had never before admitted aloud. In all three cases it is like turning over a coin and seeing the obverse. And it is a frightening image we see. The gentle and loving Hermia, who has already revealed a terrier-like courage in standing up to her father, Demetrius and Theseus, is reported as having been 'a vixen when she was at school'.

Demetrius declares, 'There's no following her in this fierce vein' (3.2.82) after she has roundly berated him for pestering her and accused him of killing Lysander. The worst transformation is that of Lysander's change from affectionate lover to a man ready to jilt her and verbally abuse her in a most hurtful way. In his new-found passion for Helena he repents 'the tedious minutes' spent with Hermia (2.2.111). In the most disturbing scene, the culmination of the mayhem in the woods, he cruelly abuses her. Rejecting her with the phrase 'Away, you Ethiope!' suggests Hermia has dark hair

---

1 'The Moon and the Fairies in A *Midsummer Night's Dream*', *University of Toronto Quarterly*, 24 (1955), 234–46.

and tanned skin. This may be a gibe at her as a representation of the Dark Lady who causes such heartache for Shakespeare in *The Sonnets*. It was certainly the case in those days that dark looks were not fashionable. Ladies went to great lengths to keep out of the sun and preserve the whiteness of their skin. Blonde hair and a pale complexion had long been the mode for beauty. Helena's fairness creates another binary. Hermia is a 'tawny Tartar [...] loathed medicine [...] hated potion' (3.2.263–4). She is a serpent to be shaken off, a cat and a burr. The latter two are things that cling, perhaps suggesting Hermia has been a little too possessive, hanging on to Lysander to indicate her ownership and her insecurity. A cat clings with its claws and this connotes her cattiness and sharp tongue, evident in the verbal attack she makes on Helena, thinking she has stolen her man: 'You juggler! You canker-blossom! You thief of love!' (3.2.282–3). Helena accuses her of having no modesty: 'no maiden shame,/No touch of bashfulness' (3.2.285–6). Both girls lack the virtue of modesty and sink into worse personal attacks. Helena calls her friend 'counterfeit [...] puppet' 'Counterfeit' suggests Hermia is over made-up, that her beauty is artificial. There was a good deal of criticism of the increasing use of make-up and other beauty aids. The word 'puppet' is a corruption of the French *poupée* (doll), suggesting Hermia is small, doll-like, childish. This is not a compliment for it carries connotations of looking unreal, having too much make-up and being undersized. The Renaissance had its ideal of feminine beauty that prioritized middling height, blonde hair, fair skin, breasts not too small and not overlarge and moderate body curves. Hermia responds by calling Helena a 'painted Maypole'. This again refers to being over made-up and also too tall and skinny. Neither girl fits the ideal. Hermia's fierce streak shows in her violent threat:

> How low am I, thou painted maypole? Speak:
> How low am I? I am not yet so low
> But that my nails can reach unto thine eyes. (3.2.296–8)

Helena reveals that Hermia is choleric and 'keen and shrewd' (has a malicious, sharp tongue), and has been since her school days. These are females reverting to animal types as their security has been lost and their civility peeled back under stress. It is, in its way, as extreme a reversal of what is thought to be female gentleness, as the monstrous half-ass half-man Bottom presents. The nastiest abuse is delivered, however, by Lysander in a vicious dismissal of his supposed lover:

> .... Get you gone, you dwarf;
> You minimus, of hindering knot-grass made;
> You bead, you acorn. (3.2.328–30)

Helena's parting comment returns to the size difference and Hermia's combativeness:

> Your hands than mine are quicker for a fray:
> My legs are longer though, to run away. (3.2.342–3)

The audience would not fail to see how Hermia's violence is a gender reversal. Once again there is reversal in Hermia being left alone. The men have stalked off to fight, Helena has fled, so Hermia, who once had two men after her and a close friend, now has no one. She is learning, perhaps, how her friend felt before. The outbreak of the row between the four is funny at first, but it takes on unsettling features. Puck rejoices in the arguments and their mistaken bases: 'this their jangling I esteem a sport' (3.2.353) and it is Oberon who commands him to 'overcast the night […] with drooping fog, as black as Acheron' (3.2.355, 357) as a preliminary to putting things right. Puck then proceeds to play with his mortal puppets one last time, leading them through the dark, keeping them from each other, but bringing them unknowingly back together in the same spot and letting them fall asleep in a group for Theseus to find next morning. He achieves this by putting a spell on them:

> Up and down, up and down,
> I will lead them up and down;
> I am feared in field and town:
> Goblin, lead them up and down. (3.2.396–9)

Addressing himself as 'Goblin' Puck reveals a more malign aspect of his self. The name goblin is of unclear origin, perhaps from the Greek *kobalos*, meaning a roguish person. In folklore and legend goblins were mischievous tending toward evil. They are usually depicted as grotesque and ugly and, depending on the source and culture, their behaviour ranges from merely aggravating to actively creating malefic mayhem by use of magic. This dark side, briefly shown, suits with the polar opposite mixes evident in the central characters.

In act 1 Helena had envied Hermia, wishing to have her eyes, voice and favour (facial good looks and appearance). She declared that if she had all the world, she would give it up (apart from Demetrius) to be like her friend: 'The rest I'd give to be to you translated' (1.1.191).

When she is in Hermia's situation, having two men madly in love with her, she hates it and is convinced it is a trick and they are complicit in mocking her. Her translation is less comforting than Bottom's. She learns that envy is a sin and is punished by finding that being in the shoes of another is not as pleasurable as dreamed.

Another failed 'translation' is Lysander's romantic imagining of the elopement:

> Tomorrow night, when Phoebe [the moon] doth behold
> Her silver visage in the wat'ry glass,
> Decking with liquid pearl the bladed grass
> (A time that lovers' flights doth still conceal),
> Through Athens' gates have we devis'd to steal. (1.1.209–13)

His experience of absconding will not be as easy or picturesque as he dreams. He is punished for presumption, for law breaking, for theft of a man's daughter and for his naivety. It is also another example of how venturing out of the cocooned comfort of the court brings you into contact with some of the nasty realities of life.

Demetrius too will be translated: from the 'spotted and inconstant' jilter of someone he was promised to, through victim of an infatuated stalker, to returned lover. It is significant that Shakespeare's most commonly referenced classical text is Ovid's *Metamorphoses*.[2] Telling the many love stories of the gods and goddesses, its recurrent narrative pattern is of change, of transformation. Helena refers to one of the most famous stories, that of Apollo pursuing the nymph Daphne and how she changes into a laurel tree to escape his lustful clutches.[3] Her chasing Demetrius is a gender and role reversal, a double transformation that suits the transgressions and reversals with which the play is replete:

> Apollo flies and Daphne holds the chase;
> The dove pursues the griffin, the mild hind
> Makes speed to catch the tiger. (2.1.231–3)

The dove (usually a symbol of gentleness) chasing the griffin (a monster hybrid; upper half eagle and lower half lion) is a foreshadowing of Titania's 'love' for the half-ass, half-man. It is nature turned upside down, normality reversed. It echoes all the other unnatural reversals and oddities of a play that rapidly metamorphoses from a courtly love comedy to an indefinable nightmare pantomime. It is noticeable that the central acts (2 and 3) are full of animal references and metaphors, symbolizing the release of chaos, the sense of the present but not visible teeming animal world of the woods, the translation from court to the wild. The other acts also have allusions to

---

2 He would have studied it at school, but certainly knew and pillaged Arthur Golding's 1567 translation.
3 Ovid, 1. 584ff. and Golding, 1.569–700.

a range of creatures, but they are fewer than in the woodland scenes. Some critics have seen the woodland setting as evoking the pastoral beauty of rural life, but a lot of the animal images are repulsive or frightening. There are worms, serpents, reremice (bats), cankers (caterpillars and grubs), newts and blind-worms (slow worms), spiders and beetles, the lynx, leopard, wild boar and bears (headless and otherwise). They are mentioned rather than seen or active, but they create a sense that the natural world is not all cuddly, cute and beautiful, but has blacker and nastier aspects too. It is part of the comedy and part of the fiction that the only 'animals' that actually 'appear' are an ass's head that speaks and is a gentle beast, and a costume lion that also speaks and is less terrifying than a tabby cat. Suitably these animals are not what they seem, but then little in this play is. Much of what is funny in the woodland scenes is pretence.

The bird and animal language that fills central scenes of the play is very evident. It is extensive, though not all the creatures referred to are of the woodlands of England or Athens. The following list of animal references displays the degree to which the texture of the play is associated with the natural world: 'a fat and bean-fed horse [...] filly foal' (2.1.45–6); 'mare', 'a rough colt', 'ox [...] crows [...] murrion flock' (2.1.93, 97); 'lion, bear, or wolf, or bull,/On meddling monkey, or on busy ape' (2.1.180–1); 'the simplicity of Venus' doves' (1.1.171); 'lark to shepherd's ear' (1.1.184); 'morning lark', 'sucking dove [...] nightingale' (1.2.77–8); 'ousel cock [...] throstle [...] wren [...] finch [...] sparrow [...] lark [...] cuckoo' (3.1.120–6); 'raven [...] dove' (2.2.113); 'screech owl', 'goose', 'my dove, 'wild geese [...] russet-pated choughs', 'cock crow' (2.1.255, 267); 'wood-birds'. Some animal references are ordinary enough: 'spaniel [...] spaniel [...] dog' (2.1.203, 205, 210); 'a horse [...] a hound [...] A hog', 'The squirrel's hoard', 'hounds [...] hounds', 'smallest monstrous mouse', 'ass', 'Moth', 'humble-bees', 'painted butterflies', 'glow-worms', 'giant-like ox-beef', 'a part to tear a cat in' (1.2.25). Others are more exotic: 'the lion's part' (1.2.60); 'wild beasts' (2.1.228); 'The dove pursues the griffin, the mild hind/Makes speed to catch the tiger' 2.1.232–3); 'ounce [...] cat [...] bear/Pard [...] boar' (2.2.29–30), 'I am as ugly as a bear [...] beasts [...] monster' (2.2.93, 94, 96); 'a headless bear' (3.1.103–4), 'mermaid on a dolphin's back' (2.1.150); 'Thessalian bulls', 'lion roars [...] wolf behowls', 'Centaurs', 'night's swift dragons', 'My mistress with a monster is in love' (3.2.6). Yet others are English but with connotations of evil and darkness: 'serpent's tongue', 'worm [...] adder [...] adder [...] serpent [...] adder', 'cat [...] serpent' (3.2.261–2); 'batty wings', 'snake', 'cankers', 'reremice', 'the clamorous owl', 'spotted snakes [...] Thorny hedgehogs [...] newts and blind-worms' [...] weaving spiders 'beetles black worm [...] snail (2.2.3,4, 6,); 'crawling serpent [...] serpent' (2.2.145, 148); 'fox', 'wormy beds', 'lion' (3.1.26); 'ass', 'ass', 'hounds [...] dog [...]

cur', 'humble-bee', 'ass', bear [...] hounds [...] hounds', 'ass', 'lion' (mentioned 13 times in act 5), 'mouse'.

There are a number of references to snakes or serpents that carry meaningful connotations. Snakes are obviously dangerous. Hidden in the undergrowth they may bite and poison the unwary or unlucky. The common phrase 'a snake in the grass' is a reference to this and a metaphor for someone whose malevolent activity is not perceived until their evil is afoot. The associations with danger and evil extend to sin and the evil, through the biblical connection with the Temptation in the Garden of Eden, being achieved by Satan shape-changed into a snake. Thus all snake/serpent/viper references reverberate with that moral warning. The first, distant hint at devious malice is cached in Lysander calling Demetrius 'spotted and inconstant'. 'Spotted' means morally tainted, but is later echoed by the song Titania's fairies sing (2.2.9–23). It is a protective charm to ward off evil and begins by warning 'you spotted snakes with double tongue' to keep away. (Other dangers/evils to be warded off are 'thorny hedgehogs', 'newts and blind-worms', 'weaving spiders', 'beetles black', 'worm' and 'snail'. Worm could mean snake as well as earthworm.) The 'double tongue' refers not just to the forked tongue of snakes but also to the lying deviousness of the Devil as serpent and to anyone who says one thing but means another, like Demetrius in his ungentlemanly, inconstant behaviour toward Helena. Further snake references emerge in Hermia's dream when she imagines a serpent is crawling on her breast, a serpent she thought 'ate my heart away' (2.2.145, 148). She has this dream (incidentally, the only 'real' dream in the play) when Lysander has done to her what Demetrius did to Helena – abandoning her for another woman. She will later accuse Demetrius of killing Lysander while he slept and scorns such dishonourable conduct:

Could not a worm, an adder, do so much?
An adder did it; for with doubler tongue
Than thine, thou serpent, never adder stung! (3.2.71–3)

Her loyalty is cruelly rewarded later in the scene when Lysander shakes her off with the comment 'I will shake thee from me like a serpent' (3.2.261). The snake too has connotations with sexuality and fertility. Its phallic shape is a part of ancient Cretan and Egyptian pictorial and religious iconography, and, like the moon, it has divers significations. The accumulating animal imagery becomes dominantly nasty. In a masque the rural imagery would include birds with beautiful songs (that is, Philomel the nightingale) and gentle creatures of the pastoral world (sheep, rabbits, cows). The woodland scenes in *Dream* are more like an antimasque to counterbalance the attempted moderation of act 1 and the achieved harmony of act 5. If the masque represents idealized values and hoped for happy outcomes, the antimasque presents all the things that can and do go wrong in the real world.

BIBLIOGRAPHY

Alford, Stephen. *The Watchers: A Secret History of the Reign of Elizabeth I*. London: Penguin Books, 2013.

Apian, Peter. *Cosmographicus liber* [Book of the universe]. Antwerp, 1524.

Ashley, Maurice. *England in the Seventeenth Century*. Harmondsworth: Pelican History of England, 1960.

Augustine. *The City of God*. Translated by Henry Bettenson. London: Penguin Classics, 2003.

———. *Confessions*. Translated by R. S. Pine-Coffin. London: Penguin Classics, 1964.

———. *On the Good of Marriage (De Bono Coniugiali)*. Edited and translated by P. G. Walsh. Oxford: Clarendon Press, 2001.

Bacon, Francis. *The Advancement of Learning*. Edited by Arthur Johnston. Oxford: Clarendon Press, 1980.

———. *The Essays*. Edited by John Pitcher. London: Penguin Classics, 1985.

Bateman, Stephen. *The Christall Glasse of Christian Reformation* (1584).

Becon, Thomas. *Golden Boke of Christen Matrimonie* (1542).

Bede, the Venerable. *A History of the English Church and People*. Translated by Leo Sherley-Price. London: Penguin Classics, 1955.

Beier, A. L. *Masterless Men: The Vagrancy Problem in England, 1560–1640*. London: Methuen, 1985.

Berry, Helen, and Elizabeth Foyster. *The Family in Early Modern England*. Cambridge: Cambridge University Press, 2007.

Bevington, David. '*But we are spirits of another sort*'. In *A Midsummer Night's Dream: New Casebook*, edited by Richard Dutton. London: Palgrave Macmillan, 1996.

Bicheno, Hugh, *Vendetta: High Art and Low Cunning at the Birth of the Renaissance*. London: Weidenfeld & Nicholson, 2008.

Book of Common Prayer. Edited by Brian Cummings. Oxford: Oxford World's Classics, 2011.

A Book of Masques. Edited by G. R. Bentley. Cambridge: Cambridge University Press, 1967.

Borman, Tracy. *Elizabeth's Women*. London: Vintage, 2010.

Brathwait, Richard. *The English Gentleman*. London, 1631.

Bullough, Geoffrey, ed. *Narrative and Dramatic Sources of Shakespeare*. New York: Columbia University Press, 1957–75.

Bunker, Nick. *Making Haste from Babylon*. London: Pimlico, 2011.

Burnet, Gilbert. *History of the Reformation*. London: Richard Chidswell, 1682.

Burton, Robert. *The Anatomy of Melancholy*. Edited by F. Dell and P. Jordan-Smith. New York: Tudor Publishing Company, 1938.

Butler, Charles. *Female Replies to Swetnam the Woman-Hater*. Bristol: Thoemme Press, 1995.

Castiglione, Baldassare. *The Book of the Courtier.* Translated by George Bull. Harmondsworth: Penguin Classics, 1981.

Chambers, E. K. *William Shakespeare: A Study of Facts and Problems.* Oxford: Clarendon Press, 1988.

Clapham, John. *Elizabeth of England.* Edited by E. Plummer Read and C. Read. Philadelphia: University of Pennsylvania Press, 1951.

Coleridge, Samuel T. *Biographia Literaria,* 1830.

———. *Coleridge's Shakespearian Criticism.* Edited by T. M. Raysor. London: Constable, 1930.

Cressy, David. *Agnes Bowker's Cat: Travesties and Transgressions in Tudor and Stuart England.* Oxford: Oxford University Press, 2000.

Crowley, Robert. *Voice of the Last Trumpet* (1550).

Dabhoiwala, Faramerz. *The Origins of Sex: A History of the First Sexual Revolution.* London: Penguin Books, 2012.

Dante. *L'Inferno,* in *The Divine Comedy.* Translated by C. H. Sisson. Oxford: World's Classics, 2008.

Daunton, M. J. *Progress and Poverty.* Oxford: Oxford University Press, 1995.

Davies, C. S. L. *Peace, Print and Protestantism.* London: Fontana Press, 1995.

Davies, Owen. *Popular Magic: Cunning-folk in English History.* London: Hambledon Continuum, 2003.

De Lisle, Leanda. *After Elizabeth.* London: Harper Collins, 2005.

Dickens, A. G. *The English Reformation.* London: Fontana/Collins, 1974.

Donne, John. *Sermons.* Edited by George R. Potter and Evelyn M. Simpson. Berkley: University of California Press, 1953–62.

Downes, John. *Roscius Anglicanus, or an Historical Review of the Stage from 1660 to 1706* (1708).

Duffy, Maureen. *Henry Purcell.* London: Fourth Estate Ltd., 1994.

Dusinberre, Juliet. *Shakespeare and the Nature of Women.* Basingstoke: Macmillan, 1996.

Elyot, Thomas. *The Boke Named the Governor.* Leicester: Scolar Press, 1970.

Erasmus. *Praise of Folly.* Translated by Betty Radice. London: Penguin Classics, 1971.

Freud, Sigmund. *The Interpretation of Dreams.* Translated by Joyce Crick. Oxford: Oxford World's Classics, 1999.

Gawdy, Philip. *The Letters of Sir Philip Gawdy.* Edited by Isaac H. Geaves. London, 1906.

Gillespie, Stuart. 'Shakespeare's Reading of Modern European Literature'. In *Shakespeare and Renaissance Europe,* edited by Andrew Hadfield and Paul Hammond. London: Thompson Learning, 2005.

Gouge, William. *Of Domesticall Duties,* 1622.

Greenblatt, Stephen, ed., *Norton Anthology of English Literature,* vol. 1. London: W. W. Norton & Company, 1962.

Guerber, H. A. *Myths and Legends of the Middle Ages.* London: Studio Editions, 1994.

Hakluyt, Richard. *Voyages.* Edited by Jack Beeching. London: Penguin Books, 1972.

Harrison, G. B. *A Jacobean Journal.* London: Routledge and Sons, 1946.

———. *A Second Jacobean Journal.* London: Routledge and Kegan Paul, 1958.

Henslowe, Philip. *Henslowe's Diary.* Edited by R. A. Foakes and H. T. Rickert. Cambridge: Cambridge University Press, 2002.

Hill, Christopher. *Intellectual Origins of the English Revolution.* London: Pamther Books, 1972.

Hill, Frances. *A Delusion of Satan: The Full Story of the Salem Witch Trials.* London: Penguin Books, 1996.

Holland, Norman N. *Representing Shakespeare*. Baltimore: Johns Hopkins University Press, 1980.

Horace. *Ars Poetica (The Art of Poetry)*.

Hutton, Ronald. *The Stations of the Sun: A History of the Ritual Year in Britain*. Oxford: Oxford University Press, 1997.

James I. *Basilikon Doron*. EEBO Editions' reprint of the 1682 edition.

———. *Demonologie*. San Diego: The Book Tree, 2002.

Jonson, Ben. *Ben Jonson: Works*. Edited by C. H. Herford, Percy and Evelyn Simpson. Oxford: Oxford University Press, 1925–52.

———. *Eastward Ho!* (in collaboration with John Marston and George Chapman). Edited by C. G. Petter. London: A. & C. Black, 1994.

———. *Oberon*. In *A Book of Masques*. Edited by G. R. Bentley Cambridge: Cambridge University Press, 1980.

King, John N., ed. *Voices of the English Reformation*. Philadelphia: University of Pennsylvania Press, 2004.

Kishlansky, Mark. *A Monarchy Transformed: Britain 1603–1714*. London: Penguin Books, 1996.

Knights, L. C. *Drama and Society in the Age of Jonson*. London: Peregrine, 1937.

Knox, John. *The First Blast of the Trumpet Against the Monstrous Regiment of Women* (1558).

Kott, Jan. *Shakespeare Our Contemporary*. London: Methuen, 1965.

Kramer, Heinrich, and Jacob Sprenger. *Malleus Maleficarum (The Hammer of Witches)*. Translated by Christopher S. Mackay. Cambridge: Cambridge University Press, 2009.

Lacan, Jacques. *Ecrits*. Translated by Alan Sheridan. London: Norton and Co., 1977.

Leggatt, Alexander. *The Cambridge Companion to Shakespearean Comedy*. Cambridge: Cambridge University Press, 2010.

———. *Shakespeare's Comedies of Love*. London: Methuen and Co., 1974.

Lovell, Mary. *Bess of Hardwick*. London: Abacus, 2014.

McFarland, Thomas. *Shakespeare's Pastoral Comedy*. Chapel Hill: University of North Carolina Press, 1972.

McIlwraith, A. P., ed. *Five Elizabethan Comedies*. Oxford: World's Classics, 1951.

McKerrow, R. B., ed. *Works of Thomas Nashe*. London: A. H. Bullen, 1904.

Machiavelli, Niccolo. *The Prince*. Translated by George Bull. Harmondsworth: Penguin Classics, 1961.

Marston, John. *The Dutch Courtesan*. Edited by David Crane. London: A. & C. Black, 1997.

Martz, William J. *Shakespeare's Universe of Comedy*. New York: David Lewis, 1971.

Meres, Francis. *Palladis Tamia*, 1598.

Middleton, Thomas. *A Mad World My Masters*. Oxford: World's Classics, 1995.

Montaigne, Michel. *The Complete Essays*. Translated by M. A. Screech. London: Penguin Classics, 2003.

Mortimer, Ian. *The Time Traveller's Guide to Elizabethan England*. London: Vintage, 2013.

Muir, Kenneth. *The Sources of Shakespeare's Plays*. London: Methuen & Co., 1977.

Nashe, Thomas. *Christ's Tears over Jerusalem*, 1593.

———. *Works*. Edited by R. B. McKerrow. Oxford: Blackwell, 1958.

Nichols, John. *The Progresses, Processions, and Magnificent Festivities of James the First*. London, 1828.

Oldridge, Darren. *The Devil in Tudor and Stuart England*. Stroud: The History Press, 2010.

Olson, Paul. 'A Midsummer Night's Dream and the Meaning of Court Marriage', *English Literary History* 1957.

Peele, George. *The Old Wives' Tale*. In *Five Elizabethan Comedies*. Edited by A. K. McIlwraith. Oxford: Oxford World's Classics, 1951.

Pepys, Samuel. *Diary*. Edited by R. G. Lathom and W. Matthews. London: Bell & Son, 1970.

Percy, Henry. *Advice to his Son*. Edited by G. B. Harrison. London: Ernest Benn, 1930.

Perkin, Harold. *Origins of Modern English Society*. London: Routledge, 1986.

Perkins, William. *The Foundation of Christian Religion* (1591).

Plato. *Phaedo*. In *The Last Days of Socrates*. Translated by Hugh Tredennick. London: Penguin Classics, 1971.

Plutarch. *Plutarch's Lives*. Reputedly translated by John Dryden, edited by Arthur Hugh Clough London: Dent, 1938.

Ripa, Cesare. *Iconologia* (1593).

Rowse, A. L. *William Shakespeare: A Biography*. London: Macmillan, 1963.

Rubin, Miri. *Mother of God*. London: Allen Lane, 2009.

Schanzer, Ernest. 'The Moon and the Fairies in A *Midsummer Night's Dream*', *University of Toronto Quarterly* 24 (1955).

Schleiner, Louise. *Tudor and Stuart Women Writers*. Bloomington: Indiana University Press, 1994.

Scot, Reginald. *Discovery of Witchcraft* (1584).

Seneca. 'On Mercy', in *Dialogues and Essays*. Translated by John Davie. Oxford: Oxford World's Classics 2008.

Sidney, Philip. *A Defence of Poetry*. Edited by J. A. Van Dorsten. Oxford: Oxford University Press, 1971.

Stone, Lawrence. *The Crisis of the Aristocracy*. Oxford: Clarendon Press, 1966.

———. *The Family, Sex and Marriage in England 1500–1800*. London: Penguin Books, 1979.

Stow, John. *The Survey of London*. London: Dent, 1970.

Strype, John. *Memorials of Thomas Cranmer*. 1690.

Stubbes, Philip. *Anatomie of Abuses*. 1583. London: Forgotten Books, 2015.

Tawney, R. H. *Religion and the Rise of Capitalism*. 1926. London: Penguin Books, 1990.

Thomas, Keith. *Religion and the Decline of Magic*. London: Penguin Books, 1991.

Tillyard, E. M. W. *The English Renaissance, Fact or Fiction?* Baltimore: Johns Hopkins University Press, 1952.

Twyning, John. *Forms of English History in Literature, Landscape, and Architecture*. London: Palgrave Macmillan, 2012.

Tyndale, William. *Obedience of a Christian Man* (1528).

Weber, Max. *The Protestant Ethic and the Spirit of Capitalism*. 1904–5. London: Unwin University Books, 1968.

Webster, John. *The White Devil*. Edited by Christina Luckyj. London: A & C Black, 1996.

Wickham, Glynne, Herbert Berry and William Ingram, eds., *English Professional Theatre, 1530–1660*. Cambridge: Cambridge University Press, 2000.

Wilson, John Dover. *Shakespeare's Happy Comedies*. London: Faber & Faber, 1962.

Wilson, Thomas. *State of England*, in *Camden Miscellany*, vol. 16. London: Camden Society (third series), n.d.

Winthrop, John, and Margaret. *Some Old Puritan Love-Letters*. Edited by J. H. Twichell. London, 1893.

Wootten, David, ed. *Divine Right and Democracy: An Anthology of Political Writings in Stuart England.* Indianapolis: Hackett Publishing Co., 2003.

Wycliffe, John. *The Wycliffe New Testament.* London: British Library, 2002.

Wyrick, Deborah Baker. 'The Ass Motif in *The Comedy of Errors* and *A Midsummer Night's Dream*', *Shakespeare Quarterly* 33, 1982.

INDEX